THE FUTURE
OF RELIGIOUS
ORDERS IN THE
UNITED STATES

THE FUTURE OF RELIGIOUS ORDERS IN THE UNITED STATES

Transformation and Commitment

DAVID J. NYGREN
AND MIRIAM D. UKERITIS

Foreword by David C. McClelland

PRAEGER

Westport, Connecticut
London

Library of Congress Cataloging-in-Publication Data

Nygren, David J.
  The future of religious orders in the United States :
transformation and commitment / David J. Nygren and Miriam D.
Ukeritis; foreword by David C. McClelland
    p. cm.
  Includes bibliographical references and index.
  ISBN 0-275-94665-7 (alk. paper)
  1. Monasticism and religious orders—United States—History—20th
century. 2. Monks—United States—Attitudes. 3. Nuns—United
States—Attitudes. I. Ukeritis, Miriam D. II. Title.
BX2505.N93   1993
255'.00973—dc20   93-19088

British Library Cataloguing in Publication Data is available.

Library of Congress Catalog Card Number: 93-19088
ISBN: 0-275-94665-7

First published in 1993

Praeger Publishers, 88 Post Road West, Westport, CT 06881
An imprint of Greenwood Publishing Group, Inc.

Printed in the United States of America

The paper used in this book complies with the
Permanent Paper Standard issued by the National
Information Standards Organization (Z39.48-1984).

10 9 8 7 6 5 4 3 2

CONTENTS

FIGURES AND TABLES

FIGURES

TABLES

FOREWORD

The authors of this book have undertaken a challenging task. They have conducted a thorough and objective study of the condition of Catholic religious orders in the United States. Impetus for this study was provided by the steep decline in the membership in such orders since the Second Vatican Council and the decline in the number of Catholic institutions generally. Such changes inevitably raise questions as to why they have occurred. The authors have left no stone unturned in searching for factors in the church as an institution, in the congregations themselves, or in their members' attitudes which might be responsible for these changes. They have pursued their search with energy, great skill, and complete objectivity. They are thoroughly grounded in, and employ, modern social science methods and theory. Being members of religious orders themselves has enabled them to interpret their findings better, but it has in no way compromised their objectivity. Furthermore it is clearly their hope that their findings will help identify "a path toward a vibrant future" for such religious orders. This book is an excellent example of "knowledge for use."

They have approached their task in a variety of ways:

- by reviewing the history of religious orders, and changes in the institutional church since Vatican II;
- by organizing focus groups of leaders of unusual vision;
- by interviewing outstanding and typical leaders of religious orders;
- by studying outstandingly caring religious; and
- by conducting an attitude survey of a large representative sample of members of different types of religious orders (apostolic, mendicant, monastic, and contemplative).

The results of this survey provide a unique source of information on how American Catholic religious feel about organizational, ethical, social, and spiritual issues of concern to the Church and all Americans.

The authors have employed many different tools of modern social science: survey research techniques, organization and management theory, job competency analysis, and personality and social structural analysis. They made a special effort to examine gender differences in congregational styles in view of the strong feminist awareness in the church. Many of their findings will be of immediate practical importance to the orders, such as their identification of competencies of outstanding congregational leaders for which new leaders can be trained when chosen. Finally, they end their report by identifying themes which inhibit and promote transformation and renewal of Catholic religious orders.

What is striking about these themes is that they deal with the central moral and religious issues in American society as they have been identified by Tipton (1982), Bellah et al. (1985), and others. In other words the book does not deal with esoteric, parochial concerns of the Catholic Church in America, but with moral issues that most Americans have struggled with in one form or another. As Tipton points out, during the 1960s Americans came to feel that the victims of poverty, racism, and sexism needed not so much charity as justice. The call shifted from helping individuals in need to an urgent drive to change the system so that it would no longer produce such victims. The Catholic Church at Vatican II also called for more people to work with the poor and disadvantaged. Many members of the church's religious orders who were in tune with the spirit of the 1960s felt this could best be accomplished by changing the system and by becoming advocates for the dispossessed. As in American society in general, many in the Catholic Church pushed for "people power," for more democracy in governance, and for greater opportunities for women, for those of other races, and for the laity to assume positions of responsibility in the church.

As the authors document, all of these trends left many members of Catholic religious orders, particularly the younger ones, confused about their role. Many orders responded to the calls for change by making membership less distinctive—by dropping distinctive habits, encouraging participation by the laity, leaving the cloister, joining in the activities of a local parish, and ceasing to sponsor and staff Catholic hospitals and educational institutions. Many Catholics were less clear about making lifelong, sacrificial commitments to the religious life, particularly so far as chastity was concerned for men and obedience for women. It was unclear how members of a religious order could contribute uniquely to the kinds of changes in the social system that many felt were needed to undo the effects of oppression of the poor, minorities, and women. So it was not surprising that membership in many orders declined or that many religious felt such a diminishment was entirely appropriate given the changes in attitudes regarding the best way to implement Christ's teachings in today's world.

It is true that at least one successful order responded to the new challenges in a very traditional way—namely, the Missionaries of Charity, founded and led by Mother Teresa of Calcutta, whose mission was to serve the poorest of the poor on an individual basis. She specifically focused on charity for persons—on giving fish to the hungry rather than on providing them with fishing rods so that they could catch their own fish, to use her own example. She demanded great sacrifice from her sisters: a lifelong, full-time commitment under vows of poverty, chastity and obedience, and the wearing of a distinctive habit. The order has spread rapidly all over the world, suggesting, perhaps, the viability of the traditional Catholic model of a charitable congregation even today.

More congregations have adapted to changed circumstances and discovered a new vision and justification for continuing. The order of the Alexian Brothers which was founded to care for victims of the plague has found a new sense of mission in caring for AIDS victims. Leadership in a Franciscan province has by precept and personal example developed a zeal for social justice among its members which matches the enthusiasm of the early followers of St. Francis. The women in a Benedictine monastery have developed an enthusiasm for, and sacrificial personal commitment to, the cause of peace which has shocked and evoked anger from more conventional Catholics accustomed to supporting the military and "just wars." Yet as its leader observed, "If we are forced to disappear as a community, I would rather we go testifying to the Christian way." Such religious orders are also thriving under the kind of inspired leaders whose qualities are a major focus of attention in this book.

Other congregations are struggling to find a renewed sense of mission. The Jesuits have re-committed themselves to the mission of their founder which was to educate the poor. Yet over the centuries they have developed a tradition of excellence in scholarship and education among elites which does not fit easily with the renewed vision. A central element in all of these religious concerns has been caring for others. And some Catholics have been drawn to caring for others on a more organized basis by improving agriculture, changing the social order, increasing self-reliance, or identifying ever more closely with the poor as advocates. It has been harder to see such approaches to caring as calling for *religious* vocations. Thus, while feeding the hungry on a loving one-to-one basis has always called for a religious vocation, it is not so clear that working to invent a new kind of rice that saves the lives of millions from dying of hunger calls for a religious vocation.

These are simply examples of the many different conflicts and sources of confusion that the authors identify as pushing religious orders toward extinction or revival in new or old forms. Although social science findings can describe the way things are, they can not be more than indicators that point the way to the future. As the authors recognize, the will of God must also be taken into account. But surely the will of God will express itself in the lives, convictions, and visions of those who read this book and continuously seek God's guidance as to what its findings mean for the future. From the religious point of view, one of the most striking findings of the authors' studies is that those religious who were truly outstanding either as congregational leaders or as caring people mentioned significantly more often that they felt closely in touch with God as they moved through life's daily activities. Theirs was not simply a *belief* that God should be important in guiding them. The outstanding leaders or caring religious showed by what they mentioned spontaneously that God's presence was guiding and supporting them and giving meaning to what they were doing more often than for other religious. This finding is supported furthermore by the fact that among religious nominated because of their vision of the future, con-templation—direct contact with the divine—was ranked as of first importance for the future.

If outstanding Catholic religious see the importance of living in continuous contact with God and in fact show signs of being in such living contact, then there is a solid basis for hope that they will be able to discern God's will for the future of religious orders, assisted as they certainly will be by the information in this book.

David C. McClelland

ACKNOWLEDGMENTS

The Lilly Endowment Inc. endorsed our request to undertake a comprehensive study of religious orders in the United States in 1989. Jeanne Knoerle, S.P., and Fred Hofheinz, officers of the endowment, encouraged us to think broadly and inclusively in order to obtain the widest possible perspective on the future of religious orders. With their constant support and encouragement, we launched the Religious Life Futures Project, a study that eventually would involve more than 10,000 participants representing more than 121,000 members of religious orders.

A project of this size could never have been accomplished by the efforts of two individuals alone. Given the scope and magnitude of our intentions, we engaged colleagues in the scientific and religious communities to assist us in designing, reviewing and drawing conclusions. In addition, many capable graduate students and administrative and technical support personnel at both Boston University and DePaul University in Chicago helped us to see our interests translated into action. In order to assist us in assessing the critical issues to be studied, making sure to incorporate the greatest possible number of constituent concerns, we formed a national advisory board, which met twice a year during the three-year project to reflect on the findings and suggest implications from the data. We are deeply grateful to those men and women who represent the apostolic, mendicant, monastic and contemplative traditions. In addition, we are grateful to the national leadership of the Leadership Conference of Women Religious (LCWR), the Conference of Major Superiors of Men (CMSM) and the National Association of Religious Brothers (NARB) for providing support, encouragement and official representatives to serve on the national advisory board. Members of the board were Patricia Fritz, O.S.F.; Adrian Gaudin, S.C.; Howard Gray, S.J.; Fred Hofheinz; James Jones, O.S.B.; Thomas Kelly, O.P.; Jeanne Knoerle, S.P.; Donna Markham, O.P.; Bette Moslander, C.S.J.; Basil Pennington, O.C.S.O.; Loughlan Sofield, S.T.; and

Barbara Valuckas, S.S.N.D. (replacing Patricia McCann, R.S.M.).

Experts in the social sciences and research design also were consulted. Jean M. Bartunek, R.S.C.J., Ph.D. (Boston College); Philip Kubzansky, Ph.D. (Boston University); Wade Clark Roof, Ph.D. (University of Massachusetts at Amherst); Charles O'Reilly, Ph.D. (University of California at Berkeley, School of Management); Bernard Bass (State University of New York at Binghamton, Center for Leadership Studies); Althea Smith, Ph.D. (Boston University); and Jeanne Hanline (*The Official Catholic Directory*) were among the scholars acting as technical advisors to the project. We are indebted to Martin Frankel, Ph.D., Senior Statistician, National Opinion Research Center, for his technical support in developing sampling and analysis plans for the National Survey questionnaire that would reflect precisely the complex populations represented by American religious. In addition, numerous other women and men religious provided further theological consultation and advice in the design of the National Survey and other research units.

One of the great benefits of working on the project at Boston University was the opportunity to work with David C. McClelland, Ph.D. From the inception of the project, he supported our efforts to design a study that would take into account the complex interrelationship of psychological rigor and constructs of faith. He encouraged us personally to pursue the points of connection between two historically distinct frames of reference. Together with Carol Franz, Ph.D., Dr. McClelland collaborated with us to undertake the Caring People Project. In this study, they discovered the motive structure of individuals who are identified as uniquely caring.

In addition to his work on the Caring People Project, David McClelland collaborated with us in designing and undertaking the Leadership Competency Assessment with the McBer Company of Boston, MA. McBer, a subsidiary of the Hay Group, which is most skilled in leadership assessment, contributed researchers, staff and managerial support to undertake the study. We are grateful to John Larrere, senior vice president of McBer, for his personal contribution and interest in the project. In addition, we are grateful to Anne Munley, I.H.M., and Michael Park, C.P., for their competence in collaborating on the study with us.

We acknowledge Vanessa Urch Druskat for her contributions to the leadership and gender analysis, Patrice O'Donnell for her work in role clarity, and Gary Reed, Jaime Pereyra, Carol Wintermyer, R.S.M., and other graduate students and faculty of Boston University for their contributions to the project.

The project would not have been possible without the competence and commitment of Dennis Ross, our data base manager, who moved with us from Boston University to DePaul University. We deeply appreciate his loyalty to the project and to us. Similarly, Sharon Farber, our project administrator at DePaul, also pulled up stakes in Boston to move with us to Chicago. She has been flawless in managing the project's finances, publications and reports. She replaced Lisa Handler, who was instrumental in launching the project and managing it with extraordinary enthusiasm and competence in the first two years at Boston University. To Dennis, Sharon and Lisa, we shall be forever indebted.

If conducting the study was the greatest challenge, disseminating the results was our greatest reward. We wanted as many members of religious orders as possible to share the results of their contribution to it. With the continued generous support of the endowment, we sought the help of individuals trained in communication to assist us in the design and execution of the dissemination phase of the project. Sheila King, chief executive of Sheila King Public Relations, Inc., enthusiastically accepted the challenge. Under her capable guidance, and assisted by a staff more ambitious than any we have ever seen before, we produced a nationwide teleconference titled, "Pathways and Promises: Reporting the Results of the Religious Life Futures Project," on October 3, 1992. Jim Gardiner, a member of the Atonement Friars of New York, graciously volunteered his time to act as executive producer for nearly six months in order to guarantee the highest quality program. Together with Frank Frost Productions of McLean, VA; WTTW Public Television of Chicago, IL; and the Catholic Television Network of America (CTNA) of Washington, DC, he exceeded our fondest hopes. We are equally indebted to Susan Anderson, our distinguished host from WBBM—Channel 2 in Chicago, IL, for delivering a thoroughly engaging review of the results. Adam Villone and Reunion Productions of Boston, MA did an extraordinary job of producing the technical and video support to the project. Finally, with the help of Sheila King, Jane Holroyd, Marianne Bankert, Cathy Bisbing, Edward Udovic, C.M., and Jennifer Alter Warden, the study results also appeared in more than 200 newspapers, periodicals and magazines nationwide. Charles-Gene McDaniel and Sean C. Peters, C.S.J., assisted us in the final editing of this text. We are thankful for their contributions in producing this work.

Jane Gerard, C.S.J., of DePaul's Institute for Leadership of Religious Organizations, contributed mightily to many parts of the project including the distribution of and accounting for the Pathways and Promises video. Her most significant contribution was, for us, her painstaking care in editing and preparing the index of this text for publication. Additional support was provided by members of DePaul University's Department of Psychology, including Jane Halpert, Ph.D.; Ching Fan, Ph.D.; Sheldon Cotler, Ph.D.; Michelle Page; Steve Allscheid; Karl Brugger; Julia Hickman; Diane Sheehan; and Keith Lavine.

Finally, we want to express our deepest gratitude to the leadership and members of our religious congregations, the Congregation of the Mission (Vincentian Fathers and Brothers, Midwest Province) and the Sisters of St. Joseph of Carondelet (Albany Province) for their willingness to grant us the time away from other possible ministries in order to undertake this study. Our own vocations have been challenged and strengthened, both by the opportunity to work together, and by interacting with so many committed individuals, without whose support this study would never have been developed.

INTRODUCTION AND PURPOSE

The changes that have occurred in religious orders in the United States since Vatican Council II opened in 1962 have been dramatic, affecting the manner in which the members live and work as they carry on sometimes centuries-old traditions of caring for those most in need. This study provides a perspective on the lives of more than 121,000 sisters, brothers and religious priests, as reflected through various social scientific methods. Its purpose was to identify the changes that must yet occur if the religious order is to remain a vital social institution in American society and the Catholic Church into the next millennium.

The study emerges at a time when the average age of the members of many congregations in the United States approaches 67 years of age for women and 60 years of age for men while, over the period ranging from 1962 to 1992, the number of members in Roman Catholic religious orders has decreased by nearly 43% for brothers and sisters and 18% for religious priests. This decline corresponds with a comparable decline in Roman Catholic health, education and social service institutions. For instance, during that time period, the number of Roman Catholic hospitals decreased by 23%, universities and colleges by 15% and private elementary schools by nearly 42%. (Both population statistics and Roman Catholic institutional demographics are elaborated in Appendix A.) The current trend of decline is itself not the focus of the study. Rather, the intention was to focus on the future of these orders and their robust histories in order to shape a perspective for the American public and for religious audiences, which will be most affected if this decline continues.

Surely, those who began to implement the changes some 30 years ago had a vision of what religious orders could become. However, the course of renewal has faced more challenges than were expected. Many of the changes appear less chosen than required in light of diminished resources. To develop new perspectives on this unique call requires courage and energy from those who began the changes. Leaders and members today continue that challenge, and thus vivify their solemn promise of caring.

HISTORICAL ROOTS OF THE RESEARCH QUESTIONS

Religious orders have a very rich history. They have spanned the centuries, expanding and contracting in size in response to particular spiritual needs and social conditions. Throughout the long history of religious life in the Roman Catholic Church, in faithful response to the great Gospel commandments of the love of God and neighbor, a countless number, and an amazing variety, of different types of religious orders of men and women have arisen continually to meet both the ongoing and the emerging challenges of the contemporary spiritual and material needs of humanity and the church. The vast majority of these religious communities have come and gone as times, conditions and needs in the world and in the church have changed. Others have endured and wondrously evolved for well over four hundred, five hundred or even a thousand years.

There were early groupings of dedicated virgins, widows and desert hermits dating from the time of the New Testament and the earliest centuries of the church's existence. Beginning in the fifth century, both in the church of the East and in the church of the West, these primitive forms of religious life for men and women gradually evolved into vast monastic and contemplative families guided by the enduring genius of, respectively, the Rule of St. Basil and the Rule of St. Benedict.

The Jesuit historian John Padberg (1984) has analyzed the broad sweep of the history of religious life in the church on the basis of need and response. For example, Padberg noted that the development of monasticism from the fifth to the twelfth centuries came as an effective response to the church's need to provide some measure of order, stability, piety and devotion at a time when Western civilization, of which the church was an integral part, was experiencing the chaos and massive societal disruption caused by the great waves of the barbarian invasions of Europe.

According to Padberg, the church next had to ask itself how it would respond to the worldliness of the emerging values of the urban, mercantile, mobile, newly wealthy civilization of the late Middle Ages. The effective response to this need was the development of the great mendicant orders, notably those of the Franciscans and the Dominicans. According to their tradition, mendicants would fulfill their work by begging for the resources that they needed for themselves and those they served. The mendicant religious orders provided invaluable services to the church and to Western civilization by, for example, appropriating successfully the body of Aristotelian thought to the service of the Gospel and by reaffirming the basic Christian virtues of simplicity, renunciation and piety. In contrast to the isolated and contemplative monastic groups, the foundations of the new mendicant orders were increasingly mobile and more directly apostolic in their service.

Several centuries later, the next great challenge posed to the church occurred with the need to respond to the emergence of the powerful individual nature of the humanism of the Renaissance and the Protestant Reformation. Innovative and imaginative forms of highly centralized, highly mobile and dynamic apostolic religious life, such as the Society of Jesus, now emerged. These new communities were more than equal to the challenge of the militancy, learning, piety and vigor of the Renaissance humanists and the Protestant reformers. Each emerging order focused on a particular need of society or addressed the issues through a particular understanding of the Gospel, such as an emphasis on mercy or reconciliation. As a result, the groups became known for the unique charism, or gift, that they brought to the church and society.

In the Age of the Council of Trent and the Catholic Reform, these communities made a wide-ranging commitment to establish specialized institutionalized apostolates, such as those dedicated to the education of men, women and children, the training of worthy clergy, and the service to the poor. These efforts were integral parts of the Tridentine renewal of the Catholic Church throughout Europe.

This was also an age of exploration and discovery, which opened vast new worlds, and the countless millions of people who inhabited them, to the preaching of the Gospel. Once again renewed, newly founded religious communities zealously took the lead in immediately responding to this need by organizing and undertaking the systematic evangelization and institutional establishment of the church in these new and largely unknown lands.

Until this era, the only opportunities for service and ministry for women in the religious life of the church were in contemplative, cloistered convents. Several initial attempts, such as those by the Ursulines and Visitandines, to broaden the opportunity for women to serve the church in religious life outside the traditional structures and limitations of the cloister had failed. It was not until the early seventeenth century and the founding of the Daughters of Charity that new women's congregations finally were able to begin freely establishing themselves and their apostolates in response to the pressing needs of the world and the church.

The cataclysm of the French Revolution and its rapid spread throughout Europe all but destroyed the institutions of both church and state of the ancien régime. When the revolutionary dust finally settled, there was next to nothing left of either the most ancient or the most recently established religious orders and congregations of men and women. To give only one example, at the dawn of the revolutionary era, more than 2,000 Benedictine foundations were scattered across the face of Europe. By 1815, however, only about 20 were still extant. This story of utter destruction was universal for all religious communities in the church, and even the absolute extinction of many communities was a not at all uncommon result. More than a few contemporaries expected that not even the church itself, let alone the structures of religious life, would be able to survive these events.

Nonetheless, within the lifetime of someone born at the beginning of the nineteenth century, at the very height of this revolutionary chaos and destruction, an extraordinary rebirth of religious life in the church would begin. Older orders and congregations that had managed to survive would be dynamically refounded, and their works reestablished. In addition, great numbers of new apostolic and missionary communities would arise to rebuild completely and greatly expand the organizational and charitable infrastructure of the church's mission, not only in Europe, but throughout the world.

Especially noteworthy in this era is the fact that a large majority of these new communities were for women. Moreover, not only were large numbers of these new communities founded, they continually attracted vocations in such large numbers that it was often difficult for them to keep up with the influx. The founding and explosive growth of all forms of religious life in the United States took place during this period.

This refounding and expansion of religious life met perfectly the perceived needs and clear expectations of the ecclesiology of the Catholic Church of the nineteenth and early twentieth centuries. This was a church which, in the spirit of the First Vatican Council (1869-1870), reacted to the challenges of the dawn of the modern era by retreating into the strengths and weaknesses of a militant ultramontane, and a deeply conservative, intellectual, spiritual and theological stance toward the modern world.

The orders in the United States reached their greatest membership in the early 1960s. Nearly 1,000 orders, with a membership of close to 200,000, were involved intensely in nearly every facet of Catholic life. Next to the federal government, religious orders developed the largest health-care delivery system in the United States, with more than 800 hospitals. Moreover, with more than 10,000 universities, colleges, secondary and primary schools in the U.S. Roman Catholic Church, no other provider or entity could compare in influence to the religious orders in the church. The orders were sustained in large measure by donations or support from works. For all intents and purposes, they labored for very little financial compensation. They operated on the assumption that constant expansion through the assimilation of younger members into their ranks would provide adequately for their continuation and retirement. It was understood that younger members would replace the older members in the ministries, which were largely corporate and would provide the economic underpinnings for the group. However, recent history reveals that this assumption was erroneous.

The Second Vatican Council (1962-1965) has had as great a revolutionary impact on the life and future of the Catholic Church and its religious orders, congregations and communities as did the French Revolution, the Protestant Reformation, the Counter-Reformation and any other of the key events in the long history of the church. Debate between reformists and restorationists will no doubt be as strong in the coming years as any other time in the history of religious orders. As in all these other previous revolutions, when the dust finally settles, some religious communities will have gone out of existence. Others will have refounded themselves successfully by creatively adapting their charisms to contemporary needs in the church and the world. Undoubtedly, other new, innovative and untraditional forms of religious life also will emerge providentially. Together, all these groups will form the next chapter in the continuing history of religious life in the Roman Catholic Church.

Members of religious orders today are motivated by distinctive drives and transcendent purposes. They live the vows of poverty, chastity and obedience, and commit, in general, the whole of their lives to the service of God, in and through their order. This study explores the views of these individuals at this critical juncture in the change process: their beliefs, attitudes and perspectives on the future. Their views are derived from the application of both qualitative and quantitative research methodologies. The framework for interpretation was developed largely through the application of organizational and psychological theories.

Some facets of the project, such as the National Survey, involving 9,999 individual members of religious orders, follow empirical design protocols. Others facets, such as the Visioning Groups, attempt to employ more innovative methods to capture the unique perspectives of those whose lives will help shape master images of the future. The research units are described in Chapter 1.

The portrait that emerges reflects both the diversity of opinion that is operative at present and the vitality among members of religious orders who, despite their increasing median age, devote enormous energies to refining their purposes and methods in order to remain vital to the church and American society. The key to the future, as the members represent it to us, is a complex dynamic of selfless generosity, a sensitivity to emerging human needs and an intimate relationship with God, whom they firmly believe calls them to ministry in the church and the world through religious life.

THE RESEARCH AGENDA

The life of members of religious orders is, in fact, unique when compared to nearly every other social category of society. However, one of the emergent concerns among members of religious orders is the increasing ambiguity with respect to the group's function in both the church and society. This study gradually reveals the nuances of transcendence and confusion in this population. In addition, because of the critical role that leadership has traditionally played in religious orders, several studies of leadership were undertaken as part of the comprehensive assessment. Each facet of the study provides a unique window into this role from the perspectives of members as well as leaders.

We worked from several assumptions in undertaking the research. First, only members of religious orders can describe their experience of God, faith, the church and their personal commitment. Second, as social researchers, we hoped to gather data that would serve these individuals in their own self-direction. Third, we believe that without significant change, religious life in the United States will continue to decline and, more important, that those who most need the help it provides will not receive it. Finally, we believe that the generosity that is so evident in the lives of members of religious orders today remains a strong model of self-sacrifice that must be articulated clearly if others are to follow Jesus in this manner.

The study sought the broadest possible contribution from leadership, membership and those with unique perspectives pertinent to a comprehensive study such as this. The data were analyzed throughout by vocation, tradition, age and gender. Chapter 1 provides the theoretical framework of transformation and the explicit purposes of the research. Chapter 2 draws the broad vision of members identified by their peers as possessing vision about the future of religious life. Chapter 3 details two distinct studies of leadership in the population. The first study explores the major issues that leaders face in developing a strategy for mission, while the second identifies the competencies required for outstanding leaders of religious orders.

Chapter 4 reports the results of the 335-item National Survey which was mailed to 9,999 members of religious orders in 1990. One of the significant findings in the National Survey was the lack of role clarity that is currently experienced by a significant number of men and women religious. Chapter 5, therefore, examines more closely the results related primarily to this factor. Chapter 6 presents the dynamic motivation of members of religious orders who are known to be exceptionally caring or altruistic. The conclusions in Chapter 7 suggest the dynamic forces currently operative among the membership and how individuals, individual congregations and the social institution of religious life in United States are likely to be transformed. This chapter also delineates the discrepancies between the vision to which members of religious orders aspire, the future shapes that religious life is likely to take, and the realities members face in trying to live the ideal. It then unfolds a formula that shows how religious orders can move from their current state to a desired future state by considering key theological, social, psychological and organizational variables. The polarities identified in this section represent the breadth of opinions represented to us throughout the various facets of the study.

In the study design, we carefully sought to ensure that it was representative and included diverse opinions. We also attempted to use a variety of traditional as well as creative methods to capture the range of beliefs and perspectives on the future. Certain limits must be kept in mind while reading the results. First, as members of religious orders ourselves, we undertook the study with the hope of identifying a path toward a vibrant future. As members of distinctly apostolic traditions, we may not have been as attuned to the other core traditions, such as the monastic or cloistered. Second, we are trained as psychologists. We employed that body of knowledge but depended on the expertise of other scholars and researchers in a variety of disciplines, as well as the opinions of a nationally recognized board, to assure that proper attention was given to the major issues facing religious life.

Third, although we used a variety of standard scientific measures in areas that are common between members of religious orders and other populations, many of the measures in the National Survey were designed specifically for this population. They are, therefore, reliable within the population but have not been standardized on other populations. Generalizing the results beyond the population of religious orders should be considered carefully. Fourth, the small number of cloistered religious limits comparability with other groups. Mean scale comparisons are valid, but statistical differences may not be reliable.

Fifth, when we began the study, many individuals suggested that we survey the laity, former members of religious orders and hierarchy of the church to determine their perspectives on this unique population. Because of resource constraints and our own specific interests, however, we limited ourselves to studying only those individuals who are currently members of religious orders. Pursuing such investigations, however, could contribute significantly to this discussion.

The conclusions drawn from all facets of the study describe, as best we can within the limits of the design, what we believe will make a difference to individual members of religious orders, the future of congregational life and the ministry of religious orders in the United States. The chapters of this book attempt, as clearly as possible, to retain internal coherence of the research units for purposes of clarity and replicability. The first and last chapters, however, consolidate both theory and results to relate to the larger project objective: a study of the transformation of religious life.

In scriptural metaphors, the concept of transformation appears in Paul's call to "be transformed into Christ." In the organizational realm and the social sciences, however, the concept of transformation refers basically to qualitative, discontinuous shifts in organizational members' shared understandings of the organization, accompanied by changes in the organization's mission, strategy, and formal and informal structures. In contrast to carrying out comparatively simple incremental changes, organizations undergoing transformation come to understand themselves and their mission very differently from their original understanding.

Studies of transformation have tended to focus on one particular level at which the change occurs: either the industry or social institution considered as

a whole, or a particular organization. Only a few studies have explored some
of the experiences of individuals whose organizations are experiencing major
change. In contrast, we investigated issues related to change in religious life on
all three levels:

- The *social institution* as one entity, "religious life": Referring to
  religious life as a social institution acknowledges the existence of the
  broad-based beliefs, attitudes and behaviors that are common across all
  religious orders. This investigation revealed that while congregations
  may differ in their expression of religious life by virtue of sex or
  tradition—for example, apostolic, monastic or contemplative—all groups
  share certain elements.
- The *congregations,* including the 816 groups that participated in the
  National Survey: Shifting understandings of how a group interprets a
  shared past, selects value priorities, allocates resources and assesses
  mission opportunities mark the experience of transformation. This
  investigation sought to identify those shifts, particularly as they related
  to different congregations. Analysis of change at the level of the
  congregation is limited to the major traditions of apostolic, mendicant,
  cloistered and monastic life.
- The *individuals,* including some 121,000 sisters, brothers and religious
  priests: Investigating the implications of transformation for the
  individual members of religious congregations is central to this study.

This approach enables a more complete understanding of how individual,
congregational and intercongregational experiences can affect each other, as well
as the means through which the various types of change occur. The conclusions
that are drawn require that hope and ambition take a hand in shaping the future.
The resolution of the change process, however, is affected deeply by the
individual and communal choices that are made along the way. The critical
component in the change effort is to imagine a desirable future for a congregation and reinforce that movement by consistency in choices based on the values
and traditions of the particular order.

THE FUTURE
OF RELIGIOUS
ORDERS IN THE
UNITED STATES

Chapter 1

DYNAMICS OF TRANSFORMATION

One of the great challenges for contemporary organizations is adapting structures to support constantly changing or expanding purposes. To describe this complex relationship, organizational theorists sometimes use the analogy that "if a bridge gets long enough, you must change the shape of it." Irwin Miller (in a film by Ault, 1991) has said that the nature of organization is reorganization. Change, which was once perceived as a phase of organizational life, is now seen as normative. Managing change is one of the distinctive competencies of outstanding leaders, although it is a process little thought of by average leaders (Nygren & Ukeritis, 1992). Senge (1990b) made the point that one of the three critical functions of leadership is the capacity to design an organization that fits the environment within which it is operating. Beckhard (1988) went so far as to say that change can only occur with the commitment of the organization's top leadership.

These dynamic forces of change provide a unique opportunity to maneuver structures, resources and the imagination into new organizational forms that serve specific purposes. As the complexity intensifies, new structures and new styles of leadership often are required to achieve a new vision of the organization. Others have warned, however, that as change happens, without a clear end state in mind, organizations can suffer from "random drift," a process of minor alterations in structures, roles, relationships and purposes that unravels previously purposeful groups, and leaves their members feeling "adrift" (Hannan & Freeman, 1986).

Thirty years ago, the historic Vatican Council II called on all religious orders in the Roman Catholic Church to institute an aggressive and reflective process that would lead to transformation and renewal. Various disciplined interpretations of this process have emerged (Cada et al., 1979; Daly et al., 1984; Lozano, 1986; Molinari & Gumpel, 1987; Schneiders, 1986, 1991; Wittberg, 1991). Pope John Paul II (1983) invited members of religious orders to employ the various research disciplines in an attempt to explain where religious orders are in the process of change and what factors will continue to shape the future of religious orders worldwide.

Since Vatican II, religious orders in the United States have changed substantially. Their missions have become more complex in ways that reflect the immediacy of those to whom they minister. Change continues to characterize the lives of both individuals and of the congregations that make up what is known as "religious" in the Catholic Church in the United States. Some individuals would say "random drift" is prevalent while others would say that changes have enlivened charisms that had become static over time.

Whatever the opinion, the data to suggest what changes must yet occur if religious life is to remain a vital institution in society and the church has heretofore been incomplete. In this study, we present a complex perspective on the past, present and future of religious life drawn from the opinions of the more than 10,000 individual members of religious orders whom we invited to participate in the process. Combined with various theoretical models, the data suggest a formula for change that will enable religious orders to survive.

THE DYNAMICS OF TRANSFORMATION

Organizations are driven by the implicit or explicit views, dreams and ambitions of those who comprise them. Individuals join a particular organization generally because the organization best reflects a set of values or has a purpose compelling enough to deserve commitment. Organizations evolve and are given shape by individual and collective action and intentions. As evolution occurs, some structure emerges that gives coherence to action. Certain patterns of action are rationalized by the members to give justification for the energy they expended to keep the organization moving. The structure that supports a specific interpretation of reality or collective action is often called a paradigm.

Every paradigm has a corresponding script that both describes and interprets the reality on which it is based. These "interpretive schemes" hold the paradigm in check and keep it operative over time. They also help make sense of organizations and, depending on their strength, attract individuals who want to participate.

Paradigms change slowly, and for a variety of reasons. They may shift because they are no longer relevant to the environment or to the members who uphold them. They may change by virtue of external forces. If the founding assumptions, myths and beliefs fade from memory, a shift in the paradigm may take place. Paradigm shifts also may occur when a gap develops between espoused values and actual behavior or when the structure of the paradigm no longer serves a specific and satisfying function.

Morgan (1980) offered four types of paradigms that appear to operate within organizations. He named them functionalist, interpretive, radical-humanist and radical-structuralist paradigms, each of which specifies particular assumptions about both the purpose and the nature of organizations.

The functionalist paradigm is based on the assumption that human existence and, indeed, organizations themselves, are oriented to produce an ordered and regulated state of affairs. Behavior is always seen as bounded by a network of social relationships. This paradigm emphasizes both regulation and behavioral objectivity.

The interpretive paradigm is based on the assumption that all social reality is merely the product of subjective and intersubjective experiences of individuals, leading to multiple interpretive schemes that support their worldview. The interpretive paradigm operates primarily from the subjectivist view of language, textual criticism and symbolic action.

The radical-humanist paradigm assumes, similarly, that all reality is socially constructed and that individuals eventually canonize their choices in ideological arguments which ultimately alienate them from themselves and one another. This paradigm is largely individualistic and opposed to organizations because they fail to elaborate subjective experience. The radical humanist is concerned with understanding how individuals can connect thought and action as a means of transcending alienation.

Finally, the radical-structuralist paradigm is based on a view of society by which some groups dominate others. Change occurs when those being held in check by those in power begin to transcend domination through constructive action.

Each paradigm is supported through complex rational descriptions, symbolic constructs and ways of interacting that attempt to externalize the internal conviction of the members. Paradigms become enacted through organizations of all types. They tend to reflect the poles of subjectivity or individualism, on the one hand, and objectivity, on the other. They also tend to be driven by interpretations or preferences for radical change and social regulation. Morgan maintained that the four types of paradigms operate in any social change process and operate on those who attempt to explain that change. Consequently, if transformation occurs, it is fostered, experienced and described in various ways, depending on some variation of the four organizational paradigms.

Tushman and Romanelli (1985) have suggested that organizational paradigms evolve in either of two ways. The first involves processes of convergence that operate, through incremental change mechanisms, to align and make consistent the complex of dynamics that support an organization's particular orientation to purpose and mission. The second involves reorientation, in which patterns of consistency are reordered dramatically toward a new sense of purpose and alignment with the external environment. Transformation occurs only when executive leadership has the capacity to engage key interventions in periods of either convergence or reorientation.

While the term *transformation* has been used to describe both incremental change and complete reorientation, in the organizational realm, it refers basically to qualitative, discontinuous shifts in its members' shared understandings of the organization, accompanied by changes in the organization's mission, strategy and formal and informal structures. In contrast to carrying out comparatively simple incremental changes, organizations undergoing transformation come to understand themselves and their mission very differently from the way they originally had understood them. Transformations are shifts in paradigms. Paradigms are altered as new implicit and explicit views of reality begin to shape new expressions of the mission within the group or the organization.

A Model for the Process of Transformational Change

Transformation usually begins with a crisis indicating that the organization's current paradigm is no longer adequate. The crisis may present itself in one of several forms: new needs emerge to which the organization may not be able to respond; current performance may be poor; leadership transitions may occur; some powerful subgroup's interests may no longer be served; management practices may no longer be successful; or, most typically, there may be a major environmental shift that confronts and challenges the already existing paradigms or interpretive schemes. The easiest response for the organization to take is to defend itself against the challenge or, perhaps, not to respond at all. For transformation to occur, the experience of crisis must be strong enough to "unfreeze" organizational members' present understandings of the organization by presenting a significant challenge to its validity.

After such "thawing" occurs, or in conjunction with it, various individuals and organizational subgroups begin developing alternative understandings. These emerging understandings lead to new types of action and, most likely, to changes in the structure of the organization. Generally, what occurs is an alteration of behavioral norms, authority relationships and foundational beliefs. Moreover, the new types of action that take place are likely to occur outside the organization's initial boundaries; for example, AT&T changed from providing telephones to include the sale of computers and other forms of communication devices. Very often, the types of structural changes that occur are likely to include the breakdown of formerly established boundaries. This change in boundaries as structures are altered has a profound effect on the individual members of the organization as the process of unfreezing occurs. Why is this so?

Boundaries within and between organizations provide a frame of reference for interpreting experience. They serve to link individuals to one another and also to separate them. Boundaries are essentially features that either differentiate one tradition from another (Cherns, 1976); pose actual or symbolic barriers to access or transfer information, goods, services or people (Katz & Kahn, [1966] 1978); or serve as points of external exchange with other organizations, clients, peers, competitors or other entities (Friedlander, 1987). In periods of transition or transformation, boundaries are renegotiated. New boundaries emerge only as the new paradigms become more clear.

Boundaries are difficult to describe concisely. They can be psychological, physical, symbolic, financial, spiritual or philosophical in character. All can serve, however, at least partly, to define how a group needs to operate within its context in order to be effective (Sundstrum, De Meuse & Futrell, 1990). When boundaries become too open or indistinct, an organization risks becoming overwhelmed and losing its identity. If its boundaries are too exclusive, the organization may lose touch with its primary constituents.

The fusion of groups within organizations occurs when boundaries are less clear or when maintaining their distinctiveness is no longer necessary. Boundaries alter as shifts in self-identity occur. Moving from a fixed identity to an alternative unfreezes assumptions and actions at the individual and group levels, and also introduces competing interpretations of a group's direction and the individual member's sense of self.

As boundaries are negotiated and as alternative paradigms emerge to explain the life and direction of a group, there is likely to be considerable conflict among the original and developing interpretive schemes and among the subgroups espousing them. Groups that hold one new perspective, for example, are likely to find themselves in conflict with individuals or groups that espouse either the original perspective or a different new one. The conflict may take various forms. One perspective may clearly dominate those holding different perspectives and may be separated from other views, or leaders of the organization may acknowledge the potential value of, and thus encourage, interaction between several perspectives.

Leaders can have a strong impact on the outcome of a conflict between perspectives. If, as Tushman and Romanelli (1985) indicated, leaders serve as the key mechanism for intervention in general, then in the context of conflict, their role is even more critical. If they support only one perspective, they are likely to decrease the potential creativity of the transformational process and the sense of involvement of organizational members whose perspectives are not taken into account. If they separate out the different perspectives, they are likely to perpetuate splits between the groups. However, if leaders enable conflicting perspectives to interact with each other, they will increase the chances of paradoxical outcomes of transformation: of new and creative shared understandings that emerge from the interaction of the competing perspectives.

The conflict among subgroups will create additional tension. When, and if, a new synthesis is reached that is experienced as acceptable, there is likely to be a sense of "rightness" and satisfaction, at least on the part of members whose perspectives have been incorporated. The transformation process continues until a desirable alternative state is determined and negotiated structures have been established to secure some degree of collective intention and, however minimally, some measure of predictability or perceived control. This refreezing or stabilization in the transformation process then allows the group to operate from the perspective of shared values, culture and vision until those basic assumptions again are challenged by new forces, whether internal or external to the group. Boundaries that reflect the new paradigm are established during this stabilization period.

The process of transformation is not affect-free. Rather, it is often paralyzing and disorienting, and it may be experienced as a sequence of deaths and rebirths. Initially, primary feelings of the various members of the organization are likely to include shock, defensiveness, grief and anger. Others feel exhilarated by the challenges and the freedom introduced by change. Throughout the development of new interpretive schemes, nearly all organization members will experience ambivalence and confusion, both at times when it is unclear that any satisfactory new understanding is developing and also when there are multiple potential perspectives.

Transformation among Religious Orders in the Roman Catholic Church in the United States

To say that paradigm shifts have been occurring in the Catholic Church in the last 30 years is to state the obvious. However, to consider why these shifts have occurred and how they affect the individual church members, as well as the structures that supported particular social roles in the church, is to undertake the study of transformation.

The concept of transformation applied to religious organizations such as religious orders implies both shifts in mission as well as in the supporting spirituality and the operative views of what it means to be a member of the church. As the paradigms of the Catholic Church changed with Vatican II, the forms to support a variety of roles in the church also were altered. Boundary changes perhaps most characterize the dynamic processes undertaken by the Catholic Church, and religious orders specifically, in the process of transformation since the council. For example, with Vatican II, the Catholic Church shifted the boundaries from believing that "outside the church there is no salvation," to highlighting the belief that "the church of Christ subsists in the Catholic Church . . . although many elements of sanctification and truth can be found outside of her visible structure" (*Lumen Gentium*, 1964, ¶8).

Among religious orders, the distinctiveness once typified by cultural artifacts, such as a standard way of dressing, yielded to a demand that internalized values comprise the fundamental ground of commitment. At the same time, the increasing contribution of the laity in the Catholic Church, which often looked similar to the values and work life of the members of religious orders, was one of the many forces that called into question the distinctive identity of members of religious orders. Increasingly, for nearly 30 years, members of religious orders and the laity in the church have cooperated in the mission of the church to such an extent that distinctions appear no longer relevant. However, in the larger ecologies of service and ministry, do religious orders provide something unique and distinctive that cannot be replicated?

THEORETICAL PERSPECTIVE: LEVELS OF CHANGE

This study of religious life investigates issues related to change on three levels: (1) the social institution referring to those broad-based beliefs, attitudes and behaviors that are common across all religious orders (2) the congregation and (3) the individual member of a religious order.

Change at the Level of the Social Institution

Some of the change that has taken place in religious life has occurred similarly in many congregations. For example, Schneiders's (1986) work described a shared shift—across many congregations—in the understanding of many of the components of religious life, including the nature of commitment, expression of community living and the locus of ministry or work. In addition, some writers have suggested that members of religious orders are meant to be "prophetic" or "counter-cultural" (e.g., Leadership Conference of Women Religious, 1985; Lozano, 1986; Schneiders, 1986, 1991; Woodward, 1987; Leddy, 1990). Such works are addressed to members of religious orders as a group, not to particular congregations.

Shifts in understanding are frequently intertwined with shifts in structures, both formal and informal. These structural shifts include not only new types of relationships and divisions among subgroups, but also the breakdown of formerly established organizational boundaries. At the level of the universal church, Molinari and Gumpel (1987) have asked, "Is the consecrated way of life a structure in the church or a structure of the church?" The latter construct implies a singular structure of divine origin, namely a hierarchical one, while the former implies the existence of multiple structures in the church. At the core of this distinction is the degree to which the hierarchical structure governs the pneumatic components, that is, those typically associated with the charismatic dimension of the church. The tradition of religious orders suggests a high degree of independence of the orders from the hierarchy of the church unless, of course, the order was established by the local bishop for service to a particular jurisdiction.

Depending on the response to the question of singular versus multiple structures, structural diversity and change will occur in very different ways. Many members of religious orders believe that their traditions represent the pneumatic or charismatic dimensions of the church, particularly as represented in the lives of their founders, and that they are better structured and controlled without the influence of the hierarchic structure. The issue is further confounded by the fact that priests who are members of religious orders also participate in the hierarchic structure by virtue of their ordination. This creates for religious priests an interesting dynamic of belonging to two reference groups; the order of priests and the religious life that they share in common with religious women and brothers in religious orders.

However, perhaps the single most significant dynamic to influence religious life has been the change in the theology of the laity. Prior to Vatican II, the distinctive vocation of religious life in the church was evident in the diversity of charisms, ministries and cultural artifacts of each religious order. A charism, that is, the unique contribution or gift that a congregation offers the church, might be to evangelize the poor, to educate immigrants or to work and pray for the world. Religious orders established ministries in line with their charism to advance Christ's mission in, for example, health, education or social services. Each order typically had distinctive rituals, dress, symbols and traditions.

What has emerged among religious orders is greater homogeneity with respect to their mission, greater openness to cooperative relationships in ministry with laity and diminished distinctiveness in the culture and tradition of the orders. The former paradigms that remained dominant for centuries have shifted, for many, and the language to describe them today is vastly different.

For instance, although historically distinct, the apostolic and mendicant traditions have, for all intents and purposes, merged into one functional entity. Members of apostolic orders of women and religious priests are involved increasingly in work that had typically been considered the domain of the diocesan clergy. The vocation of the religious brother awaits a supporting theology that contrasts his vocation with the spirituality of the laity. Perhaps the same can be said for religious sisters as well. In addition, the former "power" achieved by religious orders by virtue of their structural independence in the works of health, education and social service has been minimized for many reasons. For one, the parish seemingly has become the primary locus of Roman Catholic Church life.

Furthermore, many religious orders appear to have concluded in the last three decades that institutional ministry no longer is either sustainable or purposeful in achieving their mission. For some, this has allowed a distribution of resources in alternative ways to provide more direct service to those in need. For others that may have begun with that intention, the demise of the institutional structure witnessed a collateral decline in the acquisition of resources and personnel.

Among the monastic and contemplative traditions, vast changes occurred in the disciplines of obedience, prayer, work and leisure. In these instances, certain traditions have become aligned more closely with diocesan ministry. For some groups, this assimilation was motivated by a clear drive to be of service to the increasing demands of the invigorated Catholic populations in the parishes. For other groups, the involvement was less reflective of intention than of the needs for income, independence among members or a less bounded definition of the cloister.

Intercongregational structures (e.g., collaboration in ministry between congregations or for formation across congregations) and instances of the merger of congregations present additional manifestations of changes occurring within religious life in relation to the church and society. These suggest the magnitude of organizational change that is occurring. Questions arise frequently concerning the boundaries that distinguish members of religious orders from the diocesan clergy and the laity. The emergence of several new orders that tend to be characterized by a unique formula of higher costs of membership yielding higher commitment to the congregation is as radical in this decade as were the dramatic shifts that occurred in the years following Vatican II.

Change at the Level of Individual Congregations

The previous section documented those shifts that have emerged across religious life as a social institution. Other changes have surfaced differentially within religious orders themselves. Moreover, many of the changes that have occurred in several congregations have been experienced by members of the individual congregations as taking place uniquely within their own congregation rather than as a phenomenon that is characteristic of religious life as a whole. Thus, while evaluating how the paradigm shifts have affected religious life overall, it is equally important to observe the changes occurring within specific congregations.

For example, Bartunek (1984) described how the understanding of the educational mission in one women's congregation shifted from the mid-1960s to the late 1970s. At the beginning of the change process, education was viewed essentially as synonymous with activities that took place in the schools that the congregation administered. However, by the late 1970s, the educational mission was seen primarily as "education to justice in faith," (p. 363) which might or might not take place in formal educational settings, let alone within schools the congregation administered. Beres and Musser (1987) have described how, during that same time period, another religious order broadened its mission from particular areas of service to a general philosophy of service, with priorities shifting from an emphasis on the works of the congregation to an emphasis on its members as primary vehicles for fulfilling the mission.

Within religious orders, Nygren (1988) found that both male and female members are altering their structures and categories of membership boundaries to adapt to an emerging self-understanding. In a survey of 740 leaders of religious congregations, 70% of the female leaders indicated that they were adapting their definition of membership to include full or partial membership by laity. Among female congregations, 18% of those surveyed expected to amalgamate with another congregation, province or monastery in order to adapt to internal changes. Correspondingly, 25% of the male leaders expected to alter membership categories, and 12% of those surveyed expected to amalgamate with another entity in order to adapt to change. These expected or accomplished changes have an impact on both the existing members and the organization's self-definition. They also suggest how prevalent is the alteration of boundaries, both within and across religious orders.

In one religious order studied by Bartunek (1984), members' shifts in understanding of the order were intertwined with the development of several cross-province groups and commissions. They were also intertwined with the breakdown of formerly established external boundaries. Many of the order's members started to work with, and as a part of, groups that had been clearly outside the originally established province boundaries. These structural changes eventually resulted in a merger of the U.S. provinces of the order.

Many apostolic orders are expanding their efforts into mission work, particularly in the third and fourth worlds. Others are shifting their institutional strength from a generalized service of those in need to a concentrated systemic effort on behalf of those in severe need. For instance, some orders have intensified their health ministry through the formation of health systems that provide an economy of scale allowing them to compete effectively while providing more free care to the poor. Others have shifted their efforts to address directly areas of critical unmet need, for example, persons with AIDS.

Even though, during the period between 1962 and 1992, the institutional ministries of religious orders decreased in number, many of those that remain have become more vibrant and clear about their distinctive mission. Religious orders have taken very seriously their rights and obligations as sponsors of institutions by, for instance, crafting corporation bylaws to assure that the underlying values of the founding group continue to influence the society. As the larger paradigms or interpretations of religious life have shifted over time, so, too, have the structures and processes that operate at the level of each congregation. With 30 years of history, the challenge is to identify those structures, procedures, models and forces that have shaped the development of new understandings of individual religious orders.

As regards the processes through which these new understandings have occurred, the model articulated above suggests that the typical process of change includes an initial experience of crisis, accompanied by several strong feelings, including grief, anger and defensiveness, followed by the development of differing understandings on the part of various organizational subgroups. There are also feelings and reactions associated with this stage: ambivalence and confusion about possible interpretations, as well as conflict between groups. When a new synthesis is reached, a sense of rightness is experienced. If this fails to occur, more destructive dynamics may characterize the group's functioning.

As new self-understandings of religious orders develop, it is critical to determine from which elements of the environment the members of a particular congregation receive these messages. In particular, the impact of the hierarchical church and the laity, as well as the influence of intercongregational groups and networks on the development of self-understandings within the member congregations, must be considered. Similarly, leadership in effecting changes in religious life can contribute to either the development or the decline of organizations.

Albert and Whetten (1985) have suggested that an organization has an identity to the extent that there is a shared understanding of the central, distinctive and enduring character or essence of that organization among its members. The shifting interpretations of religious life as a social institution, as well as the dramatic changes within religious orders themselves, make establishing, maintaining or invigorating any collective identity an increasing challenge. Ashforth and Mael (1989) proposed that *wisdom* is little more than the ability to remember the lessons of previous identities, and that *integrity* is the ability to integrate and abide by them. This maxim might suggest that religious orders that slide too far to the extremes of structural regulation or radical change without grounding themselves in history may ultimately lose the integrity that they so much hope to achieve.

The Experience of Individual Members of Religious Orders

The changes that have occurred have significantly affected individual members. For example, Ebaugh (1984, 1993) showed that the changes had strong effects on the reasons why members of women's religious congregations left the congregation. The departure of more than 45% of the population of women religious has also had an impact on those who remain (see Appendix A). Others have indicated that one of the typical effects of a transformational process is an increase in the stress level of individual members of organizations in which the transformation is occurring. This increased level of stress is due to the accompanying ambiguity and conflict between subgroups.

However, the experience of individuals in periods of transformation reflects more than simply difficult feelings. For example, Bartunek and Ringuest (1987) found that members of a particular congregation whose work took them across the congregation's original boundaries during the early 1970s and who remained in their congregation eventually came to perceive themselves as more influential in the congregation than did members who continued to carry out traditional works. In other congregations, those who were committed firmly to the mission of the congregation but wearied of the change process migrated to the periphery. Some remain there while others fell out of the congregation entirely. Still others have moved closer to the center of the congregation's mission and structure as both have become clearer.

Members of religious orders are motivated to participate in a high-cost commitment that involves, at the least, lifelong vows of poverty, chastity and obedience. The conscious and unconscious processes of individuals and their spiritual convictions together propel them into a life that is quite distinct from that of either the laity or diocesan priests. Despite their apparent assimilation into either the clerical caste or the lay vocation, members of religious orders perceive themselves as retaining one social identity. Social identification is the perception of oneness with, or belongingness, to some human aggregate. In spite of the compromises to the collective identity of members of religious orders, individuals who feel called in some way to the vocation of religious life identify with the particular charism of an order and eventually tie their personal fate to the ultimate fate of the group.

Identification with a congregation is distinguishable from internalization (O'Reilly & Chatman, 1986). Whereas identification refers to an individual's membership in social or spiritual categories of belonging, internalization refers to an individual's incorporation of the order's values, beliefs and attitudes within the self as guiding principles.

Religious life, as distinct from other social organizations, assumes that members identify with the group and internalize the central values of the order. The identity of an individual religious as a member of the group may be seen as distinct from the internalization of values. One may belong to the group without acting in accord with its values. Members of religious orders, in fact, have multiple identities which they negotiate either consciously or unconsciously. For instance, they have membership in the Catholic Church, in their order, in their profession, in the local civic and religious communities, and in other groups as well. It is commonplace for some women religious today, for example, to claim a primary affiliation as a member of a religious order but to disclaim affiliation with the Catholic Church. Similarly, for male religious who are priests, their primary identity is as a member of an order and often only reluctantly extends to an identification with the priesthood.

Thus, in addition to the change taking place on the congregational and social institution levels, the experience of individual members of religious orders and particular subgroups is in a state of significant transition. Developmental issues also play a role, as does belonging to a particular age cohort, gender or tradition.

SUMMARY APPLICATION OF THE CONCEPTUAL MODEL

This study is based on the assumption that religious life in the Catholic Church operates at three levels: as a social institution, within the religious orders themselves, and among the individual religious priests, brothers and sisters. A second assumption is that each level of religious life continues in the transformational process and that the new paradigms of religious life held by significant numbers of members have not yet been fully developed. A third assumption is that the environmental change that had the greatest impact on the promotion of the transformation process is the new understandings of the church proclaimed during Vatican II and reflected shortly afterward in directives to religious congregations to begin the analysis and revision of their basic principles and practices.

Consistent with organizational theory outlined above, the current condition of religious life in the United States reflects diverse, and sometimes contradictory, understandings of religious life that have developed in different subgroups of members of religious orders. In addition, environmental forces that strongly support the development of particular understandings are present in the hierarchical church, in various segments of the laity and in society at large. The paradigms that have both guided consistency among religious orders for centuries and have in the past brought forth new strains of religious commitment appear to be in a state of flux. Many competing understandings of what a religious order should be exist in the church. The operative paradigms are wide, as Morgan (1980) described. They are characterized by extremes of both subjective and objective interpretations of Catholicism in American life, and the range of visions for the future are as varied as radical change, on the one hand, and regulation and standardization, on the other. Competing paradigms are operative. To say it another way, the current descriptions of religious life are shaped by prevailing views of the church within the various subgroups that comprise it. There is not at present, nor may there ever be again, one paradigm of religious life in the church. Whether one will develop remains to be seen.

The model of transformation identified here would suggest that those who continue to live the vocation to religious life have a unique perspective on their role and are rooted in a spirituality that sustains them. Within the framework of transformation, a comprehensive assessment would yield some measure of how change is occurring and affecting religious life at the level of the social institution, congregations and within individuals. The primary interest of this study was to answer the question, "What factors now must be addressed for religious life to remain vital in American society and the church?"

DESCRIPTION OF THE STUDY

The research project, Factors Influencing the Transformation of Religious Life in the Catholic Church in the United States (The Religious Life Futures Project), was undertaken for the purpose of examining the changes that are occurring in the experience and the understanding of religious life. The point of view of its members (sisters, brothers and religious priests) was the focal area. Specifically, the study examined the processes of, and the factors that contribute to, the transformation or decline of religious life in the United States. The broad objectives of this study were to:

1. Examine the interpretive schemes used by members of religious orders to describe the meaning structure of their commitment and their perceptions of the distinctiveness of religious life in relation to the other vocations and roles in the church. The interpretive schemes were examined from the perspectives of the psychological, theological and organizational changes that have occurred over time, with special attention to the degree to which religious orders are becoming more or less distinct;
2. Analyze the psychosocial, structural and organizational changes that have occurred and those still likely to occur in religious orders in order to anticipate the future shapes of religious life;
3. Identify specific members of religious orders who are perceived as outstanding leaders, visionaries and caring individuals and explore their unique perspectives on religious life, believing that they possess skills, attitudes or beliefs that will shape the future. Their profiles were compared with membership attitudes to assist in identifying the gap between the desired future and the present reality. These findings then suggested what changes must yet occur if religious life is to remain a vital social and ecclesial reality;
4. Describe and analyze some effects of change and perceptions of religious life on the commitment of individual religious; and
5. Describe some of the environmental and cultural influences on religious life in the United States.

Within such a diverse population of interest and commitment (not to mention age) the challenge in presenting a comprehensive view of religious life was to define who among the population could best represent various perspectives. Therefore, in addition to including members-at-large, the design of the study incorporated processes to identify those individuals known to possess vision; individuals who were noted as distinctly caring, outstanding and typical leaders; and key religious figures who have contributed intellectually to the theological history of religious life during the period since Vatican Council II.

All orders in the United States, regardless of size, were invited to participate in the study.

The Religious Life Futures Project has been a comprehensive assessment of religious orders in the Catholic Church in the United States. Within the major project, six independent studies or research units were undertaken, yielding substantive data in a variety of areas. The research units included as part of the Religious Life Futures Project are:

1. National Survey: A random sample of 9,999 from the identified population of 121,439 priests, brothers and sisters who are members of religious orders, with a return rate of 70% (6,359 usable responses). Using a stratified random sampling design, the population has been compared on all measures by tradition (apostolic, mendicant, monastic and contemplative), age, sex and vocation (sister, brother or priest).

2. Visioning Groups: Four gatherings held between October 1989 and March 1990 involved in-depth study of 92 members of religious orders identified as "visionary," that is, as possessing a sense of future vision and committed to religious life.

3. Caring People Project: David C. McClelland, Ph.D., and Carol Franz, Ph.D., collaborated in an investigation of the dynamics that characterize uniquely caring people within the population of religious orders.

4. Individual Interviews: 23 in-depth interviews with persons who are national figures or scholars in the area of religious life were conducted.

5. Leadership: In addition to four regional Leadership Workshops, leadership was also studied through:
   a. The National Survey: Using Bernard Bass's leadership scales as well as measures of spiritual leadership, the study identified both follower perceptions of leadership and leaders' own perceptions.
   b. In-depth interviews with former and current leaders, as well as some of the major theological writers, on issues of leadership in religious life in the United States yielded a range of insights that are incorporated throughout the text.
   c. Leadership Competency Assessment: Through a separate grant from the Lilly Endowment Inc., competencies that distinguish outstanding from typical performance among leaders of religious orders have been identified.

6. Historical/Theological Monograph: Elizabeth Johnson, C.S.J. (Fordham University) has written an historical monograph and John Padberg, S.J. (St. Louis University) has provided an historical postscript. These will appear in the more popular treatment of the study to follow this publication.

Chapter 2

MASTER IMAGES AND DILEMMAS:
THE VISIONING GROUPS

PURPOSE

The purpose of the Visioning Groups unit of the Religious Life Futures Project was to explore creatively the future of religious life in the United States through the eyes of individual members of religious orders who were identified as possessing a unique and future-oriented perspective. A secondary goal was to establish baseline images and attitude measures against which attitudes of the general population of members of religious orders regarding their vision of the future of religious life could be measured. In addition, specific session goals included the development of strategies to implement these predicted images of religious life.

SUBJECTS

Participants in the Visioning Groups phase of the study were recruited through a nomination process that began with a letter to the major superior of randomly selected religious orders of women and men. To ensure geographical representation, the congregations were selected from the Atlantic, Mid-Central, South and West regions of the United States.

In the letter, the superior was invited to consult with her or his council or similar group of advisors to identify one member of his or her order as a nominee to participate in the Visioning Groups gathering. A nomination criteria sheet was included with the mailing which stipulated that the nominee:

1. Be a person of vision in the congregation;
2. Be recognized for his or her ability to live the charism of the congregation in today's culture; and

3. Have concretely evidenced, and be able to articulate, a sense of hope
   and a belief in the future of religious life.

A total of 550 religious orders was invited to participate (237 men's groups and
313 women's groups). Nominations were submitted by 76 of the men's orders
(32% response rate) and 113 of the women's orders (36% response rate).

The groups met at retreat or conference centers in Connecticut, Louisiana,
Colorado and Illinois during fall 1989 and spring 1990. Twelve women and
twelve men were invited to participate at each site. The researchers also sought
a mix of brothers and priests among the men and representation from the various
traditions within religious life. To the extent possible, efforts were made to
include members of ethnic and racial minority groups.

For each gathering, some unforseen event resulted in one member's
cancellation. Hence, 23 persons participated in each of the four Visioning
Groups gatherings, yielding a total of 92 subjects. This total included 48
women and 44 men (12 brothers and 32 priests). Minority representation
included one Hispanic sister, one Hispanic priest and one African-American
priest.

METHOD

The Visioning Groups unit consisted of various processes designed to elicit
both qualitative and quantitative data. These interventions yielded information
concerning the beliefs, attitudes and choices that are shaping the future of
religious life in the United States. A multitrait, multimethod analysis was
employed throughout to gather the widest array of data possible from this select
population.

Preparatory Reflection: Hopes for the Future

Prior to their arrival, Visioning Groups participants were asked to complete
an essay entitled, "Hopes for the Future." The instructions invited them to
"write about your dream, plan, or vision for the future of religious life. In this
dream, plan or vision, describe what you are willing to put into achieving that
vision and what you would hope to see realized by it." The essays were mailed
to the researchers prior to the gathering and redistributed to their authors at the
opening session.

During the Gathering: "Components of a Future Vision of Religious Life"

Each of the Visioning Groups gatherings lasted from noon Friday to noon Sunday. After introductions and a sharing of their "Hopes for the Future" statements, each participant received a list of those elements or components thought to be basic to religious life in the future. The list was based on the "Transformative Elements," a list of ten elements thought to be critical to the future of religious life in the United States and generated at the 1989 Joint Assembly of the Conference of Major Superiors of Men (CMSM) and the Leadership Conference of Women Religious (LCWR). To ensure completeness, the researchers examined the results of a pilot research project that preceded this research endeavor, reviewed the "nonnegotiables" of religious life, as identified by some 1,000 female and male members of religious orders who participated in one of three regional Convergence Workshops sponsored by a Chicago-based religious consulting group in spring 1989, and studied recent writings on religious life, including sources ranging from Vatican writers to feminist theologians. As a result, commitment focus, conversion and community life were added to the "Transformative Elements." The resulting list of 13 characteristics was titled "Components of a Future Vision of Religious Life." They are listed, with the definitions that also were presented to the participants, in Appendix B.

A Q-sort method was used to examine the collective relationship between, and the priority given to, each of these components as they were considered relevant to a vision of the future. After private reflection, participants met in preassigned groups of three or four persons with a set of 15 cards, 1 each for the 13 components and 2 blanks, or "wild cards." Participants were then asked to discuss the theological and other facets of the components and select the eight components that most reflected the probable future content and belief about religious life. Two additional "wild card" entries were allowed to provide for the inclusion of components that the participants thought were significant but did not see included in the listing. Editing of the original concepts also was permitted so that the groups could come to a consensus on meaningful terminology.

The same process was then replicated after two groups were combined. Each group was asked to sort components again from the two independently sorted groups and select from among the originals, the edited versions and the wild cards those components and possibly two additional items, totaling no more than 15, that the group of seven or eight persons believed would characterize the future of religious life.

After this exercise, each of the groups of seven or eight participants was asked to construct images or metaphors to capture visually and graphically the relationships of the components to a whole. Identical packets of colored poster board, tape, scissors, colored markers, masking tape and a ruler were provided to each group.

The Next Step: Choosing a Vision

The larger groups presented the images that they constructed to the other participants in the Visioning Groups when gathering during the latter part of the second afternoon. All participants had the opportunity to view the images, listen to the description that accompanied each, and pose questions regarding the process or product itself.

In the early evening, the group reconvened. Instructions to the group were to "walk around the room, reflecting on each of the images, then stand by the one image that elicits the most energy for you." This was followed by a strategy-building exercise, thus actualizing the third goal of the Visioning Groups: the development of strategies to implement their images of the future. For the strategy session, the participants received the following directive: "You are a part of a group around this vision. What must you do to move yourself closer to this vision? How can we, as church, move toward the realization of this vision?"

RESULTS

"Hopes for the Future"

Each of the "Hopes for the Future" statements was read and coded by two raters for the presence of each of the 13 "Components of a Future Vision of Religious Life."

The statements also were read and coded for the appearance of the nine "Essential Elements" as defined in the Vatican document, *Essential Elements in Church Teaching on Religious Life* (1983). This document listed those elements that the Vatican Congregation for Religious and Secular Institutes considered to be distinguishing characteristics of religious life. It is a significant piece of literature insofar as it originated in the Vatican, the official seat of authority for members of the Roman Catholic Church. It elicited much conversation and consternation among members of religious orders in the United States, many of whom said that they believed it failed to reflect their current experience or expression of religious life. These elements, with descriptions taken from the text itself, are listed in Appendix B.

The purpose of this critical comparison between the components and elements was to examine the interpretive schemes of members of religious orders. As noted in Chapter 1, shifts in interpretive schemes of organizations typically mark periods of transformation and reflect operative paradigms. By examining the "Hopes for the Future" statements for the presence, priority and expression of some of the values and practices that have traditionally marked religious orders, it was possible to determine that these shifts are indeed occurring.

A comparative reading of the components and the elements themselves shows that, in many cases, similar underlying constructs appear in both lists. They can be noted in the following pairings:

Components	Elements
Commitment Focus	Consecration by Public Vow
Intentional Communities	Communion in Community
Contemplative Attitude	Prayer
Prophetic Witness	Public Witness

Articulations of the characteristic, however, reveal significant differences. Components are more typically defined in relational and global terms. Contemplative Attitude, for example, speaks of "a contemplative attitude toward all creation" and an attentiveness to "the presence of the sacred in their own inner journeys, in the lives of others, and throughout creation." In contrast, the parallel element, Prayer, is called a "habit" and described in terms of "individual, communal and liturgical" forms. This reflects a more juridical expression, one characteristic in general of the elements.

While participants had access to the information reflected in both lists, they were not apprised of the analysis to which these essays would be subjected. Hence, it is fair to assume that their accounts reflect their current ideas and images. Table 2.1 presents the data, in terms of actual frequency counts of the appearance of each of the components and the elements, and percentage based on the total number of responses in each category for the "Hopes for the Future" statements. The components are first listed in alphabetical order, followed by the alphabetical listing of the essential elements. A ranking of the items, based on their frequency of mention, is also included in Table 2.1.

As is evident from the numbers, the "Components of a Future Vision" were referred to more frequently and by greater numbers of participants in the Visioning Groups than were the "Essential Elements." Among the elements, only Prayer (rank = 11) was mentioned more frequently than any other of the Components, and Cultural Interdependence (component) tied for positions 14, 15 and 16 with the elements Evangelical Mission and Formation. One could conclude from this data that there is evidence for a shift in interpretive schemes among religious orders in the United States. An understanding of this phenomenon might provide significant areas of conversation between members of religious orders in the United States and the Vatican.

Table 2.1
**Results of Coding Visioning Group Participants' "Hopes for the Future"
for "Components of a Future Vision" and "Essential Elements"**

Component/Element	Number of References	% of Participants	Overall Rank
Commitment Focus	10	11	13
Community Life	25	28	8.5
Contemplative Attitude	36	40	4
Conversion	11	12	11.5
Cultural Interdependence	8	9	15
Distributed Power	26	29	7
Global Spirituality	30	33	5.5
Intentional Communities	46	51	1
Living with Less	16	18	10
Preferential Option for the Poor	40	44	3
Prophetic Witness	44	49	2
"We Are Church"	30	33	5.5
Asceticism	3	3	19
Communion in Community	5	6	18.5
Consecration by Public Vow	7	8	17
Evangelical Mission	8	9	15
Formation	8	9	15
Government	0	0	21
Prayer	11	12	11.5
Public Witness	1	1	20
Relationship with Church	5	6	18.5

The Q-Sort Project

At the four Visioning Groups gatherings, the combination of the small groups of three or four individuals into larger groups of seven or eight resulted in a total of 17 groups. Thus, 17 sets of rank orderings of the components and 17 images of the future were generated through this process.

This section will focus on two approaches to the Q-sort results. The first is a primarily qualitative consideration of the "wild card" entries: those items introduced by various groups because they were perceived as critical to religious life in the future but were not included on the original list. The second is a more quantitative approach, consisting of a study of the rankings assigned to the 13 components.

Additional Components

The additional components submitted by individual groups on their "wild cards" were read and categorized according to the implicit domains or logical factors that are suggested. They are:

Witness	*Sexuality*
Visionary	Intimacy/Sexuality
Partnership with Creation	Celibate Loving
Non-violence as a Way of Life	Covenanted Commitments
Faith and Spirituality	*Leadership Context*
Charism as Gospel Vision	Cross-Cultural Evangelization
Retrieval of Scripture	Apostolic Leadership
Sharing the Faith Story	Pluralism
Prayerful People	Articulated Charism
Ongoing Formation	

Their importance lies in the fact that they were derived consensually from the participants and included by at least one group in the Q-sort process. The process did not allow all the groups in any one city to develop a composite. With one exception, the additional components generally reflect the thought of a single group and do not appear in the rank ordering. The single exception to this was the component titled "God's Initiative," which emerged independently from the groups and has been included in the standardized ranking of the components in Table 2.2.[1]

The appearance of these additional components is significant in that they point to the different perspective that persons identified as "visionary" possess when compared to the formal leaders of religious orders. It was these leaders, members of the Conference of Major Superiors of Men and Leadership Conference of Women Religious, who generated the listing of the ten items that formed the basis for the components list. A second striking aspect is found in examining the category, Faith and Spirituality. Visioning Groups suggested five different components related to this area and were overall most insistent on the recognition and articulation of the role of God in life. In addition to the categories listed under this heading, consideration of the components list by the Visioning Groups participants included repeated expressions of surprise and concern regarding the absence of the mention of God, call to religious life and the role of scripture in the items presented by the conferences.

Rank Orderings

The "Components of a Future Vision of Religious Life" were rank-ordered using standardized priority scores. Each components, ranked by priority, was then subjected to content analysis and clustered according to the levels of analysis proposed in the original research protocol. Table 2.2 presents the rank ordering of the components organized according to the three levels of analysis (social institution, congregation and individual) proposed by the study. Clearly, each component has implications for all levels of analysis, but organizing according to domains is suggestive of possible interventions.

Table 2.2
Q-Sort Results Categorized by Level of Analysis

	Level of Analysis		
Rank	Social Institution	Congregation	Individual
1			Contemplative Attitude
2	Prophetic Witness		
3		Intentional Communities	
4			Conversion*
5		Charism	
6	Preferential Option for the Poor		
7	Distributed Power		
8	Global Spirituality		
9			God's Initiative*
10	Cultural Interdependence		
11		Living with Less	
12		Community Life*	
13	"We Are Church"		
14			Commitment Focus*

* Items that did not appear on the 1989 CMSM/LCWR listing of "Transformative Elements" but were added by the researchers.

Contemplative Attitude, which ranked first in the total listing, is the only component with a strong applicability to the individual domain that appeared in LCWR/CMSM's 1989 listing of "transformative elements." Prophetic Witness, the component ranked second in the overall listing, appears with the other five that cluster together with implications for religious life as a social institution. The component ranking third, Intentional Communities, is included in the domain of the congregation. Hence, in beginning with the "top three" components, the relevance of these constructs for the three levels of analysis becomes clearer.

A cursory consideration of the components most applicable to the individual domain could lead to an interpretation of support for the traditional views of religious life: God calls an individual (God's Initiative), and the individual, who is attentive to the movement of grace (Contemplative Attitude), responds. After a period of mutual discernment, the response is formalized (Commitment Focus) and the individual's life is devoted to deepening and purifying the response to that initial call (Conversion).

The articulation of those components, however, departs in several significant ways from the more traditional understandings and, consequently, has far-reaching implications for individual members of religious orders. As is also evident in Table 2.2, the spread of the rankings ranges from first to last from among the 14 components. This leaves much room for question concerning the relative significance of the components.

According to the participants in the Visioning Groups, Contemplative Attitude will be a core component in religious life of the next millennium. In its definition, it is totally inclusive: no longer does religious life promise to provide a haven of "escape from the world." This is true for members of cloistered orders as well as for the apostolic religious insofar as, with this definition of Contemplative Attitude, nothing eludes the gaze of the truly contemplative person. From within monastery walls or on the streets of the city, a sense of the interconnectedness of the universe in its proper perspective challenges both the narcissistic and the triumphalistic tendencies of an individual. It assumes the ability to integrate, to internalize, to synthesize and to implement. Such an understanding challenges any sense of passivity in an individual. It also challenges a spirituality of "avoidance of the world" and insists on an understanding of incarnational theology.

Ranking fourth in the complete listing was Conversion, the component that speaks of the penetration of the church and social order as a result of the experience of conversion and its expression through a vowed commitment and mission. As in the understanding of Contemplative Attitude, the direction is outward; in this instance, it is named as the transformation of interpersonal relationships, community and the social and global order. Conversion is a concept that involves a reverence and appreciation for process over product and a willingness to grapple with issues of growth and change.

God's Initiative, the third of the components with the clearest implications for the individual, ranked ninth in the complete listing. It recognizes the call of God in the ongoing life of the individual and the rootedness of one's being in that relationship. This, as noted above, was the only item added to the original listing of 13 components, and was included because of its widespread introduction by the Visioning Groups participants.

Commitment Focus appeared last in the rankings of the Visioning Groups participants. It is described in terms of a life-style marked by the vows of chastity, poverty and obedience which offers a positive model of community. It is interesting to note that the phrase "the vowed life" was once used as synonymous with religious life. Seeing this component ranked as last provides further confirmation of hypotheses concerning the changes that have occurred in interpretive schemes of religious women and men over the past 30 years.

Seen as a whole, the preeminence of Contemplative Attitude and Conversion over Commitment Focus marks a transition, for members of religious orders, to a focus on, and commitment to, issues beyond the limited concerns of their own life-style to a global focus and process of growth. At the very least, the more traditional words have been replaced by a vocabulary that reflects internal as well as external concerns and by a focus on relationships with persons beyond the limits of particular congregations. This provides evidence for the boundary shifts described in Chapter 1.

On the congregational level of analysis, the components of Intentional Communities, Charism, Living with Less and Community Life appear. The rankings of these components range from 3 to 12, which is the "narrowest" spread when the three domains are considered. Only the last item, Community Life, was added to the LCWR/CMSM list by the researchers. A review of the content identified in the descriptions of these four components will highlight the shifts in articulation of what is significant when considering religious life on the congregational level.

The forms of community life, as described in the Intentional Communities (rank = 3) definition and the renewal implied in the Charism (rank = 5) statement contrast with the more traditional description of Community Life (rank = 12). Living with Less (rank = 11), a description of the community, takes significantly lower priority than those with whom these members of religious orders will live. On the congregational level, there is also a gap between the ranking of Preferential Option for the Poor (rank = 6), considered as a component in the domain of the social institution, and the expected consequences, implied in Living with Less.

On the level of the social institution, Prophetic Witness, Preferential Option for the Poor, Distributed Power, Global Spirituality, Cultural Interdependence and "We Are Church" ranged in rankings from 2 through 12.

Images of the Future

As was noted in the preceding section, the division of Visioning Groups participants into subgroups resulted in the production of a total of 17 different images of the future of religious life. In terms of the actual products, the following images were presented:

spectrum	concentric circles with rays emanating
intersecting planes	amalgamation of various shapes
prism	yin/yang image
crossroads	"spiral of unitive consciousness"
mobile (2)	"contemplative symphony"
weaving	jazz band
spiral musical staff	kaleidoscope
stained glass window	fan

In presenting these images, the participants exhibited energy and enthusiasm. Typically, they also resisted the notion of a static image. Some groups used movement in their presentation. For example, one walked around the outside of the group with the completed image to depict the shifting scenes of a kaleidoscope or the variations in light as it shines through a prism. Another concluded a presentation with an invitation to the participants to join in dance. Others used language to capture the energy, in words such as, "Fan into flame the gift that God has given us," "an eruption of energy coming from a contemplative center" or "the energy that moves everything outward to a newness of life but also draws everything or absorbs everything inward to that vision." Still others, in constructing a mobile or other hanging, integrated the possibility of movement into the image itself.

Common themes in the narrative descriptions of the images included the following:

Mystery. The sense of the sacred and the unfathomable was a common theme. "We kept talking about this element of mystery, and the fact that we cannot totally understand it." It was often depicted by a central or empty space where God is found: "There is a real hole that needs to be part of this vision of the future: the surprise element, the unknown, the mystery that is always there." Another group, reflecting on the significance of the Gospel of Jesus for religious life, noted that the "vision needs to be concretized in specific forms, many of which are yet to be discovered. And that's why there's that hole [in the image], because there are many that aren't yet discovered."

Explicit mention of God and/or God's action. There was clear acknowledgment of the centrality of the divine in the life of the members of a religious order: "The reflective life, the relationship with Jesus, is the essential, the most essential, the foundational point." Religious life was described as a

"revelation of God's love to the world." "The initiative from God is the very
first thing for religious life." In the image of the crossroads, the presenter
noted: "In the middle is God. We felt that if it wasn't for God and our
relationship with God, we wouldn't be discussing this." The awareness that God
as an initiator of the process of a call to religious life also was noted frequently.
This includes a "willingness to be converted and transformed into Christ. This
is the *internal* commitment. It seemed at the very center of it all." (Emphasis
in the original.)

Incompleteness. Incompleteness took two forms. The first relates to the
status or "evolution" of the process of renewal. One group articulated it at the
conclusion of their presentation when, in turning their image to present to the
group the "back" or reverse side of their product with all of the indications of
tape and extra materials, they noted: "It looks horrendous. . . . If you've
ever done a needlepoint or a weaving, the underside looks kind of messy. So,
we're doing theology of religious life from the underside." Another group also
used the expression "messy" to describe this experience. A third group
described the experience as being "not only of motion and interconnectedness,
but something not finished and ongoing."

The second form of incompleteness was manifested in the awareness that
others, including the laity in the church, members of minority groups and,
indeed, all creation are partners in the process. One group observed: "We had
a lot of discussion around this. . . . We feel there [are many] people who
aren't here. There are people who, by our ministry, and our walking with
them, and their walking with us and our exchanges, change who we are." This
form also was stressed in the presentation of the *Contemplative Symphony 2010*
in which the group prefaced its presentation with the observation that "religious
life is really one element of the orchestra. It is represented by the string
section. The other sections of the orchestra represent all the other ways of life
that are in existence, all of which work together to produce the contemplative
symphony." For example, it was suggested that the hierarchy is analogous to
the brass.

Flexibility. Motion has been already noted in the images of the shifting
kaleidoscope, mobiles and prism. The flexibility that this entails was mentioned
as a critical value by several groups, such as those who observed, in their
production, that there is "room for change, for continual growth of conversion." The group that produced the kaleidoscope also noted that "the elements
change, depending on how you view them. . . . No matter how you turn it,
the result is always beautiful." Similarly, those who constructed the prism
observed that "as the light comes through, the colors are never the same shape,
they're always different. . . . [So, too, the shapes we cut for this presentation
will] never be that shape again. That is part of our vision. Religious life will
never be in stone again."

Permeable boundaries. Participants mentioned frequently, and constructed deliberately in their images, a sense of fluctuation with regard to boundaries, for example, "not confined within a frame." The stained glass window, for example, was "not bounded by a leaded frame. . . . It was purposely left very loose. . . . There is no way of keeping the components separate or isolated. . . . The openness is an opportunity for interchange and mutuality between religious life and the world outside." The crossroads image included a series of half-circles ("broken links") symbolizing "openness to others, in the sense that there is a receptive image in there, but it is also reaching out." "The mystery of being human breaks the boundaries, and it goes beyond the frames and is greater than any of us."

Concern for the economically poor and marginalized. This concept was articulated frequently and with conviction (e.g., "definitely, that [concern] would have to be there"), particularly in terms of where members of religious orders would be found in the future: among "the poor and marginalized, very close to the heart of God, to whom religious life of the 21st century is committed." One group noted: "We did change 'preferential option for the poor' to 'solidarity with the poor.' . . . We can't simply be giving things to the poor, we need to be with the poor."

Recognition of religious life as unique. This concept was mentioned frequently, but the essence of the uniqueness was never specified. The struggle with this concept is, perhaps, best typified in the following observation: "We are not higher or, in some ways, not different, but we are a very clear, explicit, visible, sacramental form of what our commitment to Christ is about. And it takes some specific form." A sense of possessing a unique role marks the expressions of Visioning Groups participants but, like their colleagues in religious orders, they cannot articulate it.

In all these presentations, there was an underlying sense of the tension that exists between the vision these persons have of religious life in the future and their ability and freedom to express it. The tension between the communal and individual dimensions was perhaps most clearly articulated in the image of the jazz band. Here, the group observed that in a jazz band, "all are artists and they are expected to be competent. They obviously have different competencies insofar as they are competent on different instruments." Consequently, "trust is critical." The group then observed that "one of the things the jazz band symbolizes, and we think religious life will, is that we will not let go of either the individual good or the common good. We will take a stand that both of those are important."

Another indication of the struggle experienced by members of religious orders today was manifest, as one group noted, in the tendency to "resist the need to prioritize or the importance of prioritizing" when participants were requested to rank the components. Expressions like "All are important," or "We didn't want to assign values" may reflect the resistance among members of religious orders to identify a focus for their orders lest it carry an implication that some works are "more important" than others. Statements such as, "Different parts have different weights at different times" also were common.

While resistance to establishing a priority order for the components was frequently connected to a rejection of any implication of "hierarchy," such a dynamic may paralyze a group by perpetuating the illusion that, in face of diminishing numbers of members and resources, it can continue to be "all things to all persons." The recognition of one's limits, and the fact that saying "yes" to some things frequently involves saying "no" to others, is a critical part of adult life, and of the process of a group's achievement of a corporate identity.

Interestingly, only one group addressed the need for leadership. In the jazz band metaphor, the group noted:

> Someone lays down a beat; they have to make some decisions about playing this tune rather than another tune. So, there is some definition around things. The melody is decided, and then people begin. . . . What is important [for each member] is that you do know well what it is you do, so that in fact you can play.

Related conversations brought to the surface the power of the experience and the participants' affirmation of the need for other members of religious orders to engage in similar processes. Reflections on the process itself brought significant insights to some, as when, on reflecting on taking the step to begin to cut the paper after much group discussion, one participant noted the significance of the "moment of courage in cutting the paper." Another recalled her comment, as she cut out the first figure in the jazz band, "I feel like I'm creating a new life," and the process of listening, sharing and shaping of ideas that preceded the "risk" entailed in cutting the paper to "free" the sketched image.

The Dilemma

As was described in the Methods section, at the conclusion of the presentation of the images, each person was asked to consider all the models and select one that he or she found most engaging in terms of a future vision. Participants were directed to base their choice on their willingness to make a personal commitment and to devote their energy to realizing that future vision.

This request invariably caused a dilemma for participants. The experience of a preference for a model designed by another group produced in most individuals a sense of guilt or betrayal, as well as abandonment concerns, regarding the group with which they had worked to produce an image. This phenomenon was processed at each of the gatherings, and the participants' responses were categorized according to the following three questions:

1. What factors influenced your choice?
2. What dilemmas presented themselves as you considered the various choices available?
3. How might this experience be generalized/or applied to religious life?

In terms of factors influencing the choice, ownership and familiarity played significant roles. Participants made comments such as, "I had the inclination to choose the one that I had some ownership of" or "the one I had a common experience with"; "I invested time and sharing and the energy of the group", and "I understood my own [model] and . . . [I did not have the time] I needed to really understand enough to make another commitment." A few noted an increased appreciation of their original image as they viewed the others: "There were things in each one that drew me, and yet the one was part of me"; "[After] finding within all the images something that resonated with my original creation . . . [and] then seeing my own image in a new perspective, which I hadn't seen in the creation of it because we were too close to the actual creating, . . . a perspective of distance also led me back."

Those who did shift to a new image expressed a sense of being drawn to something new and, frequently, a surprise with their ability to make the move. "I felt an inner core of attraction toward that one that I couldn't deny. I think what it was, was the element of change. . . . It was not going to stay the same." "I was surprised I could detach myself from [the model] I had created and [go] to another one." "I wanted to find one that reflected the values I had. . . . I hadn't been that excited about the process that created the one I was in. I wanted to be with the people who excited me."

Many of the dilemmas expressed by the participants reflected concern about the feelings of others: "I didn't want them to be feeling rejection;" "It was loyalty to the group." There were also personal considerations, such as, "[In changing], I was saying that [I was going to give up on] something I had done as my best work . . . and go to somebody else's work." Also evident was concern about subsequent steps: "not knowing exactly where we were going to go [with the process]."

Throughout, the relational factor played a significant role. This was not always a pleasant realization, as one participant observed: "For a while I kept trying to deny that I really liked the people in the group." Others noted, in their choice, that "there was the temptation to look at who was standing in each group and choose for the relationship with people, rather than just the values." Many forced themselves to confront the issue, "Am I choosing the image that really resonates with me, or am I choosing the group, the people in the group?" The prospect of new persons presented mixed feelings, as noted by the observation that "there were a few new people, and that was exciting, but it was also frightening. . . . I felt [that] maybe there [were] expectations." Realistically, too, participants acknowledged that "we weren't alike at all, and that was scary to me. How were we going to support each other?" Some faced yet another possibility: "What if I was alone? Would it be OK to make this choice and stand by myself with it?"

The intensity of the dilemma was articulated by several participants. "For me, the immediate thing was, 'Do I really have a choice?' We had made a commitment. We shared the energy that we had. We unleashed what is in our hearts. We trusted one another. There could be no other choice." One who opted to move to another group noted similarly:

> I felt sadness because I was letting go of something that I had helped shape for something that somebody else had. There was fear that [in] leaving, once I got to the new thing it really wouldn't be something I could own. I felt a real concern for the group, a concern for abandonment as I went to something else. Yet, I was excited by the choice I had made. When I looked around at the end, and saw the people standing there, it was like an affirmation of the choice I was making that others saw something here that might have meaning.

As the participants extrapolated these experiences to religious life and to ways in which the vision of religious life in America might be shaped, they noted the parallel of the choice within this experience to the choices about maintaining relational bonds or moving forward with a vision of the mission that many members of religious orders must face in their own congregations. The psychological dynamics of history in a group, particularly as regards relational bonds and affiliational motives, can be a significant force inhibiting creativity and the achievement of vision. Similarly, the need is clear to attend to the feelings of rupture, disloyalty and even violence when individuals do leave. One participant summarized this in the comment, "Any choice we make usually calls us to die [sic] towards something else." Another commented on "the importance of people being involved in shaping the vision, to have ownership."

In summary, this process replicated the dilemma that many members of congregations experience in wanting to be involved in achieving a compelling vision of the future while desiring also to maintain existing relational bonds. Although this sense of loyalty or affiliation that inhibits change is not unique to religious groups, it does represent a critical factor in how groups move toward the future. Affiliation is generally a stronger force than vision.

IMPLICATIONS

Implications for Religious Life as a Social Institution

Religious life as a social institution is defined both within the structure of the church and among the domains of organizations in society. Religious life as a social institution in the church refers to the unique contribution that members of religious orders attempt to make to the ministry of the church which is generally distinct from both the form and substance of what laity and clergy contribute. Religious life in relation to society is marked by social boundaries and characteristics that specify both its intensely spiritual quest and its existence as an alternative to the dominant culture in which it is engaged in the United States and, for that matter, in the church itself.

When the various "components" of religious life are organized according to their primary level of analysis, religious life as a social institution will be characterized by six components: prophetic witness, a preferential option for the poor, distributed power, global spirituality, cultural interdependence and the attitude that "we are church."

The content and ranking of the components and the participants' spontaneous verbalizations in the presentations of images of the future of religious life suggest that the structures, mission and resources of religious life will be rooted in Christ, the values of the Gospel, and some recognition of the poor as a source of conversion. The outcome of such intensity will be a presence to the world, whether enacted by cloistered, monastic or apostolic religious, which, by its very nature, challenges social systems that do not acknowledge the rights of the poor. Moreover, the manifestation of life lived in simplicity will speak as well to the anticipation of the reign of God to the extent that religious life remains allied with its espoused dedication to the poor. The narratives presented here of the various images of the future support this view.

The practical consequence of a commitment to prophetic witness and a preferential option for the poor will be a simplicity in life-style, a chosen austerity equal to that of the poor, with openness to the natural beauty of the earth, sacred ritual and a life of prayer and good works conducted in a community of equals. The implication of distributed power is that structures of religious life will continue to reflect a transition to collective activities, where a corporate exchange will be a more compelling vision than the individualism that has characterized both the therapeutic and technological influences in religious life in recent years. At the same time, the motive of distributing power among equals will predominate, leading to increasing demands by groups to clarify the responsibility of leadership. The tyranny of consensus to which many members of religious orders refer as they struggle to understand the role of leadership in religious life must yield to shared understandings of the necessity to clarify leadership for some, to the decline of other groups into a state of chaos, and to the emergence among a few groups of workable models reflective of the structures of utopian or feminist collectives. The resistance to engaging in a task of setting priorities that appears to operate in many of the groups gives additional significance to the issue.

In addition, the expanding consciousness of the globe as the locus of redemption will alter the content of prayer and prayer styles, the choices made by members of religious orders to share in the world's suffering, and the rigidity of continental, juridical and regional thinking. Similarly, as the interchange of multiple cultures occurs, the idioms of faith, the context of belonging, the shared symbolic life and even the primary languages of some communities will be transformed. The flexibility and fluidity of boundaries noted in the presentation of the images points, too, to a need for boundary maintenance lest religious orders regress to a primarily associational form of collective.

Implications for Individual Religious Congregations

Religious congregations ought to provide opportunities for structural expressions of emerging forms of religious life. To do so, they will have to discern the contemporary expression of their founder's charism, redefine or establish boundaries for membership and behavior, and confront the discrepancies between espoused and lived values.

Structural demonstrations are efforts to isolate and highlight a particular manifestation of a charism, not as an end in itself but as a representation of a possible direction for the congregation. At present, such efforts to regain the founding spirit are often viewed by the majority of members as marginal. The presence of those who may have the vision to move the group to the future but rather opt, on the basis of affiliational needs, to conform to group norms may in fact undermine revitalization.

The role of leadership in shaping such a dramatic transformation of religious life will require a new set of competencies. Change will figure more prominently in this period than in the period since Vatican II. Leadership cannot be comprised simply of influence and inspiration. Rather, it will be tied to the work that must be accomplished if, in fact, a prophetic witness is to be achieved. Leadership will require mobilizing people to that critical challenge and getting them to take responsibility for collective action. The leaders of religious congregations must be willing to manage the process of social learning among their members and facilitate the future in specific ways.

Groups will learn their way as they go forward in the context of the work to be done. A vision of religious life that does not also contain some notion of the work or ministry in which members are invited to participate may leave members feeling motivated but without an outlet for their determination. The role of leadership in creating a vision will be strengthened in proportion to the clarity they have about the work that they intend to do.

Hard choices will be made to enable the membership to participate in the collective witness that presents a shared focus that is rooted in tradition and responsive to evident need. Individuals will be called to take stock of the crisis in which they find themselves as groups that increasingly lack a focus, and they must examine their part in it. Leadership may distill the wishes of the group, but leadership must also build relationships within the group while at the same time keeping it focused on the task as defined by the group's own tradition and aspirations. Structural demonstrations of new forms of Gospel life and ministry may be the primary way to evidence desirable change. Such a pioneering view will require the choice to be poor and absolute faith to remain faithful to what it is that members of religious orders understand to be their unique contribution to the church and the world.

Implications for Individual Members of Religious Orders

For individuals who are currently members of religious congregations, the call to change may demand a shift in perspective from an internal focus to a sense of global appreciation, the possible acquisition of new interpersonal skills, and the willingness to accept the implications of ongoing growth and development for personal stability and security. The shift in identity of religious life from a state of life that is relatively self-contained to one that has expressed concern for the whole earth has a range of implications. Individuals who, at one point in their lives, may have been discouraged from informing themselves regarding even local or national events are now expected to think globally. For individuals who are less than adequately stable and mature, these shifts may involve more than such persons may be able to handle. Evidences of psychopathology resulting from the dissolution of structures of religious life that provided for some, a sheltered workshop environment have been noted already in individuals whose psychic structure necessitated such an environment and, as a consequence, may have been attracted to earlier forms of religious life.

A serious appropriation of these components will also provide a challenge to those members of religious orders who, over the past three decades, have moved toward an increased sense of autonomy and independence. The call toward a recognition of the interconnectedness of all creation, even within the church, challenges the sense of privatism and individualism that marks our culture and has permeated religious life. While attention to the sacredness of one's own journey and the action of God in one's life will be key in religious life of the future, individuals, challenged to express this awareness in their ministry and life-style, will face a call to relinquish much of what may now be perceived as nonnegotiable. In light of this challenge, honest discernment may again lead to a significant number of departures from religious life.

The concern about future members of religious congregations also poses a host of issues. Clearly, in this time of diminishing numbers of members and unclarity of focus in many congregations, it can be difficult to evaluate critically individuals who apply for membership. The qualities of docility and dependence, which were once highly valued in potential candidates, do not bode well for the lived expression of many of the chosen components. In addition to the experience described in the God's Initiative component, new members of religious orders will need a maturity that enables them to live a life-style that continues to be countercultural and that also places them in positions of leadership in the global and church communities. The experience of positive interpersonal interactions, the ability to sustain intimate relationships within the context of a celibate commitment, and the manifestation of a variety of personal resources and professional competencies will be critical factors in the admission of candidates to membership in religious congregations. Persons involved in candidate development and leadership positions will face many difficult decisions with regard to this issue over the coming years.

NOTE

1. The "God's Initiative" component was defined in the following manner: "Religious life exists because of God's initiative in the ongoing life of the individual and in the formation of particular religious groups shaped by God's call and grace."

Chapter 3

LEADERSHIP

IMAGINATION AND STRATEGIES OF LEADERS

As noted in the opening chapter of this volume, religious orders of the Roman Catholic Church are undergoing a time of profound transformation. This experience was precipitated when the Second Vatican Council called religious communities to conduct an intense reexamination of their life and structures. The process led most religious orders to study their histories, including for many a first-time investigation of the life and motivation of their founders, and to probe the order's charism. It also called them to examine critically, and then re-write their constitutions. Over three decades, structures of religious orders and their models of governance were altered in response to the mandate for all areas of church life to adjust to contemporary realities and to incorporate principles of subsidiarity and collegiality into decision making.

In addition to the adjustments required as a result of the challenge of the Second Vatican Council, members of religious orders in the United States have also faced shifting demographic trends—most notably, declining enrollment and aging membership—as well as the challenges presented by the secularization of American society. Some members of religious orders welcomed eagerly the new directions set by the church, yet others resisted efforts to update. A wide range of emotional consequences has accompanied the external adaptations, sometimes in the form of immobilizing pain, fear and anger. For many members of religious orders, this has been not simply a time of turmoil, but a time of crisis. For others, however, this has been a period of exhilaration.

With these changes and the accompanying shifts in understandings of authority and leadership and new structures of governance, the role of leaders in Roman Catholic religious orders is an increasingly critical area of investigation. The voices of leaders as they articulate the struggles they face and the strategies they use to address these issues present the unique perspective of individuals charged with managing the complexities that mark an organization in a period of transformation. The population of religious orders presents an additional unique component insofar as it offers precedents to a number of organizations facing similar circumstances and guidance to their leaders.

PURPOSE

In order to confront the question of how leaders can participate in the transformative process that their organizations are experiencing while attending simultaneously to their responsibilities to maintain the organization, leaders of Roman Catholic religious orders were invited to participate in a workshop entitled "Leadership in the '90s." The stated purposes of the sessions were to encourage leaders to explore their experiences as leaders, to confront the issues that they face in their positions and to develop strategies for dealing with the future. In preliminary information circulated to potential participants, the central questions posed were:

1. What were your hopes when you began leadership?
2. Where did you expect to lead?
3. How has the reality of daily stewardship impacted these expectations/ hopes?
4. What are the issues/concerns we share as men and women religious in leadership?
5. How can we shape the future of religious life in the church?
6. What can we do collaboratively to encourage creative leadership?

SUBJECTS

Leaders of religious orders learned of the workshops through mailings from their respective leadership organizations, the Conference of Major Superiors of Men and the Leadership Conference of Women Religious. Offering the workshops in four different geographical regions ensured the participation of leaders from all areas of the United States. Recognizing the significantly greater number of female than male leaders of religious orders, registration limits of 30 women and 20 men at each site helped to achieve gender balance as well as allow for an optimal number of participants. A total of 185 leaders of women's and men's religious orders chose to participate in these sessions. The length of involvement in leadership of their orders ranged from a few months to 10 or more years.

METHOD

Each of the workshops spanned a three-day period, beginning with the evening meal on the first day and concluding with lunch on the third day. During the opening session, after a brief orientation, participants were invited to spend the remainder of the evening writing a letter to the members of their order. In the letters, they were to express their hopes and dreams for the future of their order. It was suggested that they consider their order's mission to the church and society, their sponsored works and corporate mission, and their relationship to other groups within the church and to the laity, as well as their hopes for individuals and their local communities. The exercise was designed to elicit images of the future of religious life and possible strategies for achieving them. It also sought to reveal what factors would contribute to the evolution of religious life.

During the opening session, the workshop facilitators also introduced the participants to the goals of the Religious Life Futures Project. While exerting every effort to preserve each person's sense of freedom regarding participation in this project, the participant-leaders were invited to share a copy of their letter with the facilitators for analysis by the researchers. Through this process of invitation and response, 70 women and 35 men submitted their letters for inclusion in the investigation.

The letters were analyzed initially using an open coding method, which involved an unrestricted reading of the material to derive themes or categories for analysis. This led to the first division of leadership styles as evidenced in themes from the letters: Individuals who are able to envision the future and those who are not. In the next stage of analysis, modified axial coding was used to further refine these divisions and analyze the resulting categories (Strauss, 1987).

RESULTS

Through the process described above, four categories of leadership styles emerged. These categories are characterized by the four themes of response to the exercise and were developed into a typology of leadership styles which is described below. The four categories are: value based, visionary, conflicted and incognizant.

These categories are posed as an heuristic tool for understanding the letters from the perspectives both of their content and their writers. Great variability exists within the letters themselves and few of them could be easily placed in their entirety into one or the other of the categories. The same is true of the leaders themselves: while many do reveal a predominant leadership style in their letters, it is quite possible that a leader would possess a combination of approaches, the most common combinations being conflicted and value-based. Table 3.1 lists the four typologies of leadership and gives definitions of each.

Table 3.1
Typology of Leadership Styles Derived from *Leadership in the '90s* Workshops

Style	Definition
Conflicted	Leaders who have a sense of the direction in which they would like their congregation (or religious life) to develop, and express it in terms of the *conceptual and/or cultural aspects* of religious life. Often, this is articulated as a need to be responsive to, or concerned with a constituent group or a social issue.
Visionary	Leaders who have a sense of the direction in which their congregation (or religious life) ought to develop, and the forms that it might take. They discuss the future in terms of the *structural and/or organizational* aspects of religious life. Generally, they are suggesting images of community or apostolate.
Conflicted	Leaders who, because of personal attributes and/or situational characteristics are hindered in their ability or attempts to address issues of change. While the factors that impede movement may or may not be evident, many leaders experience particular frustration with their membership.
Incognizant	Leaders who do not address any of the issues being experienced by American religious today. Their language is basically rhetorical, and within the context of leadership, ineffective.

Leaders Able to Envision the Future

Among those able to envision the future, the first and most common theme of response involves values. Values reflect what is important to members of religious orders about who they are, who they should be and how they should live their lives in order to best achieve their orders' goals. Values typically represent the cultural foundations of religious life and they are presented as such, without an enabling strategy. An example of this is found in a letter in which the writer expressed concern about environmental problems but offered no suggestion as to how they might be corrected. Other examples are found in statements regarding "oppressive structures" and the need to eradicate them and in references to feminism, environmentalism, multicultural concerns, cooperation, collaboration and hospitality. These writers clearly have an image of how they would like to see their communities and religious life, as a social institution, develop. The values most likely reveal many core elements that will characterize religious life in the future.

The second theme of response concerns vision. A vision is, as the name implies, a concrete image of the future of religious life as the author would like to see it. Unlike values, these visions frequently relate to concrete structural or organizational aspects of religious life and are accompanied by an enabling strategy. For example, a leader may propose a new form of community that includes nonvowed members and also outline the guidelines by which these members might be able to participate in the community's governance. As would be expected, the strategies proposed in this kind of letter are often congregation-specific, reflecting the context in which the letters were written.

Leaders Unable to Envision the Future

Looking next at those leaders who do not envision the future, letters marked by the conflicted style do reflect persons who (for reasons that may or may not be evident in the content of their letters) showed clearly that they were unable to form, or were hindered in articulating, either visions or directions for the future of their individual religious orders or religious life in general. Sometimes these leaders hinted at values or vision, but most of their energy was focused on the problems that they saw and felt. In some instances, the writers emphasized the challenges that they had faced and survived. Often, they did this in retrospective, tracing their history from the founder's time or since Vatican II. In other letters, rather than cajoling their membership, leaders covertly or overtly expressed their anger, frustration and sadness. The leaders whose letters fell into this category displayed different intensities of conflict. For some, the anger and frustration had been immobilizing. Others were able to acknowledge the conflict and attempt to imagine, and sometimes progress toward, the future.

The "incognizant" style of leadership marks the letters in which the leader-authors stopped short of any firm prediction. Instead, they tended to express vague, often rhetorical hopes that lacked substantive images of change or progress. Given their frequently rhetorical nature, they also lacked an expression of what could be the guiding values for change. These letters were written by members of religious orders who were either oblivious to the currents of change around them or who were simply unable to cope in ways that are constructive and provide movement.

DISCUSSION

The following discussion of leadership, incorporating the typology identified from the letters, presents their content and themes in terms of three central questions related to leadership:

1. For those leaders who have a view of the future of religious life, what is the future?
2. For those who do not have a sense of future, why do they lack it?
3. What are the implications for religious life?

Reflections from Leaders Who Have a View of the Future

As religious leaders face the future, the question of self-definition is one of the most significant issues presenting itself to both leaders and members of religious orders in the United States. The symbols and functions that had previously defined members of religious orders, both to the world and to themselves, are no longer available to provide the comfort and security that comes from knowing who one is and what is one's relationship to the world. The resulting ambiguity and identity crisis has led to a long and, for many, painful process of redefinition. This process has demanded that members of religious orders identify, individually and corporately, the essence of what it means to be a member of a religious order. Once identified, this understanding must be internalized in order to continue the process of change without reliance on roles and symbols that are either no longer valid or have lost their meaning. One leader reflected on this reality as she wrote:

> I believe the future holds . . . still more unknowns, still more uncertainties, still more changes, but I envision them at a deeper level than those of the last 20 years. There is something in our future much more radical—something which will take the reality of our smaller numbers, our limited resources and cast us once more to Gospel images of being salt and leaven and light. The future will demand much more authenticity of each of us, much more interior strength and stamina to withstand the conversion to which we will be called.

Articulating the role of members of religious orders. A close reading of the leaders' writings indicates a struggle to define the role of members of religious orders in today's church and society. This was also true for participants in the Visioning Groups gatherings. In the National Survey, role clarity for members of religious orders, defined as the knowledge of what it means to be a member of a religious order in the church today, also surfaced as a critical factor.

As they struggle with this issue, leaders express values that are indicative of changes in the cultural structure of religious life. The issues they addressed reflect their views of the relationship of members of religious orders to the world and the church. The values are also suggestive of the national and global elements that exert an influence on the transformation of religious life in the United States. In most cases, these elements are regarded as the "needs of our times." It is interesting to note that although these workshops took place between four and ten months prior to the August 1989 CMSM/LCWR Joint Assembly, many of the concepts that emerged from the joint assembly in the form of the "Transformative Elements" appear in these letters.[1]

Many of the leaders, for example, wrote in their letters about the responsibility of members of religious orders to fight against oppressive economic and social structures. This was called Prophetic Witness in the listing of the Transformative Elements and was ranked first by the joint assembly. These letters would indicate that, for at least some of the leaders, Prophetic Witness is a central goal of religious life. The demand that members of religious orders become politically or systemically involved, insofar as this position proposes a course of action, might be considered a strategy for the struggle against injustice and oppression. One leader wrote:

> We will need strength. Strength for what? For changing systems and laws, for setting new priorities in church and in society. We'll become more politically active, more vocal in church and society. This privilege [of tax exemption] silences our song in high places and clips our wings. I believe that we have got to take every means available to challenge the injustice which demeans and impoverishes people and the planet even to the point of risking old privileges like the tax exempt status we've enjoyed.

Another leader expressed clearly the call for members of religious orders to act for justice within the church:

> I dream of us being inspirers, motivators, catalysts, instructors and challengers in a church which is beset by fears and cautious to the extreme. That we would reach out to the poor and oppressed, demand justice for all, seek peace for the troubled, speak out fearlessly for what is right even if we end up in prison as did our foundress.

Several other leaders also spoke of the need for change in the larger society. Again, the Transformative Element theme of the Preferential Option for the

Poor, that of being for and with the powerless and the poor, emerges. A typical
example, beginning with "I have a dream," went on to say:

— One day we as a community will lead in the areas of spirituality
  and prayer; of concern for and solidarity with the poor; of being
  a voice for the powerless and at the same time helping the
  powerless gain power; of taking a stand against the abuse of
  persons, against injustice; and of working to transform unjust
  structures.
— One day our community will use its influence for truth and
  goodness and responsible leadership in the Catholic schools—challenging students to think critically, to develop their gifts and talents
  and potential, to be responsible Christian leaders.

The first point is fairly typical of the way in which these values are described
by other leaders: the values themselves are explicit, but the mode of enactment
remains vague. The second point suggests a way in which these values can be
incorporated into the context of the order's ministry.

This leader went on to describe her dream that "one day our community,
with its varied nationalities, will model for the larger community, unity and
respect for all peoples—from every race and culture and creed." This desire to
become a community that embodies egalitarianism was expressed in many of the
letters and is reminiscent of themes found in the Transformative Elements of
Intentional Communities, Distributed Power and Cultural Interdependence.

Working with Others. Collaboration, a word that is widely used by
members of religious orders today, is another theme frequently mentioned by
those who expressed a view of the future. By definition, collaboration embodies
the values of unity and respect, but because of its frequent use, it is sometimes
difficult to gauge the actual depth of understanding or commitment of the letter
writers to this value. Several examples of their hopes follow:

It is my hope that materialism, racism and sexism will give way
to collaborative sharing, respect and cooperation.

My dream is that we can collaboratively effect changes in our
government so that our earth will be preserved for those who will
come after us.

We must change our mind-set so that we are self-sufficient to
openness to collaboration and networking to achieve the relief of
misery.

My dream is that we will continue this process towards collaboration in several areas, especially formation, housing, ministry
and health care/retirement facilities.

Leaders related the emphasis on collaboration and echoed the words of CMSM/LCWR's description of Global Spirituality by placing an importance on having a global perspective, that is, on recognizing that all people are members of a global community. One leader presented his hope in this area, along with one of the few specific expressions of strategy to be found in the letters, particularly as it relates to values:

I dream of having all of us spending some time outside of the U.S., outside of the U.S. culture, with the *poor*, and *acquiring a global perspective*, and *becoming global citizens* rather than simply U.S. citizens in order to renew our works that are more directly, explicitly oriented toward peace and justice for all people. [Emphasis in the original.]

Inclusivity, collaboration and global thinking are core elements presented in these letters. Although these concepts are not always identified as "feminist," the style of their articulation in several instances does reflect the influence of feminism, particularly, but not exclusively, on women leaders. Explicitly feminist issues were identified in some of the letters, often in words similar to the following:

I encourage us as we move toward a vision for the future to claim our identity as women in this world and challenge us to join our hearts and beings with other women in continuing to name and offer our gifts to our church and world. I urge us to join suffering women in their struggle to find wholeness and fulfillment.

Other women used political or metaphorical language, such as "I hope that we continue to model full incorporation of women into the church and to birth our priestly stance." While the role of women within the church is clearly an area of tension for American women religious, a reading of their leaders' letters indicates that it does not impede the relationship between women religious and the world around them, or their relationship to other women religious.

Some of the leaders' views for the future of religious life were reflected in exhortations to "be with the poor and oppressed," to witness collaboration, to explore nonhierarchical models of organization and to respond to calls to care for the environment. All these value-based visions speak to religious leaders' increased awareness of external demands and their perception of a continued need for transformation within society and the church. They also speak to the tensions that develop between those who approach these issues differently: "We must keep these two faces turned toward each other—the faces of direct relief of misery and the addressing of the causes of misery in order to effect radical change." The ability of leaders to balance these approaches, along with the tensions that will, no doubt, result, promise to present challenges for years to come. This distinctive competence among leaders will help shape the future of community and ministry in religious life and the church.

The content of the letters containing themes of the visionary leadership style suggests also that as ambiguity in identification lessens and as clarity of purpose is gained, visions will become sharper and clearer and strategies for movement may follow more readily. Answers to the questions that were posed by some leaders regarding the uniqueness of religious life and their role in the world around them undergird the visions of the future.

Struggles related to institutional commitments. Sponsorship, a structural issue that is frequently raised in the leaders' letters, provides some clear examples of the connection between the role of leader and vision. Responding to declining populations, one of the most pressing environmental factors facing religious orders, many communities have opted to divest themselves of institutions that they had formerly sponsored or operated. As a result, many of their members are now engaged in the same ministries but instead pursue them in institutions or organizations not directly connected with the religious order.

Where sponsorship has been maintained, staffing patterns have shifted dramatically. Institutions staffed previously by members of religious orders alone now employ primarily lay women and men. These shifts have caused emotional pain and role ambiguity among both individual religious and their congregations. Closing institutions that have been expressions of the central focus of mission and ministry within a community not only causes grief, but also stimulates reflection on the nature of vocational commitment. Given the pull between two or more positive values, the leaders' writings reflect much ambivalence with regard to institutional commitments.

Frequently the letters conveyed the leaders' belief that their corporate identity does not lie necessarily in a particular sponsored institution but rather in the essence of the institution's ability to address areas of critical need. This distinction, or the ability to recognize it, often flowed directly from the leader's values of being with the poor, needy and oppressed. Many of these leaders tended to point out that being with these disadvantaged individuals can truly be accomplished only with mobility, a characteristic that they frequently perceive as unattainable in the face of large institutional responsibilities.

> We have never attempted a real analysis of [our founder's] time and
> place in history and have thus assumed that establishing schools was
> his gift to the church. Instead of holding on to our founding story,
> we have settled for the secondary myths of our congregation; namely
> that we run fine schools, etc. We need a new beginning. The
> Constitution calls us to be apostolically mobile—ever on the move.
> We must become missionaries again instead of rooting ourselves to
> institutions. Missionaries who get an evangelizing project going that

can be handed over to others while we move on to other urgent needs
in our United States.

Some leaders did speak to the issue of how institutional commitments can
hinder an order's ability to respond to the "needs of the time." Leaders used
this expression repeatedly in the letters, clearly indicating that one of the central
purposes of religious life is to respond to critical unmet needs. While there is
little consensus regarding which needs are most urgent, the letters do suggest
some agreement that among the most pressing are ministry among persons with
acquired immune deficiency syndrome (AIDS), work with homeless persons and
victims of domestic violence and helping those with unique educational needs.

In general, the letters provide little evidence of the leaders' ability to think
structurally or to provide creative solutions to help institutions function as
conduits of mission. Few, if any, leaders suggested strategies whereby the
institutions themselves can be transformed to respond to absolute human need.
The following is a typical example:

> The clear-cut sense of mission which was ours but a generation ago
> has given way to a plethora of needs beckoning us from all direc-
> tions. Our institutional ministries can seem strangely irrelevant to our
> broken times. Could this not be God's call to leave our sanctuaries,
> our tried and true works of mercy, to turn towards works of justice?
> Could this not be the cutting edge of religious life, as schools and
> hospitals and mission once were?

New understandings of community. The challenge to respect the unique
gifts of individual members of religious orders, while simultaneously defining
the corporate mission of the order, is one that all leaders face. Some struggled
with it in their letters. "One of my dreams is that we find creative ways of
spreading our presence: of being leaders of leaders, of changing our focus to
individual works and to include the reality that where *one* is we *all* are present
(emphasis in the original)."

Traditionally, "witness to community," as expressed through group life in
a convent or monastery, has been a basic element of religious life. Living in
this fashion became one of the external and visible symbols of being a member
of a religious order. The current formulation that "where one is, we all are"
challenges the notion of communal witness and poses yet another challenge to
leaders of religious orders today. The ramifications of reworking the myriad
understandings and expressions of community are enormous, both for individual
religious orders and for religious life itself as a social institution. If religious
women and men no longer live with members of their congregations, what
constitutes the community and what defines membership? If members are
scattered, how does recruitment take place? To what place are prospective

members invited? As members of religious orders live with members of other congregations or with laity, how do individual members maintain a sense of connectedness with their orders?

One leader spoke very concretely to these issues. Her vision is built on the idea that members will have spiritual strength, enabling them to live the life she describes.

> Because of our spiritual strength we shall not need to live in groups of ourselves—except for certain periods of renewal—but we shall live and work as members of basic Christian communities, living our vows of poverty, chastity and obedience in the midst of families. We shall continue bonding with each other as soul-sisters, needing to share our experiences and discernment in regular gatherings.
>
> We shall have regular in-depth sharings with members of religious orders of other congregations (men and women), as well as with religious leaders (inclusive of various traditions) to the extent that these persons are willing and open to share.

Another leader, challenging her community to continue on the course of changes it had already begun, urged her members to reconsider their definitions of community in relation to mission:

> In our ministries we have succeeded in moving from institutional settings to pastoral settings. . . . I would like to suggest that an equally necessary shift has to take place in how we structure our local community settings. Our *mission* should determine who we live with, where we live and how we live as community. I encourage you to explore inter-community with other religious congregations and also community with the laity who share our same vision and mission. A new understanding and experience of community will give us new energy for mission. (Emphasis in the original.)

The relationship between ministry and individuals was raised in the letters almost as frequently as the question of community and institutions. The importance placed on individual members and their talents, desires and gifts is another reflection of the shifts taking place within religious life. It is a natural outcome of the church's shift from acting as a "total" institution to becoming less encompassing, and is a reflection of cultural trends toward individualization. Many of the leaders also expressed concern that their members' gifts were not being used to their full advantage, for either the member or the community. Therefore, they assert, more attention should be paid to recognizing and honoring the individual in ministry. As one leader stated:

The gifts of each member should be used to extend the Kingdom of God. In the apostolate of the schools it is becoming more and more difficult for Brothers to teach the areas for which they are the most gifted. What do we do? Most often we force them into areas for which they are unqualified. Why can't they minister anywhere that their gifts can be used for the sake of service in the church? Why must we force people to remain teaching in the classroom when their gifts are so obviously in other areas of church ministry?

One of the ironies of the emphasis on individualism among religious orders is that the existing ethos of individualism within American society is being questioned increasingly by critics of the culture (Bellah et al., 1985, 1991). While it is true that members of religious orders, too, have identified the dangers of such an attitude, they themselves have not been spared from these tendencies.

Boundary concerns. Several leaders wrote about the inclusion of associate members as well as experiences of intercommunity living. With new structures and several experimental situations, leaders frequently alluded to the need to allow nonmembers to be a part of governmental structures and described the resultant shifts in relationships and in organizational boundaries. In one of the most detailed examples, one leader sketched this scenario:

> I would like to see lay missioners thoroughly integrated into [the order] in the next four years. People who stay with us for more than five years would be eligible to head units overseas, to be on regional councils, be heads of any department/office and be represented on the General Council.
>
> At the same time, I would like to see the lay missioners and the brothers maintain a certain strong self-identity and "power" of their own, out of which this integration flows. In a further development, I would like to see long-term, top-level "employees" be integrated at decision-making levels in both Society/Congregation. Such people would have an official status within [the order] and would be present "with a vote" at General Council and Department levels.
>
> I would like to see us develop an approach to overseas mission from the basis of two realities: shorter-term and long-term members. This can be done effectively, we now know. We must develop for lay persons a "career status" such as Protestant missionary groups developed in this century.

Yet another leader observed:

Our community form must move away from the all-male celibate life
and invite others to live with us with full membership to share our
[community name] identity. We must be willing to let others be part
of our governmental structures and share in a new creative vision of
serving God in education.

These and other examples refer clearly to forging relationships with the laity and
incorporating into them an order's governance structure. Another possible
connection mentioned by several leaders involves intercongregational bonding.
As one leader suggested:

We must continue to build collaborative models of living and working
with other religious orders. In the process, we must be willing to
join our charism with others and build an identity apart from our own
religious gifts as [members of the community]. We must study with
them the possibility of forming a new religious order in the church
that works with all the People of God in an equal manner.

The struggle with boundaries can be exacerbated by the crisis of identity
regarding the role of members of religious orders and by the decreasing number
of candidates. This leader's struggle provides an example of an attempt to
address the pain:

Our numbers are greatly reduced because so many of our finest have
walked out the front doors of our community houses. As we cry in
our hearts over their departures, is not the noise of our sobs drowning
out the gentle taps on our back doors being made by lay people
wanting to join our ranks. Their commitments, being non-permanent
and non-celibate, may be more modest, but are they any less sterling
and true?

Vows. Beyond apostolate and community, few other structural aspects of
religious life were addressed by leaders. For example, only one of the leaders
discussed the vows, raising questions such as:

Is celibacy so essential? How does this vow re-enforce the sexual
violence imposed by church authorities in its teachings about sex? Is
the obedience that we vow to the Pope or to the community? Does
personal surrender of goods and money allow corporate greed among
us? What vows will best free us today for the tasks ahead?

She suggested alternate vows that flow directly from her beliefs about the
importance of the political role of members of religious orders.

The absence of challenge, attempts to redefine, or direct discussion of the vows is noteworthy. While the leaders presented images of community in which nonvowed and vowed members shared life and living, the leaders' visions contained little or no discussion concerning the content or significance of the vows. In some respects, this is to be expected. Without negating the spiritual role that vows play in the life of members of religious orders, it is reasonable to say that vows are also an important symbolic delineator. The ambiguity in the relationship between members of religious orders and laity, mentioned above, does not exist when approached from the vantage of the vows. In adopting collaborative models and egalitarian frameworks, many members of religious orders hold the belief that they are not more holy than the laity, but simply that they have chosen, or are called, to live their holiness in a different way. Viewing themselves as different is functional until, as discussed earlier, the symbols of being different come to be called into question or lose their meaning. While dimension after dimension of religious life is being called into question, reevaluated and altered, accelerating the blurring of distinctions between members of religious orders and the laity, the vows continue to distinguish members of religious orders. In symbolic and profound ways, the traditional vows of poverty, chastity and obedience continue to characterize members of religious orders.

Leaders with Difficulties in Envisioning the Future

Leaders who could not envision the future wrote letters that typically reflected an enmeshment in past or current concerns. They presented themselves as unable to move beyond the narrow vision of day-to-day problems or the aftermath of yesterday's battles. A sense of the urgency of the present situation, as related to the mission of the order, was typically absent.

Leaders' sense of impotence. Many leaders reflected a state of conflict in their writings, although the range of intensity varied. Although some leaders, despite either their own or their congregation's sense of conflict, seemed able to imagine the future, in general, those who presented their frustrations were not able to move beyond them. It is clear from the tone of the letters and the issues that are raised within them that leaders are greatly affected by the atmosphere that they perceive within their community. Many continued to feel burdened or stymied by the fear and anger that members of their congregations experience; their letters convey feelings of sadness and even despair. Other letters are filled with anger, usually directed at the community members themselves.

Many of the leaders who did not articulate a vision of the future were clear about their concern that so doing might incur the displeasure of their members. The distance and the tensions experienced by leaders in their relationships with members, and the resultant apologetic and self-deprecating tone that underlies some of the letters, are striking. Some leaders acknowledged directly that they felt a lack of trust and support.

My dream may come as a shock to you for several reasons. It is a presumption on my part that you will take the time to entertain *dreams* and *this dreamer*. (Emphasis in the original.)

I am writing to tell you how much I wish we could be a loving healing community. I feel we are spending too much of our precious energies and time on non-important things such as me things. We need to be more for God/others.

It may be hard to ask you to trust the leadership. They are not seeking to do damage to the religious institute which they equally love. As a leader, please know that I am always eager to learn more about how that work can be done today. I am exploring along with many others.

Many of the sisters need a tremendous amount of *affirmation/support*. This works both ways and the leadership must be able to feel a sense of affirmation/support. (Emphasis in the original.)

I see the 1990s as a time for healing past hurts and freeing ourselves from what I call the "we-they syndrome." I have observed that there is unresolved anger and hurt toward the community. The leadership is always referred to as "they."

The struggle reflected in these letters is even more striking when one recalls that they were written in response to the directive, "Write a letter to the members of your order expressing your hopes and dreams for the future of your group." Many of the leaders chose to express, in varying degrees, their frustration with what one leader termed "the apparent lack of interest, enthusiasm, creativity. A satisfaction with the status quo."

Exhortations, reassurance and remembrance. In response to malaise in the community, a common approach to the letter-writing assignment was for the leaders to exhort their members to reenergize themselves and each other, and to reexamine and recommit themselves to the goals of religious life and their community. Often, leaders never reached the point of articulating goals for their communities or for religious life in general, focusing instead on individual or communal exhortations:

Wake up! The time is *NOW*, the place is *HERE* and we are the ones called to wake from lethargy and fear into the light and hope of this

day! We embody the charism and spirit of [founders]: care-filled in
word and deed to share life with others in humility, simplicity,
charity. (Emphasis in the original.)

We are carrying too much baggage and are preoccupied with the trip
worried whether we'll "get there," wherever *that* is. We are "bent
over" with limited vision to see the path, hiding past hurts and pain;
wondering if we'll have "enough" as we get older. Could we stand
up straight as Jesus asked the bent-over women? Ask for forgiveness
and forgive one another? God is with us. I believe our future
together lies in conversion of heart. (Emphasis in the original.)

It seems to me that some of our members are unconcerned. They
seem to have lost the original enthusiasm of their religious calling to
life. Life has become drudgery for them and membership in our
congregation a burden. Nothing we do, or try to do, seems to change
this picture and it is of great concern to me. . . . We must work to
come to an acceptance of where the church has brought us.

This style is perhaps best typified by one leader who began her letter by saying:
"I have a dream. I would like to see each of us remember back to our early
days of religious life and draw on that enthusiasm to re-commit ourselves to God
and one another and our ministry of service to others." After naming areas
where she felt her community should change, mostly in terms of being more
caring, loving and open, she concluded with six directives, which she listed as
"the practical":

Be positive; stop murmuring. Act out of positive thinking.
In conflict, confront the person involved. Do not share with others
    not involved.
Be caring but don't meddle in what needn't concern you.
Trust one another in their sincerity as you want to be trusted.
Take on some global concerns.
Take matters into your prayers.

On the community or micro level, these directives may be very important, if not
critical, to this group's well-being. However useful, though, the first four
directives address primarily interpersonal relations and focus on individual rather
than communal or corporate efforts. This list suggests the emotional drain that
internal issues presented for this leader and illustrates how focusing on such
issues can preclude the development of broader images.
    Some leaders varied their approach by reassuring their membership, rather
than exhorting them:

I have wished that each of you could share these privileged glimpses
into the hearts of our Sisters. We would surely reverence one
another more and judge so much more gently.

I want to affirm the many efforts toward growth and wholeness I
have seen.

If these leaders' energies are being consumed with the task of reassuring or
exhorting individuals to recommit themselves to the goals of community and
religious life, it will be difficult for them to focus themselves and their members
simultaneously on the images of the future.

A third form that reassurance/exhortations takes is manifested in the
"retrospective letters" which trace some portion of a congregation's history. In
these, the leaders combined reassurances with the exhortations, and the message
imparted is: "Be reassured. We have survived and we will continue to survive.
Don't worry." It is expressed in the following ways:

These past several years in community leadership provided me with
some insights I would not have thought possible years ago. Despite
the many dark moments and events of our history (both past and
recent) I find myself filled with a sense of hope for our future.

The changes in our lives over the last twenty years have taken away
a sense of security we seemed to have. We have more questions than
answers but I recall in the beginning of renewal we were told the
questions were far more important than the answers.

We see new life in our community in our new candidates and
novices. Along with the new members we have witnessed a renewal
in our members. . . . We have begun an honest effort to look at our
continuing formation called for in our new Constitution. All these
are signs of hope for our future—signs of life.

Leaders who are unconscious or unaware. "Unconscious or unaware" is
one of the definitions for "incognizant." These characteristics mark the
incognizant style of leadership, and provide yet another set of answers to the
question of leaders' inability to envision the future. Leaders writing in this style
are those who seem not so much unable to move along the path but rather,
unable to find it. Using language that is often rhetorical, these leaders wrote
letters that do not reflect any awareness of the crisis or concerns faced by either
their communities or religious life in general.

In the example that follows, the leader's letter contains no reference to her
religious order or to the members:

Dear God,
My dreams are simple and not far beyond my reach. To know you and to achieve union with you. Ultimately, that is the only desire I can control. The past is no longer before me, the future is not yet. There tends to be much confusion in my life right now. The uncertainty need not become certainties; the light can transform the darkness. Help me enter into the "sunshine and the sunset." Let me be comfortable in my discomfort.

Another leader sketched the points to be developed in addressing his confreres:

1. There is no secular history/profane history, there is only sacred history. God is present in everything and in all. God journeys with us, with all people.
2. Let's listen to that God who's present in everything and in all. Develop an ear, an eye, a heart that can hear, see, perceive God who's speaking in nature, events and people (national and international level). What prevents me/us from listening?
3. Let's enter into a dialogue with God for the sake of discerning the message to me/us, to humanity.
4. Let's commit ourselves to our tasks—discovered in dialogue and in listening—in a collaborative model.
5. The listening, the dialogue and the collaborative commitment are present at every moment.

Other examples of absence of vision replaced by an iteration of spiritual generalities focus on God and the need for a relationship with God. While these are critical issues for members of religious orders, these leaders failed to communicate to the members the import of God or the role that healthy relationships with God can have in their lives as individuals, as a religious order and as people of the church. While choosing to focus on God, they failed to address or offer reflections on their particular community, the unique role of members of religious orders in the church, their relationship as religious to society, or any of the other issues with which other leaders dealt. By oversimplifying the complex reality in which they and their God reside, they remained unable to cope with the threats posed by that very reality:

As we look to the answers provided by our rich tradition, questions being raised today move us to beseech our God to provide us with better ones, such as will help us truly learn with the conviction that "the greatest misfortune is to live and die without knowing God."

In my own heart I am experiencing myself called to religious life—what is striking is its utter newness. It's like the God I always wanted to call is calling. . . . It's happening to me personally—but I sense it is happening to me as part of being part of [community]. I want mostly for you—each of you—to experience God's holding on to you so that you, too, can let go of boxes, perimeters, limits you put on your experience.

What are my imaginings? That we will accept our relative power-lessness to save, or do anything remarkable for the world, yet be willing to believe that we are earthen vessels—and that God's clay works in us powerfully.

IMPLICATIONS

While many of the leaders quoted in the preceding sections may not have developed very comprehensive visions of the future, some exhibited a certain level of awareness, and even acceptance, of where their communities are in the process of change. As leaders, they have been affected and burdened by these challenges, but they continue to cling to their hope and optimism. At this point, though, one has to ask about the role of leadership in the process of change. Is struggling to maintain hope and optimism enough in light of the demands of the present and the future? The answer would have to be, "No." Although important, hope and optimism alone cannot move a congregation forward. Neither can the recollection of God's saving work among the members of the order, nor the offering of spiritual bouquets alone. The inability to transform their hope and optimism into vision and/or strategies or to connect the rich spiritual heritage of a religious order to the needs of today's world are some of the reasons for leaders' inability to shape successfully their orders' futures.

Religious communities and their members have experienced, and continue to experience, turmoil after Vatican II. Leaders of religious communities have faced the same turmoil. Governmental structures have changed, and with them, expectations of leadership. Increasingly there is a sense among many that a "crisis" in leadership exists. Where and how are the leaders to lead? The letters they wrote indicate clearly that many of the current leaders of religious orders lack the skills needed to negotiate the complexities of organizational transformation.

Many leaders lack clear images of themselves as leaders, of their communities and of religious life. They are unable to identify the elements that are key to their identity, their mission or their role as members of religious orders. Many congregations struggle with the very fundamental, and often profoundly frightening, questions of, "Who are we? What is our purpose? Whom do we serve?" In some cases, the leaders' inability to answer these questions hindered their ability to provide direction as their communities sought to identify these elements corporately.

One of the critical internal blocks for leadership is an inability to formulate strategies. Strategies—that is, directives for actions that enable goal achievement—were rare within the letters. The difficulty that leaders experience in developing strategies has major implications. A vague sense of a direction is not enough to ensure movement. Strategies help ensure movement and can be strengthened or inhibited by various forces. In the context of religious leadership, increasing emphasis must be given to overcoming the inhibiting forces that continue to restrict leaders' ability to imagine a future for their congregations. Strategy can be supported through programs, structures, purposeful action, training and various other avenues. The lack of strategies in the letters and the number of leaders who appeared "conflicted" suggest that many congregations remain fixated on maintenance issues. Clarifying values and developing strategies will provide impetus for and direction to the movement.

Another related issue, which is of particular importance to those with value-based and conflicted styles, is the importance of thinking structurally. The conceptual groundwork that values provide can best fulfill their role if structural frameworks are built on them. What are the structures that will facilitate collaboration in ministry and community? Do they include spiritual growth and depth? What about commitment to charisms, community, and God? Visioning new structures is a critical element of choosing corporate goals and choosing goals is the first step to forming strategies on how to attain them.

For the leaders who had images of the future, specifically those identified as vision and value-based leaders, there are many issues to be addressed. In their letters, leaders often questioned the role of institutions in their communities. This issue alone has highly significant implications for sponsorship in religious life, for the church in general and for society at large. Continuing shifts in congregational relationships to traditionally sponsored institutions is, no doubt, one of the factors that will continue to exert pressure on religious life. Given demographic shifts, persistent cultural values that stress individuality, and the challenges to be more "authentic" and responsive to the "needs of the times," religious communities will, no doubt, continue to analyze their need to be involved in the ministries by which they have historically defined themselves.

The corporate ability to be flexible and creative in understanding charisms and founders and to allow history to be freeing rather than binding will determine much of the future of both individual congregations and religious life itself. Leaders who are able to understand the difference between who they are and what they do will be critical in this process. Some of the letters suggested that leaders understand this distinction, as seen in the attention that they pay to the questions of sponsorship and the ministry. In many instances, the leaders' ability to examine critically the role of sponsored institutions in congregational ministry is questionable. Moreover, the very idea that institutions are relevant and sufficient conduits of congregational mission is similarly suspect, given the current cultural and ecclesial ethos.

Leaders who do not have visions of the future or are impeded in their articulation of their vision, as well as leaders who have been described above as "conflicted," raise a very different set of issues. Because conflicted leaders do not propose structural changes in their communities, and because they cannot suggest values by which they would like to be guided, conflicted leaders do not provide many insights into the external forces that will shape religious life. They do, however, suggest many of the internal issues with which communities will continue to grapple.

The most important issue indicated by the letters is commitment, or rather, the intensity of commitment. Leaders did not appear overly concerned with the fact that people are not choosing to commit to (join) religious life. They are very concerned, however, about the level of commitment of those who are members of their congregations. They speak of the lack of commitment, passion, energy and intensity in language filled with anger, frustration and deep sadness. The negativity that leadership experiences appeared to drain the energies of those who were struggling to maintain vibrancy.

The lack of intense commitment, or the perception that there is a lack of commitment, poses a challenge for leadership. How do leaders respectfully disengage from those among their membership who are depressed, angry and frightened in order to facilitate the growth of those who have the creative energy on which the future of the congregations and religious life depends? How do congregations respond structurally to the reality of people's waning energies? If, over the course of life, individuals become less passionate and less energized, how can the structures of congregation and religious life accommodate that, capturing the energy when it is there and allowing people to move on if they no longer feel passionate involvement? There is an inherent tension between the demands for lifetime commitment (duration) and intense commitment (intensity). Already, the beginnings of structural responses are being discussed to alleviate this tension. Temporary vows and forms of associate membership are examples. However, the question remains salient for members of religious orders who have taken permanent vows and have lived in community for years.

The discernment that began 30 years ago will continue if religious life is to remain "healthy" for many years to come. While leaders have a unique opportunity to help shape the process and to provide direction, the letters suggest that there is a discrepancy for some leaders between their responsibilities and their abilities. Many lack the competencies to function effectively or are impeded in functioning by other factors.

As leaders, and as members of religious orders in general, continue to process the issues that they face, identifying the elements of their lives that they hope to preserve as well as the elements that they need to leave behind, they will build a solid foundation for the future. One of the key elements will be the ability to identify, with clarity, the essence of religious life at all its levels: for individual religious, for religious congregations and for the institution of religious life. Having identified the essence and purpose of religious life, congregational strategies must be developed to enable structures and individuals to be mission-oriented with respect to the needs of individual religious, the various congregations and all the people of God.

A second key element is to identify those leaders of religious orders who have exhibited excellence in their leadership ability and to determine the characteristics that enable them to perform in an outstanding fashion. This investigation provides the basis for Part II of this chapter.

A COMPETENCY MODEL
FOR LEADERS OF RELIGIOUS ORDERS

The analysis of the visions for the future that leaders articulated in the workshop series, as well as a host of individual interviews with experts in religious life and conversations with several members of religious orders, identified the urgency of selecting and training leaders. These leaders must not only manage the complexity of religious life which is predicted to intensify during the next ten years due to aging populations, but also must respond to the increased regulation of religious institutions such as hospitals and schools. With membership involved in increasingly diversified ministerial activities and fewer financial resources, they also need to focus their members' attention on an authenticating vision that will unite individual efforts in the realization of a corporate mission.

As has already been noted, the most striking deficit among leaders of religious orders is their inability to formulate a strategy to achieve a purpose or mission. Without a strategic or goal-oriented focus as part of their leadership, an incrementalism that emphasizes maintenance concerns over mission tends to mark their style. As has been noted repeatedly, leadership is an ever-increasing concern among both leaders and members in Roman Catholic religious orders.

Additional influences on the state of leadership in religious orders include an increasing number of consensual processes used in selection. On the surface, such consensual processes have appeared to be a significant enhancement of collegiality and subsidiarity in the church, increasing participation by some members in processes critical to their lives. However, declining membership, aging populations among religious orders and the residue of therapeutic concerns have also precipitated, in some instances, the selection of the less than stellar leaders. In other instances, particularly where greater influence could be achieved outside the leader position, well qualified members asked not to be considered.

Nygren (1988) has shown that effective leaders attend to the future of their organization, its viability and the apt use of resources toward specified ends. This approach assumes a range of competencies that enable the leader to attend equally to organizational and managerial realities and the theological foundations that support the purpose of religious life.

Leadership competency requirements are the skills and characteristics that predict superior performance in the position of leadership: success in job tasks, responsibilities, performance standards and—in the case of religious leadership—ability to tap the spiritual energies of the group.   A congregation's mission, strategy and structure may also influence the content of the leadership role and the levels of competencies required to function effectively as a leader.

PURPOSE OF STUDY

The Leadership Competency Assessment of Leaders of Religious Orders addressed the concerns outlined above. Its aim was to identify the principal competencies required for the excellent leadership of religious orders. The focus was on groups whose membership exceeded 150 and which had significant institutional commitments as part of their responsibility.

RESEARCH METHOD

Competency assessment, an established and validated technique for determining the characteristics required for outstanding performance in organizational leadership positions (Boyatzis, 1982), was used to identify competencies that are critical to outstanding religious leadership.[2]

This process drew on data from three sources: (1) resource panels of experts both within and outside the organizations, (2) in-depth interviews with current and former leaders of religious congregations and (3) compendia of competencies known from prior research to characterize outstanding performance in similar leadership positions. Detailed procedures on the use of these sources is outlined in the following discussion of project phases.

Phase 1: Expert Panel

A resource panel composed of excellent leaders, notable former leaders and scholars of leadership was convened for two purposes. The first was to identify leadership tasks and responsibilities and the performance standards by which effectiveness in the position might be determined, as well as competency behaviors and characteristics that would be expected to be shown by excellent leaders. Within religious life, panel members defined levels of skills and knowledge required for effective performance by those individuals who have successfully negotiated change and have developed strategies to direct the membership toward a congregational mission.

The second task of the panel was the nomination of leaders for interview. Each member of the panel was invited to nominate as many as ten women and ten men who, in his or her opinion, had provided or were providing outstanding leadership for religious life. While reviewing criteria for outstanding leadership was helpful in preparing nominators for this process, it was emphasized that they need not use or refer to the criteria in making their recommendations. Their task was simply to name those individuals who, in their opinion (and for whatever reason) had provided outstanding leadership in spiritual and or-ganizational realms. In order to focus more clearly on the excellence of leadership in the institutional realm, nominators were asked to consider as two additional criteria those leaders who had been responsible for a congregation or province of not less than 150 members and whose order has a substantial base of sponsored institutions.

The criterion group, or primary group of interest, consisted of individuals who were doing, or had done, an outstanding job. A control or comparison group, composed of typical leaders, included persons who were doing, or had done, an adequate, but not noteworthy, job. Persons considered for interview included the leaders who had been nominated independently by at least two nominators. The control group of typical leaders was matched for age, tradition, length of tenure, and other factors with the criterion group.

Phase 2: Behavioral Event Interviews with Persons in Leadership Positions

The Behavioral Event Interview (BEI) asks interviewees to identify critical situations, including those with positive and negative outcomes, that they have encountered in their leadership role. They then describe what happened in these situations (in considerable narrative detail), including what led up to the situation; who was involved; what the interviewee thought about, felt and wanted to accomplish in the situation; what he or she actually did; and the outcome.

Six trained researchers conducted two- to three-hour BEIs with 24 members of religious orders (8 priests, 3 brothers and 13 sisters) who had been identified through the nomination process as outstanding leaders, as well as with a comparison sample of 15 individuals (4 priests, 2 brothers and 9 sisters) whose performance was viewed by nominators as satisfactory or typical. The larger number of outstanding leaders selected for interviews is based on the belief that there are more ways to be excellent than to be average. In other words, research has shown that excellent leaders exhibit a wider array of outstanding behaviors than do typical leaders.

Individuals selected for interview knew only that they had been chosen to be interviewed because they were leaders; they did not know about the excellent/typical distinctions that had been applied to sample selection. Similarly, the interviewers were not apprised of the category to which the interviewee had been assigned.

Phase 3: Definition of Competencies

The tape-recorded interviews were transcribed, read and coded carefully (according to a competency lexicon) by a panel of experts. This lexicon, a proprietary document developed by McBer & Company of Boston, included competencies determined previously through this method to be important for more successful leadership behavior in other organizations, as well as those based on previous research with this population. The competencies coded may be categorized according to goal and action competencies (achievement, efficiency, initiative); intellectual/cognitive competencies (information seeking, conceptual thinking, analytical thinking); people competencies (responsiveness to members' needs, responsiveness to needs of client groups, developmental, interpersonal understanding); organizational competencies (mission orientation, community leadership, directiveness/personal assertiveness, impact and influence); and personal competencies (self-confidence, positive expectations, negative reactions, concern for moderation/control of excess, stress resistance, spiritual support, spiritual dynamism). This process also provided for the emergence of unique competencies, namely, those characteristics that have not surfaced in previous investigations of this type. Most competencies had several levels in order to differentiate the application, as well as the relative strength or weakness within them.

The data were then analyzed for differences between outstanding and typical leaders in both level and frequency of occurrence of each of the competencies. The outcome of the analysis of the BEI protocols obtained from outstanding and typical religious leaders follows. It provides a model of both the threshold or baseline competencies required for adequate leadership and the competencies needed for outstanding performance in this role. Differences between competencies demonstrated by outstanding male and outstanding female leaders are also presented.

RESULTS

The interviews with the outstanding and typical leaders were comparable in length, with each group averaging about 37 typed pages, and in the number of competencies coded per interview, with approximately 98 and 87 for outstanding and typical leaders, respectively. Thus, differences in frequency of occurrence of competencies cannot be ascribed to differences in level of articulateness between leadership groups. Each interview was blind-coded as to leadership status by two different judges for all the competencies in the lexicon, and differences in coding were adjusted to fit the scoring criteria. Reliability of the coding was determined by having two additional judges recode the same material. Reliability of coding varied by competency, averaging 74% overall.

Threshold Competencies

In studies of this kind it is customary to find that a number of competencies occur about equally often in the interviews of outstanding and typical performers. They are referred to as threshold competencies because they appear to be essential characteristics for all people attempting to carry out a particular role. The present study yielded a number of such threshold competencies. Mission orientation is one example. It is essential for all leaders of religious congregations not only to be mindful of their mission, but also to be able to articulate it to internal and external constituents. In this study, the question is whether outstanding leaders focus their attention more than typical leaders on the mission of the congregation in everyday activities. If so, mission orientation would be categorized as a competency associated with outstanding leadership. However, both typical and outstanding leaders reported incidents or activities focusing on the congregation's mission about equally often, as Table 3.2 shows. Therefore, mission focus is foundational to the leadership role: a threshold competency that all leaders should demonstrate. Some examples of mission orientation follow.

> Every one of the boards of our congregationally owned schools and other schools as well has to realize that the charism of our community is outreach to the poor—to aid the poor. That's the type of thing that annually I would remind the boards of: I would remind them that our mission has a religious purpose. Therefore, we would expect very strong religious education programs in our schools—opportunities for not only prayer, but opportunities for service ministries. It's just not enough to tell the students about the poor; ideally they themselves should be doing some service for the poor. That is what we were founded for and that has to be kept in view.

When we went there, it was poor. That was many years ago. We
came out of there about six years ago because it was no longer a poor
school. So we really focused, we looked for schools in areas that
were poor.

Table 3.2 lists a number of other threshold competencies that characterize
typical as well as outstanding leaders. Summary examples of each competency
also follow. In addition to mission, mentioned above, both groups also
mentioned administering the business of the congregation.

We were planning as a team in the first years. We always seemed to
begin with each one's role as regional—being a representative to all
the members in a specific region and relating to other institutions.
Then, in addition, one might relate to the government committee,
another might relate to the social justice committee, and so forth. It
was wonderful for me because it left me free for national things.

Table 3.2
**Competencies That Characterize Typical as Well as Outstanding Religious
       Leaders**

Frequency of Reference to:	Typical Leaders (T)		Outstanding Leaders (O)		Diff. O-T	p
	Mean	SD	Mean	SD		
Mission Orientation	7.00	4.26	7.26	4.16	.26	ns
Manages Meetings Well, Administratively Skillful	.92	1.56	1.22	1.35	.30	ns
Information Seeking	4.83	2.19	3.65	2.44	-1.18	ns
Conceptual Thinking	8.67	5.79	8.39	4.94	-.28	ns
Analytical Thinking	2.50	3.00	3.09	5.60	.59	ns
Efficiency Orientation	2.58	3.48	1.09	1.53	-1.49	ns
Self-Confidence	3.00	1.91	3.74	2.26	.74	ns
Concern for Moderation	2.08	1.78	2.52	2.86	.44	ns

Both typical and outstanding leaders were active in seeking information to help them better perform their duties as leaders.

> The problems would still be there because what they weren't doing was empowering themselves with the skills to deal with those problems. I tried to say to them from the beginning, "Who in the group has skills for personnel issues? Who can deal with these troubled people? Who knows how to make interventions? Who can take the time to become more knowledgeable about the high schools and work with these high schools?"

Given the cognitive and educational levels of religious leaders, it is not surprising that the typical as well as the outstanding leaders are expert at using concepts to make sense of confusing situations or to see things in a new way. Both groups are also skilled in analyzing events to discover causal sequences or establish priorities.

> What's the value of it [corporate commitment]? First, it gives purpose, conscious purpose, focused purpose to the group. Secondly, it gives identity. Thirdly, it answers to the prophetic role of religious life in a society. Fourth, it bonds a community around a common goal. Fifth, it gives a community a prophetic presence in society without the necessity of institutionalization. You don't build a special building for corporate commitment. And sixth, it enables that community to continue to refine, nurture, develop or close the institutions that it is now supporting without losing a central and, I hope, sanctifying center to its life.

> How often do we talk about values? Not very often. Values, visioning and planning should be considered in that order. We go right into planning. "Well, we've got to do some planning now so let's have this meeting." You know, it's like a shot in the dark! But we need to talk about values and the things that are non-negotiable.

Nor is it surprising to discover that a concern for efficiency and moderation, as well as a degree of self-confidence, are characteristic of both typical and outstanding leaders.

> I did 150 house meetings in about 90 days. That was the way that we recruited volunteers.

I would say it was a successful action. It identified the candidate
with people who were minority and poor and that was the whole
campaign.

The more we renew corporately in a believable and realistic way for
our times, the healthier we are as a group, the higher the self esteem,
the less our sense of fragmentation, of falling apart, and breakdown.

We couldn't negotiate our way out of it without compromising our
principles, so I said we have to be willing to lose the hospital.

From the point of view of leadership, I think the council felt I
handled the situation extremely well. In a crisis, you also have to
create a sense of vision and direction, and I think I kept those two
things in tension, in balance.

Competencies That Differentiate

Of particular interest are those competencies that characterize the
outstanding, as compared with the typical, leaders. These will be summarized
under several main headings and then followed by a summary of differences in
outstanding leadership styles for men's and women's congregations.

Figure 3.1
Achievement Motivation of Religious Leaders

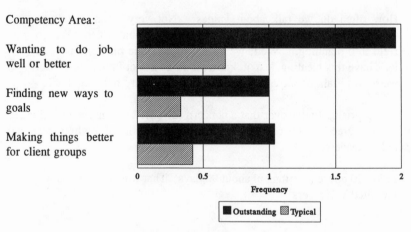

Note: Differences are significant on all scales.

Outstanding leaders are more achievement-oriented and active, and tend to plan ahead. As Figure 3.1 indicates, the outstanding leaders showed several signs of greater achievement motivation. More often than the typical leaders, they expressed a desire to do things well or better. They set goals and sought new and more effective ways to achieve them. In addition, they more often tried to make things better for client groups served by the congregation.

Some examples of achievement motivation expressed by religious leaders include:

> One of my goals for this four years is to find a way to better coordinate our hospitals so that the general superior and the other council members don't spend as much time running from place to place to place.

> When I came here I worked to strengthen relations with minority groups. There was not really an out-reach to the multicultural scene here, so I immediately invited into the place leaders from the local churches, especially the Hispanics. "How can we do a better job?" And little by little we built programs for the training of ethnic persons and also the writing of manuals for ethnic ministry.

There is no difference in the frequency with which the two kinds of leaders mentioned taking initiative to deal with immediate problems. Thirty-three percent of the typical leaders mentioned taking the initiative, as compared with 39% of the outstanding leaders. However, there is a major difference in the frequency with which the two types of leaders took the initiative to solve problems that might arise in the future: from one to two months to as long as more than a year ahead, as Figure 3.2 illustrates. More then two-thirds of the outstanding leaders reported frequently planning ahead in this way, as compared with only a quarter of the typical leaders. Some examples include:

> I genuinely knew in 1980 that we probably were not ready to close that academy. So I worked for 10 years to help it happen. Time at every single Chapter meeting was devoted to a very rigorous and in-depth analysis of the ongoing conditions in the academy. This brought the community to the point where they voted in Chapter that the academy could not incur more than $80,000 debt. I held the position that we ought not to be bartering our future to pay for our past. I had seen too many small communities begin this silent, secret subsidy of a dying institution. Then, you've put so much money into it by that time that you've got to make it successful or you've dropped everything down a dry well. It took 10 years but I want you

to know that we closed that academy with a united community, with a certain degree of pain, but with a lot of class.

I knew that the church was going to have to have lay catechists for the parishes in the rural areas where there were no religious women even available, even no possibility of religious women. So I began to develop the theology department at the college in a way that would lean toward the training of lay catechists.

Figure 3.2
Anticipatory Problem Solving by Religious Leaders

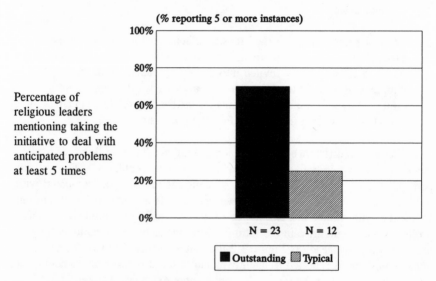

Note: Difference is statistically significant.

Outstanding leaders exert more power to attain group goals and to mobilize commitment to the goals from the membership. To be effective, leaders must act assertively or powerfully to influence individuals and groups. Although the difference is not statistically significant, there is a tendency for the typical leaders to focus on individuals more often than the outstanding leaders. The following example illustrates this competency: "When it came time to sign that he would be willing to do these things, he didn't know if he could in conscience sign. I said, 'There is no way you can go back to Lourdes if you don't sign. You know that.' So then he signed." Figure 3.3 demonstrates that both types of leaders acted assertively on individuals by telling them what to do, confron-

ting them about performance problems or threatening sanctions to control
behavior.

Figure 3.3
Religious Leaders' Use of Power

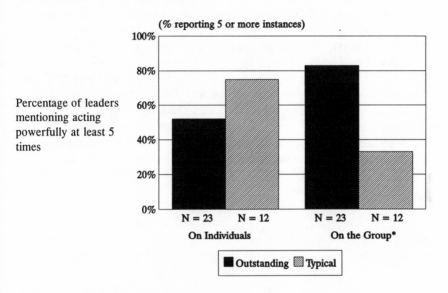

* Indicates difference is statistically significant.

As the figure indicates, the outstanding leaders, much more often than the
typical leaders, acted powerfully to influence group decisions or behavior.
Examples of action to influence the group follow.

> With regard to raising the Province tax: I brought the subject up my
> second year as Provincial. I was turned down by my consultants.
> They didn't think we should do it. I said to myself, "I'm going to do
> it by the time that I leave." And I ultimately got the consultants to
> agree to it. I did this by giving them the basic facts of life like the
> budget (the income and the expenditures weren't matching except by
> soft money—gifts and donations). God is very good to us, we always
> have that soft money coming in, so the budget was relatively in the
> black, but not as measured against income. So I convinced them we
> had to get more hard income and raising the Province tax would be
> one of the ways. My other, more telling, point was it hadn't gone up
> in over ten years and everything is going up everyplace else. We

can't give a false impression out there that the Province is a bottom-less pit. It's not an eternal lactation machine, where the milk is always there, never ending. I said, "We've got to change that mentality, and therefore we have to raise it." And I convinced them.

We had identified these convents we would like to use, but the pastors out there didn't know that any of this was afoot. I had talked with the diocese, but I was concerned that if the diocese would start to say to them, "Oh, you're to give your convent over in a long-term lease to the sisters," all hell could break loose. So I decided, "No, before I get back to the diocese at all, I will go and talk to each of these pastors and bring them aboard with the situation." I did, and they were all very, very responsive, very charming. And I was very pleased about that. Again, it was a confirmation for me that I do negotiate well, and I do approach things like that well. I have my facts ready and can state my case and can listen to whatever comes back. They were all, each one in his own way, quite positive.

Table 3.3
Power Matrix

Source of Power:

	Others	Self
Focus: Self	I. Dependent	II. Independent
Others	IV. Interdependent a. consensual b. resourceful	III. Assertive a. personalized power b. socialized power

In conventional motivational terminology, using power for the good of some cause is called *socialized power motivation* (or s Power; McClelland, Davis, Kalin & Wanner, 1972). The outstanding leaders demonstrated exerting power more often to attain group goals and less often to influence individuals than did typical leaders. The Power Matrix[3] (Table 3.3) suggests graphically how socialized power differs from other types of power. It is interesting to note that men are more likely to reach Stage III while, of those who attain Stage IV, women constitute the majority.

Within the area of use of power and authority, there were also differences in whether the source of authority was seen as based in the institution, such as belonging to the office of being a provincial, or as based on consensus of the membership. As Figure 3.4 shows, the typical leaders more often acted out of the authority granted them by virtue of their position, whereas the outstanding leaders more often worked to create or gather a consensus among the members by which they felt more authorized to make a decision. The more democratical-ly inclined leaders were not passive, simply waiting for guidance from the group. Rather, they actively solicited ideas from others, built community spirit or positioned themselves as leaders so that the members responded to the mission, goals or policy of the congregation.

> He would give me a report before I went there and when I arrived I would know how things were going and I could pursue that on a more authoritative level. So, the assistant kept on top of all of the mechanics of apostolate. He gave me a report so that I would have a good sense of what the trouble spots are. There weren't many surprises.

> In our society, the leadership lost control some years ago over what goes on in the houses. The Provincial is supposed to approve major policies, but all kinds of major policies got approved without his awareness. Since assuming office, I have insisted a lot more that I approve major policies. I am aware of it so that we can keep our community together.

> You can't make a decision if you can't see what the options are. And helping them clarify that is often the best thing. I usually have confidence a group will make the right decision, but only if they have the right information and see clearly what the options are.

Outstanding leaders are less focused on the personal adjustment of members. The typical leaders were much more involved in dealing with the personal problems of members in contrast to dealing with problems of the congregation as a group. As Figure 3.5 shows, there are trends suggesting that typical leaders, more than outstanding leaders, report being responsive to members' needs and work hard to establish good relations with others. Above all, however, typical leaders mentioned much more often than outstanding leaders supervising, counselling, and coaching members, as well as more frequently arranging for their special training, such as therapy.

Figure 3.4
Type of Authority Exercised by Religious Leaders

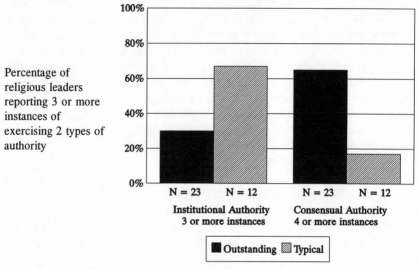

Percentage of religious leaders reporting 3 or more instances of exercising 2 types of authority

Note: Differences are statistically significant.

Figure 3.5
Interpersonal Relationships of Religious Leaders

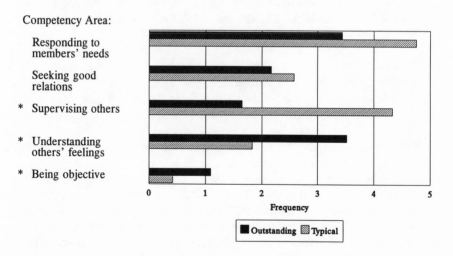

* Indicates significant difference.

Typical leaders are more involved in day-to-day personnel problems than outstanding leaders, as the following examples indicate.

I realize I have to talk to one of the people and say, "Have you any sense of how harshly you come across?" I tried a couple of times to say, "Why do you have to be so angry about things that don't necessarily please you? Can't you deal with the issue rather than getting personally angry? If you could only move a little bit, you'd be ever so much more effective." It's just not always easy to do that.

I had strongly encouraged her to get into counseling and had found a counselor for her within her area. I just sort of felt that she needed to begin to sort out a lot of things.

My instincts would have told me, for a long time anyway, that this is one person that counseling would benefit. So I was able to suggest it and she said, "Yeah, and would you find somebody for me?" I mean, she was very, very open to it. So I did and she started counseling.

On the other hand, the outstanding leaders significantly more often reported that they understood and were influenced by the feelings of others; they were able to be objective and see things from different perspectives.

I think the letter was disrespectful because it didn't respect the commitment of our members. It didn't respect whatever reasons they had for making the statement, and besides, it was actually poorly worded.

I had to do some damage control in mending the fences there, particularly with the chairman of the board, who's an attorney.

It's that personal relationship between me and the board chair, the lay chair of each of those boards, that is important. Then, if they run into difficulty or anything, they feel as though they have a right to call me.

Such understanding can clearly contribute to better management of the group. It does not lead, however, to trying to help individual members to such an extent that collective goals are neglected.

Outstanding leaders show signs of greater spiritual sensitivity. One aspect of the conceptual thinking competency is the tendency to find and understand the deeper spiritual meaning of life events. Leaders would sometimes explain explicitly how an activity furthered the congregational mission or spirituality. While only 1 out of 12, or 8%, of the typical leaders mentioned finding a spiritual meaning in events three or more times, 52% of the outstanding leaders did so. In other words, the outstanding leaders were more apt to see and mention the spiritual or religious significance of events. In general, the outstanding leaders grounded their lives in an awareness of the presence of God.

> Were we willing simply to cast our lots and accept a plurality, if that was necessary, rather than a majority? The entire community agreed. What was crucial here was that we had agreed to agree. What was crucial was not what we agreed upon, but that the whole community agreed that there ought to be such a thing as a community witness. Instead of just bringing a lot of isolated people together to live independently, I was very concerned about the fact that people join a group in order to do together what they cannot possibly do alone. And so I was very intent on developing, reclaiming, revitalizing, renewing the notion of the community witness.

> I think we have done well on this. The outcome is all in God's hands. Like this morning's Gospel, the seed will be scattered and we go to bed and get up in the morning and we hope that it is going to grow as seeds do. But whether it will be something really stable for the future or not, we don't know.

An awareness of God's presence and support in dealing with leadership problems was spontaneously mentioned more often by the outstanding than the typical leaders. The nature of this assistance was different for women and men. Among the men, the outstanding leaders more often mentioned the immediacy of spiritual support for what they were doing than did the typical leaders. Means were 1.17, SD=0.69, and 3.00, SD=2.09, for the typical and outstanding leaders, respectively; difference = 1.83, t=2.51, p<.02.

> I can honestly say that God has sent new support to us so that we would not be abandoned, would not be left alone to die in the desert without any help whatsoever.

> You find the motivation with prayer. I mean it's as simple as the simplest prayer of petition: "Help me do the right thing, and not hurt anybody by this." "Show us the way." "Get us out of this." And it drives you back to your own resources for prayer because you have to give voice to the mission, to the cause.

Among women, awareness of God's presence as source of energy and dynamism distinguished the outstanding from the typical leaders.   Means were 1.75, SD=2.45, and 2.87, SD=2.19, for the typical and outstanding leaders, respectively; difference = 1.12, ns.

> Spiritually, I've always had a very close relationship with God. So often when I'm in situations I'm aware of God's presence and that has been very helpful.

> The situation of greatest danger is often the situation of greatest grace. I was very much aware of God's presence in that situation. I wrote and said and did things that I could not do by myself, I know that.

Since these statements appear to be two different ways of expressing an awareness of the presence of God that are more readily mentioned among both types of outstanding leaders, the results have been combined and are summarized in Figure 3.6. About two-thirds of the outstanding, as compared to one-third of the typical, leaders mentioned their awareness of God at least twice in their interviews (χ^2 test for the difference = 6.21, p < .02).

Figure 3.6
Awareness of the Presence of God among Religious Leaders

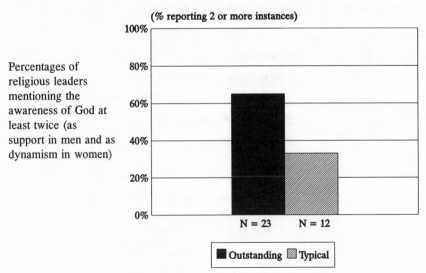

Note: Difference is statistically significant.

The foundation for excellence in religious leaders appears to be a potent awareness of the presence of God amidst the challenges they face in addressing the role of their congregation in the modern world. The combination of this awareness and a concern for the larger potential impact of the congregation on the world yields for them a degree of meaning that allows them to focus on group goals.

Both this and the competence of finding meaning indicate that the outstanding leaders are more attentive to the spiritual aspects of their work. They more often see and talk about the spiritual significance of what is happening and draw more often on divine assistance in supporting or energizing their leadership role.

Gender Differences in the Characteristics of Outstanding Leaders of Religious Orders

Figure 3.7 displays some of the differences in the ways that outstanding men and women lead their congregations. The men were more likely than the women to start new projects to deal with expected problems, while the women were more likely than the men to take actions designed to persuade the group to make a certain decision.

Figure 3.7
Gender Differences in Characteristics of Outstanding Religious Leaders

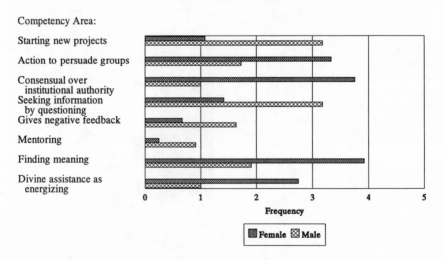

Note: All differences are statistically significant.

Some examples of these competencies include:

> In 1972 we had an Assembly and, through letters I had written, I encouraged them to start a research and planning committee. We needed to move into the future as a result of making decisions, and not just back into the future as we were forced to do at so many times in the past.

> She was not so sure that there was a need for change; I was convinced there was. I remember after that conversation going home and thinking "Somebody has got to do it!" I remember a clear sense that I probably was one of those, or at least I should get involved in trying to make changes happen. So, when the processes opened up for committee work, as they did for the special General Chapters of those years, I began to get very involved in committees that would effect change.

One reason why outstanding women leaders spend more time persuading people is that they may be more focused on the importance of building consensus and support for decisions than are men. They mention building a consensual basis for authority significantly more often than relying on an institutional authority as compared with the male leaders of religious orders.

> I began to pull together information for the education of the congregation around the issue. I started out by pulling together a lot of printed material from a variety of different sources that would explain what [the issue] was, what the legal ramifications of signing the Covenant were, what implementing it meant, what it meant for each sister in terms of what she could be expected to do if she agreed that we as a group should sign this Covenant.

The men appeared more assertive than the women, tending to seek information by direct questioning and more often giving negative feedback on behavior to individual members.

> This is the Constitution, and this is what we said, and this is the chapter document. If you don't want to live it, if you are not called to religious life in this congregation, why don't you do something else? Do something that gives you life.

> I told him, "You are assigned here in Dallas. You have to come down." So I made him come to Dallas.

The outstanding men mentioned mentoring or providing opportunities for others to develop leadership capacities more often than did the outstanding women. This may be because men tend to view authority more in terms of succession than do women (Jacobs, 1991).

> I was his Novice Master. I saw that there was a depth to this man. He made his temporary vows, and after one year of temporary vows we let him teach Scripture in our school of theology. He did a fine job of teaching, and it became clear that he was a well organized man and that he was a thinker. There was depth to him. We had him teach then. Subsequently, we made him vice rector of the college, which is sort of the chief office of the college. Through this, he had acquired experience. He'd proven himself to be a pretty good administrator. My intention was to see to it that, at the time when the former rector would have to step aside, this person would be in a position to assume that office.

> There is a guy who I think is one of our most talented people. He has loads to offer, as well as a few rough edges. He has tremendous potential for leadership. I think that it is important for guys who have good ideas and energy to begin to express it together. Certainly, that can feed into our visioning process. I made certain that this guy is on the visioning committee I'll be working on. That will be very helpful to him and to us.

The outstanding women leaders were more apt to point to the spiritual significance of what was happening and to see God as actively informing and providing energy and direction to their efforts.

> There are moments when you really can let God be part of that life which is going to be the life of those with whom we minister. It's not my life, it's their life. And, it's about people taking charge of their own lives. I had a health project. People would come and weigh their babies and get milk for them, and then six months later the babies were healthier and things changed. Then the people would say, "Well, why don't we change this so we can get milk regularly." And then you say, "Yeah, let's start a cooperative, why not?"

> In the gospel, it says that unless you lose your life you cannot save it. It doesn't say unless you become a perfect person you ain't gonna get to heaven. It's tough. Losing your life isn't easy. Losing your life can happen many ways. For some, it means losing the opportunity to be with their parents at their death bed, or for others it can

mean losing the opportunity to be with somebody they'd really like to be with for these few years, or it can mean losing the opportunity to be, to use, all one's skills and talents.

Figure 3.8
Percentage of Male and Female Outstanding Leaders Mentioning Stress and Positive Expectations of Others

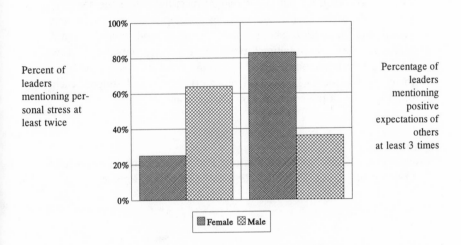

As Figure 3.8 shows, outstanding men mentioned stress more often than did outstanding women, whereas the latter stated more positive expectations about people than the former.

> I really anguished during that period, in terms of what was I doing, what wasn't I doing. I reached a point where I really was just uptight. And I left, took one week away, right before Holy Week.

> One time I passed out, as it were. I was awake, but didn't know what was going [on] for a whole weekend. I am sure it was from tension.

> I'm real excited about what went on at this last Assembly and the theme was "The Sister in and for the World of Today." It's ever, ever new, you know.

Another way to look at gender differences is to compare the way in which typical and outstanding leaders behave within men's and women's congregations.

Figure 3.9 shows that while outstanding female leaders displayed much more interest in establishing consensual authority than did typical female leaders, the difference on this dimension is much less and is not as significant for the comparison between outstanding and typical male leaders. However, the outstanding male leaders seemed to be moving in the direction of the outstanding female leaders.

> I think we need to do a lot more about getting our heads together. There's no reason we can't have regular meetings across the country; we can afford to do it. We need to develop a sense of common vision and ownership about where is priesthood today. What direction is the church taking? How do we position ourselves? How do we get each person involved in owning a vision? Also, we have to let guys come to know each other effectively and support each other and develop a common bond and a sense of unity.

Figure 3.9
Consensual Authority and Anticipatory Problem Solving Differentiate Outstanding from Typical Religious Leaders by Gender

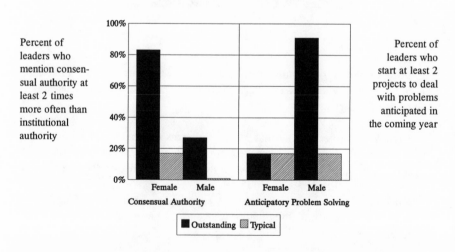

Note: The consensual authority figure represents the percentage of leaders who reported consensual authority at least two times more than institutional authority. In anticipatory problem solving, the figure represents the percentage of leaders who started at least two projects to deal with anticipated problems. The difference is statistically significant.

Outstanding male leaders were more apt to start projects than typical male leaders (shown also in Figure 3.9). There was no such difference between outstanding and typical female leaders, however, very few of whom were involved in starting new projects.

Figure 3.10
Threatening, Terminating Behavior Differentiates Outstanding from Typical Religious Leaders by Gender

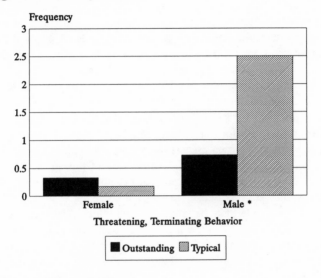

Threatening, Terminating Behavior

■ Outstanding ▨ Typical

* Difference is statistically significant.

Figure 3.10 shows that while male leaders reported generally more behavior that threatens to terminate a member for failing to live up to the requirements of his vocation, this was particularly true of typical male leaders. The outstanding male leaders were more like the female leaders, who were less inclined to dismiss a member from a congregation. It is interesting to note, however, that outstanding female leaders are more inclined to engage in terminating behaviors than are the typical female leaders.

> I determined with my Council that he was not to continue. He wasn't strong enough.

> I pushed a person to leave our formation program. They said he wasn't really shaping up inside. They had given him warnings. So we said to them, "Have him make the retreat with the other tem-

porary professed, but at the end he will not renew his vows; he does
not have permission to renew his vows. Give him a period of time
where you can test him out, and tell him that." He continued to goof
off and not do anything time and time again. So I wrote him a letter.
I said, "At this time, you do not have a call to be a member of our
congregation."

RELATIONSHIPS BETWEEN LEADERSHIP COMPETENCIES

Pearson correlation coefficients between competencies were calculated
separately for outstanding and typical leaders. Tables 3.4 and 3.5 give the
correlation matrixes for the two types of leaders. A correlation matrix of the
competencies for all leaders can be found in Appendix C. The correlational
patterns suggest, as consistent with the t tests noted in the previous section, that
the competency correlates vary with leader success; outstanding and typical
leaders show distinct correlational patterns. In order to determine if differences
between the correlations for outstanding and typical leaders were significant, t
tests were performed for each association above .50, which was significant for
either outstanding or typical leaders. The results of this analysis are given in
Table 3.6. Because of the large number of calculations, only differences with
significant z values are reported.

The distinct correlational pattern for outstanding leaders will be discussed
in the following section, along with models built on a combination of the
correlational results and the t-test results noted in the previous sections. T-test
results were used in addition to the correlations to reflect not only the
relationships among the competencies for outstanding leaders, but also the
frequency of their occurrence. Only correlations exceeding .50 were included
in the models.

CONCLUSIONS

Foundations of Leadership for Religious Orders

Figure 3.11 portrays the model of threshold competencies described in the
previous section. These competencies are necessary for anyone aspiring to meet
at least typical standards for leadership in a religious organization. Here we see
that the basic skills of seeking information, administrative adeptness and an
orientation toward efficiency—combined with the cognitive abilities to
conceptualize and think analytically, plus an attitude of mission awareness—are
necessary threshold competencies. They must be bounded by personal qualities

Table 3.4
Correlations among Competencies: Outstanding Leaders

Competency	1	2	3	4	5	6	7	8	9
1. Achievement	-								
2. Initiative: Short-term	-.39	-							
3. Initiative: Long-term	.55**	-.56**	-						
4. Objectivity	.08	.41	-.03	-					
5. Information Seeking	.44*	.26	.35	-.06	-				
6. Conceptual Thinking	.27	.06	.09	.63**	-.14	-			
7. Finding Meaning	.04	.40	.02	.56**	-.13	.27	-		
8. Analytical Thinking	.36	.53**	.59**	.15	.32	.29	.05	-	
9. Resp. to Members	.12	.54**	.41*	.35	.22	.15	.61**	.34	-
10. Resp. to Clients1	.28	.28	.32	.13	.35	.21	-.01	.80***	.11
11. Resp. to Clients2	-.19	.10	-.01	.18	-.17	.14	.25	.16	.12
12. Developmental	-.24	.04	.08	-.21	-.10	-.13	-.12	.43*	.02
13. Mentor	.26	.06	.32	-.16	.05	.05	.24	.24	.51*
14. Empathy	.00	.24	.14	.59**	.05	.42*	.63**	.10	.43*
15. Interpersonal Understanding	.20	.04	-.12	.23	.42*	.05	.23	.05	.23
16. Mission Orientation	.04	.04	.16	-.32	-.05	-.07	.17	.15	.40
17. Community Leadership	-.08	-.01	-.05	.27	.08	.35	.03	.11	.02
18. Command Authority	.24	.61**	.60**	.33	.31	.28	.36	.62**	.63**
19. Consensual Authority	.01	.17	.22	.30	-.04	.26	.36	-.13	.18
20. Directiveness	-.10	.08	-.09	.02	.01	-.19	.00	-.12	.03
21. Socialized Power	.60**	.60**	.37	.49**	.29	.30	.43*	.41	.34
22. Self Confidence	.46*	.21	.31	.05	.26	.24	.16	.42*	.31
23. Positive Expectations	.05	.41*	.27	.68***	-.06	.55*	.57**	.33	.41
24. Negative Expectations	.04	.01	-.10	.53**	.08	.37	.20	-.05	.02
25. Moderation	.33	.31	-.01	.34	.23	.34	.55**	.09	.36
26. Stress	.35	-.01	.19	.19	.08	.41	-.08	.03	.03
27. Support	.29	.12	.24	.15	.27	.37	.31	.00	.36
28. Dynamism	-.03	-.20	-.36	.43*	.06	.30	.19	-.24	-.00

Table 3.4 (continued)

Competency	10	11	12	13	14	15	16	17	18
1. Achievement									
2. Initiative: Short-term									
3. Initiative: Long-term									
4. Objectivity									
5. Information Seeking									
6. Conceptual Thinking									
7. Finding Meaning									
8. Analytical Thinking									
9. Resp. to Members									
10. Resp. to Clients1	-								
11. Resp. to Clients2	.15	-							
12. Developmental	.45*	.32	-						
13. Mentor	.05	-.11	.09	-					
14. Empathy	.24	.41	.06	-.01	-				
15. Interpersonal Understanding	.34	-.14	.07	.13	.34	-			
16. Mission Orientation	-.02	.30	.08	.56**	.10	-.15	-		
17. Community Leadership	.15	-.21	.14	.04	.23	.02	-.19	-	
18. Command Authority	.42*	-.07	.11	.30	.31	.06	.25	.30	-
19. Consensual Authority	-.18	-.18	-.38	.05	.26	-.09	.09	.24	.07
20. Directiveness	-.04	.18	.09	-.16	.01	-.01	.27	.11	.24
21. Socialized Power	.36	.19	-.30	.04	.38	.30	.03	-.18	.30
22. Self Confidence	.05	.23	-.10	.33	.01	-.09	.46*	.02	.28
23. Positive Expectations	.20	.33	.03	-.22	.73***	.05	-.04	.14	.51*
24. Negative Expectations	.19	.16	-.16	-.08	.49**	.30	-.03	.44*	.26
25. Moderation	-.08	.10	-.29	.10	.38	.07	.37	.15	.36
26. Stress	-.02	-.26	.00	.30	.13	.32	-.07	.31	.12
27. Support	-.07	-.01	-.10	.12	.56**	.27	.16	.11	.18
28. Dynamism	-.20	.02	-.34	-.02	.39	.09	-.11	.29	-.22

Table 3.4 (continued)

Competency	19	20	21	22	23	24	25	26	27	28
1. Achievement										
2. Initiative: Short-term										
3. Initiative: Long-term										
4. Objectivity										
5. Information Seeking										
6. Conceptual Thinking										
7. Finding Meaning										
8. Analytical Thinking										
9. Resp. to Members										
10. Resp. to Clients1										
11. Resp. to Clients2										
12. Developmental										
13. Mentor										
14. Empathy										
15. Interpersonal Understanding										
16. Mission										
17. Community Leadership										
18. Command Authority										
19. Consensual Authority	-									
20. Directiveness	-.35	-								
21. Socialized Power	.25	-.13	-							
22. Self Confidence	.08	.08	.43*	-						
23. Positive Expectations	.22	-.07	.40	.20	-					
24. Negative Expectations	-.05	.58**	.18	.04	.24	-				
25. Moderation	.42*	.18	.37	.51*	.45**	.24	-			
26. Stress	-.23	.11	-.09	.08	.01	.42*	.13	-		
27. Support	.32	-.31	.19	.20	.50*	-.02	.57**	.36	-	
28. Dynamism	.65**	-.38	.18	.10	.22	.15	.28	-.07	.28	-

* p<.05   ** p<.01   *** p<.001

85

Table 3.5
Correlations among Competencies: Typical Leaders

Competency	1	2	3	4	5	6	7	8	9
1. Achievement	-								
2. Initiative: Short-term	.12	-							
3. Initiative: Long-term	-.25	.73**	-						
4. Objectivity	.00	-.37	-.05	-					
5. Information Seeking	.47	.17	.13	.17	-				
6. Conceptual Thinking	-.05	.29	.43	.24	.19	-			
7. Finding Meaning	-.15	.65*	.46	-.08	.17	.26	-		
8. Analytical Thinking	-.07	.05	.03	.07	-.26	.73**	.06	-	
9. Resp. to Members	-.26	-.23	.26	.25	-.12	.39	.08	.13	-
10. Resp. to Clients1	-.36	.33	.28	-.14	-.52	.54	.44	.72**	.22
11. Resp. to Clients2	.00	.20	.14	-.29	.30	.31	-.19	.26	-.30
12. Developmental	.38	-.11	.23	.35	.49	.35	-.14	.07	.33
13. Mentor	.00	-.22	-.20	-.20	.02	-.35	.05	-.26	.02
14. Empathy	-.08	-.03	-.02	-.21	-.09	.37	-.32	.15	.19
15. Interpersonal Understanding	-.37	-.07	.42	.38	-.30	.56	.16	.47	.78**
16. Mission Orientation	.33	.54	.44	-.22	.36	.51	.46	.33	.32
17. Community Leadership	.27	-.31	-.19	.30	-.11	-.08	-.39	-.18	.45
18. Command Authority	.31	.24	.01	-.16	-.39	.35	.23	.57	.28
19. Consensual Authority	.00	.81***	.74**	-.35	.07	-.01	.25	-.27	-.23
20. Directiveness	.24	-.12	-.32	-.14	-.31	-.09	-.30	.09	-.04
21. Socialized Power	.13	.09	.11	.13	.49	.69*	.32	.54	.31
22. Self Confidence	-.11	.13	.34	-.21	-.40	.22	-.13	.29	.31
23. Positive Expectations	.26	.81**	.29	-.45	.21	.14	.52	.17	-.52
24. Negative Expectations	.09	.11	-.18	-.31	-.44	-.23	-.29	.22	-.47
25. Moderation	.06	.67*	.47	-.26	-.11	.50	.60*	.57	.15
26. Stress	.06	-.06	.18	-.01	-.20	-.07	-.33	.02	.07
27. Support	.00	.47	.57	-.34	-.14	.00	-.15	-.04	-.19
28. Dynamism	-.16	.18	.12	-.12	.22	.22	.41	.35	.02

Table 3.5 (continued)

Competency	10	11	12	13	14	15	16	17	18
1. Achievement									
2. Initiative: Short-term									
3. Initiative: Long-term									
4. Objectivity									
5. Information Seeking									
6. Conceptual Thinking									
7. Finding Meaning									
8. Analytical Thinking									
9. Resp. to Members									
10. Resp. to Clients1	-								
11. Resp. to Clients2	-.18	-							
12. Developmental	-.20	.04	-						
13. Mentor	-.20	-.25	.13	-					
14. Empathy	.01	.48	-.09	-.19	-				
15. Interpersonal Understanding	.48	-.23	.33	.09	.01	-			
16. Mission Orientation	.24	.25	.20	-.30	-.02	.21	-		
17. Community Leadership	-.29	-.29	-.06	-.18	.24	.18	.10	-	
18. Command Authority	.70*	-.36	.06	-.08	.00	.36	.41	.13	
19. Consensual Authority	-.03	.31	-.11	-.32	.09	-.18	.29	-.13	-.12
20. Directiveness	.24	-.45	-.28	-.03	.10	-.10	-.14	.44	.46
21. Socialized Power	.31	.16	.29	-.19	-.07	.27	.68*	-.06	.25
22. Self Confidence	.53	-.19	.26	-.33	.03	.30	.15	-.06	.51
23. Positive Expectations	.23	.40	-.32	-.38	-.09	-.43	.56	-.35	.18
24. Negative Expectations	.23	-.03	.55	-.18	-.13	-.25	-.08	.14	.24
25. Moderation	.65*	.16	-.07	-.37	-.10	.30	.80**	-.16	.62*
26. Stress	-.11	-.02	.32	.61*	.03	.39	-.23	.06	.05
27. Support	.05	.34	.26	-.18	.12	-.04	.02	-.32	.00
28. Dynamism	.20	.30	-.17	-.19	-.37	.08	.61*	-.22	-.04

Table 3.5 (continued)

Competency	19	20	21	22	23	24	25	26	27	28
1. Achievement										
2. Initiative: Short-term										
3. Initiative: Long-term										
4. Objectivity										
5. Information Seeking										
6. Conceptual Thinking										
7. Finding Meaning										
8. Analytical Thinking										
9. Resp. to Members										
10. Resp. to Clients1										
11. Resp. to Clients2										
12. Developmental										
13. Mentor										
14. Empathy										
15. Interpersonal Understanding										
16. Mission										
17. Community Leadership										
18. Command Authority										
19. Consensual Authority	-									
20. Directiveness	-.23	-								
21. Socialized Power	-.31	.01	-							
22. Self Confidence	.19	.30	.03	-						
23. Positive Expectations	.58*	-.12	.20	-.07	-					
24. Negative Expectations	.10	.67**	-.12	.17	.30	-				
25. Moderation	.35	-.14	.44	.29	.68*	.12	-			
26. Stress	.05	.04	-.35	.03	-.38	.10	-.21	-		
27. Support	.74**	-.23	-.42	.55	.23	.06	.18	.36	-	
28. Dynamism	-.04	-.31	.65*	-.17	.46	.10	.56	-.40	-.29	-

* $p < .05$ ** $p < .01$ *** $p < .001$

Table 3.6
T-tests between Correlation Coefficients of Outstanding and Typical Leaders

Competencies	Typical	Outstanding	Z-Value*
Achievement/Initiative2	-.25	.55	3.53
Achievement/s Power	.13	.60	2.26
Initiative1/Analytical Thinking	.05	.53	2.18
Initiative1/Resp. for Members	-.23	.54	3.39
Initiative1/s Power	.09	.60	2.44
Initiative1/Find Meaning	.65	.17	-3.86
Initiative1/Positive Expectations	.81	.41	-2.80
Initiative2/Analytical Thinking	.03	.59	2.60
Initiative2/Command Authority	.01	.60	2.75
Initiative2/Consensual Authority	.74	.22	-2.94
Objectivity/Conceptual Thinking	.24	.63	2.01
Objectivity/Finding Meaning	-.08	.56	2.88
Objectivity/Empathy	-.21	.59	3.56
Objectivity/Positive Expectations	-.45	.68	5.32
Objectivity/Negative Expectations	-.31	.53	3.69
Conceptual Thinking/Analytical Thinking	.73	.29	-2.56
Finding Meaning/Resp. to Members	.08	.61	2.54
Finding Meaning/Empathy	-.32	.63	4.34
Analytical Thinking/Moderation	.57	.09	-2.27
Resp. to Members/Mentor	.02	.51	2.20
Resp. to Members/Interpersonal	.78	.23	-3.30
Resp. to Members/Positive Expectations	-.52	.41	4.09
Empathy/Positive Expectations	-.09	.73	4.16
Empathy/Negative Expectations	-.13	.49	2.67
Empathy/Spiritual Support	.12	.56	2.07
Command Authority/Positive Expectations	.18	.51	-3.77
Consensual Authority/Spiritual Support	.74	.32	2.47
Consensual Authority/Spiritual Dynamism	-.04	.65	-3.34
s Power/Conceptual Thinking	.69	.30	-2.18
s Power/Spiritual Dynamism	.65	.18	2.41
s Power/Mission	.68	.03	-3.23
Mission/Moderation	.80	.37	2.88
Mission/Mentor	-.30	.56	3.81
Mission/Spiritual Dynamism	.61	-.11	-3.31
Moderation/Resp. to Clients1	.65	-.08	-3.46

Note: All reported Z-values are significant beyond the $p < .05$ level.

of self-confidence and a concern for moderation. These competencies are considered as thresholds because they are used equally by both outstanding and typical leaders (See Appendix C for t-test results). The model does not include the correlation coefficients between the competencies, because none of the correlations exceeded the .50 cutoff for inclusion.

Figure 3.11
Threshold Competencies for Religious Leadership

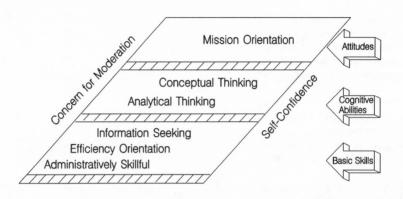

Figure 3.12 presents the model for excellence in religious leadership and the relationships among the various competencies beyond those considered as threshold competencies or those in evidence in both the typical and outstanding groups of leaders. These characteristics of outstanding religious leaders function within a more general framework of the threshold competencies outlined in Figure 3.11. That is, such leaders must also have such basic competencies as mission focus, self-confidence, a concern for moderation, and good intellectual and administrative skills.

As the diagram indicates, moving from the base of the model to the top, outstanding religious leaders are deeply rooted in the awareness of the presence of God operating in the world and in their own lives. This was reflected in the frequencies at which outstanding and typical leaders mentioned the presence of God. Though both leader types have an awareness of God, awareness of God was mentioned more frequently by outstanding leaders (Figure 3.6). Though both male and female outstanding leaders possess a strong awareness of God, they differed in their expression of this awareness. Outstanding women leaders saw God's presence as a source of energy and dynamism, while outstanding men leaders emphasized spiritual support.

The presence of a strong awareness of God led outstanding leaders to discern and speak of the spiritual meaning in what is happening in the world around them. Their deep and ever-present sense of spiritual concern arouses two types of motivation that are central to their leadership role: namely, a strong desire to make things better (achievement motivation) and an equally strong desire to make things happen, to implement changes for the congregation that are needed to make things better (socialized power motivation). This is evident from the strong correlation between the achievement and socialized power motives for outstanding leaders (r = .60, p < .01).

Figure 3.12
Foundations of Religious Leadership

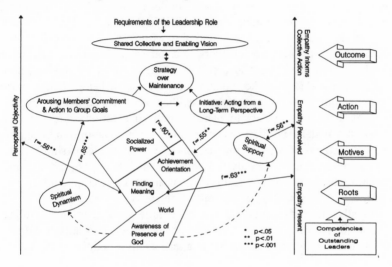

As with awareness of God, achievement and socialized power motives usually express themselves somewhat differently in men and women leaders. The men tended to think of power more in terms of replacing old, less effective ways of getting things done and of achievement more in terms of starting new projects that will replace the old ways of doing things (initiative). This was reflected by the significant correlation of achievement and long-term initiative for outstanding leaders (r = .55, p < .01).

The women leaders were inclined to think of power more in terms of building resources out of developing a strong sense of commitment from the membership: resources that can be shared and used to attain a commitment to group goals. The distinct expression of awareness of God and motivation among outstanding women leaders is strongly supported by the significant association between spiritual dynamism and consensual authority (r = .65, p < .001).

The foundations of the religious leadership model suggests that the outcome of all leadership activity is a shared, collective and enabling vision to which members can commit. The leader's action in the process must focus on strategy over maintenance. Strategy is defined as a pattern of congregational purposes and goals that defines the intention or unique service to which the congregation commits itself. A strategy is a statement that differentiates a congregation from all others. Its purpose is to create a sustainable advantage for the congregation by defining its uniqueness. Outstanding leaders consistently affected change in the congregation, whereas typical leaders seldom did.

The motivational and strategic approaches characteristic of outstanding leaders are more likely to be successful in developing collective and enabling visions because the outstanding leaders are able to perceive objectively what is going on in their congregations and the world and to empathize with or understand the feelings of members and others with whom they interact. Empathy plays a role at three levels. First, it helps the leaders understand what needs to be attended to in the congregation. Second, when it occurs, empathy builds commitment from the members as they feel attended to and understood, and third, it enables leaders to plan for collective action more successfully because they understand their members. The strong relationship of perceptual objectivity and empathy to the foundations of outstanding leadership is reflected in the correlations of objectivity to finding meaning (r = .56, p < .01) and the associations between empathy and finding meaning (r = .63, p < .001), spiritual support (r = .56, p < .01) and perceptual objectivity (r = .59, p < .01).

Finally, the model suggests that the requirements of the leadership role, including job requirements and threshold competencies, also inform and interact with the dynamic process of outstanding leadership in religious orders.

The Leadership Motive Syndrome and Leadership Selection

In several studies of large business organizations, it has been found that outstanding managers are characterized by strong socialized power motivation and a relatively weaker involvement with interpersonal concerns, as represented by the need for affiliation (McClelland & Boyatzis, 1982; Jacobs, 1991). This combination has been called the leadership motive syndrome.

These two characteristics are also associated in this study with outstanding performance among leaders of religious congregations. In fact, if the two characteristics are taken together, they identify a high percentage of the 23 outstanding leaders studied. Using the criteria of at least five references to the use of socialized power (Figure 3.3 and Table 3.2) and three or fewer references of interpersonal concerns (supervising or counselling others, Figure 3.5) in an interview, these two criteria alone identify 78% of the 23 outstanding leaders (7 of 11 men and 11 of 12 women). The same criteria characterized only 2 of the 12 typical leaders (1 man and 1 woman), $\chi^2 = 12.44$, $p < .01$. Thus, if one were to look for characteristics most likely to identify outstanding, as contrasted with typical, leaders in this sample, once again it would be those that define the leadership motive syndrome: a high need for exercising power in attaining group goals and a relatively low need for involvement in interpersonal concerns.

Figure 3.13 depicts the leadership motive syndrome ($\underline{n}$ s Power > Aff) among leaders of religious orders, along with other competencies that have relevance for leadership selection processes. The correlations among the competencies for outstanding leaders, as discussed in the previous section, are also included in this figure. The uniqueness of the model lies in the degree to which faith and the presence of God provide the foundation for what religious leaders actually do as leaders. Outstanding religious leaders score higher in achievement motivation than typical leaders, but even achievement has a direction or purpose to it: that is, for the congregation to have a larger social impact. The outstanding leaders direct their efforts beyond members' needs, and even beyond affiliation with the group, to concern for the effectiveness of the group in achieving a broader mission.

Figure 3.13
Religious Leadership Selection Model

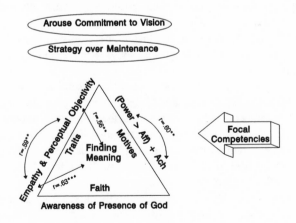

In a leadership selection process, faith, personal traits and a combination of motives should be considered. Faith is demonstrated among outstanding leaders by the degree to which they refer to and root their actions in an awareness of God. Specific traits include the expression of empathy and perceptual objectivity in matters of significance. Among outstanding leaders, socialized power or concern with congregational impact is greater than the need for affiliation with the group. When socialized power is combined with achievement motivation, the leadership motive syndrome would predict a greater probability that these leaders would focus on strategy over maintenance of the congregation. In addition, it appears only within this combination of faith, traits and motives that the members' commitment to a collective vision is aroused.

IMPLICATIONS

This study identified competencies common to leaders of religious orders (larger than 150 members and with significant institutional commitments) in the Roman Catholic Church in the United States. It also identified those competencies associated uniquely with outstanding leadership of religious orders.

Outstanding leaders were characterized by what has been called the leadership motive syndrome, as identified in other studies of successful leaders in large organizations (McClelland & Boyatzis, 1982; Jacobs, 1991). In short, outstanding, as compared to typical, religious leaders are more concerned with exerting power and influence to attain congregational goals and less concerned with supervising and counselling individual members of the congregation to make sure they live up to their vocation. Admittedly, these are matters of relative emphasis. All leaders are involved to some extent in both these activities, but the priorities are different for outstanding leaders, as reflected in what they report concerning their thoughts and actions during the interviews for this investigation.

This finding demonstrates that one essential element in the success of religious leaders, that is, the leadership motive syndrome, is the same as an essential element in the success of leaders in other organizations. Additional competencies associated with outstanding religious leadership, such as a strong achievement motivation and taking a great deal of initiative to deal with problems before they occur, have also been found in studies of the more successful managers in the business world.

Two competencies associated with outstanding leadership appear to be relatively unique to the position of major superiors of Roman Catholic religious orders in the United States today. The first centers on the outstanding leaders' grounding in spirituality. This showed itself in the greater ability of outstanding, rather than typical, leaders to find and express the spiritual significance in everyday affairs and in their greater reliance on God either as a source of support (more typical for the men) or as a source of direction and energy (more typical for the women).

While one might expect that all leaders of religious congregations would be oriented toward interpreting events in religious terms and relying heavily on the awareness of the presence of God, it is important to distinguish between what Argyris (1982) called "espoused theories," which are said to be important in reference to what guides behavior, and "theories in use," which actually do guide behavior. There is little doubt that both typical and outstanding leaders would endorse equally the importance of such a religious orientation. However, the interviews showed that in spontaneously recounting their experiences, the outstanding leaders more frequently cited instances of actions consistent with the religious theory that they would espouse. Such reports went beyond saccharine spiritual interpretation of events. Instead, outstanding leaders communicated a genuine sense of their awareness of God's presence in their lives.

The second competency unique to this population centers on the importance of using the authority of the leadership position to mobilize commitment, building consensus or helping members to "own" projects and policies of the congregation and other agencies. Traditionally, full authority is vested in a leader by the congregation and, to a considerable extent, typical leaders act as if this were the case. Compared to outstanding leaders, they do not spend as much time trying to get the members' commitment to a decision or policy of the congregation. Outstanding leaders act more often through persuasion and use a variety of means to influence the members to support and commit themselves to group goals. It is as if they believe that power lies in the members as well as in the office they hold as leaders.

The emphasis on building consensual authority has a strong historical tradition in the Western democracies and in the United States. As Baltzell (1979) pointed out, the Religious Society of Friends (Quakers) played an important role in the early settlement of the United States, yet its view of religious authority was quite different from the view among the Puritans in New England or the Roman Catholics in Maryland. Quakerism holds that there are no intermediaries, such as priests or pastors, between the individual and God. It is said that Christ speaks directly to individual members at a Quaker meeting. Therefore, the "sense" of a group of Quakers in a meeting for worship, as gathered by a clerk of the meeting, is the ultimate religious authority. There is no group of religious experts who can speak with greater authority. While Quakerism quickly died out as a major influence in the colonies (even in Pennsylvania), Baltzell argued that this view of authority reinforced the political democratic tradition and influenced subsequent organizational development in the United States. He believed that the tradition of having a board of directors, whom the top executive of a public or a private corporation serves, owes much to Quaker influence. Here, the ultimate authority is in the peer group, and not in the hands of the person in charge, who may nonetheless be the most expert.

The opinion of others, as represented often in the mass media, has a great influence on the opinions of people in the United States (McClelland, Sturr Knapp & Wendt, 1958). These authors suggested that this may be due, not only to the strong democratic tradition in this country, but also to the fact that in a country comprised of many recent immigrants, individuals had to turn to others to find out what to do. McClelland (1961) also found that this kind of "other-directedness" was associated with more rapid rates of economic growth across a number of countries in the 1950s, perhaps because it allowed for more flexibility in adapting to changing conditions than traditional authority directedness.

In the present study, the outstanding female leaders were more oriented than the outstanding male leaders toward viewing the members as a source of authority. There is a school of thought among those who have studied successful women managers in business that women have a different style of leadership. Rosener (1990), for example, argued that women executives often fail to follow the traditional male authority role of command-and-control. Rather, they have an interactive leadership style in which they encourage the participation of those they lead and share power and information, energizing others and enhancing their self-worth.

While other observers disagree with this analysis, it is worth noting that outstanding female leaders of religious orders in this study did, in fact, behave in these ways more often than did the outstanding male religious leaders. Jacobs (1991) has evidence that successful female managers more frequently use power as a resource to be shared with others in an interactive style, rather than in an assertive command-and-control manner, a style more frequently attributed to male leaders. From this point of view, women may be changing their understanding of religious leadership to include a greater emphasis on the importance of gaining commitment of the members to the direction set by leaders.

The changing understanding of leadership and authority in religious life has produced satisfaction for some but confusion for others. Some orders today operate by nearly absolute consensus or distributed authority, while others retain centralized control by authority recognized solely in the person of the leader. Pushing the source of authority to either extreme can be a potential hazard.

Revolt against traditional hierarchical authority developed when it had to be obeyed even when the person occupying an office was unworthy of respect or made unjust or unwise decisions. Few would want to go back to the extreme of obeying a leader simply because of the authority granted the office. Nor, on the other hand, does it seem wise to insist that all decisions made by a superior should be reviewed and approved by the membership. In fact, the outstanding female religious leaders certainly used the authority of their office in a variety of skillful ways to arouse consensus and commitment in the membership. They felt that it was much more part of their job as a leader to do so than did the outstanding male leaders.

Assumptions underlying authority and leadership in part shape the operative paradigms of religious life. And, the shifting paradigms of authority have implications for religious orders as organizations as well. Most congregations were founded to respond to a particular social or ecclesial need. Members attracted to a particular community traditionally understood that by pronouncing their vows in that congregation, they were positioning themselves to be sent in service of their congregation's mission, usually by someone to whom they were accountable under their vow of obedience. If authority resides solely in the group, there is little problem with accountability to the group, but there may be significant difficulties with being sent by the group to act on its behalf. Examples of such difficulty were noted particularly in areas of placement (assignment of ministry) and organizational responsibility. Many leaders observed that they no longer assign members to ministerial activities because their placement policies are based on the premise that all individuals in the group share the responsibility to discern and initiate a change in ministry. Such a reinterpretation of authority frequently precludes the congregational leader from initiating a change in another's assignment, even when pressing need is involved.

On an organizational level, the religious congregation has specific purposes to accomplish. Many leaders noted that in attempting to focus the group on a collective action, responsibility to do so is often thwarted because of the leader's lack of authority to act. Thus, opportunities for impact are lost because the group lacks a process for decision making in such realms.

Similarly, most religious orders sponsor educational and health care institutions. Leaders bear the burden of responsibility for monitoring the policies and establishing the direction of these institutions, but frequently do not possess the authority to exercise this responsibility. Current congregational structures for policy formulation and decision making do not typically reflect the linkage necessary to effectively address the major moral, financial and legal obligations that these institutions present.

In the research process, leaders could readily tell the story of how the congregation began and gained members through the founder's commitment to some corporate action or mission. Many leaders described in detail how the congregation developed objectives over time that differed from those of the founder. Many described a lack of fit between an espoused value (the original mission) and the operative theory in practice (what activates the order today). Numerous examples of a founding mission of service to the poor which, though still espoused, has little bearing on the life or work of the congregation today emerged. As Argyris (1982) observed, when espoused theories and theories in use do not agree, organizational malfunctioning occurs.

These religious orders started with enthusiasm and entered an entrepreneurial phase during which they attracted members to accomplish the vision that motivated them. Most of today's orders do reflect the development into a more stable, bureaucratic phase of organizational development. The original vision has grown somewhat dimmer with time, and the problem has become more one of system maintenance, making sure that the organization survives as an organization. Vatican II did provide an impetus toward renewal, but as many of the congregations attempted to discover and develop enthusiasm about renewed missions, other personal and organizational agendas detracted from their ability to develop a clear congregational focus or mission.

It remains that organizational survival depends less on management competencies than on the ability of leaders to interpret the founding purpose in current metaphors and idioms and to find new and exciting means by which to address the most pressing human needs: in a style and spirit not necessarily identical with, but clearly similar to, those of their founding members. At present, leaders are trying to manage organizations that often lack a clear, compelling vision. Results of this study have shown that outstanding leaders possessing the competencies described in the foundation of this religious leadership model have been able to move their groups in this direction.

NOTES

1. Refer to Appendix B, Table B.1 for a listing and definition of these constructs.

2. A competency is defined as a measurable characteristic of a person which reliably distinguishes outstanding from typical performers in a particular job. These characteristics predict superior performance.

3. Adapted from D.C. McClelland (1975). Power: the inner experience. New York: Irvington.

Chapter 4

ATTITUDE AND BEHAVIORAL
MEASURES OF MEMBERSHIP
A NATIONAL SURVEY OF MEMBERS OF RELIGIOUS ORDERS

PURPOSE

The National Survey component of the Religious Life Futures Project had two purposes: to collect information concerning the beliefs, values and practices of members of religious orders regarding their personal, spiritual, community and ministerial life and to establish a significant data base for the study of religious life on the individual, congregational and social institution levels. The National Survey was also the primary method of measuring perceptions of the future of religious life in the total population of sisters, brothers and religious priests.

The 335-item instrument, which was constructed during the first year of the grant from Lilly Endowment Inc., was piloted with an appropriate number of subjects and reviewed by both the national advisory board and other prominent social scientists. It appears in Appendix D.

METHOD

Developing the National Population Listing

This portion of the project began with the compilation of the names of major superiors of religious orders in the United States. Several inquiries confirmed the fact that no such official listing existed. Fortunately, the national offices of the Conference of Major Superiors of Men (CMSM), the Leadership Conference of Women Religious (LCWR) and the Tri-Conference Retirement Office, along with the editor of the *Official Catholic Directory,* provided access to their mailing lists. As a result of intensive efforts to reconcile the listings, eliminate duplicates and verify the incumbents, a listing of 1,138 names of persons identified as major superiors of congregations in the United States was completed.

In January 1990, these superiors received a letter requesting the names and addresses of the members of their congregations. Over the months that followed, a second request was made by phone to those superiors from whom listings had not been received. As a result of that letter and the phone requests, directories were obtained from a total of 816 distinct congregations or provinces of congregations.

To interpret as an indication of nonparticipation the difference between the 1,138 letters sent and the 816 congregations that participated in the study is not accurate. While some congregations chose not to participate, in most of the instances the failure to respond resulted from the fact that the individuals listed on the original mailing list had been included inappropriately, inasmuch as they represented parish convents, small local communities or persons who were counselors or in other administrative positions; there were also individuals whose names had been listed as "interested persons" in the files of groups from whom project mailing lists were obtained and previously unidentified duplicates. Based on the number of religious in the United States listed by the *Official Catholic Directory* for 1990 (128,571), this process identified by name and address 94.6% of the population. The listings received were sorted by gender and tradition, and a coded identification number was assigned to each. Table 4.1 summarizes the number of orders that responded, according to tradition and members' vocations.

Table 4.1

Number of Congregations Responding to Request for Directories

Tradition	Type of Congregation			
	Sisters	Brothers (only)	Brothers & Priests	Priests (only)
Apostolic	419	29	87	6
Mendicant	36	1	31	2
Contemplative	95	0	12	0
Monastic	51	1	45	1
Total	601	31	175	9

The acquisition of congregational listings presented a variety of additional questions. Some groups identified members alphabetically, and others, by length of time in the order. In many of the women's groups, where living with members of other religious groups is common, members of the other orders living with a community member were also listed. Several groups have oblate, lay associate or other forms of affiliates who also were included in the membership listings. Many groups included foreign members who are part of regions or missionary areas of a particular province or order. After reviewing the various issues presented by the myriad forms of congregational listings, criteria for inclusion in this study as a "member of a congregation" in a particular order were developed. They included:

1. All persons listed under an address in the United States unless it was clear that a particular individual was a member of another congregation or province;
2. Professed members of the U.S. group serving in foreign countries;
3. Members listed as on sabbatical, away for study or on leave of absence;
4. Individuals in stages of initial formation: postulants, candidates, novices and seminarians; and
5. Individuals designated as "infirm."[1]

Each member who met the criteria for inclusion was assigned a "within-congregation" number. Persons who were listed as an oblate, associate member or co-member, and those identified as on exclaustration or as away without permission (*vagi*) were not included.[2] Persons clearly identified as members of a foreign province or region were also excluded from the sample.

Table 4.2
Actual Distribution of U.S. Congregations by Vocation and Tradition

Tradition	Vocation			Total
	Sisters	Brothers	Priests	
Apostolic	79,276	6,459	12,468	98,203
Mendicant	8,951	1,330	4,594	14,875
Contemplative	1,692	211	241	2,144
Monastic	4,250	656	1,535	6,441
Total	94,169	8,656	18,838	121,663

Anticipating analyses by vocation, members of men's congregations were identified by vocation (brother or priest). Persons clearly designated as "Fr.," "Rev.," or "Deacon" were counted as priests while novices, candidates, postulants and seminarians were counted as brothers. When staff were unable to make this determination from available information, the order was contacted by telephone. Using this process, a total of 121,663 religious priests, brothers and sisters was identified (see Table 4.2). As was noted above, this represents 94.6% of the 128,571 member of religious orders in the United States identified by the *Official Catholic Directory* 1990.

The Sampling Plan

Accounting for tradition. Determination of the traditional groupings of religious life (apostolic, monastic, mendicant, or contemplative) to which a congregation belonged posed several issues. Lack of clarity among members with regard to this determination and concerns that this might result in significant problems with regard to both sampling issues and data analysis led to the decision to collapse the four traditions into two categories for the sample selection: apostolic/mendicant and contemplative/monastic. Previous research and current practice supported this decision.

Sample design and selection.[3] The general purpose of a sample design is to provide a scientifically valid sample of one or more populations in such a way as to satisfy the statistical needs of a research project. The goals identified for this portion of the Religious Life Futures Project included:

1.   The development of basic descriptive and analytical statistics for all members of religious congregations of the Roman Catholic Church in the United States: sisters, brothers and religious priests, across all traditions (apostolic, monastic, mendicant and contemplative);

2.   The development of basic descriptive and analytical statistics for various groupings, such as vocation and tradition, within the population. This includes separate descriptive estimates for sisters, brothers and priests, each as a separate group, and further sub-divisions of each of these groups.

The sampling plan thus developed aimed to respond to the basic descriptive and analytical   statistical goals and to provide for scientific validity and statistical flexibility.

Table 4.2 shows the distribution of the members of religious congregations of the Roman Catholic Church in the United States with respect to vocation and tradition. The distribution of the members of religious orders is highly skewed with respect to the vocational and tradition groupings. For example, apostolic sisters alone comprised approximately 65% of the total population while, at the other extreme, contemplative brothers comprised less than 1%. This lack of symmetry in the frequency distribution had a substantial impact on the basic sample design strategy.

Overall sample size. Given the size of the population and the overall project goals, the total sample size and desire to compare across groups required special consideration. At this juncture, the theoretical world of statistical precision, power functions and optimization equations met the practical world of project resources—human, temporal and financial—in relation to overall project goals. Typically, project objectives indicate a sample size as large as possible, and the basic questions to be answered involves a determination of whether the maximum affordable sample size will generally support the statistical or inferential goals of the project.

Resources for this project would support a sample size of approximately 7,500 completed questionnaires. A sample of this size provided sufficient support for descriptive and analytical goals, as described in the previous section.

Allocation between and among the primary groupings of vocation and tradition was considered. The skew of the population (already noted) presented a significant challenge in the development of a sample allocation that would satisfy both the stated statistical goals. This dilemma results from the fact that the optimal sample design for meeting the first goal involves strict proportional allocation of the sample with respect to each population segment, while the optimal sample design for satisfying the second goal requires an equal allocation among the six population groups.

Concretely, as regards the first goal of the development of basic descriptive and analytical statistics for members of religious orders, proportional allocation entailed distribution of the sample among the six basic groups (three vocations grouped by two traditions) in proportion to the population size. Based on a total sample size of 7,500 completed surveys, this proportionate allocation is shown in Table 4.3. In this distribution, apostolic and mendicant sisters, who account for 72.5% of the population, would be represented by 5,439 apostolic/mendicant sisters, or 72.5% of 7,500.

Table 4.3
Optimal Sample Allocation for Goal 1 by Vocation and Tradition

Tradition	Vocation		
	Sisters	Brothers	Priests
Apostolic/Mendicant	5,439	480	1,052
Contemplative/Monastic	366	53	109
Total	5,805	533	1,161

The optimal sample design for the second goal, the description of the various vocation and tradition groupings, results in a sample that was allocated equally, rather than proportionally, among the six basic groups. Under this model, each cell, no matter what its population percent, would be allocated one-sixth (16.7%) of the total sample. Table 4.4 displays this distribution. In order to satisfy, as well as possible, both objectives while maintaining the statistical integrity of the sampling procedure, a stratified random sample using partially disproportionate allocations was used. Based on a sample of 7,500, the allocation that provides for achieving both goals is shown in Table 4.5. This stratified design aims for a minimum of 500 completed questionnaires for each of the basic design groups.[4]

Table 4.4
Optimal Sample Allocation for Goal 2 by Vocation and Tradition

	Vocation		
Tradition	Sisters	Brothers	Priests
Apostolic/Mendicant	1,250	1,250	1,250
Contemplative/Monastic	1,250	1,250	1,250
Total	2,500	2,500	2,500

Table 4.5
Sample Allocation for Achieving Goals 1 and 2 by Vocation and Tradition

	Vocation		
Tradition	Sisters	Brothers	Priests
Apostolic/Mendicant	3,000	1,500	1,500
Contemplative/Monastic	500	500	500
Total	3,500	2,000	2,000

Sample size modified for response rate. Based on previous research with this population of sisters, brothers and religious priests, a response rate of 75% appeared reasonable. Thus, the initial sample selected within each of the six basic design cells was increased by a constant factor ($1/.75 = 1.333$) to result in an initial sample size of 10,000 (or 7,500/.75).

Subject Identification, Survey Distribution and Follow-Up

In the survey described earlier, each potential subject was assigned an identification number, enabling the participant to be identified by religious order, individual within the order, vocation and tradition. Using a program for generating random numbers, individual subject numbers were identified. During

October 1990, surveys with printed identification numbers were mailed directly to those individuals who were selected in this process. A cover letter and postage-paid return envelope were included in each packet. Recipients were asked to return the survey by November 15, 1990. A total of 9,999 questionnaires was mailed. Table 4.6 summarizes the distribution of questionnaires sent to each of the vocation and tradition groupings.

Table 4.6
National Survey Distribution by Vocation and Tradition

Tradition	Vocation			Total
	Sisters	Brothers	Priests	
Apostolic	3,590	1,674	1,465	6,729
Mendicant	398	321	538	1,257
Contemplative	194	161	92	447
Monastic	477	504	585	1,566
Total	4,659	2,660	2,680	9,999

Approximately four weeks after the initial mailing of the questionnaires, follow-up was begun. A reminder postcard was sent to the subjects, thanking them if they had returned the questionnaire, requesting that they do so if they had not yet returned it, and inviting them to call or write the project office in the event that they had not received the questionnaire. Three weeks later, an intensive program of telephoning was initiated. Efforts were made to contact each respondent who resided in the United States whose completed survey had not been received and for whom a phone number was available. This phase of follow-up was implemented by a research firm that had trained professionals in the area of response conversion related to survey research.

March 31, 1991, was set as the final date for the receipt of surveys considered for use in this study. At that time, the actual number of returned questionnaires was 7,736, yielding an overall response rate of 77%. Of this number, 6,359 surveys were usable in the analysis.

Determination of Sample Proportions and Weights

The complexities of the sample design and decisions made to address these concerns have been outlined above. The factors accounting for this included the fact that the ratio of women religious to men religious is approximately three-to-one, as well as the determination to consider differences relative to vocation (priest, brother, or sister) and tradition (apostolic, mendicant, monastic, or contemplative). These factors also had a great influence on the data analysis.

Because a process of proportional weighting is based on an estimate of the actual population size as well as the size of each group to be considered, it was necessary to sort from among the survey recipients the actual number of responses from among the vocational and tradition groupings, the size of the potential population, and the estimated adjusted size of the groups indicated by the number of nonrespondents and data received from the nonusable responses. To achieve this, a complex system of disposition codes was devised, and each of the 9,999 individuals contacted was assigned a code. A listing of these disposition categories, as well as the numbers of the survey sample in each, is included in Appendix E.

Table 4.7
Summary of Eligibility Categories Used in Determining Sample Weights

Group	Eligible		Not Eligible [2]	Not Sure [3]	No Disposition	Total
	Completed	Did not Respond [1]				
Sisters						
Apostolic	2,560	256	356	163	255	3,590
Mendicant	294	32	39	22	11	398
Contemplative	123	35	30	5	1	194
Monastic	375	24	56	14	8	477
Brothers						
Apostolic	1,004	198	120	189	163	1,674
Mendicant	180	52	30	29	30	321
Contemplative	72	16	21	28	24	161
Monastic	285	84	59	54	22	504
Priests						
Apostolic	787	225	86	197	170	1,465
Mendicant	313	75	28	67	55	538
Contemplative	38	11	5	16	22	92
Monastic	328	103	61	67	26	585
Total	6,359	1,111	891	851	787	9,999

[1] Disposition codes included: LANG, REFN, REFP, UNUS, CHNG, SENN, SENT, RETR.
[2] Disposition codes included: INFI, DEAD, LEFT.
[3] Disposition codes included: ANSF, UNKN, DISC, NOCT, PHOS.

Coefficients used for proportional means for the total population of members of religious orders and for weighted subgroup means were calculated. Table 4.7 presents the actual numbers of those determined as eligible, not eligible and uncertain that were used in the computation of population weights. In the data analysis, responses from the 6,359 usable questionnaires were weighted in light of the above-mentioned variables. The type of analysis—for example, between or within particular groups—and the nature of the statistic, such as descriptive or level of significance, also determined which weights were to be used in a particular view of the data. Reports of survey results include statistics computed by using the appropriate weights and reproportioned samples.

Response rates for the various subgroups also were determined. When the response rates for the traditions were considered, the differences were of a magnitude to suggest separating the apostolic/mendicant and contemplative/monastic combinations. Thus, analyses by tradition were run as four distinct groups: apostolic, mendicant, contemplative and monastic.

DEMOGRAPHICS OF RESPONDENTS TO THE NATIONAL SURVEY

Information regarding the respondents to the National Survey is divided into four basic areas. For each of these sections, respondents were grouped by vocation (sister, brother, or priest); tradition (apostolic, mendicant, contemplative, or monastic), and age cohort (19-45, 46-60, 61-73 and 74-96). The areas considered are:

1. Who responded to the survey? This section contains information regarding age, race/ethnicity, length of time in their current orders, history in religious life relative to their current status, and similar issues.
2. What are the respondents like professionally? In this portion, issues related to education, field of study, current ministerial/professional involvement, and future study and ministerial/professional plans are reported.
3. What is the role of formal prayer in their lives? Here, information regarding the frequency of, and circumstances related to, attendance at a variety of communal prayer experiences, as well as the individual's own frequency of prayer, are considered.
4. What about their living situations? This section reviews the range of living situations of members of religious orders, their satisfaction with these arrangements and expectations for the future.

Who Responded to the Survey?[5]

As was noted, significant emphasis was placed on the distributions by vocation and tradition in the selection of survey participants. Table 4.8 lists the distribution by these groupings.

Table 4.8
Distribution of Survey Respondents by Vocation and Tradition

Tradition	Sisters	Brothers	Priests	Total
Apostolic	2,559	920	872	4,351
Mendicant	294	155	338	787
Contemplative	124	66	43	233
Monastic	373	269	346	988
Total	3,350	1,410	1,599	6,359

Your present age?
Number of years in religious life?
Age at entrance?

The 6,359 members of religious orders who responded to the survey ranged in age from 19 to 96 years. As Table 4.9 indicates, their mean age was 58.6 years. They had been members of religious orders for an average of 37.5 years, and had entered, on the average, at 20.6 years of age. When considered by vocation, the sisters had the highest mean age. Inasmuch as the age data for this survey includes only those member of religious orders who were well enough to complete the survey, this information is consistent with the Tri-Conference Retirement Office survey which, for 1991, reported the average age of religious men to be 59 for both active and contemplative groups, and sisters' mean age to be 66 for active groups and 64 for contemplative groups.[6]

Corresponding with the highest mean age, sisters also had the highest mean number of years in religious life. Their age at entrance was approximately two years younger than that of their male counterparts. Similarly, members of apostolic groups, who represented 68.4% of the respondents, had the highest mean age, the greatest mean years in religious life, and the youngest mean age at entrance. Contemplatives had the oldest mean age at entrance and the lowest mean number of years in religious life.

Table 4.9
Demographics Relative to Age and Number of Years in Religious Life

Group	N	Current Age		Age at Entrance		Years in Religious Life	
		Mean	SD	Mean	SD	Mean	SD
Vocation							
Sisters	3,350	62.6	13.6	19.8	4.6	42.2	14.3
Brothers	1,410	52.9	14.6	22.2	7.4	30.1	16.0
Priests	1,599	55.6	14.6	21.0	5.0	34.0	16.1
Tradition							
Apostolic	4,351	59.6	14.54	19.9	4.7	39.1	15.3
Mendicant	787	56.6	15.2	21.2	5.4	35.1	16.7
Contemplative	233	57.7	14.5	24.4	8.5	32.4	15.6
Monastic	988	56.4	15.6	22.4	7.2	33.4	17.6
Cohort							
19-45	1,287	37.4	6.1	21.8	4.9	15.2	8.2
46-60	1,970	53.3	4.3	19.7	4.9	33.0	6.5
61-73	1,809	66.6	3.8	20.9	6.3	45.2	7.4
74-96	1,143	79.1	4.4	20.5	5.9	57.8	7.6
Total Sample	6,359	58.6	14.8	20.6	5.6	37.5	16.0

Note: Due to 150 missing observations, the total sample for age cohorts equals 6,209 rather than 6,359.

A consideration of age by cohort groupings provides many interesting contrasts. These age groups were determined by a joint consideration of adult developmental tasks and the age distribution of the respondents. Hence, efforts were made to group members who would be facing similar developmental issues. Simultaneously, care was taken to ensure that the age categories would be roughly comparable in size. Thus, the 19-45 cohort, the group with the greatest age span, covers the greatest range of developmental tasks. The fact that the mean age for this group is 37.4 speaks to the skew of the distribution to the older end of the range. In fact, while this cohort represents 20.7% of the respondents whose age is known (150 survey respondents left this item blank), only 228 (3.7%) of these respondents are 30 years old or younger. A similar number (223) represents those whose ages fall between 31 and 35. Thus, the remaining 806 members (62.6%), of the 19-45 cohort are 36 years of age or older.

110

THE FUTURE OF RELIGIOUS ORDERS

Table 4.10
Age Cohorts by Vocation and Tradition (based on sample of 6,359 with 150
missing observations)

Group	19-45	46-60	61-73	74-96
Vocation				
Sisters	390	1,023	1,026	819
	30.3%	51.9%	56.7%	71.7%
Brothers	462	466	325	132
	35.9%	23.7%	18.0%	11.5%
Priests	435	481	458	192
	33.8%	24.4%	25.3%	16.8%
Tradition				
Apostolic	788	1,339	1,270	846
	18.6%	31.6%	29.9%	19.9%
Mendicant	189	262	192	122
	24.7%	34.2%	25.1%	15.9%
Contemplative	39	81	83	23
	17.3%	35.8%	36.7%	10.2%
Monastic	271	288	264	152
	27.8%	29.5%	27.1%	15.6%
Total	1,287	1,970	1,809	1,143
	20.7%	31.7%	29.1%	18.4%

Table 4.10 provides the organization of cohorts by vocation and by tradition. While among the 19-45 age group, the 1,287 members are divided fairly equally among the vocational groupings of sister, brother and priest, more than 71% of those in the 74-96 cohort are sisters, with the remainder divided fairly equally between brothers and priests. In the middle two cohorts, sisters account for slightly more than 50% of the members, reflecting the proportions of sisters who responded to the survey. Among the traditions, the 19-45 cohort includes more than 24% of the respondents of the contemplative and nearly 28% of the monastic traditions, while among the apostolic and mendicant groups fewer than 19% of the respondents are 45 or younger. The 74-96 cohort includes slightly more than 10% of the contemplative respondents and nearly 20% of the members of apostolic groups.

Table 4.11
Distribution of Respondents by Race/Ethnicity (based on number of
    responses to this question)

Group	U.S. Citizen	Caucasian	African-American	Latino-Hispanic	Pacific Rim	Other
Vocation						
Sisters	3,291	2,786	15	63	25	351
	98.6%	86.0%	.5%	1.9%	.8%	10.8%
Brothers	1,378	1,208	12	35	33	88
	97.9%	87.8%	.9%	2.5%	2.4%	6.4%
Priests	1,546	1,458	10	29	21	62
	96.9%	92.3%	.6%	1.9%	1.3%	3.9%
Tradition						
Apostolic	4,246	3,695	27	89	61	353
	97.8%	87.5%	.6%	2.1%	1.5%	8.4%
Mendicant	771	701	2	15	3	47
	98.6%	91.3%	.3%	2.0%	.4%	6.1%
Contemp.	224	181	3	7	7	30
	96.1%	79.4%	1.3%	3.1%	3.1%	13.2%
Monastic	974	875	5	16	8	71
	98.8%	89.7%	.5%	1.6%	.8%	7.2%
Cohort						
19-45	1,224	1,129	18	56	43	29
	95.3%	88.5%	1.4%	4.4%	3.4%	2.3%
46-60	1,932	1,796	11	40	19	81
	98.1%	92.2%	.6%	2.0%	1.0%	4.2%
61-73	1,793	1,565	5	20	11	169
	99.1%	88.4%	.3%	1.1%	.6%	9.5%
74-96	1,132	877	1	5	3	194
	99.3%	81.2%	.1%	.5%	.3%	18.0%
Total Sample	6,215	5,452	37	127	79	501
	98.0%	88.0%	.6%	2.0%	1.3%	8.1%

Are you a U.S. citizen?
Race/Ethnicity: Caucasian? Black/African-American? Mexican-American?
Other Hispanic? Asian-American? Native American? Asian or Pacific
Islander? Other?

Members of religious congregations are typically U.S. citizens and predominantly white. Brothers account for the greatest percentage of racial/ethnic minorities represented in the survey population: 0.9% African-American, 2.2% Mexican-American or other Hispanic, and 2.4% of Pacific Rim origin. Table 4.11 presents the details.

Some difficulty was encountered in efforts to identify what portion of the respondents were Native Americans. While 1990 U.S. Census categories were used in describing the racial and ethnic groupings in the survey question, evidence of confusion in the respondents' understanding of "Native American" surfaced during the data analysis. A disproportionately high number (6.5%) of respondents indicating "Native American" as their background prompted investigation, and it was determined that this response was used by some who understood it to mean "born in the United States." Hence, this category was combined with "Other."

Have you ever belonged to another congregation?
Have you ever held a position of leadership?
Are you currently in formation?

This portion of the demographics continues to respond to the question of who responded to the survey? through a consideration of the history of an individual in religious life and the status in the congregation. This information is presented in summary form on Table 4.12.

Membership in another community was listed as part of the experience of 3.5% of the sisters, 5.9% of the brothers and 3.8% of the priests. Among the four traditions, the percentages reported were similarly small except for the contemplatives, among whom 22.1% of those who responded reported having been a member of another community. There is also a correlation with age: 6.1% of the 19-45 group reported having been members of another religious congregation, as did 5.3% of the 46-60 group. The percentage drops to 2.6% and 2.0%, respectively, for the next two cohorts.

Among the respondents, 15.8% of the priests, 11.9% of the sisters and 6.0% of the brothers have held positions of leadership. The fact that, in order to conform to the goals articulated in the sampling plan, men's orders were sampled more densely makes the difference in percentage between men and women leaders understandable. The smaller percentage of brother-leaders reflects the church's insistence, through canon law, that in religious orders consisting of ordained and nonordained members, the major superior must be a priest.

Table 4.12
Distribution of Respondents by Position/Status in Religious Order:
Those Answering "Yes" to Questions Posed

Group	Have you ever been a member of another congregation?	Have you ever held a position of major superior in your congregation?	Are you in formation?
Vocation			
Sisters	115	390	109
	3.5%	11.9%	3.3%
Brothers	83	83	149
	5.9%	6.0%	10.7%
Priests	61	252	155
	3.8%	15.8%	9.8%
Tradition			
Apostolic	126	459	239
	2.9%	10.7%	5.6%
Mendicant	19	115	67
	2.4%	14.9%	8.7%
Contemplative	51	43	27
	22.1%	18.7%	11.7%
Monastic	63	108	80
	6.4%	11.1%	8.2%
Cohort			
19-45	79	56	311
	6.1%	4.4%	24.3%
46-60	104	255	44
	5.3%	13.0%	2.3%
61-73	47	248	32
	2.6%	13.9%	1.8%
74-96	23	151	22
	2.0%	13.6%	2.0%

Analysis by tradition points to the contemplative group as having the greatest percentage of members who report having held a position of leadership (18.7%) while the apostolic members have the lowest (10.7%). Given the fact that contemplative groups tend to be smaller in size and the apostolic groups much larger, this is understandable. Save for the 19-45 cohort (in which 4.4% reported having held positions of leadership), percentages of persons who have held leadership positions are fairly equal across the 46-60, 61-73 and 74-96 cohorts: 13.0%, 13.9% and 13.6%, respectively.

Corresponding with the age distribution among the vocational groups, a greater percentage of the brothers (10.7%) and priests (9.8%) reported being in formation than did the sisters (3.3%). By tradition, contemplatives had the highest percentage (11.7%), while the apostolic religious had the lowest (5.6%). An analysis of the cohorts' responses to the formation question yields the expected outcome: 24.3% of the 19-45 group were in formation, while even in the next cohort (46-60), the percentage dropped dramatically, to 2.3%.

What Are the Respondents Like Professionally?

To answer this question we reviewed variables such as level of education and current ministry. In an effort to tap future prospects for ministry, we also considered areas of study and future ministerial pursuits.

What is the highest level of education or degree you have completed?

The level of education for the respondents is reported in Table 4.13. It is no surprise to see that, as a whole, the group is highly educated. Master's degrees are the highest level of education for 56.8% of the sisters, 42.2% of the brothers and 54.2% of the priests. A tabulation of all the post-bachelor's degree education (combining "some graduate," master's degree and doctoral degree categories) includes 68.0% of the sisters, 59.4% of the brothers and 81.8% of the priests. A past history of neglect in brothers' education, which was often noted in the spontaneous comments appended to the questionnaire, is reflected in the 15.9% of the brothers who reported an educational level of high school or less. This stands in stark contrast to 1.0% for priests and 5.6% for sisters. Sisters accounted for the smallest percentage of doctoral degrees (4.0%), while 18.9% of the priests and 6.4% of the brothers were educated through the doctoral level.

As has been noted in other areas, contemplatives continue to be unique among members of religious orders. With respect to education, 34.3% reported having a high school education or less, compared with 4.5%, 7.5% and 9.5% for the apostolic, mendicant and monastic respondents, respectively. Among these three latter groups, percentages of members holding doctoral degrees is comparable, averaging around 9%. Members of apostolic orders have earned the greatest percentage of master's degrees (57.5%), followed by mendicants (48.9%), monastics (43.7%) and contemplatives (17.8%).

Table 4.13
Highest Educational Level Attained by Respondents (N = 5,995)

Group	Grade School Only	High School	Some College/ Associate Degree	Bachelor Degree	Some Grad. School	Master's Degree	Doctoral Degree	Other
Vocation								
Sisters	55	120	188	576	227	1,780	126	62
	1.8%	3.8%	6.0%	18.4%	7.2%	56.8%	4.0%	2.0%
Brothers	42	172	170	128	145	566	86	33
	3.1%	12.8%	12.7%	9.5%	10.8%	42.2%	6.4%	2.5%
Priests	5	11	31	145	132	824	287	84
	.3%	.7%	2.1%	9.5%	8.7%	54.2%	18.9%	5.5%
Tradition								
Apostolic	49	137	210	578	312	2,354	334	118
	1.2%	3.3%	5.1%	14.1%	7.6%	57.5%	8.2%	2.9%
Mend.	10	47	55	106	72	369	71	24
	1.3%	6.2%	7.3%	14.1%	9.5%	48.9%	9.4%	3.2%
Contemp.	18	55	43	26	11	38	12	10
	8.5%	25.8%	20.2%	12.2%	5.2%	17.8%	5.6%	4.7%
Monastic	25	64	81	139	109	409	82	27
	2.7%	6.8%	8.7%	14.9%	11.6%	43.7%	8.8%	2.9%
Cohort								
19-45	3	39	83	158	173	685	75	24
	.2%	3.1%	6.7%	12.7%	14.0%	55.2%	6.0%	1.9%
46-60	9	97	111	187	143	1,091	193	59
	.5%	5.1%	5.9%	9.9%	7.6%	57.7%	10.2%	3.1%
61-73	42	107	103	232	110	900	159	62
	2.4%	6.2%	6.0%	13.5%	6.4%	52.5%	9.3%	3.6%
74-96	46	49	79	252	68	431	62	31
	4.5%	4.8%	7.8%	24.8%	6.7%	42.3%	6.1%	3.0%

By age groups, the 74-96 cohort had the greatest percent with a high school education or less (9.3%). More than 55% of each of the three youngest cohorts reported having either completed a master's degree or pursued some graduate work. The oldest and youngest cohorts were comparable in the level of doctoral education, with 6.1% and 6.0%, respectively, reporting a Ph.D. as their highest level of education. This contrasts with the 46-60 cohort, in which 10.2% of the respondents reported education at the doctoral level and, similarly, with 9.3% in the 61-73 cohort. The lower proportion of doctoral degree holders among the younger members may lend support to some concerns about younger members of religious orders demonstrating less interest in formal education in favor of pursuing ministries that entail direct service to those who are in need. Alternately, it may simply reflect the fact that members of religious orders do not tend to earn doctorates before their mid-40s.

If you have received a higher degree, what is the field of study that represents your highest (or most recent) qualification?
If you are currently enrolled in a degree program, or you plan to begin full-time or part-time study at any college or university in the near future, indicate the field of study.

The listing of areas of study, as well as the numbers of respondents who have or who plan to pursue study in each of the categories, can be found in Tables 4.14 and 4.15. This review of the information began with the identification of all the fields of study that claimed at least 10% of a group. Among sisters, for example, more than half of those who listed higher degrees had earned them in one of two fields: education (39.5%) and theology (13.6%). Education and theology were similarly high categories for brothers' studies, accounting for 19.5% and 16.8%, respectively, of their degrees. Humanities, at 10.6%, was also frequently mentioned. Priests earned most of their degrees in theology (45.1%) and humanities (16.5%).

Two fields alone account for more than 50% of the apostolic respondents: education (30.1%) and theology (20.4%). Using the same 10% criterion, there are no other fields of study that account for a large portion of apostolic respondents. Among mendicants, a pattern similar to that in the apostolic group presents itself, with theology (33.4%) and education (18.9%) accounting for more than half of the respondents of that group (those two areas being the only ones in which members earned more than 10% of their degrees). Consistent with an apparent deemphasis on degree study, as indicated by the "highest level of education" responses, contemplatives most frequently checked "Does Not Apply" (23.0%). Theology accounts for 19.5% of their remaining responses in this area. Among monastic groups, 26.4% earned their degrees in theology, 19.3% in education and 12.8% in the humanities.

Table 4.14
Field of Study for Highest Degree (N = 4,912)

Field of Study	Vocation			Tradition				Cohort			
	Sister	Brother	Priest	Apos.	Mend.	Cont.	Mon.	19-45	46-60	61-73	74-96
Does Not Apply	139 / 5.4%	87 / 8.8%	38 / 2.8%	147 / 4.3%	43 / 7.4%	26 / 23.0%	48 / 6.3%	47 / 4.1%	74 / 4.5%	81 / 5.9%	55 / 8.1%
Medicine	20 / .8%	4 / .4%	2 / .1%	15 / .4%	3 / .5%	4 / 3.5%	4 / .5%	8 / .7%	7 / .4%	7 / .5%	4 / .6%
Law	7 / .3%	5 / .5%	15 / 1.1%	19 / .5%	2 / .3%	2 / 1.8%	4 / .5%	10 / .9%	8 / .5%	5 / .4%	3 / .4%
Bio. Science	42 / 1.6%	19 / 1.9%	29 / 2.2%	66 / 1.9%	9 / 1.5%	-	15 / 2.0%	14 / 1.2%	33 / 2.0%	25 / 1.8%	18 / 2.7%
Phys. Sci.	41 / 1.6%	27 / 2.7%	26 / 1.9%	72 / 2.1%	5 / .9%	4 / 3.5%	13 / 1.7%	12 / 1.1%	28 / 1.7%	34 / 2.5%	18 / 2.7%
Social Sci.	126 / 4.9%	79 / 8.0%	87 / 6.5%	201 / 5.8%	35 / 6.0%	6 / 5.3%	50 / 6.6%	80 / 7.0%	75 / 4.6%	93 / 6.8%	41 / 6.0%
Humanities	168 / 6.5%	105 / 10.6%	221 / 16.5%	331 / 9.6%	56 / 9.6%	10 / 8.8%	97 / 12.8%	112 / 9.8%	146 / 8.9%	139 / 10.1%	83 / 12.2%
Mathematics	66 / 2.6%	36 / 3.6%	27 / 2.0%	100 / 2.9%	5 / .9%	1 / .9%	23 / 3.0%	17 / 1.5%	38 / 2.3%	43 / 3.1%	30 / 4.4%
Engineering	3 / .1%	13 / 1.3%	7 / .5%	12 / .3%	5 / .9%	3 / 2.7%	3 / .4%	12 / 1.1%	2 / .1%	6 / .4%	3 / .4%
Education	1,017 / 39.5%	194 / 19.5%	94 / 7.0%	1,039 / 30.1%	110 / 18.9%	9 / 8.0%	147 / 19.3%	170 / 14.9%	423 / 25.8%	427 / 31.2%	258 / 38.0%

Table 4.14 (continued)

Field of Study	Vocation			Tradition				Cohort			
	Sister	Brother	Priest	Apos.	Mend.	Cont.	Mon.	19-45	46-60	61-73	74-96
Social Work	59	23	12	77	9	1	7	33	34	14	12
	2.3%	2.3%	.9%	2.2%	1.5%	.9%	.9%	2.9%	2.1%	1.0%	1.8%
Agriculture	1	3	1	2	-	-	3	1	2	2	-
	.0%	.3%	.1%	.1%			.4%	.1%	.1%	.1%	
Business	70	61	22	109	11	5	28	46	57	40	10
	2.7%	6.1%	1.6%	3.2%	1.9%	4.4%	3.7%	4.0%	3.5%	2.9%	1.5%
Theology	351	167	606	706	195	22	201	391	422	240	55
	13.6%	16.8%	45.1%	20.4%	33.4%	19.5%	26.4%	34.3%	25.8%	17.5%	8.1%
Art	30	21	8	38	5	3	13	16	19	15	8
	1.2%	2.1%	.6%	1.1%	.9%	2.7%	1.7%	1.4%	1.2%	1.1%	1.2%
Counseling	82	49	56	139	26	4	18	30	86	56	10
	3.2%	4.9%	4.2%	4.0%	4.5%	3.5%	2.4%	2.6%	5.3%	4.1%	1.5%
Pastoral Counseling	38	15	24	55	12	2	8	27	31	16	2
	1.5%	1.5%	1.8%	1.6%	2.1%	1.8%	1.1%	2.4%	1.9%	1.2%	.3%
Health Professions	176	21	9	156	16	4	30	45	65	59	34
	6.8%	2.1%	.7%	4.5%	2.7%	3.5%	3.9%	4.0%	4.0%	4.3%	5.0%
Other	140	64	59	172	36	7	48	68	88	68	35
	5.4%	6.4%	4.4%	5.0%	6.2%	6.2%	6.3%	6.0%	5.4%	5.0%	5.2%
Total	2,576	993	1,343	3,456	583	113	760	1,139	1,638	1,370	679

Table 4.15
Current Field of Study or Anticipated Degree (N = 1,716)

Field of Study	Vocation			Tradition				Cohort			
	Sister	Brother	Priest	Apos.	Mend.	Cont.	Mon.	19-45	46-60	61-73	74-96
Does Not Apply	459	175	180	559	96	33	126	126	262	257	149
	55.5%	38.4%	41.6%	47.6%	40.7%	68.8%	48.8%	18.9%	49.6%	78.8%	88.7%
Medicine	6	2	2	7	1	-	2	6	2	2	-
	.7%	.4%	.5%	.6%	.4%		.8%	.9%	.4%	.6%	
Law	-	1	3	3	-	-	1	4	-	-	-
		.2%	.7%	.3%			.4%	.6%			
Bio. Science	5	2	1	6	1	-	1	3	2	2	1
	.6%	.4%	.2%	.5%	.4%		.4%	.4%	.4%	.6%	.6%
Phys. Sci.	1	-	1	1	-	-	1	-	-	1	1
	.1%		.2%	.1%			.4%			.3%	.6%
Social Sci.	4	5	12	15	2	-	4	17	2	2	-
	.5%	1.1%	2.8%	1.3%	.8%		1.6%	2.5%	.4%	.6%	
Humanities	6	12	17	22	7	2	4	27	8	-	-
	.7%	2.6%	3.9%	1.9%	3.0%	4.2%	1.6%	4.0%	1.5%		
Mathematics	3	2	-	4	-	-	1	1	3	-	1
	.4%	.4%		.3%			.4%	.1%	.6%		.6%
Engineering	-	1	1	2	-	-	-	2	-	-	-
		.2%	.2%	.2%				.3%			
Education	46	33	8	69	9	-	9	55	27	5	-
	5.6%	7.2%	1.8%	5.9%	3.8%		3.5%	8.2%	5.1%	1.5%	

119

Table 4.15 (continued)

Field of Study	Vocation			Tradition				Cohort			
	Sister	Brother	Priest	Apos.	Mend.	Cont.	Mon.	19-45	46-60	61-73	74-96
Social Work	22 2.7%	10 2.2%	3 .7%	26 2.2%	6 2.5%	1 2.1%	2 .8%	18 2.7%	15 2.8%	1 .3%	-
Agriculture	1 .1%	-	-	-	1 .4%	-	-	-	1 .2%	-	-
Business	19 2.3%	11 2.4%	10 2.3%	25 2.1%	5 2.1%	-	10 3.9%	26 3.9%	14 2.7%	-	-
Theology	118 14.3%	125 27.4%	132 30.5%	233 19.8%	72 30.5%	10 20.8%	60 23.3%	249 37.3%	84 15.9%	32 9.8%	7 4.2%
Art	6 .7%	4 .9%	6 1.4%	10 .9%	1 .4%	-	5 1.9%	9 1.3%	4 .8%	2 .6%	1 .6%
Counseling	23 2.8%	23 5.0%	13 3.0%	49 4.2%	7 3.0%	-	3 1.2%	32 4.8%	20 3.8%	4 1.2%	3 1.8%
Pastoral Counseling	38 4.6%	15 3.3%	26 6.0%	56 4.8%	13 5.5%	-	10 3.9%	31 4.6%	38 7.2%	8 2.5%	-
Health Professions	25 3.0%	8 1.8%	2 .5%	28 2.4%	2 .8%	-	5 1.9%	18 2.7%	14 2.7%	3 .9%	-
Other	45 5.4%	27 5.9%	16 3.7%	59 5.0%	13 5.5%	2 4.2%	14 5.4%	44 6.6%	32 6.1%	7 2.1%	5 3.0%
Total	827	456	433	1,174	236	48	258	668	528	326	168

In the 19-45 cohort, 34.3% earned their highest degree in theology and 14.9% in education. Education and theology each claim 25.8% of the highest degree areas for the 46-60 group. Among the 61-73 cohort, 31.2% earned their highest degree in education, 17.5% in theology and 10.1% in the humanities. For the oldest cohort, education (20.2%) and humanities (17.3%) were the most frequently studied areas.

Respondents acknowledged little interest in considering future study. Of the total 6,359 respondents to the survey, only 14.2% currently pursue, or indicate the intention of pursuing, a formal course of study. Those who reported being currently engaged in or anticipating any study include 11.3% of the sisters, 20.3% of the brothers and 16.2% of the priests. Theology was the only area that included 10% or more of the group: 14.3% for sisters, 27.4% for brothers and 30.5% for priests. Admittedly, the mean age of 58 years for this group has implications for the energies available for the rigors of formal study. However, the lack of interest and/or energies for study and training has significant implications for the preparation of religious to work, in an effective and professional manner, to remedy the current pressing needs. Tools for involvement in systemic change, preparing for administrative positions in their own orders and in sponsored institutions, and acquiring the necessary retraining to meet changing needs in ministry do not appear to concern the members of this group.

The pattern holds true across the traditions: theology is the only field in which 10% or more respondents in any of these groups indicated current, or anticipated future, study. Looking at the question of future study by cohort presents a more optimistic picture. A full 42.0% of the 19-45 group reported involvement in, or plans to pursue, a formal program of study. Theology is the field that 37.3% of this cohort designated. While it may appear to be the most logical response, the identification of theology as the current or intended field of study by the largest group of members of religious orders may also reflect overtones of social desirability. Similarly, it might also be construed as an indication of assimilation into the ecclesiastical culture. Needs for training in administration, the social sciences, humanities and education are not likely to be met if choices are left to individual members. Skills for addressing pressing social needs will not be developed if persons pursue their current projections for education.

The primary ministry in which you are currently involved.
The ministry you intend to pursue in the future.

The religious orders were fairly dispersed in their areas of ministry. Education was currently the primary ministry for 23.6% of the sisters who responded to the survey. The next highest category is "other," which was selected by 13.4% of that group. The list of ministries may be found in Table

4.16. None of the remaining 24 areas accounts for more than 10% of the members. Among the brothers, 24.6% are involved in education and 14.1% indicated "other." Parish ministry is the primary activity for 27.9% of the priests, followed by "other" (12.4%), higher education (10.3%) and education (10.2%).

The ministries that accounted for the greatest proportions of apostolic religious are education (22.9%), "other" (12.5%) and parish ministry (11.1%). For mendicants, the areas are the same, with the order of magnitude differing slightly: parish ministry (24.0%), "other" (19.3%) and education (13.1%). The fact that a greater proportion of the mendicant group are priests may account for this distribution. Apostolate of prayer was listed by 47.5% of the contemplatives, as might be expected given their focus. "Other" was also named by 19.3% of the group. Education (18.2%), "other" (17.7%) and parish ministry (10.4%) occupied the monastics' time. Given their tradition, an involvement in parish ministry at the level of 10.0% may be an area of concern for monastic religious.

Education (21.8%), "other" (15.7%) and parish ministry (12.9%) are the areas in which most of the 19-45 year old respondents currently ministered. The same three areas occupied the energies of the next two cohorts as well, and in about the same percentages. Among the 73-96 cohort, 32.5% indicated "retired," but 12.0% were engaged in education and 11.8% in "other" work.

In listing "the ministry you intend to pursue in the future," 15.1% of the sisters listed "retired." Education was named by 12.1% and "pastoral visiting" by 10.6% (see Table 4.17). This last category is currently, for many members of religious orders, a preretirement move and may provide further verification of the sisters' sense of their dwindling energies. Brothers planned to continue in education (20.4%), though not in as strong numbers. Priests intended to continue in parish ministry with slightly less strength (26.3%). Given the historic tension between the institutional aspect of the church (typified by priesthood) and the prophetic element (seen in religious life), the fact that one-fourth of the religious priests are currently involved, and expect to continue, in parish ministries, a part of the institutional structure, is most interesting. Priests continue to be the only group in which ministry in higher education claims the interest of at least 10% of members.

Considering the respondents by tradition, apostolics are the only group to project a clear increase in the number of those involved in parish ministry (13.1%), with 12.0% projecting that they will be retired. Parish ministry (22.0%) and "retired" (10.5%) are the main categories listed for future ministry among mendicants. The percentage of contemplatives anticipating the apostolate of prayer increased to 56.5%. Interestingly, only 1.9% of this group indicated "retired." The response may reflect something of the mind-set here, for all other traditions scored over 10% in listing "retired" as an area of anticipated ministry. Among monastics, for example, 11.3% anticipated being "retired."

Table 4.16
Current Area of Ministry

Area of Ministry	Vocation			Tradition				Cohort			
	Sister	Brother	Priest	Apos.	Mend.	Cont.	Mon.	19-45	46-60	61-73	74-96
Parish Min.	236	60	424	449	177	2	92	161	258	224	62
	7.7%	4.7%	27.9%	11.1%	24.0%	1.1%	10.4%	12.9%	13.7%	13.5%	6.6%
Hosp. Admin	14	7	6	20	4	-	3	2	14	6	5
	.5%	.5%	.4%	.5%	.5%		.3%	.2%	.7%	.4%	.5%
Con./Prov. Leadership	53	8	27	52	9	4	23	12	52	22	-
	1.7%	.6%	1.8%	1.3%	1.2%	2.2%	2.6%	1.0%	2.8%	1.3%	
Cong./Prov. Admin.	47	35	44	88	16	2	20	28	55	35	6
	1.5%	2.7%	2.9%	2.2%	2.2%	1.1%	2.3%	2.2%	2.9%	2.1%	.6%
Social Serv.	54	38	4	78	9	-	9	18	31	32	12
	1.8%	3.0%	.3%	1.9%	1.2%		1.0%	1.4%	1.7%	1.9%	1.3%
Educ. Admin	182	90	55	254	19	3	51	99	140	74	10
	6.0%	7.1%	3.6%	6.3%	2.6%	1.7%	5.7%	8.0%	7.5%	4.5%	1.1%
Higher Ed.	114	84	157	244	45	2	64	83	135	108	23
	3.7%	6.6%	10.3%	6.1%	6.1%	1.1%	7.2%	6.7%	7.2%	6.5%	2.5%
Engineering	4	10	-	8	2	1	3	1	7	4	1
	.1%	.8%		.2%	.3%	.6%	.3%	.1%	.4%	.2%	.1%
Education	718	314	155	923	97	5	162	272	425	351	112
	23.6%	24.6%	10.2%	22.9%	13.1%	2.8%	18.2%	21.8%	22.6%	21.1%	12.0%
Health Care	273	38	39	252	45	5	48	63	130	106	45
	9.0%	3.0%	2.6%	6.2%	6.1%	2.8%	5.4%	5.1%	6.9%	6.4%	4.8%
Communications	29	13	15	39	6	1	11	6	15	26	10
	1.0%	1.0%	1.0%	1.0%	.8%	.6%	1.2%	.5%	.8%	1.6%	1.1%
Past. Visiting	128	21	46	139	37	-	19	20	33	58	77
	4.2%	1.6%	3.0%	3.4%	5.0%		2.1%	1.6%	1.8%	3.5%	8.2%
Agriculture	11	25	4	16	2	3	19	4	16	16	3
	.4%	2.0%	.3%	.4%	.3%	1.7%	2.1%	.3%	.9%	1.0%	.3%

Table 4.16 (continued)

Area of Ministry	Vocation			Tradition				Cohort			
	Sister	Brother	Priest	Apos.	Mend.	Cont.	Mon.	19-45	46-60	61-73	74-96
Eucharistic Ministry	27 .9%	4 .3%	8 .5%	29 .7%	4 .5%	3 1.7%	3 .3%	1 .1%	5 .3%	10 .6%	21 2.2%
Business & Finance	86 2.8%	54 4.2%	30 2.0%	112 2.8%	11 1.5%	5 2.8%	42 4.7%	29 2.3%	47 2.5%	53 3.2%	39 4.2%
Art	21 .7%	13 1.0%	1 .1%	25 .6%	2 .3%	-	8 .9%	7 .6%	12 .6%	8 .5%	7 .7%
Retreat Min.	50 1.6%	29 2.3%	65 4.3%	91 2.3%	19 2.6%	5 2.8%	29 3.3%	31 2.5%	54 2.9%	45 2.7%	13 1.4%
Prison Min.	12 .4%	8 .6%	9 .6%	18 .4%	6 .8%	-	5 .6%	8 .6%	8 .4%	5 .3%	7 .7%
Social Work	47 1.5%	21 1.6%	6 .4%	57 1.4%	9 1.2%	1 .6%	7 .8%	21 1.7%	24 1.3%	20 1.2%	5 .5%
Apostolate of Prayer	108 3.5%	48 3.8%	23 1.5%	55 1.4%	4 .5%	86 47.5%	34 3.8%	39 3.1%	38 2.0%	47 2.8%	52 5.6%
Counseling	43 1.4%	35 2.7%	20 1.3%	79 2.0%	7 .9%	2 1.1%	10 1.1%	22 1.8%	42 2.2%	27 1.6%	6 .6%
Pastoral Counseling	32 1.0%	6 .5%	19 1.3%	36 .9%	13 1.8%	-	8 .9%	7 .6%	24 1.3%	22 1.3%	2 .2%
Retired	287 9.4%	81 6.4%	62 4.1%	327 8.1%	50 6.8%	3 1.7%	50 5.6%	2 .2%	6 .3%	107 6.4%	304 32.5%
Format/Voc.	48 1.6%	49 3.8%	99 6.5%	118 2.9%	37 5.0%	12 6.6%	29 3.3%	100 8.0%	70 3.7%	21 1.3%	4 .4%
Peace & Justice	17 .6%	3 .2%	12 .8%	21 .5%	8 1.1%	1 .6%	2 .2%	14 1.1%	13 .7%	5 .3%	-
Other	407 13.4%	180 14.1%	188 12.4%	503 12.5%	100 13.6%	35 19.3%	137 15.4%	195 15.7%	223 11.9%	230 13.8%	110 11.8%
Total Responding	3,048	1,274	1,518	4,033	738	181	888	1,245	1,877	1,662	936

Table 4.17
Anticipated Area of Ministry

Area of Ministry	Vocation			Tradition				Cohort			
	Sister	Brother	Priest	Apos.	Mend.	Cont.	Mon.	19-45	46-60	61-73	74-96
Parish Min.	240 9.6%	76 6.9%	352 26.3%	449 13.1%	140 22.0%	2 1.3%	77 10.6%	173 14.8%	262 15.9%	180 13.0%	40 6.3%
Hosp. Admin	10 .4%	4 .4%	5 .4%	14 .4%	3 .5%	-	2 .3%	5 .4%	8 .5%	3 .2%	3 .5%
Con./Prov. Leadership	8 .3%	2 .2%	6 .4%	8 .2%	2 .3%	1 .6%	5 .7%	6 .5%	7 .4%	3 .2%	-
Cong./Prov. Admin.	11 .4%	11 1.0%	17 1.3%	26 .8%	6 .9%	-	7 1.0%	12 1.0%	17 1.0%	9 .6%	1 .2%
Social Serv.	39 1.6%	23 2.1%	10 .7%	61 1.8%	6 .9%	-	5 .7%	14 1.2%	31 1.9%	21 1.5%	5 .8%
Educ. Admin	73 2.9%	57 5.2%	36 2.7%	130 3.8%	12 1.9%	-	24 3.3%	73 6.2%	58 3.5%	28 2.0%	6 .9%
Higher Ed.	75 3.0%	80 7.3%	137 10.3%	195 5.7%	41 6.4%	2 1.3%	54 7.4%	118 10.1%	106 6.5%	58 4.2%	7 1.1%
Engineering	3 .1%	8 .7%	1 .1%	6 .2%	1 .2%	1 .6%	4 .6%	4 .3%	4 .2%	3 .2%	1 .2%
Education	303 12.1%	225 20.4%	119 8.9%	482 14.1%	60 9.4%	2 1.3%	103 14.2%	200 17.1%	243 14.8%	164 11.8%	34 5.3%
Health Care	169 6.8%	28 2.5%	26 1.9%	164 4.8%	28 4.4%	1 .6%	30 4.1%	50 4.3%	98 6.0%	58 4.2%	14 2.2%
Communications	19 .8%	15 1.4%	26 1.9%	46 1.3%	4 .6%	1 .6%	9 1.2%	17 1.5%	20 1.2%	19 1.4%	3 .5%
Past. Visiting	266 10.6%	42 3.8%	42 3.1%	269 7.9%	43 6.8%	3 1.9%	35 4.8%	27 2.3%	107 6.5%	140 10.1%	65 10.2%
Agriculture	13 .5%	14 1.3%	4 .3%	14 .4%	2 .3%	3 1.9%	12 1.7%	5 .4%	12 .7%	13 .9%	1 .2%

Table 4.17 (continued)

Area of Ministry	Vocation			Tradition				Cohort			
	Sister	Brother	Priest	Apos.	Mend.	Cont.	Mon.	19-45	46-60	61-73	74-96
Eucharistic Ministry	34 1.4%	13 1.2%	14 1.0%	40 1.2%	7 1.1%	3 1.9%	11 1.5%	8 .7%	9 .5%	27 1.9%	16 2.5%
Business & Finance	45 1.8%	33 3.0%	16 1.2%	60 1.8%	9 1.4%	1 .6%	24 3.3%	25 2.1%	36 2.2%	25 1.8%	8 1.3%
Art	37 1.5%	19 1.7%	8 .6%	39 1.1%	7 1.1%	1 .6%	17 2.3%	14 1.2%	26 1.6%	15 1.1%	6 .9%
Retreat Min.	78 3.1%	35 3.2%	86 6.4%	124 3.6%	31 4.9%	6 3.9%	38 5.2%	49 4.2%	93 5.7%	44 3.2%	11 1.7%
Prison Min.	10 .4%	9 .8%	6 .4%	18 .5%	4 .6%	-	3 .4%	8 .7%	9 .5%	4 .3%	3 .5%
Social Work	55 2.2%	32 2.9%	7 .5%	75 2.2%	10 1.6%	-	9 1.2%	34 2.9%	37 2.3%	19 1.4%	2 .3%
Apostolate of Prayer	210 8.4%	47 4.3%	33 2.5%	141 4.1%	16 2.5%	87 56.5%	46 6.3%	39 3.3%	53 3.2%	103 7.4%	90 14.2%
Counseling	68 2.7%	62 5.6%	44 3.3%	133 3.9%	18 2.8%	2 1.3%	21 2.9%	65 5.6%	70 4.3%	31 2.2%	4 .6%
Pastoral Counseling	67 2.7%	37 3.4%	33 2.5%	103 3.0%	16 2.5%	1 .6%	17 2.3%	41 3.5%	60 3.7%	27 1.9%	6 .9%
Retired	377 15.1%	89 8.1%	98 7.3%	412 12.0%	67 10.5%	3 1.9%	82 11.3%	2 .2%	57 3.5%	244 17.6%	239 37.6%
Format/Voc.	20 .8%	24 2.2%	40 3.0%	46 1.3%	14 2.2%	3 1.9%	21 2.9%	38 3.2%	34 2.1%	8 .6%	3 .5%
Peace & Justice	53 2.1%	16 1.5%	27 2.0%	72 2.1%	15 2.4%	2 1.3%	7 1.0%	37 3.2%	36 2.2%	13 .9%	7 1.1%
Other	219 8.8%	101 9.2%	143 10.7%	296 8.6%	75 11.8%	29 18.8%	63 8.7%	107 9.1%	150 9.1%	130 9.4%	61 9.6%
Total Responding	2,502	1,102	1,336	3,423	637	154	726	1,171	1,643	1,389	636

This is second only to education (14.2%). Approximately the same number of individuals as are currently involved (10.6%) anticipate parish ministry.

Looking to the future, responses from the 19-45 cohort indicated that education will continue to be a significant ministerial area. However, while 17.1% of the members of this cohort indicated their intention to pursue ministry in this area, this represents a decrease from the 21.8% of this group who reported education as their current ministry. Parish ministry is the anticipated ministry site for 14.8%. When the 46-60 group looked to the future, only parish ministry (15.9%) and education (14.8%) exceeded the 10% mark. Reflecting a sense of reality, 17.6% of the 61-73 cohort listed "retired" as their anticipated future ministry, and 13.0% and 11.8% listed parish ministry and education, respectively. Pastoral visiting was named by 10.1% of the 61-73 cohort. *Apostolate of prayer*, often the phrase used by members of religious orders to describe their ministry in retirement, was identified as the probable future ministry of 14.2% of the 74-96 cohort but was identified by only 7.4% of the 61-73 group. A full 37.0% of the 74-96 cohort listed "retired" as their anticipated future ministry, and 10.2% named pastoral visiting.

As has been hinted throughout this section, the information gleaned in response to the five questions presents cause for concern. Congregational leadership/administration, hospital administration and educational administration, respectively, were the primary ministries for 3.7%, 0.5% and 5.6% of the respondents. When they looked to the future, however, the interest of members of religious orders in pursuing ministry in these areas dropped, as reflected in percentages of 1.1%, 0.4% and 3.4%, respectively. This has serious implications, both for the future of sponsored institutions and for the leadership interests within the orders themselves. The minimal interest in educational pursuits, particularly as related in these areas, does not bode well for the future. Similarly, formation/vocation was listed as their primary ministry by 3.4% but was anticipated by 1.7%. This reflects little interest in the task of incorporating new members into the orders.

Another area in which shifts are indicated is in the traditional realm of education. The current 20.3% of members of religious orders involved in this ministry is projected by this group to drop to 13.1%. Health care will also see a decrease in personnel, from a current 6.0% to an expected 4.5%. Where are increases expected? Though the numbers are often in the 1-4% range, the percentage of members of religious orders involved in pastoral visiting, eucharistic ministry, art, counselling, pastoral counselling, and peace and justice is expected to double or more.

What Is the Role of Formal Prayer in the Lives of Members of Religious Orders?

Over a typical week, how often is Eucharistic liturgy a part of your routine?

Daily Eucharist is normative for 62.8% of sisters, 58.2% of brothers and 69.7% of priests (see Table 4.18). The fact that 95.3% of the members of cloistered orders attend daily Eucharist most likely reflects some consistency with their tradition, as does the 60.5% of members of apostolic groups and 62.5% of mendicants who attend. A full 70.0% of the members of monastic groups reported attending Eucharistic liturgy daily. Reviewing the data by cohorts reveals a clear split. Eucharistic liturgy is part of the daily routine for 44.6% and 50.4% of the two youngest cohorts, and for 75.2% and 87.7% of the two oldest cohorts. This may be more a function of opportunity or availability of time.

Over a typical week, how often is the Liturgy of the Hours a part of your routine?

Liturgy of the Hours is part of the daily lives of 67.2% of the sisters, 59.3% of the brothers and 61.6% of the priests who responded to this item. Given the obligation of daily recitation of the Office for priests, their statistic reflects a gap between the expectation and the practice. It is even more striking that of those who responded "almost never," the priests, at 12.1%, represent the greatest percentage. (For sisters and brothers, the percentages are 10.8% and 9.3%, respectively.) Members of apostolic and mendicant groups reported daily Liturgy of the Hours as part of their practice at levels of 57.3% and 61.9%, respectively. Contemplatives and monastics, for whom this form of prayer is basic, reported daily celebration of the Liturgy of the Hours for 93.9% and 88.5%, respectively. At least 50% of respondents in each cohort reported daily Liturgy of the Hours. "Almost never" is true for 13.5% of the 19-45 cohort, 15.5% of the 46-60 cohort, 8.4% of the 61-73 group and 6.1% of the 74-96 group.

Table 4.18
Frequency of Participation in Eucharist and Liturgy of the Hours [1]

Group	Eucharistic Liturgy						Liturgy of the Hours					
	1	2	3	4	5	6	1	2	3	4	5	6
Vocation												
Sisters	2,088	516	429	243	23	24	2,228	390	238	29	71	359
	62.8%	15.5%	12.9%	7.3%	.7%	.7%	67.2%	11.8%	7.2%	.9%	2.1%	10.8%
Brothers	813	266	206	92	15	4	823	268	104	31	33	129
	58.2%	19.1%	14.8%	6.6%	1.1%	.3%	59.3%	19.3%	7.5%	2.2%	2.4%	9.3%
Priests	1,108	266	168	41	7	-	975	219	128	24	46	191
	69.7%	16.7%	10.6%	2.6%	.4%		61.6%	13.8%	8.1%	1.5%	2.9%	12.1%
Tradition												
Apostolic	2,616	787	572	288	37	21	2,464	672	375	73	120	597
	60.5%	18.2%	13.2%	6.7%	.9%	.5%	57.3%	15.6%	8.7%	1.7%	2.8%	13.9%
Mend.	487	126	112	45	4	5	482	143	65	7	17	65
	62.5%	16.2%	14.4%	5.8%	.5%	.6%	61.9%	18.4%	8.3%	.9%	2.2%	8.3%
Contemp.	221	9	1	1	-	-	216	7	2	1	-	4
	95.3%	3.9%	.4%	.4%			93.9%	3.0%	.9%	.4%		1.7%
Monastic	685	126	118	42	4	2	864	55	28	3	13	13
	70.1%	12.9%	12.1%	4.3%	.4%	.2%	88.5%	5.6%	2.9%	.3%	1.3%	1.3%
Cohort												
19-45	570	294	265	121	19	9	659	247	133	25	40	172
	44.6%	23%	20.7%	9.5%	1.5%	.7%	51.6%	19.4%	10.4%	2%	3.1%	13.5%
46-60	985	409	351	177	20	13	1,016	327	194	42	67	303
	50.4%	20.9%	18%	9.1%	1%	.7%	52.1%	16.8%	10%	2.2%	3.4%	15.5%
61-73	1,350	239	138	60	4	4	1,272	217	98	11	39	151
	75.2%	13.3%	7.7%	3.3%	.2%	.2%	71.1%	12.1%	5.5%	.6%	2.2%	8.4%
74-96	995	87	34	15	1	2	974	72	33	2	4	41
	87.7%	7.7%	3%	1.3%	.1%	.2%	86.5%	6.4%	2.9%	.2%	.4%	3.6%

[1] *Frequency Codes:*   1 = Every day   2 = 5-6 times per week   3 = 2-4 times per week
4 = Once each week   5 = Less than once a week   6 = Almost never

How often do you pray or meditate privately?

Personal prayer is important in the lives of members of religious orders. In responding to the question regarding the frequency of private prayer, 81.5% of the sisters, 67.2% of the brothers and 69.7% of the priests responded, "daily" (see Table 4.19). An additional 14.2%, 22.3% and 22.5%, respectively, responded "several times a week." "Seldom or never" was the response for only 0.7% of the sisters, 3.0% of the brothers and 1.9% of the priests.

As would be expected by virtue of their life-style, 95.9% of the con-templatives reported daily prayer or meditation. For the remaining tradition groupings, responses for daily prayer ran between 72% and 78%. The "several times a week" response brought totals for all other groupings of tradition to at least the 90% level. Age does not discriminate significantly among those who pray. Combining "daily" and "several times a week" responses accounts for 90.3% of the 19-45 cohort, 90.9% of the 46-60 folks, 95.6% of the 61-73 group and 98% of the 74-96 cohort.

Table 4.19
Frequency of Private and Group Prayer[1]

Group	Pray or Meditate Privately						Pray with a Group					
	1	2	3	4	5	6	1	2	3	4	5	6
Vocation												
Sisters	23	28	65	460	2,643	22	151	341	191	778	1,681	84
	0.7%	.9%	2.0%	14.2%	81.5%	.7%	4.7%	10.6%	5.9%	24.1%	52.1%	2.6%
Brothers	40	29	62	298	898	9	97	103	63	298	753	19
	3.0%	2.2%	4.6%	22.3%	67.2%	.7%	7.3%	7.7%	4.7%	22.4%	56.5%	1.4%
Priests	28	39	45	338	1,047	5	140	202	146	354	625	28
	1.9%	2.6%	3.0%	22.5%	69.7%	.3%	9.4%	13.5%	9.8%	23.7%	41.8%	1.9%
Tradition												
Apostolic	60	56	135	794	3,093	25	290	515	319	1,135	1,798	98
	1.4%	1.3%	3.2%	19.1%	74.3%	.6%	7.0%	12.4%	7.7%	27.3%	43.3%	2.4%
Mend.	14	19	16	157	540	1	45	75	41	219	350	11
	1.9%	2.5%	2.1%	21.0%	72.3%	.1%	6.1%	10.1%	5.5%	29.6%	47.2%	1.5%
Contemp.	-	-	2	6	212	1	4	6	2	4	199	4
			.9%	2.7%	95.9%	.5%	1.8%	2.7%	.9%	1.8%	90.9%	1.8%
Monastic	17	21	19	139	743	9	49	50	38	72	712	18
	1.8%	2.2%	2.0%	14.7%	78.4%	.9%	5.2%	5.3%	4.0%	7.7%	75.8%	1.9%
Cohort												
19-45	27	25	60	349	776	8	77	107	95	332	608	21
	2.2%	2.0%	4.8%	28.0%	62.3%	.6%	6.2%	8.6%	7.7%	26.8%	49%	1.7%
46-60	38	50	70	425	1,300	15	149	247	144	521	802	33
	2.0%	2.6%	3.7%	22.4%	68.5%	.8%	7.9%	13.0%	7.6%	27.5%	42.3%	1.7%
61-73	21	16	29	230	1,407	8	104	194	106	375	885	42
	1.2%	.9%	1.7%	13.4%	82.2%	.5%	6.1%	11.4%	6.2%	22.0%	51.9%	2.5%
74-96	4	3	11	78	988	4	52	79	47	169	699	29
	.4%	.3%	1.0%	7.2%	90.8%	.4%	4.8%	7.3%	4.4%	15.7%	65.0%	2.7%

[1] *Frequency Codes*:   1 = Seldom or never   2 = On special occasions   3 = About once a week
                          4 = Several times each week   5 = Daily   6 = Other

Other than celebration of the Eucharist, how often do you pray with a group?

"Daily" was the response to this question for 56.5% of the brothers, 52.1% of the sisters and 41.8% of the priests. Each group averaged around 23% for the "several times a week" response. Again, praying with a group is more typically a daily experience for contemplatives (90.9%) and monastics (75.8%). This figure appears low for members of the monastic tradition, whose rule is based on *ora et labora* (prayer and work). When the "seldom or never" and "special occasions" categories are combined, the resulting percentages account for 10.5% of the monastic members. This raises questions (already posed) concerning the integrity and/or gap between the ideal and practice of monastic life.

The combination of the same two categories ("seldom" and "special occasion") includes 19.4% of the apostolics and 16.2% of the mendicants who responded to this question. Such a high percentage appears significant in light of the stated value of community, shared living and focus on the spiritual dimension of life. It is also, perhaps, reflective of the dispersion of members of religious orders, not only in their physical connectedness but also in their focus.

Older members of religious orders are more likely to report praying with a group. Frequencies of "several times a week" combined with "daily" were reported by 80.7% of the 74-96 cohort. Middle groups are more likely than either the oldest or youngest cohort to report "seldom/never" or "special occasion"; a combination of the two responses represents 20.9% of the 46-60 group and 17.5% of the 61-73 group. The fact that younger members are more likely to pray together than their immediately older peers may be explained by the fact that a greater proportion of this group was involved in the phase of religious formation, as well as by the stated desire and the broader experience of younger members to pray with others. Many of those in the 46-60 and 61-73 cohorts struggled to free their orders from often meaningless periods of "prayer in common."

I find attending Mass has become so difficult for various reasons that I no longer attend.
I find attending Mass is not difficult at all. It is usually a very important form of prayer and worship for me.
I find attending Mass difficult, but it remains a very important form of prayer and worship for me.
I find attending Mass is not difficult, but it is not a very important form of prayer and worship for me.

The sense of the significance of the Eucharist and the emotional difficulty experienced by persons who attend is an area of considerable controversy among members of religious orders. This item sought to account for some of the reasons for attending or not attending the Eucharistic liturgy, as well as to learn some of the attitudes regarding Eucharist (see Table 4.20). Among the sisters, 70.2% reported that Mass is not difficult and continues to be an important form of prayer. Another 24.3% of the sisters responded that although it is difficult to attend, it continues to be important. Fewer brothers (65.6%) than sisters reported that Mass is both important and not difficult to attend. The brothers for whom Mass was difficult but important represent 23.8% of the respondents, while 9.0% of the brothers said that while Mass is not difficult for them, neither is it important. Smaller totals of 5.5% of the priests and 3.9% of the sisters gave the same response. It is interesting to note that women comprise the smallest percentage of those who say that Mass is not significant to them.

Table 4.20
Difficulty and Importance of Attending Eucharist (N = 6,259)

Group	I find attending Mass has become so difficult for various reasons that I no longer attend.	I find attending Mass is not difficult at all. It is usually a very important form of prayer and worship for me.	I find attending Mass difficult, but it remains a very important form of prayer and worship for me.	I find attending Mass is not difficult, but it is not a very important form of prayer and worship for me.
Vocation				
Sisters	55	2,315	801	129
	1.7%	70.2%	24.3%	3.9%
Brothers	18	914	332	130
	1.3%	65.6%	23.8%	9.3%
Priests	10	1,250	219	86
	.6%	79.9%	14.0%	5.5%
Tradition				
Apostolic	61	3,034	964	222
	1.4%	70.9%	22.5%	5.2%
Mendicant	12	571	152	38
	1.6%	73.9%	19.7%	4.9%
Contemp.	-	201	16	15
		86.6%	6.9%	6.5%
Monastic	10	673	220	70
	1.0%	69.2%	22.6%	7.2%
Cohort				
19-45	36	706	416	114
	2.8%	55.5%	32.7%	9.0%
46-60	36	1,253	538	107
	1.9%	64.8%	27.8%	5.5%
61-73	10	1,414	275	88
	.6%	79.1%	15.4%	4.9%
74-96	-	992	102	26
		88.6%	9.1%	2.3%

Considering the traditions, contemplatives reported the least difficulty with attending Mass, with 86.6% of that group rating it as both important and not difficult. Monastics, at 69.2%, accounted for the lowest percentage among tradition groupings in their rating of Mass as both important and not difficult. Apostolics and monastics are close in the proportion of respondents who rated mass as difficult but still important (22.5% and 22.6%, respectively). This response was also chosen by 19.7% of the mendicants and 6.9% of the contemplatives.

The selection of the "Mass is important and not difficult" response ranged from 55.5% for the 19-45 group to 88.6% for the 74-96 cohort. The "Mass is difficult but still important" percentages ranged in the opposite direction, from 32.7% for the 19-45 cohort and 27.8% for the 46-60 group to 9.1% for the oldest group. In the 19-45 cohort, 9.0% reported that "Mass is not difficult, but not important."

What about the Living Situations for Members of Religious Orders?

At present I live . . .
In the future, I expect to live . . .

When describing their current living situation, 80.0% of those responding indicated that they lived with one or more same sex members of their congregation, 9.0% lived alone and 5.8% lived in intercommunity settings. This accounts for 94.9% of those who answered this question (see Table 4.21).

Considered by vocation, 9.1% of the sisters, 5.7% of the brothers and 12.0% of the priests lived alone, while 78.0% of the sisters, 85.0% of brothers and 47.1% of priests lived with one or more members of their congregation. More sisters (7.1%) than either brothers (4.9%) or priests (4.1%) lived in intercommunity situations. Fewer than 2% of any of the vocation groups lived in mixed communities. Apostolic and mendicant respondents most frequently reported living alone (9.3% and 12.8%, respectively).

The middle two age cohorts presented similar pictures regarding living situations. Nearly 76% of the 46-60 cohort lived with one or more members of their congregations, 12.2% lived alone and 6.5% lived in intercommunity settings. Slightly more than 10% of the 61-73 cohort also lived alone; 79.3% lived with one or more members of their congregation. Reports of intercommunity living are fairly even across age groups (around 5.3%). This may reflect an increased sharing of resources such as retirement facilities for older members of religious orders.

Table 4.21
Current Living Situation

Group	Alone	In a community with more than one other person of my congregation	With one other member of my congregation	With member(s) of other congregation (same sex)	In a mixed community of men and women religious	In a community that includes men and women, married and celibate	With an elderly or ill parent/ relative	Other
Vocation								
Sisters	281	2,109	312	219	11	6	31	118
	9.1%	68.3%	10.1%	7.1%	.4%	.2%	1.0%	3.8%
Brothers	75	1,056	58	64	11	10	4	32
	5.7%	80.6%	4.4%	4.9%	.8%	.8%	.3%	2.4%
Priests	182	1,097	101	62	20	9	3	47
	12.0%	72.1%	6.6%	4.1%	1.3%	.6%	.2%	3.1%
Tradition								
Apostolic	378	2,887	345	240	23	17	33	132
	9.3%	71.2%	8.5%	5.9%	.6%	.4%	.8%	3.3%
Mend.	94	499	66	41	8	6	4	17
	12.8%	67.9%	9.0%	5.6%	1.1%	.8%	.5%	2.3%
Contemp.	9	181	1	7	-	-	-	16
	4.2%	84.6%	.5%	3.3%				7.5%
Monastic	57	695	59	57	11	2	1	32
	6.2%	76.0%	6.5%	6.2%	1.2%	.2%	.1%	3.5%
Cohort								
19-45	79	962	79	73	10	8	2	39
	6.3%	76.8%	6.3%	5.8%	.8%	.6%	.2%	3.1%
46-60	228	1,232	183	122	17	8	15	63
	12.2%	66.0%	9.8%	6.5%	.9%	.4%	.8%	3.4%
61-73	173	1,195	141	89	13	5	17	52
	10.3%	70.9%	8.4%	5.3%	.8%	.3%	1.0%	3.1%
74-96	46	784	48	52	2	3	4	38
	4.7%	80.2%	4.9%	5.3%	.2%	.3%	.4%	3.9%

In describing where they expect to live in the future, 74.7% of those surveyed said they expected to live with one or more members of their community (see Table 4.22). Living alone was projected by 5.6%, and another 5.8% projected living in an intercommunity setting. Their alternatives covered 86.1% of those responding, a contrast to the 94.9% for whom these categories accounted in response to the question, "At present I live . . ." Fewer than 1% projected living with ill or elderly parents or relatives, but 2.1% (up from 0.7%) expected to live with male and female members of religious orders, and 3.7% expected that they would be a part of communities consisting of women and men, vowed members of religious orders and married and single people (this was in contrast to the 0.4% who reported this as their current living situation). Though numerically small, this change would represent an increase in the range of 900%.

A projection of future living experiences shows that the percentage of those living alone will drop from 9.1% currently to 5.6% in the future (the decrease is true across all vocation groups). The reason for this shift is not clear. It may reflect an intentional move toward the communal aspects of religious life, a reading of demographic and financial realities or other factors.

Table 4.22
Anticipated Future Living Situation

Group	Alone	In a community with more than one other person of my congregation	With one other member of my congregation	With member(s) of other congregations (same sex)	In a mixed community of men and women religious	In a community that includes men and women, married and celibate	With an elderly or ill parent/ relative	Other
Vocation								
Sisters	146	1,912	159	227	56	118	24	268
	5.0%	65.7%	5.5%	7.8%	1.9%	4.1%	.8%	9.2%
Brothers	57	943	41	50	35	45	7	72
	4.6%	75.4%	3.3%	4.0%	2.8%	3.6%	.6%	5.8%
Priests	110	1,073	63	48	27	46	8	76
	7.6%	73.9%	4.3%	3.3%	1.9%	3.2%	.6%	5.2%
Tradition								
Apostolic	227	2,616	201	251	78	160	33	277
	5.9%	68.1%	5.2%	6.5%	2.0%	4.2%	.9%	7.2%
Mend.	44	478	40	34	24	31	3	45
	6.3%	68.4%	5.7%	4.9%	3.4%	4.4%	.4%	6.4%
Contemp.	6	154	1	5	-	-	1	31
	3.0%	77.8%	.5%	2.5%			.5%	15.7%
Monastic	36	680	21	35	16	18	2	63
	4.1%	78.1%	2.4%	4.0%	1.8%	2.1%	.2%	7.2%
Cohort								
19-45	70	834	57	76	40	71	4	74
	5.7%	68.0%	4.6%	6.2%	3.3%	5.8%	.3%	6.0%
46-60	142	1,114	104	129	45	98	20	124
	8.0%	62.7%	5.9%	7.3%	2.5%	5.5%	1.1%	7.0%
61-73	73	1,200	73	74	26	25	7	123
	4.6%	75.0%	4.6%	4.6%	1.6%	1.6%	.4%	7.7%
74-96	20	703	19	35	4	10	7	85
	2.3%	79.6%	2.2%	4.0%	.5%	1.1%	.8%	9.6%

Fewer people in the middle two cohorts expected to live alone (8.0% and 4.6%). However, 8.0% of the 46-60 group expected to live in some form of mixed-gender community (compared to the current experience of 1.3% for that cohort). Of those currently between 46 and 60, 68.6% expected to live exclusively with other members of their orders. Projections for the youngest cohort are similar: 72.6% expected to live exclusively with members of their order, 5.7% expected to live alone, 6.2% anticipated intercommunity settings and 9.1% expected to live in a mixed community (either exclusively celibate or with celibate and married members).

I am satisfied with my present living situation.

Responses to this item reflected high levels of satisfaction: 84.3% of the sisters, 81.4% of the brothers and 83.9% of the priests agreed or agreed strongly with this statement (see Table 4.23). Analysis by traditions also indicates general satisfaction among the apostolic, mendicant, contemplative and monastic groups. Only among the mendicant group did the proportion of those who disagree with the statement reach 10.0%. The analysis by cohort reveals where the dissatisfaction with living situations could be found. Among the 19-45 cohort, 15.7% disagreed with the statement. In the 46-60 group, 12.0% also disagreed; they were not satisfied with their present living situation. On previous sorts, levels of disagreement at or beyond 10.0% were found only among brothers (11.1%), priests (10.3%) and mendicants (10.0%).

My congregation allows me sufficient freedom in determining my living situation

Agreement with this item was expressed by 84.6% of the sisters, 72.8% of the brothers and 73.0% of the priests. However, the percentage of brothers and priests who disagreed with this statement (14.2% and 12.0%, respectively) is striking in contrast to that of sisters (7.5%).

In general, members of the apostolic and mendicant groups reported greater satisfaction with the amount of freedom they experienced in determining their living situations. The proportion of those who disagreed with the statement is approximately 9%, while 19.2% of the contemplatives and 14.2% of the monastics disagreed. These two groups agreed at only 62.0% and 70.0%, respectively. This compares with 81.1% agreement for apostolics and 83.6% for mendicants.

The 19-45 group expressed strongest disagreement (18.1%). Of this group, 19.1% were also uncertain. For all the worry about how older individuals feel about living arrangements, 90.6% of the 74-96 cohort indicated a sense that their congregation allows them sufficient freedom in determining one's living situation. By contrast, only 62.8% of the 19-45 cohort agreed. Agreement for the 46-60 group was 76.7% and for the 71-73 group, 86.5%.

Table 4.23
Responses to Items re Significance of Living

		Vocation			Tradition				Cohort			
		Sister	Brother	Priest	Apos.	Mend.	Cont.	Mon.	19-45	46-60	61-73	74-96
I am satisfied with my present living situation.	Agree	2,760 84.3%	1,125 81.4%	1,113 83.9%	3,532 82.8%	647 84.3%	193 85%	826 85.9%	964 75.6%	1,555 79.9%	1,545 87.5%	1,008 92.6%
	Uncertain	239 7.3%	103 7.5%	91 5.8%	319 7.5%	44 5.7%	14 6.2%	56 5.8%	111 8.7%	155 8.0%	109 6.2%	49 4.5%
	Disagree	274 8.4%	154 11.1%	161 10.3%	413 9.7%	77 10.0%	20 8.8%	79 8.3%	200 15.7%	236 12.1%	112 6.3%	32 2.9%
My congregation allows me sufficient freedom in determining my living situation.	Agree	2,723 84.6%	984 72.8%	1,128 73.0%	3,416 81.1%	633 83.6%	132 62%	654 70.0%	795 62.8%	1,483 76.7%	1,506 86.5%	940 90.6%
	Uncertain	254 7.9%	175 13.0%	222 14.4%	400 9.5%	63 8.3%	40 18.8%	148 15.8%	242 19.1%	207 10.7%	132 7.6%	60 5.8%
	Disagree	242 7.5%	192 14.2%	195 12.6%	394 9.4%	61 8.1%	41 19.2%	133 14.2%	229 18.1%	243 12.6%	103 5.9%	37 3.6%
My present living situation detracts from my prayer life.	Agree	223 7.0%	144 10.7%	150 9.8%	341 8.2%	68 9.1%	12 5.6%	96 10.3%	178 14.1%	171 8.9%	110 6.4%	50 5.0%
	Uncertain	254 8.0%	129 9.6%	151 9.9%	385 9.3%	68 9.1%	11 5.1%	70 7.5%	150 11.8%	197 10.2%	135 7.9%	43 4.3%
	Disagree	2,703 85%	1,074 79.7%	1,224 80.3%	3,430 82.6%	615 81.9%	193 89.3%	763 82.2%	940 74.1%	1,563 80.9%	1,472 85.7%	907 90.7%
My present living situation enhances my sense of belonging to my congregation.	Agree	2,461 76.5%	1,029 75.9%	1,056 68.4%	3,093 73.7%	545 72.3%	190 85.6%	718 76.1%	885 70.1%	1,345 69.7%	1,311 75.3%	905 86.1%
	Uncertain	459 14.3%	178 13.1%	249 16.1%	634 15.1%	134 17.8%	13 5.8%	105 11.1%	191 15.1%	341 17.7%	255 14.7%	76 7.2%
	Disagree	298 9.2%	149 11.0%	240 15.5%	472 11.2%	75 9.9%	19 8.6%	121 12.8%	186 14.8%	243 12.6%	174 10.0%	71 6.7%
Ministry is the primary factor in determining my living situation.	Agree	1,828 57.9%	759 56.7%	1,025 66.6	2,706 65.1%	451 60.1%	72 35.1%	383 41.4%	701 55.2%	1,209 62.7%	1,089 63.0%	530 54.1%
	Uncertain	440 13.9%	231 17.2%	186 12.1%	539 13.0%	101 13.4%	42 20.5%	175 18.9%	172 13.6%	225 11.7%	239 13.8%	206 21.1%
	Disagree	891 28.2%	350 26.1%	327 21.3%	911 21.9%	199 26.5%	91 44.4%	367 39.7%	395 31.1%	493 25.6%	401 23.2%	242 24.8%

My present living situation detracts from my prayer life.

Disagreement with this statement, reflecting a sense of congruence with one's living situation and prayer life, was indicated by 80 to 85% of sisters, brothers and priests. Disagreement was above 81% for each of the four tradition groupings. Those who agreed most with this statement are the monastics (10.3%). Consistent with what appears to be a pattern relative to satisfaction with living situation, 14.0% of the youngest cohort agreed with this statement, with an additional 11.8% claiming to be "uncertain" (unable/unwilling to disagree). Members of the 46-60 cohort were not overwhelmingly delighted (80.9% disagree) but were not as strong in their agreement (8.9%) as the youngest group.

My present living situation enhances my sense of belonging to my congregation.

The statement that their present living situation enhances the sense of belonging to one's congregation is true for 75.0% of the sisters and brothers who responded to this item and for 68.0% of the priests. The level of disagreement was 15.6% for priests and around 10% for sisters and brothers. Contemplatives agreed most (85.6%) with this statement. Members of other traditions agreed at levels of 72 to 76%. Only the oldest group agreed beyond the 80% level (86.1%) on this item. Nearly 15% of the youngest cohort disagreed, as did 12.6% of the 46-60 group and 10.0% of the 61-73 cohort. "Uncertain" was selected more frequently on this item than for any other of the statements regarding living situation. Perhaps a sense of "belonging to the congregation" is not typically considered in relation to one's living situation.

Ministry is the primary factor in determining my living situation.

This item drew the greatest diversity in response. It was accurate for 57.8% of the sisters, 56.7% of the brothers and 66.6% of the priests. On the other hand, 28.2% of the sisters, 26.1% of the brothers and 21.3% of the priests disagreed. Contemplatives reflected much diversity in their responses: approximately 20% of the group is represented in each of the five points on the scale. Perhaps the "ministry" construct was not significant in their thinking. Among the monastics, 39.7% disagreed and 41.4% agreed with the statement. Members of apostolic and mendicant groups are stronger in their agreement: 65.1% and 60.1%, respectively. About 13% of each of these groups also reported themselves to be "uncertain." The members of the 19-45 cohort also reflected much diversity: 31.1% disagreed, 55.2% agreed and 13.6% were uncertain. In the two middle cohorts, which probably represent the greatest segment of members of religious orders in active ministry, 62.7% and 63.0% agreed.

PERSONALITY CHARACTERISTICS

Because the intent of the National Survey was to obtain baseline information concerning the beliefs and practices of members of religious orders in the United States rather than a psychological profile of the population, the temptation to include a wide range of personality measures was avoided. However, recognizing the potential of personality factors to influence the outcome of the responses, the Positive and Negative Affect Schedule (PANAS) was included as a means of obtaining information concerning the general affect state of the respondents. This instrument, which was developed by Watson and Clark, has proven reliability and validity (Watson, Clark & Tellegen, 1988).

The PANAS consists of a listing of 20 adjectives (ten reflecting positive affect, ten reflecting negative affect). Positive affect (PA), according to Watson, Clark and Tellegen (1988), reflects the extent to which a person feels positive emotion, such as pleasure and enthusiasm. A person high in positive affect is in a state of high energy, concentration, and pleasurable activity, while a person low in positive affect is characterized as lethargic and sad. Negative affect (NA), in contrast, reflects the extent to which a person feels negative and aversive emotions (anger, contempt and guilt are examples). Low negative affect reflects a state of calmness and serenity. Following the directive to "indicate to what extent you generally feel this way, that is, how you feel on the average," the respondents to the National Survey rated a number of adjectives on a five-point scale ranging from "very slightly or not at all" (1) to "extremely" (5). The adjectives that comprise the scales and group means for each of the adjectives appear in Table 4.24.

Analysis by vocation indicates that the mean scores of PA items were consistently higher for sisters than for priests. This also tended to be true for NA items. Brothers, however, had consistently higher scores on negative affect and lower scores on positive affect. Nygren and Piedmont (1988) found in their study of brothers that some of these men felt that their contributions were overshadowed by their ordained confreres and that the value of their contribution was frequently minimized. This finding, coupled with a history that is marked by a perception of lower status ascribed to men choosing to be brothers rather than priests, particularly in orders that include both vocations, is consistent with the National Survey data relative to brothers' affect. Brothers often inappropriately compare themselves to priests, who are perceived to have more recognition (Nygren & Piedmont, 1988). This comparison, then, could result in higher negative affect and lower positive affect. The same theory can also be used to explain why sisters, who do not have a similar social comparison group, score highest on the positive affect scale.

Analysis by tradition did not present as clear a picture. On NA, members of contemplative groups tended to have the lowest mean scores, while monastics tended to score highest. Among respondents from apostolic and mendicant

orders, means for NA adjectives typically fell between those of the contemplatives and monastics. No clear pattern emerged in the PA means for
groups by tradition.

Table 4.24
Positive and Negative Affect Scales (PANAS): Mean Ratings for Groups

	Vocation			Tradition				Cohort			
	Sister	Brother	Priest	Apos.	Mend.	Cont.	Mon.	19-45	46-60	61-73	74-96
POSITIVE AFFECT											
Active	4.02	3.96	3.99	4.04	4.00	3.69	3.88	4.12	4.12	3.94	3.69
Alert	3.9	3.74	3.78	3.86	3.83	3.75	3.73	3.84	3.89	3.83	3.70
Attentive	3.93	3.75	3.84	3.89	3.85	3.87	3.76	3.86	3.88	3.86	3.83
Determined	3.91	3.83	3.85	3.88	3.86	3.98	3.85	3.93	3.93	3.86	3.72
Enthusiastic	3.66	3.56	3.63	3.65	3.68	3.63	3.54	3.67	3.66	3.65	3.54
Excited	3.02	2.94	3.00	3.02	3.06	2.60	2.95	3.20	3.08	2.91	2.70
Inspired	3.47	3.28	3.40	3.40	3.50	3.49	3.37	3.42	3.43	3.40	3.38
Interested	4.11	3.95	4.07	4.07	4.05	4.11	4.00	4.01	4.05	4.08	4.08
Proud	3.19	3.16	3.03	3.19	3.16	2.71	3.02	3.33	3.25	3.06	2.87
Strong	3.42	3.32	3.42	3.41	3.39	3.30	3.39	3.45	3.48	3.37	3.23
NEGATIVE AFFECT											
Afraid	1.65	1.66	1.54	1.62	1.63	1.52	1.64	1.75	1.67	1.52	1.57
Ashamed	1.36	1.50	1.43	1.40	1.42	1.51	1.45	1.46	1.42	1.37	1.41
Distressed	1.93	1.95	1.90	1.91	1.97	1.77	2.00	2.14	2.07	1.77	1.63
Guilty	1.56	1.72	1.66	1.61	1.65	1.58	1.67	1.78	1.66	1.54	1.48
Hostile	1.38	1.54	1.51	1.43	1.46	1.38	1.51	1.50	1.56	1.37	1.30
Irritable	1.93	1.97	1.90	1.92	1.92	1.91	1.99	2.02	1.98	1.86	1.85
Jittery	1.54	1.59	1.49	1.54	1.53	1.35	1.59	1.59	1.52	1.50	1.59
Nervous	1.95	2.01	1.84	1.95	1.94	1.80	1.92	2.01	1.95	1.86	1.97
Scared	1.64	1.62	1.52	1.61	1.60	1.47	1.61	1.76	1.65	1.50	1.48
Upset	1.87	1.89	1.82	1.86	1.87	1.65	1.92	2.03	1.98	1.76	1.63

The results showed that age had a significant effect on PA and NA scores.
As age increased, the mean scores for PA items diminished in general. The
exception to this pattern was seen in the positive affect adjective "interested,"
where the mean increased with age. NA scores for the oldest cohorts also
tended to be the lowest. There is some precedent for this pattern in Diener et
al. (1985), who noted that the individuals who experience PA intensely are also
those who experience NA intensely. The reverse, as demonstrated in the older
cohorts, is also true. The reason for the pattern, however, remains unclear.
Some explanations may be found in a developmental pattern consistent with

aging in general, or in generational differences in awareness and ease in naming and expressing emotions.

A review of the means for each of the adjectives does not present a picture of members of religious orders as particularly passionate people. Among the items on the PA scale, only "interested" and "active" approached a rating of 4.0 ("quite a bit") for any of the analysis groups. "Excited" and "proud" were reported as least frequently experienced of the PA items, with a mean around 3.0 ("moderately"). Among members of religious orders, where humility is important, an adjective such as "proud" may have a negative valence. However, if members of religious orders are to be credible in their vocation, some elements of healthy pride and excitement must be kindled.

While no item on the NA scale received a mean rating beyond 2.2 (2 = "a little"), "irritable," "distressed" and "nervous" had the highest means. At the other end of the scale, "ashamed," "hostile" and "jittery" received the lowest ratings. Evidence of those feelings of sadness, anger, loss, ambivalence and confusion that typically accompany various phases of transformation (as mentioned in Chapter 1) is lacking. Considering the decline and diminishment experienced over the past three decades, as well as the current state of religious life and projections for the future, the low means on all the NA items do raise some concern regarding the apparent denial on an emotional level of the current state of affairs as well as for future prospects for orders.

PRINCIPAL COMPONENTS FACTOR ANALYSIS: OVERVIEW

Items contained within the Religious Life Futures Project National Survey were used to conduct principal components factor analyses with varimax rotation. Factor analysis is a data reduction technique, which is used to reduce a large number of items to a smaller, more manageable group of factors. These factors represent groupings of items that share something in common. The commonality between the items is determined through an examination of the items in the group using a varimax rotation. Varimax rotation is an orthogonal rotation performed on the data to simplify the columns of a factor matrix. In this survey, 27 factors emerged from more than 300 survey items. In addition to the 27 factors, items from four areas of interest were examined: commitment to the poor, diversity, support of sponsored institutions and influence (see Appendix F for the complete listing of factors and items). It should be noted that some items with dual variability (that is, that were "loaded" on more than one factor) were either discarded or grouped with an appropriate factor. The factors were determined and then grouped into three categories (and still further, into components of the categories). For the present discussion, the three categories are: (1) social institution factors, (2) congregation factors and (3) individual factors. Table 4.25 outlines the major factors according to their level of analysis. Where single items are significant, mean scores are generally reported. Respondents rated all items using a 5-point Likert-type scale (for example, 1 = strongly disagree; 5 = strongly agree). Factors of major importance to the future of religious life are elaborated.

Table 4.25
Categorization of Factors

Social Institution	Congregation	Individual

STRUCTURES
  Role Clarity
  Permanent Commitment
  External Authority
  Systemic Change
  Hierarchical Alliance
	LEADERSHIP
	  Spiritual Intensity
	  Charisma/Individual
	    Consideration
	  Intellectual Stimulation/
	    Inspirational
	  Laissez-Faire
	  Active Management by
	    Exception
	  Contingent Reward
		SPIRITUALITY
		  Oneness with God
		  Intensified Spirituality
		  Structured Prayer
		
		BELONGING
		  Congregational
		    Commitment
		  Affiliation

INNOVATIONS
  Expanding Lay Roles
  Greater Inclusion
  (Diversity)		

RESTRAINTS
  Cultural Threats
	DYNAMICS
	  Community Living
	  Involvement
	  Ongoing Development
	  (Influence)
		ACTION
		  Faithfulness to Vows
		  Works of Mercy

CREDIBILITY
  Anomie
  (Commitment to the
    Poor)
	GUIDANCE
	  Procedural Clarity
	  Effects of Renewal
	  (Support of Sponsored
	    Institutions)	

Note: Parentheses indicate items that did not emerge as factors but are of interest.

PRINCIPAL COMPONENTS FACTOR ANALYSIS:
SOCIAL INSTITUTION

This section of the analysis examines the means of vocations, traditions and cohorts on scales that are most appropriately examined within the social institution domain. The scales at this level were grouped into four major categories: (1) Structures, (2) Innovations, (3) Restraints and (4) Credibility. The scales comprising structures included role clarity, hierarchical alliance, permanent commitment, external authority and systemic change. The innovations scales included expanding lay roles, greater inclusion and dimensions of diversity. The scale comprising the restraints category included cultural threats. Credibility was comprised of anomie and the commitment to the poor. Means, standard deviations, valid sample sizes, F values and effect sizes for social institution domain factors by vocation, tradition and age cohorts are presented in Table 4.26-4.28. Because of the significance of the role clarity findings, an extended discussion of this issue follows in Chapter 5.

Three statistical comparisons were made for each factor: vocation, tradition and age cohort. All means in the present report are *weighted* means. Since the sample size in this study was very large, the majority of analyses were statistically significant at levels of $p < .05$ or greater. However, the practical significance of the analyses may not be as great as the statistical significance might indicate. Therefore, readers are advised to examine the effect sizes of statistical tests (e.g., eta^2) and use caution when making judgments regarding the power of the effect size.

Structures

Role clarity. Religious role clarity was defined as the individual's perceived level of understanding regarding his or her purpose and function within the current structure of the church. The role clarity scale was constructed from two survey items: "The role of the religious in the church is sufficiently clear to me," and "I know what it means to be a religious in the church today." The alpha reliability coefficient for this scale is .79.

Respondents were divided into three groups, indicating high, moderate and low role clarity, based on their scores for this measure. Subjects responded to a 5-point scale, ranging from 1 (strongly disagree) to 5 (strongly agree), with 3 designated as "neither agree nor disagree." A score of 4.0 was set as the threshold level for inclusion in the high clarity group. Subjects scoring below 4.0 but at or above 3.0 were assigned to the moderate clarity group, while subjects scoring below 3.0 were assigned to the low clarity group. Based on this criterion, 59% of the population was high in role clarity, 13% was in the moderate group, and 28% was low.

Table 4.26
Social Institution Factors by Vocation

		Sister	Brother	Priest	F Value	p	eta²
STRUCTURES							
Role Clarity	Mean	3.57	3.73	3.79	37.60	<.001	.01
	SD	.91	.86	.88			
	N	3,271	1,394	1,582			
Permanent	Mean	3.16	3.28	3.50	94.81	<.001	.03
Commitment	SD	.80	.85	.83			
	N	3,270	1,391	1,581			
Hierarchical	Mean	3.03	3.27	3.37	157.34	<.001	.05
Alliance	SD	.71	.59	.58			
	N	3,019	1,330	1,514			
External Authority	Mean	2.31	2.54	2.43	37.26	<.001	.01
	SD	.89	.88	.83			
	N	3,141	1,348	1,516			
Systemic Change	Mean	3.34	3.10	3.37	27.46	<.001	.01
	SD	1.10	1.16	1.07			
	N	3,122	1,336	1,515			
INNOVATIONS							
Expanding Lay	Mean	1.98	1.95	1.78	32.31	<.001	.01
Roles	SD	.78	.75	.67			
	N	2,665	1,198	1,392			
Greater Inclusion	Mean	2.47	2.30	2.27	23.60	<.001	.01
	SD	1.08	1.03	1.04			
	N	3,030	1,309	1,483			
RESTRAINTS							
Cultural Threats	Mean	3.11	3.02	3.00	11.93	<.001	.00
	SD	.83	.82	.77			
	N	3,082	1,337	1,518			
CREDIBILITY							
Anomie	Mean	3.61	3.58	3.61	.72	n.s.	
	SD	.78	.74	.71			
	N	2,980	1,308	1,488			

Table 4.27
Social Institution Factors by Tradition

		Apostolic	Mendicant	Contemp.	Monastic	F Value	p	eta^2
STRUCTURES								
Role Clarity	Mean	3.61	3.59	4.05	3.69	18.92	<.001	.01
	SD	.91	.90	.86	.87			
	N	4,519	770	229	965			
Permanent	Mean	3.19	3.26	3.82	3.40	54.03	<.001	.02
Commitment	SD	.82	.80	.81	.78			
	N	4,510	775	224	975			
Hierarchical	Mean	3.10	3.07	3.65	3.15	44.17	<.001	.02
Alliance	SD	.71	.65	.58	.60			
	N	4,208	716	205	907			
External Authority	Mean	2.32	2.39	2.97	2.50	44.71	<.001	.02
	SD	.88	.87	.99	.83			
	N	4,346	739	204	929			
Systemic Change	Mean	3.34	3.41	2.20	3.28	74.90	<.001	.04
	SD	1.09	1.06	1.28	1.13			
	N	4,319	735	212	926			
INNOVATIONS								
Expanding Lay	Mean	1.94	1.91	1.87	2.01	2.98	<.05	.002
Roles	SD	.76	.76	.74	.78			
	N	3,754	637	160	817			
Greater Inclusion	Mean	2.43	2.47	1.83	2.43	21.14	<.001	.01
	SD	1.06	1.11	.99	1.05			
	N	4,195	721	202	907			
RESTRAINTS								
Cultural Threats	Mean	3.08	3.11	3.11	3.13	1.29	n.s.	
	SD	.82	.81	.79	.81			
	N	4,275	732	204	924			
CREDIBILITY								
Anomie	Mean	3.60	3.60	3.86	3.64	8.50	<.001	.004
	SD	.77	.75	.74	.72			
	N	4,149	703	203	901			

Table 4.28
Social Institution Factors by Cohort

		19 - 45	46 - 60	61 - 73	74 - 96	F Value	p	eta^2
STRUCTURES								
Role Clarity	Mean	3.36	3.47	3.71	3.90	75.41	<.001	.04
	SD	.95	.93	.87	.79			
	N	1,279	1,942	1,767	1,102			
Permanent	Mean	3.27	3.16	3.22	3.30	8.32	<.001	.00
Commitment	SD	.85	.81	.83	.78			
	N	1,274	1,950	1,770	1,100			
Hierarchical	Mean	2.88	2.84	3.23	3.51	298.52	<.001	.14
Alliance	SD	.70	.67	.63	.56			
	N	1,277	1,865	1,648	963			
External Authority	Mean	2.05	2.04	2.46	2.85	285.55	<.001	.13
	SD	.75	.73	.85	.93			
	N	1,254	1,885	1,716	1,014			
Systemic Change	Mean	3.45	3.38	3.33	3.13	18.67	<.001	.01
	SD	1.05	1.05	1.11	1.18			
	N	1,251	1,892	1,688	1,007			
INNOVATIONS								
Expanding Lay	Mean	1.62	1.80	2.04	2.34	187.32	<.001	.10
Roles	SD	.63	.70	.74	.81			
	N	1,204	1,737	1,438	748			
Greater Inclusion	Mean	2.78	2.72	2.26	1.94	183.34	<.001	.09
	SD	1.05	1.05	1.01	.94			
	N	1,224	1,859	1,665	943			
RESTRAINTS								
Cultural Threats	Mean	3.05	3.05	3.11	3.11	3.10	<.03	.002
	SD	.80	.82	.84	.81			
	N	1,255	1,884	1,683	974			
CREDIBILITY								
Anomie	Mean	3.49	3.56	3.65	3.74	23.01	<.001	.01
	SD	.69	.71	.79	.81			
	N	1,232	1,852	1,632	916			

Although a significant difference in religious role clarity was found between vocation groups on the this scale (p < .001; eta^2 = .01), all groups agreed moderately that they experienced role clarity. Similarly a significant difference was found between traditions on the role clarity scale (p < .001; eta^2 = .01) even though members of the apostolic, mendicant and monastic orders had moderate agreement that they experienced role clarity. Members of the contemplative tradition, however, agreed that they experienced role clarity. A significant difference was found between cohorts on the role clarity scale (p < .001; eta^2 = .04). Members of the 19-45 and 46-60 cohorts experienced relatively low degrees of role clarity. Members of the 61-73 cohort had higher levels, and the 74-96 cohort experienced the highest levels of role clarity.

In summary, there are significant groups that appear unclear about their role as members of religious orders in the church. Those groups include both the youngest cohort and, generally, women, who report less clarity than their male counterparts. This difference for women is notable particularly because it is one of the few factors in the study on which women and men religious consistently showed a difference.

Research on role clarity in general has demonstrated that ambivalence regarding one's role can lead to anxiety, reduced ability to meet role requirements, decreased ministerial satisfaction, lower trust and self-confidence, an increased sense of futility and a greater propensity to leave a religious order. The lack of role clarity that a high percentage of members of religious orders experienced may contribute to a further diminishment in number of members in religious orders. The lower clarity among some groups may also be a function of the fact that they described themselves apart from any particular church identity which, if their perceptions are true, suggests a greater problem of alienation from the church to which they are still committed. There may also be some connection between statistics showing that equal numbers of women and men are entering religious life (in contrast to the approximately three-to-one ratio of prior years) and the greater numbers of women who experienced low role clarity. Taken together, this data signals the essential need for role clarity if religious orders in the United States are to be revitalized. Without this clarification, over time the relationship between the church and religious orders could be jeopardized.

Reactions to the stress of role transitions, such as those experienced since Vatican II on the part of members of religious orders who have become more involved in active ministries, include a tendency to fall back on old roles, compartmentalism of conflicting life spheres and passive or active withdrawal. According to Allen and van de Vliert (1984), the response that is chosen depends on the perceived legitimacy of the new role, anticipated sanctions, personal capacity to implement the role and the existence of the situational facilities necessary for role fulfillment.

Myerson and Martin (1987) have maintained that, in the management of change, it is crucial to create a sense of psychological safety in order to allow role ambiguity to be confronted and worked through. Ambiguity can be channeled or it can be acknowledged as a paradox and legitimized. The least effective strategy in the face of ambiguity is denial of the lack of clarity.

As subsequent factors in this analysis suggest, the process of clarifying the role of members of religious orders must mean more than an ecclesiastical pronouncement. There is a strong relationship between lack of role clarity and other factors, such as alienation from the hierarchy and anomie. Since many of the members of religious orders who experience role ambiguity are willing to work through this period of transition, findings suggest that involving them intensely in the clarification process may, paradoxically, lead to a resolution of both role ambiguity and conflict among themselves and with others in the church.

Permanent commitment. The scale of permanent commitment is defined as the expectation that lifelong commitment is normative for religious life. All groups (considered by vocation, tradition and age group) registered barely moderate agreement, indicating doubt about the nature of permanent commitment. Based on a scale on which 1 represents "strongly disagree" and 5 represents "strongly agree," the group means ranged between 3.1 and 3.5 in indicating their agreement that permanent commitment is the norm.

A significant difference was found between vocations on the permanent commitment scale ($p < .001$; $eta^2 = .03$). Sisters and brothers expressed the greatest doubt that permanent commitment would be the norm for religious life. Priests moderately agreed that permanent commitment would be the norm for religious life. A significant difference was found between traditions on the permanent commitment scale ($p < .001$; $eta^2 = .02$). Members of the apostolic, mendicant and monastic traditions moderately agreed that permanent commitment would be the norm for the future of religious life. Members of the contemplative tradition, however, strongly agreed that permanent commitment would be the norm for the future of religious life. While there was a significant difference between cohorts on the permanent commitment scale ($p < .001$; $eta^2 = .00$), members of all cohorts agreed at, at least, a moderate level that permanent commitment is the norm for the future of religious life.

Most religious orders traditionally have had as a criterion for membership the willingness and ability to make and sustain a permanent commitment. This generally involved a commitment to the vows of poverty, chastity and obedience. Several dynamics since Vatican II help to explain the population's ambivalence about permanency. First, many alternative forms of membership have developed that allow temporary commitment or affiliative membership. In these instances, the vows are not necessarily essential. Second, the years since the Vatican Council have brought redefinitions of the vows for some individuals. In various facets of the research, some members of religious orders have suggested that the formality and rigor of the classic vows be replaced, for instance, by vows of solidarity, cosmic reverence and creativity. In this instance, permanence is not necessarily a meaningful criterion. Others have argued adamantly that without the expectation of permanence, religious life will continue to decline because there are myriad alternative ways of expressing voluntary Christian action without becoming a member of an order. Still others believe that the notion of temporary commitment undermines the possibility of bonding among members who live intentionally in relationship from year to year with no intention beyond a limited horizon. In defense of temporary commitment, others have argued that in American society, individuals cannot expect the permanence that was once associated with marriage or religious life. Some would argue theologically that the notion of temporary vows is incompatible with religious life. This particular view is challenged, however, by the Daughters of Charity who annually renew their commitment while intending to remain members for life.

It would seem important, in light of the divergence of opinion regarding permanency, that members of religious orders themselves must address the question and determine the conditions or contexts in which permanency is desirable and those where temporary commitment is to be promoted. The data suggest that both life-styles are, in fact, supported. The issue is to be clear on how permanency or temporary commitment categories and requirements interrelate. Keeping requirements of either state vague will undermine the commitment of existing members and make recruitment extremely difficult. Boundary clarity enhances the sense of belonging, clarifies relationships and allows some degree of predictability for members.

Hierarchical alliance. Hierarchical alliance is defined as the relationship between church hierarchical authority and its influence on members of the congregations. The cluster of items related to the positive relationship between hierarchy and religious orders as well as the influence of church hierarchy and magisterial authority were typically not rated highly by members of religious orders.

For hierarchical alliance, statistically significant differences were found among the three vocation groups. Sisters expressed the least amount of hierarchical alliance, while religious priests reported stronger hierarchical alliance ($p < .001$; $eta^2 = .04$). All four tradition groups reported moderate levels of agreement to items identifying this scale. Mendicants expressed the least hierarchical alliance, while contemplatives reported the most ($p < .001$; $eta^2 = .02$).

All age cohorts reported moderate levels of agreement with the items assessing hierarchical alliance. The younger age groups expressed the least hierarchical alliance, while those 74-96 years of age reported the most hierarchical alliance ($p < .001$; $eta^2 = .14$). Clearly, it is among the younger members of religious orders and the members of apostolic congregations that a sense of hierarchical alliance is the lowest. Unlike the older members and the contemplatives, they do not experience a strong sense of collaboration with the hierarchy. The implications of these findings are clear enough. Religious orders which traditionally have cooperated with the hierarchy to effect the church's mission will not continue to do so without respect for the hierarchy.

External authority. External authority is defined as the tendency to seek influences or commands regarding thought, opinion or behavior from sources outside oneself (for example, church or group authority). All respondents tended to disagree with a belief that reliance on external authority would favorably influence the future of religious life. There was a general rejection of the tendency to seek influence regarding thought, opinion or behavior from outside sources such as the church or group authority, which was indicated by the fact that, on the 5-point scale described above, means for all groups were between 2.5 and 3.1.

A significant difference was found on the external authority scale between members of each vocation (p < .001; eta^2 = .01). Sisters, brothers and priests, however, all moderately disagreed that external authority would favorably influence the future of religious life. A significant difference was found among members of the traditions on the external authority scale (p < .001; eta^2 = .02). Members of the contemplative tradition moderately agreed that external authority would be favorable for the future of religious life. Members of the apostolic, mendicant and monastic traditions, however, moderately disagreed that external authority would have a favorable influence on the future of religious life.

There was a significant difference among cohorts on the external authority scale (p < .001; eta^2 = .13). Members of the 19-45 and 46-60 cohorts had moderate disagreement that external authority would have a favorable influence on the future of religious life. Members of the 61-73 cohort, however, moderately agreed that external authority would have a favorable influence on the future of religious life. The 74-96 cohort, though, believed that an external authority would have an even more favorable influence on the future of religious life.

The issue of external involvement in the affairs of religious orders, particularly in defining their rights and authority, has been a serious concern among members of religious orders since Vatican II. Some members of religious orders blame external authority, such as the hierarchy, for undermining their place in the church following the council. They would argue, for instance, that the failure of the hierarchy to endorse health, education and social service delivery through conventional means left many members of religious orders scrambling for corporate identity. Similarly, many members of religious orders resented the control exercised by the hierarchy in the establishment of new constitutions. Given the decline of their membership during this time, religious orders are not willing to have the hierarchy determine their future any longer. Hence, with either Synodal dialogue (Vatican Synod Secretariat, 1992) or in discussion with the American bishops on the role of religious orders in the church, members of religious orders want to remain in control of their choices and self-definition. This is not to say, however, that they are unwilling to support the fundamental mission of the church. It does mean though, that the hierarchy's involvement in their governance or in the affairs of their institutions will be unwelcome.

Systemic change. The scale of systemic change is defined as efforts to influence the social and political structures that tend to discriminate against disadvantaged persons. The scale attempted to estimate the extent to which participation in efforts at systemic change is integrated with individual spirituality and fulfillment. It was originally hypothesized that those individuals most involved in aspects of systemic change on behalf of the poor would find greater fulfillment in religious life. Sisters, brothers and religious priests experienced little connection between their work for systemic change, defined as "efforts to influence the social and political structures which tend to discriminate against disadvantaged persons," and their personal and spiritual fulfillment. All means were greater than 3.0 and less than 3.4. This did not change when considered by age groups or tradition.

A significant difference was found between vocations on the systemic change scale ($p < .001$; $eta^2 = .01$). However, members of all vocations believed that systemic change has limited impact on their personal and spiritual fulfillment. A significant difference was also found between traditions on the systemic change scale ($p < .001$; $eta^2 = .04$). Members of all four traditions, however, indicated that systemic change had doubtful value as a contributor to their personal and spiritual fulfillment. Another significant difference was found between cohorts on the systemic change scale ($p < .001$; $eta^2 = .01$). The youngest cohort believed that involvement in systemic change was significantly more important to their personal and spiritual fulfillment than among the older cohorts. These results suggest that undertaking work for systemic change may not be necessarily as strongly related to either spiritual motives or personal fulfillment as might have been anticipated. It could be that members of religious orders see systemic change as anchored more in political power motives, but based on these measures there is no evidence of a strong relationship between personal or spiritual fulfillment and involvement in systemic change. These conclusions suggest a counterintuitive direction to what is espoused as a constitutive factor directing religious orders. It may, however, explain in part the distribution of those members of religious orders who intend to work among the poor and those who do not.

Innovations

The National Survey included items measuring participants' responses to trends in religious life that produce greater diversity in the composition of Christian community living. These include the expanding role of laity and lay associations among religious orders, the conscious inclusion of persons who have declared their homosexual orientation, and the general membership's perception of the comfort level of minority-group members in its congregation.

Expanding lay roles. The expanding lay roles scale is defined as the degree to which increasing the scope of the functions assumed by lay persons in the church is believed to threaten religious life even though a significant difference was found between members of the three vocations on the expanding lay roles scale ($p < .001$; $eta^2 = .01$), priests, sisters and brothers all disagreed that involvement of the laity and alternative expressions of ecclesiology pose threats to the future of religious life.   A significant difference was found between members of the four traditions on the expanding lay roles scale ($p < .05$; $eta^2 = .002$).   Members of the monastic tradition believed that new understandings of the church would pose moderately little threat to the future of religious life, while members of the apostolic, contemplative and mendicant traditions believed that expanding lay roles would pose little threat to the future of religious life.   A significant difference was also found among cohorts on the expanding lay roles scale ($p < .001$; $eta^2 = .10$).   The 19-45 and 46-60 cohorts believed that expanding lay roles would pose little threat to the future of religious life. The 61-73 and 74-96 cohorts, though, believed that expanding lay roles would pose moderately little threat to the future of religious life.

This factor is particularly interesting when considered in the context of role clarity among members of religious orders.   It might be assumed that the increasing role of the laity since Vatican II has somehow precipitated the decline in role clarity among religious orders. However, the data does not bear this out. To the contrary, members of religious orders view the increasing emphasis on lay ministry as a critical enhancement to ministry in the church. The strength of the monastic concern may reflect the boundary-spanning function that most monasteries play between popular culture and solitude. Potential confusion does arise, however, when issues of lay involvement with the congregation are raised.

Many orders have expanded the definition of lay associates and now grant them the full rights and privileges of vowed members. In a very few congregations, the number of lay associates actually exceeds the number of vowed members. In these circumstances, the concerns of asset control are particularly relevant. However, the broader questions that emerge with the construct of lay associations relate to the meaning of membership and the boundaries that are necessary to maintain some sense of cohesion among the members. Consequently, while members of religious orders do not regard the involvement of the laity in the church as a threat, they may be less clear about the psychological impact of lay associates and degrees of membership on the existing members.

Greater inclusion. Greater inclusion is defined as the expectation of positive effect of structural changes to include the influence of feminist thought and the presence of persons of both gender, including married persons, in the community and among the ordained clergy. Tables 4.29, 4.30 and 4.31 elaborate additional items by vocation, tradition and cohort, respectively. There was also a significant difference among members of the vocations on the greater inclusion scale (p < .001; eta² = .01). Sisters, brothers and priests, however, all believed that greater inclusion will moderately positively influence the future of religious life in only limited ways. Sisters believed that greater inclusion will more positively influence religious life than do brothers and priests.

A significant difference was found among traditions on the greater inclusion scale (p < .001; eta² = .01). Members of the contemplative tradition believed that greater inclusion would not favorably influence the future of religious life. Members of the apostolic, mendicant and monastic traditions, however, believed that a greater inclusion of feminist thought and married people are likely to influence the future of religious life in only limited ways.

A significant difference was found among cohorts on the greater inclusion scale (p < .001; eta² = .09). Members of the 19-45 and 46-60 cohorts believed that greater inclusion would be a more positive influence on the future of religious life. Members of the 61-73 cohort, however, believed that greater inclusion would have moderately little influence on the future of religious life. Finally, members of the 74-96 cohort believed that greater inclusion would have little favorable influence on the future of religious life.

This measure reflects the belief among membership that the future of religious life will not be shaped to any significant degree by the inclusion of married persons or by the establishment of mixed-sex communities. This measure is but one of several in which the gap between the leadership's view of the future of religious life, as espoused in the "Transformative Elements of Religious Life," as well as the visionary members' views, do not correspond with the perspective of the membership.

Admitting homosexual persons. Survey participants were asked to respond to the statement, "Declaring a homosexual orientation would not exclude an individual from being admitted to my congregation." Sixty-four percent of all respondents indicated either agreement with the statement or uncertainty, and the remaining 36% disagreed. (See Tables 4.29, 4.30 and 4.31 for means for all subgroups.)

Table 4.29
Selected Items of Interest by Vocation

		Sister	Brother	Priest	F Value	p	eta²
I am committed to working with the poor	Mean	3.43	3.22	3.36	17.31	<.001	.01
	SD	1.13	1.15	1.12			
	N	3,292	1,394	1,584			
Declaring a homosexual orientation would not exclude one from admission to my congregation	% Agree	16.4%	34.6%	43.3%			
	% Uncertain	48.9%	24.9%	21.7%			
	% Disagree	34.8%	40.5%	35.1%			
Members of minority groups may feel uneasy in my congregation	% Agree	32.0%	39.1%	39.9%			
	% Uncertain	23.3%	21.3%	20.0%			
	% Disagree	44.7%	39.6%	40.1%			
Inclusion of lay associates may undermine the meaning of membership in my congregation	Mean	2.12	2.44	2.43	68.46	<.001	.02
	SD	1.05	1.07	1.12			
	N	3,288	1,387	1,581			
I am willing to work in an institution sponsored by my congregation	% Yes	92.1%	93.7%	93.8%			
	N Yes	2,953	1,286	1,470			
I am willing to live in an institution sponsored by my congregation	% Yes	84.5%	91.5%	91.6%			
	N Yes	2,717	1,254	1,436			
My opinions are considered in decisions made about my congregation	Mean	3.65	3.41	3.42	48.09	<.001	.02
	SD	.93	1.01	1.01			
	N	3,113	1,398	1,584			

Table 4.30
Selected Items of Interest by Tradition

		Apostolic	Mendicant	Contemplative	Monastic	F Value	p	eta²
I am committed to working with the poor	Mean	3.44	3.35	2.85	3.13	36.18	<.001	.02
	SD	1.13	1.14	1.03	1.11			
	N	4,551	769	212	980			
Declaring a homosexual orientation would not exclude one from admission to my congregation	% Agree	25.6%	38.4%	23.3%	28.4%			
	% Uncertain	38.7%	31.7%	23.3%	33.1%			
	% Disagree	35.8%	30.0%	53.4%	38.5%			
Members of minority groups may feel uneasy in my congregation	% Agree	36.3%	36.4%	27.6%	33.6%			
	% Uncertain	22.3%	22.9%	20.0%	20.9%			
	% Disagree	41.4%	40.8%	52.4%	45.5%			
Inclusion of lay associates may undermine the meaning of membership in my congregation	Mean	2.17	2.22	2.60	2.44	27.10	<.001	.01
	SD	1.07	1.06	1.18	1.03			
	N	4,536	773	218	977			
I am willing to work in an institution sponsored by my congregation	% Yes	92.9%	91.5%	90.6%	94.0%			
	N Yes	3,946	701	163	899			
I am willing to live in an institution sponsored by my congregation	% Yes	87.2%	87.4%	89.4%	90.8			
	N Yes	3,705	768	168	863			
My opinions are considered in decisions about my congregation	Mean	3.58	3.64	3.78	3.70	7.56	<.001	.0004
	SD	.95	.96	.94	.97			
	N	4,561	782	230	976			

Table 4.31
Selected Items of Interest by Cohort

		19-45	46-60	61-73	74-96	F Value	p	eta²
I am committed to working with the poor	Mean	3.61	3.48	3.32	3.27	24.41	<.001	.01
	SD	1.10	1.15	1.13	1.11			
	N	1,279	1,953	1,783	1,109			
Declaring a homosexual orientation would not exclude one from admission to my congregation	% Agree	44.9%	33.7%	18.6%	10.7%			
	% Uncertain	24.0%	35.1%	41.1%	45.9%			
	% Disagree	31.2%	31.2%	40.3%	43.4%			
Members of minority groups may feel uneasy in my congregation	% Agree	51.8%	43.8%	25.6%	53.3%			
	% Uncertain	17.6%	20.2%	23.9%	26.9%			
	% Disagree	30.6%	36.0%	50.4%	19.8%			
Inclusion of lay associates may undermine the meaning of membership in my congregation	Mean	1.99	2.00	2.26	2.52	77.57	<.001	.04
	SD	.97	1.00	1.07	1.11			
	N	1,276	1,952	1,777	1,108			
I am willing to work in an institution sponsored by my congregation	% Yes	92.3%	90.8%	93.9%	93.8%			
	N Yes	1,267	1,743	1,643	1,008			
Am willing to live in an institution sponsored by congregation	% Yes	85.2%	83.3%	90.7%	93.8%			
	N Yes	1,080	1,599	1,581	1,018			
My opinions are considered in decisions about my congregation	Mean	3.57	3.59	3.62	3.59	1.01	n.s.	-
	SD	.97	1.00	.92	.92			
	N	1,281	1,955	1,787	1,124			

When considered by vocation, only 16% of sisters agreed with the statement and nearly 50% expressed uncertainty. This was significantly different from the responses of religious priests and brothers. Agreement of religious priests registered at 43%, with 22% uncertain. Thirty-five percent of the brothers agreed, with 25% uncertain. Among the four traditions, 53% of contemplatives indicated disagreement, implying the least expectation that persons declaring a homosexual orientation would be admitted to their congregations. "Agree," "uncertain" and "disagree" percentages were more evenly split among the other traditions. Among monastics, the greatest percentage (39%) agreed. Thirty-eight percent of the members of apostolic groups (again the greatest percentage) indicated uncertainty regarding the admission of candidates with a known homosexual preference.

When considered by age groups, 45% of the members under 46 expressed their belief that a person with a homosexual orientation would be admitted to their congregation. Forty-three percent of the oldest age group felt that homosexual persons would not be admitted and 46% of the same age group expressed their uncertainty.

Many orders operate with policies that delineate criteria for admission into the vowed life. The purpose of this measure was to assess the perception of members regarding the admission of homosexuals, regardless of their knowledge of official policy. Clearly, men acknowledged to a much higher degree the probable reality that a fair percentage of their members are indeed homosexual and they, therefore, indicated on the survey the acceptance of that fact. Curiously, the majority of women religious did not perceive the admission of homosexual members into their order as likely. Explaining the discrepancy between men's and women's responses is beyond the scope of this study. However, the psychological implications of both inclusion and exclusion should be examined.

Members of minority groups. When asked to respond to the statement, "Members of minority groups may feel uneasy in my congregation," the sentiment among members of religious orders in general was fairly evenly split: 36% agreed, 22% were uncertain and 42% disagreed. This response pattern reflected the response pattern of sisters, brothers and religious priests, and the same was true for apostolic, mendicant and monastic members of religious orders. Fifty-two percent of contemplatives disagreed with the statement, while 27% agreed.

Analysis by cohort reveals the greatest differences. Fifty-two percent of the youngest and 44% of the next age group (46-60) indicated their belief that members of minority groups would feel uneasy. In contrast, half of the 61-73 age group and 53% of the oldest group did not believe that minority-group members would feel uneasy in their orders. At present, less than 10% of the members of religious orders in the United States are members of ethnic minorities. In the near future, 50% of the U.S. Catholic population will be

Hispanic. Clearly, the reality of multiculturalism must be addressed by religious orders.

Restraints

Cultural threats. The cultural threats scale is defined as aspects of contemporary American culture such as capitalism, technology and affluence. There was a significant difference among the vocations on the cultural threats scale ($p < .001$; $eta^2 = .00$), although there was not an effect size. Sisters, brothers and priests all believed that affluence, capitalism and technology posed a limited threat to the future of religious life.

No significant difference was found among members of the four traditions on the cultural threats scale. Members of the contemplative, apostolic, mendicant and monastic traditions all believed that cultural threats posed a moderate threat to the future of religious life. There was a significant difference among the four cohorts on the cultural threats scale ($p = .03$; $eta^2 = .002$). However, members of all cohorts believed that cultural threats posed a moderate degree of threat to the future of religious life. Members under 61 years old viewed cultural threats as less significant than members aged 61 and older.

The general conclusion from these findings would suggest that members of religious orders are not at war with the culture. They see themselves as embedded within the culture and feel that the dynamics of culture do not pose a significant threat to religious life. Perhaps these data reflect the degree of assimilation of religious orders into the Euro-American culture. Members may see themselves as one with the culture rather than at variance with it.

Without exaggerating the analogy, it is hard to imagine a prophetic force being relatively unattuned to the cultural forces shaping religious life. Although we should not derive greater significance from this measure than is warranted, in other facets of the research project (for instance, in individual interviews and in the Visioning Groups process), individual members of religious orders frequently spoke about the assimilation of members of religious orders into the culture and how domesticated members of religious orders had become. They often use the immobility that has set into religious consciousness as an example of the shift from being set apart from the culture to being grounded in it. If religious orders are to fulfill their espoused function as critics of society and the church, their prophetic role would seem to require significant distance from the cultural forces that could co-opt their power.

Credibility

Social institutions achieve credibility if, in the context of their service, they evidence that they are faithful to their purpose and responsive to a real need. Credibility will be at stake if social institutions violate the expectations of the environments or societies within which they are operating. However, as social institutions change from one form to another, it also can be true that the challenge to their credibility is less a case of their not exercising their responsibilities appropriately than it is that those who witness the new forms either do not understand or do not agree with the prevailing direction.

Both threats to the credibility of religious orders seem to be operative. By their own measure, the orders are not as thoroughly committed and active as they want to be. On the other hand, they are changing, or have changed their direction and, in some instances, have done this so vastly that they are not thought to be credible in some sectors. Thus, the challenge to remain credible in the society and the church is indeed an issue. Without credibility, resource acquisition will be difficult, recruitment will be marginal, and efforts to achieve a coherent and important mission may be thwarted.

Organizations that espouse particular values are held to those values by various constituents. Religious orders have had high degrees of social credibility. They appeared to live and work in accord with their espoused values. Certainly, there always have been exceptions and both written and oral histories of religious life can recount abuses. Nonetheless, the mainline traditions of religious orders are characterized by high social credibility and, consequently, durability over the centuries. In the National Survey, two factors emerged that relate to the dynamic processes of the credibility of social institutions. The first relates to the congruence of attitudes and behaviors among members, especially with respect to serving the poor. The second addresses a degree of anomie or indifference among individual members of religious orders that could lead to an undermining of the social institution of religious life in American society.

Anomie. The anomie scale is defined as a cognitive or emotional state in which normative standards of conduct and belief are weak or lacking. It is characterized by disorientation, anxiety and isolation. There was no significant difference between vocations on the anomie scale. Sisters, brothers and priests all believed that the loss of faith or conviction about the vows, lack of clarity about the role of members of religious orders, reactance to authority, lack of corporate mission and ministry and disillusionment with leadership pose moderate threats to the future of religious life.

There was a significant difference among members of the four traditions on the anomie scale ($p = .001$; $eta^2 = .004$). Members of the contemplative, apostolic, mendicant and monastic traditions, however, all thought that anomie would pose a moderate degree of threat to the future of religious life.

Contemplatives were most concerned about the impact of anomie. There was a significant difference on the anomie scale as well among cohorts, although the practical significance is limited ($p < .001$; $eta^2 = .01$). As the cohorts increased in age, so did their belief that anomie poses a moderate threat to the future of religious life.

The anomie factor was intended to measure the degree of threat that various attitudes or contingencies posed to religious life. All religious traditions, vocations and age groups identified indifference or further deterioration of stable practice as potentially harmful to religious life. By reinforcing consistency with respect to prayer, optimism about the future, the relevancy of church involvement through work and role identity as members of religious orders, the degree of threat felt by members of religious orders is likely to diminish. The measure suggests that members of religious orders may desire more predictability with respect to the core beliefs and practices that supposedly underlie religious commitment. Without this consistency, the members worry about stronger levels of indifference and, resulting lower impact and satisfaction.

Commitment to the poor. To measure a member's stated commitment to work personally with the poor, survey participants were asked to respond to the statement, "Although there is increasing talk about working with the poor, I feel little commitment to that." Mean scores for all vocations, traditions and age groups did not exceed 3.5. Sisters, members of apostolic groups and members of religious orders in the 19-45 age group yielded the highest means in their respective groupings. Thus, members of congregations express limited commitment to participate in an activity that has become increasingly an espoused value for many congregations and has been quite explicitly promoted by the church.

A difference in the commitment of members of religious orders to work with the poor was found between vocations. Women religious were more likely to express the intention to work with the poor than either priests or brothers. A difference was found among traditions on commitment to work with the poor. Members of the apostolic and mendicant traditions, not surprisingly, expressed greater degrees of interest in working with the poor than the monastic and contemplative traditions. A difference was also found among cohorts on commitment to work with the poor. The younger a member of a religious order, the greater the likelihood that he or she was committed to working with the poor.

These findings suggest that the greatest commitment to work with the poor would be found in a young apostolic sister. This group currently shows the smallest tendency to increase in size.

Conclusions: Social Institution Level of Analysis

The church can be viewed as a shared entity that exists across congregations. This is the focus of the social institution level of analysis. The study found a diversity of understandings at this level among vocations, traditions and age groups concerning the Structures, Innovations, Restraints and Credibility.

One of the most significant findings from the analyses regarding perceptions of social institution was the overriding lack of role clarity among members of religious orders. The most significant differences in role clarity were found among age groups. Younger religious members reported the least amount of role clarity. These findings may be explained by the fact that those who have the greatest amount of tenure with an organization tend to develop well-defined roles. However, it is important to note that a lack of role clarity may have detrimental effects. Role ambiguity has been associated with anxiety, lower satisfaction and an increased propensity to leave an organization. With newer members reporting low levels of role clarity, it may be critical to help members define their purpose in order to decrease turnover.

Another interesting finding regarding the structures factors concerns the reports of low to moderate levels of hierarchical alliance and perceptions of the influence of external authority on the future of religious life. The most meaningful differences were found among vocational subgroups and age cohorts. Although all three vocations reported low levels of external authority and low to moderate levels of hierarchical alliance, sisters reported significantly lower levels than did either brothers or priests. These findings suggest that sisters experience difficulty working with the hierarchy of the church and may experience more incidents of conflict with the institutional church. In addition, sisters are less likely to view the institutional church and external authority as a favorable influence in the future of religious life. It is possible that communities of women religious view their mission as relatively autonomous from that of the institutional church, more so than male communities. The strength of feminism's advances in power equalization will certainly continue to impact women in the church, and consequently the church itself, but feminism itself is not consciously perceived by women or men in religious orders as having an overwhelming impact on religious life.

Age groups also reported differences in both hierarchical alliance and external authority. Those respondents between 19 and 60 years of age consistently reported less alliance with the hierarchy and influences by external authority than the oldest age group (means less than 3.0). These findings are important since younger age groups represent the newest members of religious orders and, thus, the future of religious life.

Also significant regarding the structures factors was the perception of permanent commitment. Respondents across subgroups reported only moderate agreement with the belief that permanent commitment will be the norm of

religious life.   This factor alone could have the single greatest impact in
religious life, to the extent that personal commitment to the vowed life also has
a profound impact on the sense of interpersonal commitment in community.
Similarly, the role of leadership in collectives of temporarily committed persons
would be significantly different than today, perhaps involving less emphasis on
retirement and greater emphasis on planning.

Equally important is the significance of working for systemic change
among members of religious orders. Respondents generally saw activities such
as support for the causes of minority peoples, work for better political
leadership, participation in social justice activities, action on behalf of the ill and
participation in ecumenical activity as having relatively little value in contributing to their own personal and spiritual fulfillment. The only meaningful
difference regarding systemic change was found among the tradition subgroups.
Not surprisingly, contemplative members reported the least fulfillment in
working for systemic change (2.2 on a 5-point scale). Such a finding is
reflective of the nature and mission of their tradition.

However, working for systemic change through advocacy efforts or
transforming institutions to better serve those in need seems to us to be
important in light of the nature of American society. Perhaps this measure
reflects more of a personalized form of ministerial involvement than a
congregational focus, and should, therefore, not be overinterpreted.

PRINCIPAL COMPONENTS FACTOR ANALYSIS: CONGREGATION

This section of the analysis examines the scales that have the most
relevance to the congregational level. The scales of this level are grouped into
three categories: Leadership, Dynamics and Guidance.

Within the leadership category, scales, which were based primarily on
Bass's Multifactor Leadership Questionnaire (Bass, 1985), are further
categorized as transformational or transactional in nature. The transformational
scales included spiritual intensity, charisma/individual consideration and
intellectual stimulation/inspirational. The transactional scales included laissez-
faire, contingent reward and active management-by-exception.

Scales comprising the dynamics category are community living, involvement, influence and ongoing development. The scales comprising the guidance
category are procedural clarity, effects of renewal and support of sponsored
institutions. See Tables 4.32-4.34 for means, standard deviations, valid sample
sizes, F values and effect sizes for congregational domain factors by vocational
groups, tradition and age cohorts.

Table 4.32
Congregational Factors by Vocation

		Sister	Brother	Priest	F Value	p	eta^2
LEADERSHIP							
Spiritual Intensity	Mean	3.92	3.50	3.41	174.97	< .001	.06
	SD	.92	1.00	1.02			
	N	3,127	1,339	1,521			
Charisma/Individual	Mean	3.67	3.44	3.36	60.86	< .001	.02
Consideration	SD	.89	.95	.97			
	N	2,794	1,272	1,448			
Intellectual Stimulation/	Mean	3.57	3.41	3.39	31.12	< .001	.01
Inspiration	SD	.80	.86	.87			
	N	2,922	1,292	1,484			
Laissez-Faire	Mean	2.13	2.38	2.48	88.95	< .001	.03
	SD	.81	.90	.91			
	N	2,798	1,318	1,473			
Contingent Reward	Mean	1.62	1.78	1.70	15.51	< .001	.005
	SD	.84	.90	.84			
	N	2,950	1,308	1,488			
Active Management	Mean	2.06	2.38	2.26	81.23	< .001	.03
by Exception	SD	.79	.82	.78			
	N	2,918	1,319	1,484			
DYNAMICS							
Community Living	Mean	4.09	3.95	3.94	32.15	< .001	.01
	SD	.70	.73	.77			
	N	3,083	1,321	1,504			
Involvement	Mean	3.98	3.94	3.92	6.79	< .002	.002
	SD	.56	.54	.59			
	N	3,244	1,385	1,569			
Ongoing Development	Mean	3.97	3.97	3.91	4.69	< .01	.002
	SD	.65	.73	.74			
	N	3,153	1,374	1,562			
GUIDANCE							
Procedural Clarity	Mean	3.77	3.52	3.51	97.48	< .001	.03
	SD	.67	.72	.77			
	N	3,175	1,381	1,544			
Effects of Renewal	Mean	3.75	3.40	3.45	163.20	< .001	.05
	SD	.66	.74	.78			
	N	3,231	1,375	1,569			

Table 4.33
Congregational Factors by Tradition

		Apostolic	Mendicant	Contemp.	Monastic	F Value	p	eta²
LEADERSHIP								
Spiritual Intensity	Mean	3.82	3.74	3.74	3.72	3.56	.01	.002
	SD	.96	.99	1.02	.98			
	N	4,321	746	207	929			
Charisma/Individual	Mean	3.59	3.62	3.57	3.66	1.72	n.s.	
Consideration	SD	.91	.93	.98	.96			
	N	3,898	694	184	873			
Intellectual Stimula-	Mean	3.52	3.57	3.46	3.59	2.96	<.05	.002
tion/	SD	.81	.84	.93	.88			
Inspiration	N	4,063	711	190	911			
Laissez-Faire	Mean	2.20	2.24	2.38	2.35	8.94	<.001	.005
	SD	.84	.85	.90	.91			
	N	3,932	690	185	883			
Contingent Reward	Mean	1.62	1.74	1.67	1.76	8.92	<.001	.005
	SD	.83	.84	.92	.91			
	N	4,114	700	196	911			
Active Management	Mean	2.08	2.21	2.42	2.34	34.82	<.001	.02
by Exception	SD	.79	.79	.94	.79			
	N	4,065	709	194	913			
DYNAMICS								
Involvement	Mean	3.96	3.97	4.18	4.00	11.15	<.001	.005
	SD	.56	.56	.48	.55			
	N	4,484	756	222	975			
Community Living	Mean	4.06	4.03	4.24	4.09	5.07	<.002	.003
	SD	.72	.73	.65	.73			
	N	4,280	724	194	908			
Ongoing Develop-	Mean	3.96	3.96	3.83	3.90	3.89	<.01	.002
ment	SD	.66	.71	.79	.77			
	N	4,380	750	214	938			
GUIDANCE								
Procedural Clarity	Mean	3.71	3.65	3.89	3.68	6.49	<.001	.003
	SD	.70	.70	.72	.73			
	N	4,396	755	208	943			
Effects of Renewal	Mean	3.69	3.59	3.70	3.62	6.54	<.001	.00
	SD	.69	.74	.74	.71			
	N	4,461	766	221	962			

Table 4.34
Congregational Factors by Cohort

		19-45	46-60	61-73	74-96	F Value	p	eta^2
LEADERSHIP								
Spiritual Intensity	Mean	3.62	3.75	3.84	3.96	25.13	< .001	.01
	SD	.97	.96	.94	.95			
	N	1,267	1,894	1,695	1,002			
Charisma/Individual Con-	Mean	3.47	3.51	3.64	3.79	26.79	< .01	.02
sideration	SD	.95	.92	.90	.86			
	N	1,192	1,765	1,535	853			
Intellectual Stim./Inspiration	Mean	3.59	3.56	3.53	3.43	6.60	< .001	.004
	SD	.83	.84	.79	.81			
	N	1,212	1,813	1,611	907			
Laissez-Faire	Mean	2.27	2.22	2.17	2.21	3.56	< .02	.002
	SD	.91	.84	.84	.79			
	N	1,202	1,742	1,543	888			
Contingent Reward	Mean	1.64	1.57	1.63	1.78	14.07	< .001	.008
	SD	.81	.79	.84	.91			
	N	1,213	1,814	1,623	939			
Active Management by Excep	Mean	2.15	2.03	2.10	2.24	16.82	< .001	.009
tion	SD	.81	.77	.77	.83			
	N	1,191	1,803	1,630	922			
DYNAMICS								
Involvement	Mean	4.03	3.97	3.96	3.94	6.23	< .001	.00
	SD	.52	.59	.55	.56			
	N	1,276	1,934	1,761	1,083			
Community Living	Mean	3.84	3.95	4.12	4.30	93.44	< .001	.05
	SD	.84	.75	.67	.55			
	N	1,245	1,888	1,683	971			
Ongoing Development	Mean	4.04	3.99	3.96	3.83	19.14	< .001	.01
	SD	.76	.67	.64	.62			
	N	1,277	1,939	1,737	985			
GUIDANCE								
Procedural Clarity	Mean	3.56	3.66	3.74	3.83	34.35	< .001	.02
	SD	.72	.72	.67	.67			
	N	1,271	1,928	1,719	1,029			
Effects of Renewal	Mean	3.57	3.68	3.76	3.65	20.02	< .001	.01
	SD	.74	.71	.65	.69			
	N	1,269	1,934	1,760	1,072			

Leadership

Bass (1985) developed the Multifactor Leadership Questionnaire (MLQ) to investigate transformational and transactional leadership. The instrument has helped to determine quantitatively the behaviors contributing to transformational and transactional leadership. It is also a useful measure of transformational and transactional leadership orientations.

The previously standardized Multifactor Leadership Questionnaire (MLQ, form 8Y, Bass & Avolio, 1990) was included in the questionnaire to measure members' perceptions of transformational and transactional leadership. A series of questions pertaining to the members' perceptions of their leader as a spiritual leader was developed specifically for this survey. Respondents were instructed to choose the person or group in their congregation to whom they considered themselves accountable and to keep that individual or group in mind as they completed the scale.

Transformational leadership. Transformational leadership accounts for three of the six scales in the leadership category: spiritual intensity, charisma/individual consideration and intellectual stimulation/inspirational. The scale of spiritual intensity is defined as that characteristic of transformational leadership marked by the ability to model credibly and exert effectively a positive influence over activities pertaining to spirituality and mission. The charismatic attraction of transformational leaders is seen in their referent power, their value as role models, and the trust and confidence followers place in them. They have self-confidence; self-determination; insight about the needs, values and hopes of their followers, and strong convictions regarding the righteousness of their beliefs. Followers idealize them and identify with their goals and mission (Bass, 1985).

Transformational leaders are also inspirational. They are persuasive, set high expectations and manage meaning and impressions (Bass, 1988). They influence subordinates' self-expectations and inspire them to reach beyond their own self-interest. Inspirational leaders make use of metaphors, symbols, ceremonies and insignias to communicate their visions. These traits were coupled with individual consideration in the second scale in the transformational leadership factor. These leaders are developmentally oriented, giving consistent and personal feedback and linking the needs of members to the order's mission. They work at developing their members to their fullest potential. The leaders' skill at recognizing individual needs and elevating these needs when the time calls for it boosts their ability to advance the organization during times of change and crisis.

Finally, transformational leaders stimulate their subordinates intellectually. They assist in interpreting and analyzing problems in new ways, support contemplation and questioning before action, and arouse imagination and creativity in problem solving. Intellectual stimulation develops problem-solving abilities, which improves organizational functioning. This requires that the leaders' abilities be superior to those of followers, but not so superior that communication breaks down (Bass, 1985).

An examination of means for all leadership scales shows that across all groupings in the analysis, leaders are rated as being more transformational than transactional. Mean scale ratings on transformational factors are consistently higher for women leaders. In considering the vocation groups, sisters rated leaders highest with reference to spiritual intensity (mean = 3.92). Mean scores for brothers and priests were 3.50 and 3.41, respectively ($p < .001$; $eta^2 = .05$). Sisters, brothers and priests evidenced a similar pattern for charisma/individual consideration ($p < .001$; $eta^2 = .02$) and intellectual stimulation/inspirational leadership ($p < .001$; $eta^2 = .01$).

In considering the tradition subgroups, members of apostolic orders rated their leaders higher in spiritual intensity (mean = 3.82) than any of the other three traditions. Although statistical significance was found in the difference among the means, they did not approach practical significance ($p < .01$; $eta^2 = .002$). Groups by tradition reported similar levels of charisma/individual consideration. Differences among means on intellectual stimulation/inspiration were again statistically, but not practically, significant ($p < .05$; $eta^2 = .002$).

Spiritual intensity was the most highly rated behavior by all cohort groups. The oldest age group reported the highest levels of spiritual intensity leadership behaviors overall. These differences were statistically significant ($p < .001$; $eta^2 = .01$). In addition, cohorts' ratings of charisma/individual consideration increased with age, with means ranging from 3.47 to 3.79 ($p < .01$; $eta^2 = .02$). Intellectual stimulation/inspiration means were around 3.5 for all cohort subgroups ($p < .001$; $eta^2 = .004$).

Transactional Leadership. The leadership cluster also yielded three transactional leadership scales: laissez-faire, active management-by-exception and contingent reward. Laissez-faire leadership is practiced by leaders who avoid any intervention. There is no attempt to monitor or motivate followers. These leaders avoid making decisions and display an absence of initiative. Active management-by-exception describes transactional leaders' intervention when subordinates have done something that the leader deems a mistake. Active management-by-exception is used when the leader monitors worker activities and watches for deviations from standards, taking corrective action when this occurs. Reinforcement consists of criticism, negative feedback and negative contingent reinforcement (Bass & Avolio, 1990). Finally, transactional leaders make rewards contingent upon progress. These leaders recognize the needs of followers and respond to these needs as long as the job gets done. Followers receive positive reinforcement for work done well. Effective transactional leaders know how to facilitate subordinate goal achievement and fulfill subordinate expectations (Kuhnert & Lewis, 1987).

Mean scores for all groups were much lower for the transactional leadership dimensions than for the transformational scales. In contrast to the consistently higher ratings on transformational scales by women for their leaders, men were consistently higher than women in rating their leaders on transactional scales.

By vocation, sisters, brothers and priests rated their leader as exhibiting low levels of laissez-faire behaviors (means between 2.13 and 2.48, $p < .001$; $eta^2 = .03$), even lower levels of active management by exception (means between 2.06 and 2.38, $p < .001$; $eta^2 = .03$), and the lowest levels of transactional behavior in contingent reward (means between 1.62 and 1.70, $p < .001$; $eta^2 = .005$). Members of all tradition subgroups also reported that their leaders exhibited low levels of laissez-faire ($p < .001$; $eta^2 = .005$), active management-by-exception ($p < .001$; $eta^2 = .02$) and contingent reward ($p < .001$; $eta^2 = .005$) behaviors. Among age groups, respondents once again reported low ratings for all three transactional scales, with contingent reward receiving the lowest ratings. There was no consistent pattern of ratings among the age groups, but differences were significant among all subgroups on all scales.

These findings suggest that transformational leadership qualities are relatively frequent among leaders of religious orders. Spiritual intensity was consistently the most highly rated scale among all groups. This scale included items traditionally ascribed to religious leaders. Many of the other qualities of the transformational leadership style are also consistent with the espoused values of religious life. Organizational moves toward shared decision making and recognition of the individual member's gifts, talents and interests reflect the requirements of a transformational leadership style. The transformational leader is concerned with advancing the organization toward an adaptable and desired future, a major concern for religious orders at this point in history. The qualities of transformational leadership are also similar to those qualities identified as characterizing women's preferred style of leadership (Rosener, 1990). Conversely, the culture among men's religious orders may more easily support the laissez-faire, active management-by-exception behaviors characteristic of the transactional leaders.

Transactional leadership alone works well in stable organizations or during times of organizational stability. Transactional leaders do not, however, stimulate the high levels of motivation, innovation and creativity provided through transformational leadership. The need for transformational leadership arises during times of growth, change or crisis when leadership must provide new solutions, inspire and develop subordinates, and energize motivation (Bass, 1985). Transformational leadership works best when there is a need to develop the work force in order to keep pace with a constantly changing environment. It also works well in a highly educated work force. Both characteristics—the changing pace and a highly educated work force—characterize the current state of religious orders.

It should be remembered, however, that some minimal level of transactional leadership skills is required for the maintenance of an organization. The need here is not for "either/or" as much as "both/and" with regard to transactional and transformational leadership qualities. To ensure that the organization survives the transformation, someone within the leadership of the group must also attend to transactional concerns.

Dynamics

The dynamics grouping includes those factors that encompass interaction of the congregation and members in terms of community living, involvement, influence and ongoing development.

Community living. Community living is defined as the degree of satisfaction with the current living situation, including impact on affiliation and spirituality. An analysis of the individual items in this scale is included in the demographics section. Considered as a factor, high levels of satisfaction with community living were reported by sisters, brothers and priests. All factor means were beyond 3.9. Significant differences among vocations on this scale were found ($p < .001$; $eta^2 = .01$). Sisters reported higher satisfaction with community living than brothers and priests.

Members of all tradition subgroups reported high levels of satisfaction with regard to community living. Although statistically significant differences were found among these means, they did not approach practical significance ($p < .002$, $eta^2 = .003$). In addition, all cohort groups also reported high levels of satisfaction with community living, with significant differences found among mean responses ($p < .001$; $eta^2 = .05$). While the youngest religious (19-45 and 46-60 cohorts) reported the least satisfaction on this factor, their means, reflecting satisfaction, were high (between 3.8 and 4.0).

Changes and adaptations in religious orders have had a significant impact on the context and style of community living. This area comprises, perhaps, the realm in which the effects of renewal of religious life are most notable. Movement toward openness to visitors and guests, alteration of a strict schedule of work, prayer, recreation and silence, and even physical changes in furniture and its arrangement both reflect and influence changes in the experience and expression of community living. Many groups self-select, frequently with a sense of intentionality, rather than come together as a function of congregational assignment. Large institutional settings of 15 or more members have given way to small groups of 3 to 6 members. Policies in communities typically provide for groups of individual members to exercise initiative in the establishment of local communities. Hence, the relatively high levels of satisfaction in this area are not surprising. Gender differences may reflect the greater emphasis that sisters have placed on addressing this aspect of religious life in their renewal processes.

Involvement. Involvement is defined as the experience of having, and the desire to be engaged in, activities related to the life of one's congregation. The call to broader participation in the affairs and decisions of the order, including the renewal of religious life, has heightened the expectation of involvement in affairs pertaining to one's religious order. Sisters, brothers and priests all indicated high levels of involvement in their congregations, beyond a mean of 3.9. The pattern was similar for members of all traditions, with contemplatives and monastics indicating consistently higher levels of involvement in their congregations (means greater than 4.0). Clearly, this result is consistent with what would be expected for these traditions. Although statistical differences were found among the subgroups, these differences did not have much practical significance ($p < .002$, $eta^2 = .002$).

All ages reported mean levels of involvement greater than 3.9. Analysis of variance revealed significant differences among groups ($p < .001$, $eta^2 = .00$). Means for the youngest (19-45) cohort were highest (4.03) and decreased with age.

The high levels of reported involvement in this scale are consistent with the reported levels of commitment to the congregation. Behavior connected with involvement confirms the cost of the commitment to a religious congregation and serves to enhance one's sense of ownership in the group. The processes for studying foundational writings and updating structures to be consistent with the spirit of the founder and current conditions that were constructed by religious congregations elicited a great deal of involvement on the part of members. For many, this move introduced a new set of normative behaviors: in the past, one listened to the voice of the superior and silently obeyed; however, the "new order" called for much consultation and participation by members, with "dialogue" and "communal discernment" being core words in a new vocabulary.

Influence. Influence was measured by the item, "My opinions are considered in decisions made about my congregation." Means for subgroups may be found in Tables 4.29-31. Sisters reported the highest level of influence, with a mean of 3.67. Brothers and priests reported lower levels of agreement with this item, with means of 3.40 and 3.45, respectively. When considering the responses to this item by tradition, contemplatives reported the greatest levels of agreement (mean = 3.76). Apostolic, mendicant and monastic groups reported moderate agreement, with means of 3.53, 3.57 and 3.57, respectively.

It is important to contrast these responses with the ratings for involvement in their orders. While the members' sense of involvement in their congregations was high, their sense of influence was consistently lower. This situation may ultimately precipitate a sense of futility on the part of members relative to their efforts to further the mission and ministry of the order or to influence internal politics, which, in turn, are crucial to the future direction of a congregation.

There appears, however, to be little interest in expending the energies needed to narrow the gap. For example, when the members' aspirations to participate in administrative and leadership function of their orders are considered (see Tables 4.16 and 4.17), members of religious orders do not plan to pursue the paths that would typically provide avenues of influence. When questioned regarding their desire for "more influence in establishing the future of my congregation," members of religious orders in general expressed low agreement. Means for all groups are below 3.45.

Ongoing development. The ongoing development scale is defined as satisfaction with opportunities for continuing education and formation. The mean scores for sisters and brothers were identical (3.97). The priests' mean was 3.91. While this difference was statistically significant ($p < .01$; $eta^2 = .002$), it has little practical significance.

With contemplatives as the only tradition subgroup with a mean below 3.9, a significant difference was found among traditions on the ongoing development scale ($p < .01$; $eta^2 = .002$). A significant difference was also found among cohorts on the ongoing development scale ($p < .001$; $eta^2 = .01$). Members of the 19-45 age cohort were most clearly satisfied with their opportunities for development (mean = 4.04). Satisfaction with opportunities for ongoing development decreased as age increased. It is unclear, however, whether the fact that the 74-96 cohort were least satisfied (mean = 3.83) reflects dissatisfaction with community policy or with the individual's own diminished capacity to participate in such activities.

On the congregational level, attention to the ongoing development of members has increased over the past several decades. Even before the Second Vatican Council, focus on the need to prepare professionally for the classroom was evidenced in the Sister Formation Movement of the 1950s. As a result of the call of the church, religious orders of women placed greater emphasis on the education of their members, particularly as regards their competency of professional preparation. In more recent times, the encouragement of sabbatical time and other longer periods of renewal, as well as retraining for new ministries have become common among members of religious orders. Much of this reflects population trends of retooling for second and third careers.

All this may present a mixed blessing in religious congregations. On the one hand, it has the effect of reflecting a process notion of life, a sense that one is never finished with growth, development and the possibilities for expanding one's potential. However, this trend also can serve to eclipse a member's commitment to the mission and ministry of the congregation, inflating the expectations that unending development for the individual is a right that supersedes other ministerial commitments. Furthermore, in an era of declining resources, members may face further constraints on opportunities for ongoing development and encounter a frustration of expectations that have been raised.

Guidance

The category of guidance includes those factors that are related to the direction and ordering of the life of the congregation. It includes procedural clarity and the effects of renewal.

Procedural clarity. The scale of procedural clarity is defined as the degree to which a congregation's policies and procedures are perceived to be clear to its members. Items on this scale were related to the availability of information regarding whom to contact regarding various personnel and ministry issues, channels of communication, and mission and goals of the congregation. Sisters reported the greatest degree of procedural clarity (mean = 3.77), while brothers and priests expressed slightly lower levels. Differences in means for these responses were statistically significant (p < .001; eta^2 = .03).

Members of apostolic, mendicant, contemplative and monastic orders all reported levels of procedural clarity beyond a mean of 3.6. Contemplatives had the highest level of procedural clarity. The difference in the means for these subgroups was statistically significant (p < .001; eta^2 = .003). Among the age groups, levels of procedural clarity ranged from moderate to moderately high and were related to increasing age. Older respondents reported the most procedural clarity. These responses were found to be statistically significant (p < .001; eta^2 = .02).

Clarity of policy and procedure is a significant element in the life of a group, particularly as the size of the group increases. In a time of transformation, with shifts occurring in all levels of an organization, it would not be expected that the members' ratings of their perception of the clarity of procedure and policy would be high. These low ratings are also consistent with findings related to role clarity and corporate identity. If, however, an organization is to continue to be effective in the accomplishment of mission, there must be an accompanying movement toward greater clarity. This shift typically occurs during the "refreezing" period of a transformation process that was described in Chapter 1.

Effects of renewal. The effects of renewal scale is defined as the result of efforts to remain faithful, or return, to the spirit of a congregation's founder and to the prophetic nature of religious life. A significant difference was found among women and men on the effects of renewal scale (p < .001; eta^2 = .05). Sisters voiced greater agreement that efforts for achieving renewal have been successful in their congregation (mean = 3.75). Brothers and priests, with means below 3.5, did not indicate as positive a sense of the success of these efforts.

While a statistically significant difference emerged from a comparison of the means of traditions subgroups on the effects of renewal scale (p < .001; eta^2 = .00) means for all four traditions ranged between 3.54 and 3.70.

The 61-73 age group reported the most satisfaction with the effects of renewal (mean = 3.76). It is interesting to note that in most congregations, members of this age cohort were leaders of renewal efforts 30 years ago. The youngest members were least satisfied. The differences among cohorts on the effects of renewal scale were significant (p < .001; eta^2 = .01).

Efforts at renewal and at regaining a sense of the founder's spirit have marked the agendas of chapter meetings and documents circulated among religious orders since the Second Vatican Council. The current crisis and decline among religious orders, with the accompanying lack of clarity, may cause many to call into question the effectiveness of these efforts. However, the vibrancy and renewed mission and vigor seen among many congregations attests to their effectiveness. Those who are members of the youngest (19-45) cohort entered their religious order at the beginning of the renewal period or well into it. For these persons, renewal efforts have been identical with their experience of religious life. Hence, the youngest members may be unaware of the magnitude of change that has occurred and, thus, may lack a perspective in their assessment. Their ratings may also reflect the struggle between what is ideal and what is possible that typically marks young adulthood. Alternately, they may reflect a renewed vision and intensified energies that will characterize the future.

Support of sponsored institutions. Chi-square analyses were conducted with the two items within the National Survey that were identified as support of sponsored institutions (see Tables 4.29-31). These items reflected the willingness of a member to live and/or work in an institution sponsored by the congregation. Although the items were not derived from the previously described factor analyses, the results of chi-square analyses are included here due to the relevance of their meaning to the overall heading under which they have been placed. Item 272 stated, "I am willing to work in an institution sponsored by my congregation," and item 273 stated, "I am willing to live in an institution sponsored by my congregation."

Significant differences were found among subgroups in all three areas of analysis (vocation, tradition and cohort). While sisters, brothers and priests varied in their level of agreement that they would be willing to work in institutions sponsored by their congregations (χ^2 = 6.16, p < .05), more than 90% of each of these subgroups indicated this willingness. Indications of willingness to live in institutions sponsored by the order decreased with all groups (and particularly so for sisters), but still beyond the 80% level for the three vocation subgroups (χ^2 = 73.25, p < .001).

Members of the apostolic, mendicant, and monastic traditions indicated the greatest willingness to work in sponsored institutions. The response for contemplatives was lowest and, given the uniqueness of their life-style, this question may not have seemed appropriate to many contemplative respondents. Differences among the subgroups were significant (χ^2 = 12.10, p < .01). In terms of their willingness to live in sponsored institutions, there was also a significant difference among the members of the apostolic, mendicant, contemplative and monastic traditions ($\chi^2=13.65$, p < .001).

Finally, differences among the age subgroups varied both in terms of their agreement that they would be willing to work in sponsored institutions ($\chi^2=16.98$, p < .001) and in terms of their agreement that they would be willing to live in sponsored institutions ($\chi^2=93.88$, p < .001).

In spite of the significance of differences among subgroups, a surprisingly large percentage of all analysis groups indicate a willingness to serve in institutions sponsored by their congregations. Admittedly, not all members may be prepared or possess the qualifications to work in such settings. The strength of this finding, particularly for congregations with a history of sponsored institutions, stands in stark contrast to the general trend for religious orders to divest themselves of their institutional commitments. This is particularly true among sisters. Creativity in melding the founding charism, the response to absolute need and the members' energies is critical in this area.

Conclusions: Congregational Level of Analysis

Changes studied at the congregational level considered those aspects of religious life that are specific to individual congregations. Included among these are factors related to leadership, dynamics and guidance.

Members' perceptions of their leaders were measured using a series of questions related to the functioning of the leader as a spiritual leader and Bass's (1985) transformational and transactional leadership scales. The clearest finding among the leadership factors was the consistent rating of leaders as transformational rather than transactional. Spiritual intensity scale scores were the highest of all leadership scales, indicating member perceptions of their leader in spiritual terms. These items included such behaviors as inspiring loyalty to the congregation, speaking about global concerns and focusing attention on the poor and neglected. Sisters reported that their leader exhibited greater spiritual intensity behaviors than did either brothers or priests. Such a view could indicate that for women, God, mission and spirituality play a more crucial role in their explicit leadership activities than for male religious. Men tended to rate their leaders higher on certain transactional qualities (management-by-exception and contingent reward) than women. However, no differences were found between subgroups in their reporting of the frequencies of transformational and transactional behaviors exhibited by their leader.

With regard to the dynamics of individual congregations, trends emerged that were consistent with the findings at the social institution level of analysis. While all subgroups reported a generally high level of involvement within their congregation, they consistently reported lower levels of felt influence. The finding that the perceived level of influence within one's congregation is lower than an individual's experience or desire to be involved in the group raises serious concerns regarding members' commitment and may be related also to issues of role clarity.

With regard to levels of satisfaction with opportunities for ongoing development and formation, the small percentage of members of religious orders (particularly among those in the 46-96 age range) who indicated interest in further study presents another set of interesting questions. Are individual members satisfied with the opportunities offered because of the low level of their aspirations for ongoing development and formation? Have they moved to the less rigorous route of participating in workshops and institutes rather than formal programs of study due to decreased energies or decreased interest in learning? In light of the fact that Catholics are now among the most highly educated group in the United States, positive answers to many of these questions may raise further concern regarding the future vitality of congregations and their ability to speak credibly to an increasingly well-educated laity.

The guidance factors within the congregational level of analysis also showed relatively few differences among the subgroups considered. Overall, members of religious orders reported only a moderate sense of clarity regarding their congregation's policies and procedures. The consistency of this state with the dynamics associated with transformation have already been observed. Leaders should note that any move toward the necessary clarification of policy and procedures may meet with resistance among the members who have themselves become accustomed to the freedom that this stage affords. Leaders and those influencing decision making with regard to ministerial commitments might take note of the large percentage of members who stated that they would be willing to work in sponsored institutions.

Differences in opinion regarding the effectiveness of efforts of renewal may help in understanding the more subtle dynamics that surface when policy and related conversations occur within congregations. Vagueness regarding the desired end state of renewal, which may have been in the minds of many members at the time when renewal began and then subsequently lost, may be coloring those conversations. Energies spent on developing a clarity with regard to both the policy and the mission of a congregation will enhance members' connectedness with their congregations.

PRINCIPAL COMPONENTS FACTOR ANALYSIS:
INDIVIDUAL LEVEL

This section of the analysis will examine the means of vocations, traditions and cohorts on scales that are most appropriately examined at the individual, personal domain. The individual domain scales were grouped into three major categories: spirituality, belonging and action. Scales comprising the spirituality category were oneness with God, intensified spirituality and structured prayer. The scales comprising the belonging category were congregational commitment and affiliation. The scales comprising the action category were faithfulness to vows and works of mercy. Means, standard deviations, valid sample sizes, F values and effect sizes for individual domain factors by vocation groups, traditions and age cohorts are presented in Tables 4.35-4.37.

Table 4.35
Individual Factors by Vocation

		Sister	Brother	Priest	F-Value	p	eta^2
SPIRITUALITY							
Oneness with God	Mean	3.97	3.64	3.75	91.47	<.001	.03
	SD	.79	.85	.80			
	N	3,235	1,358	1,551			
Intensified	Mean	2.65	2.49	2.53	68.96	<.001	.02
Spirituality [a]	SD	.43	.49	.47			
	N	3,233	1,371	1,544			
Structured Prayer	Mean	4.31	4.11	4.16	49.31	<.001	.02
	SD	.68	.74	.70			
	N	3,203	1,351	1,529			
BELONGING							
Congregational	Mean	4.51	4.28	4.32	102.50	<.001	.03
Commitment	SD	.53	.60	.65			
	N	3,223	1,380	1,563			
Affiliation	Mean	3.98	3.88	3.84	27.88	<.001	.01
	SD	.57	.61	.69			
	N	3,176	1,353	1,535			
ACTION							
Faithfulness to	Mean	4.02	3.75	3.70	169.09	<.001	.05
Vows	SD	.58	.67	.68			
	N	3,283	1,382	1,573			
Works of Mercy	Mean	3.99	3.55	4.04	80.91	<.001	.02
	SD	1.27	1.41	1.17			
	N	2,290	981	1,199			

[a] Responses to this item were on a 3-point scale: 1 = Less than it was when I took my vows; 2 = About the same as it was when I took my vows; 3 = More than it was when I took my vows.

Table 4.36
Individual Factors by Tradition

		Apostolic	Mendicant	Contemp.	Monastic	F Value	p	eta^2
SPIRITUALITY								
Oneness with God	Mean	3.91	3.88	4.09	3.86	5.28	< .001	.00
	SD	.80	.80	.80	.82			
	N	4,456	762	221	959			
Intensified	Mean	2.62	2.58	2.77	2.64	11.64	< .001	.005
Spirituality [a]	SD	.45	.45	.38	.45			
	N	4,451	762	224	957			
Structured Prayer	Mean	4.27	4.21	4.77	4.30	18.72	< .001	.02
	SD	.69	.70	.43	.65			
	N	4,418	745	215	956			
BELONGING								
Congregational	Mean	4.47	4.42	4.57	4.44	4.49	< .004	.00
Commitment	SD	.56	.58	.53	.59			
	N	4,457	757	220	962			
Affiliation	Mean	3.94	3.92	4.18	4.03	16.78	< .001	.008
	SD	.60	.60	.52	.61			
	N	4,386	749	215	948			
ACTION								
Faithfulness to	Mean	3.96	3.88	4.02	3.89	6.29	< .001	.003
Vows	SD	.62	.63	.71	.64			
	N	4,521	774	226	972			
Works of Mercy	Mean	4.00	4.13	2.72	3.65	65.30	< .001	.04
	SD	1.24	1.14	1.64	1.42			
	N	3,218	540	157	690			

[a] Responses to this item were on a 3-point scale: 1 = Less than it was when I took my vows; 2 = About
the same as it was when I took my vows; 3 = More than it was when I took my vows.

Spirituality

Spirituality is one of the most basic elements in the life of a member of a religious order. While a specific form of spirituality may be identified with many congregations (for example, Ignatian for the Jesuits or Franciscan or Dominican), this particular category is concerned with the individual's experience of God and religious practices.

Table 4.37
Individual Factors by Cohort

		19-45	46-60	61-73	74-96	F Value	p	eta^2
SPIRITUALITY								
Oneness with God	Mean	3.77	3.86	3.93	4.04	23.47	<.001	.01
	SD	.78	.81	.81	.78			
	N	1,269	1,930	1,745	1,074			
Intensified	Mean	2.50	2.58	2.64	2.72	48.09	<.001	.02
Spirituality [a]	SD	.47	.47	.44	.40			
	N	1,237	1,914	1,757	1,093			
Structured Prayer	Mean	3.92	4.03	4.41	4.69	390.55	<.001	.16
	SD	.71	.70	.61	.45			
	N	1,262	1,913	1,719	1,063			
BELONGING								
Congregational	Mean	4.26	4.36	4.57	4.61	121.41	<.001	.06
Commitment	SD	.63	.61	.49	.46			
	N	1,265	1,927	1,750	1,073			
Affiliation	Mean	3.89	3.85	3.98	4.09	43.04	<.001	.02
	SD	.61	.64	.58	.51			
	N	1,262	1,904	1,715	1,051			
ACTION								
Faithfulness to	Mean	3.73	3.83	4.02	4.15	125.83	<.001	.06
Vows	SD	.63	.65	.59	.53			
	N	1,273	1,943	1,776	1,106			
Works of Mercy	Mean	3.92	4.08	3.99	3.77	10.19	<.001	.007
	SD	1.20	1.14	1.30	1.46			
	N	1,024	1,542	1,225	634			

[a] Responses to this item were on a 3-point scale: 1 = Less than it was when I took my vows; 2 = About the same as it was when I took my vows; 3 = More than it was when I took my vows.

Oneness with God.   Oneness with God is defined as an individual's experience of the state of unity or harmony with God. Items on this scale include frequency reports of one's feelings of being at one with God or Christ, of being personally loved by Christ and of being in God's presence. Sisters' means relative to the questions assessing oneness with God were highest. The differences between women and men (brothers and priests) were significant (p < .001; eta^2 = .03). All traditions reported high ratings with reference to the items identifying oneness with God. Consistent with expectations related to their tradition, contemplatives had the highest means. These differences reached statistical significance but did not show an effect size (p < .001, eta^2 = .00).

All age groups also reported a moderately high frequency, with significant differences found between mean responses ($p < .001$; $\text{eta}^2 = .01$) on this scale. Reports of oneness with God increased directly with age.

Given the nature of religious life, these results are not surprising. The data do support the stereotypes of gender (with women more inclined toward the spiritual dimension), definitions of tradition (with contemplatives rating these experiences as more frequent) and research on adult development (as age increases, awareness and value of the spiritual increases).

Intensified spirituality. Intensified spirituality is defined as a heightened value of religious life or deeper belief in Jesus Christ and/or the value of prayer. This scale determined differences over time in one's belief in Jesus Christ, commitment to prayer and the value of religious life. Responses were made on a 3-point scale (1 = less than it was when I took my vows, 2 = about the same as it was when I took my vows and 3 = more than it was when I took my vows). Overall, sisters expressed the greatest levels of intensified spirituality (mean = 2.65), while brothers expressed the least amount of intensified spirituality (mean = 2.49). The results of the analysis demonstrated significant differences between these means ($p < .001$; $\text{eta}^2 = .03$).

Analyses conducted to investigate differences in traditions indicated that contemplatives expressed the greatest levels of intensified spirituality (mean = 2.77) while mendicants expressed the least (mean = 2.58). Similar analyses run on the cohort groups showed that the oldest age group expressed the greatest levels of intensified spirituality (mean = 2.72) while younger respondents expressed the least amount of intensified spirituality. The differences among these means were significant ($p < .001$; $\text{eta}^2 = .02$).

Once again, reports of spiritual experiences were high and are consistent with religious life in general and issues related to each of the analysis groupings.

Structured prayer. Structured prayer is defined as the regular exercise of spiritual practices such as common prayer, confession, devotion to Mary and annual retreat. While sisters rated these exercises higher than brothers or priests (the difference was significant, $p < .001$; $\text{eta}^2 = .02$), all means exceeded 4.1 in members' agreement that these exercises contributed significantly to their spiritual fulfillment.

A significant difference was also found on this scale among the tradition subgroups ($p < .001$; $\text{eta}^2 = .02$). Members of the contemplative tradition rated structured prayer as highly related to their personal and spiritual fulfillment (mean = 4.77). The "lower" means for members of apostolic, mendicant and monastic groups were at the level of 4.2 on a 5-point scale.

A significant difference also exists among cohort subgroups on the structured prayer scale ($p < .001$; $\text{eta}^2 = .16$). Members of the 19-45 cohort believed that structured prayer had the least value for their personal and spiritual fulfillment than any other age group (mean = 3.92). Attribution of the value of structured prayer to personal and spiritual fulfillment increased with age, with members of the 74-96 cohort rating structured prayer as a very valuable contributor to their personal and spiritual fulfillment (mean = 4.69).

The high value of structured prayer reported by members of religious orders challenges much of the criticism regarding the lack of a spirit of prayer among religious. It is not surprising that more traditional forms of structured prayer are more valued by older, more traditional groups. The voices of newer members, their preferences for emerging forms of prayer and their potential for contribution in this realm need to be acknowledged.

Belonging

Congregational commitment. Congregational commitment is defined as the satisfaction with and an indication of a person's intention to remain indefinitely as a member of the congregation. While sisters reported the highest levels of congregational commitment (mean = 4.51), all vocation subgroups indicated high agreement, beyond a mean of 4.2, with these items. Differences among the means were significant (p < .001; $eta^2 = .03$). Similarly, the tradition groupings of apostolic, mendicant, contemplative and monastic as well as the four age cohorts reported high levels of congregational commitment. Members' reports of their intention to remain (one of the questions asked explicitly in this scale) were consistently high and indicated the resolve of current membership to continue as members of their congregations. These findings challenge some of the prevalent notions of discontent-bordering-on-departure among members of religious orders.

Affiliation. Affiliation is an individual's concern over establishing and maintaining a positive relationship with members of his or her congregation as well as with the congregation as an entity. The scale included measures of the individual's perception of feeling an important part of the congregation, experience of satisfaction in connection with the congregation and its members, and the significance of the religious order in the person's life. Sisters, brothers and priests reported moderately high levels of affiliation. Mean scores for sisters, brothers and priests were 3.98, 3.88 and 3.84, respectively. The differences among the means are significant (p < .001; $eta^2 = .01$).

Contemplative and monastic groups reported the highest levels of affiliation (mean = 4.18 and 4.03, respectively). Apostolic and mendicant groups' means were around 3.92. Significant differences were found among the traditions (p < .001; $eta^2 = .008$). As was the case for the previous scales, affiliation increased steadily with age. These differences resulted in statistical significance (p < .001; $eta^2 = .02$).

High means for affiliation are consistent with levels of reported congregational commitment. Members intend to remain and are satisfied generally with their congregations. This fact is important as regards morale. It also has strong significance for those orders whose roots are based on affectional bonds. High affiliation is not always a positive quality among members of groups such as religious orders. Dynamics related to affiliation may impede movement toward new or challenging ministries or needs of constituent groups. They may also inhibit the vision that is necessary among both leaders and members to address the challenges of transformation. Finally, as noted in the Leadership Competency of Religious Orders (see Chapter 3) research, excellence in leadership involves the leader's ability to move beyond the affiliational ties and exercise power and influence for the good of the group.

Action

The category of Action includes the factors that reflect a translation of the values and commitments made as a religious to actual behaviors. It includes faithfulness to vows and works of mercy.

Faithfulness to vows. Faithfulness to vows includes three items reporting the individual's faithfulness to the vows of obedience, chastity and poverty. A significant difference was found among sisters, brothers and priests on the faithfulness to vows scale ($p < .001$; $eta^2 = .05$). The sisters' mean regarding agreement that they had been faithful to their vows was 4.02, while for brothers and priests, means were 3.75 and 3.70, respectively.

A significant difference was found among the tradition subgroups on the faithfulness to vows scale ($p < .001$; $eta^2 = .003$). Means ranged from 3.88 to 4.02. A significant difference was also found among cohorts on the faithfulness to vows scale ($p < .001$; $eta^2 = .06$). Members of the 19-45 and 46-60 cohorts had moderate agreement that they remained faithful to the vows, while members of the 60-73 and 74-96 cohorts agreed that they had remained faithful to their vows.

Admittedly, the content of fidelity was not assessed. That is, exactly what faithfulness to each of the vows entails was left to the determination of the individual religious. These questions were included not so much to assess the particulars of adherence to vows as to determine the perception of faithfulness to commitments made and the possible impact such a self-image might have in living out other areas of one's religious commitment.

Works of mercy. The works of mercy scale included those items that name direct action to help the sick or poor as an important part of one's spiritual fulfillment. The difference among the means of sisters, brothers and priests on the works of mercy scale was significant ($p < .001$; $eta^2 = .02$). Priests (mean = 4.04) and sisters (mean = 3.99) believed that direct action to help the sick or poor was a more valuable contribution to their spiritual and personal fulfillment than did brothers (mean = 3.55).

The difference was also significant among tradition subgroups (p < .001; eta² = .04). Members of contemplative groups found the least fulfillment in the works of mercy (mean = 2.72). This rating demonstrates once again the uniqueness of the contemplative tradition. Members of the apostolic and mendicant traditions reported that works of mercy were quite valuable (mean of 4.0 or greater) to their personal and spiritual fulfillment. A significant difference was also found between cohorts on the works of mercy scale (p < .001; eta² = .007). The oldest (74-96) cohort indicated the least reliance on works of mercy for their personal and spiritual fulfillment, while the 46-60 group reported the greatest value (mean = 4.0).

These data, particularly in terms of the tradition and cohort analyses, most likely reflect the definition of contemplative and monastic life and the constraints of age. In contrast to ratings by members of religious orders on the systemic change items (efforts to influence social structures), the contribution of the actual works of mercy to the spiritual and personal lives of these individuals is very significant.

Conclusions: Individual Level of Analysis

The individual domain is concerned with the effects of transformation on individual members of religious orders. This focus from the National Survey data concerns belonging, spirituality and action factors. Spirituality was considered in terms of the experience of a sense of oneness or harmony with God, the degree of increased spiritual intensity and the value of structured prayer to personal and spiritual fulfillment. All subgroups reported high levels of both oneness with God and intensified spirituality. Differences did exist, however, among age groups in regard to the value of structured prayer. The experience of structured prayer as personally and spiritually fulfilling increased with age. Younger respondents reported only moderate levels of fulfillment (3.92), while older respondents reported the highest levels (4.96). The general absence of explicit talk about God, and of a common language for this discourse, may be a source of the belief in some circles that religious have lost their sense of God. Efforts to address this may be the focus of congregational and intercongregational collaboration. The fact that the spiritual leadership aspects of religious superiors was rated so highly gives some indication of the members' openness to such interventions.

All traditions, vocations and age groups reported a strong sense of belonging to their congregation as reflected in their commitment to the congregation, intention to remain and affiliation with their community. However, it is interesting that religious report a strong sense of belonging despite their felt lack of influence in their congregation and their lack of a sense of procedural and role clarity. Such inconsistencies may be a cause for concern and further investigation.

Within both vocations and cohorts, divergent trends existed in reports concerning faithfulness to vows of the church. Responses were similar with regard to faithfulness to poverty and obedience, but women reported greater fidelity to the vow of chastity than did men. However, individual item analyses revealed that vocation subgroups differed in the extent to which they were faithful to each of the three different vows. More specifically, both brothers and priests reported that chastity was the most difficult and least meaningful of the three vows. Sisters, on the other hand, rated chastity as least difficult and most meaningful. Sisters consistently rated obedience more difficult than brothers or priests.

The traditions reported differences in the extent to which they engaged in works of mercy. Members of the apostolic and mendicant groups reported action to help the sick and the poor to be the most meaningful. However, although religious members reported having a strong sense of spirituality and belonging to a religious congregation, their actions were not always consistent with the espoused values of their orders.

GENERAL CONCLUSIONS

This chapter reports results of the National Survey offers the following summary conclusions, based on each of the levels of analysis.

Social Institution

The social institution of religious life in the United States continues to reflect the dynamics of an organization in significant transition. The lack of role clarity for a large percentage of members of religious orders and their ambivalence regarding permanent commitment to the classic vows leaves the social institution vulnerable to innumerable other social and cultural forces. The results would indicate that the population of religious in general is moving toward a much more permeable system of membership, commitment, autonomy and inclusion.

While, on the one hand, this reinforces the innovations that include diversity and broadened assumptions about religious life, the research also indicates that members of religious orders do not see how clearly they are influenced by cultural assimilation. Similarly, for many, their own credibility may be threatened in the eyes of those they serve and the society in which they function because of the discrepancies between their espoused values and their practice. By their own admission, members of religious orders see indifference and a lack of passion to be a major threat to themselves as persons and to the broader scheme of religious life in relation to other social systems in the society.

Congregation

Leadership is one of the critical forces that can assist in clarifying the role identity of religious in the United States. Within congregations, and particularly among women, there exists a fair degree of satisfaction with leadership. The hidden side of the satisfaction is that it may signal complacency among members who, at the same time, find it difficult to influence the direction of the congregation.

For many, the congregation lacks a coherent approach to collective action, particularly in regard about to sponsored institutions. In addition, the efforts at renewal have not met individual hopes. Community life continues to engage members. They feel committed deeply to congregational life and are willing to be more involved than they currently are. However, they feel less influential with leadership and in setting the direction of the congregation. The high need for affiliation noted in the survey is consistent with high ratings of satisfaction in community life. For some congregations, this is an affirmation of their tradition or expression of their charism. In celebrating these results, however, members of religious orders should be aware that these dynamics can also stifle the creativity necessary to move groups into the future.

Individual

One of the facets of the research that addresses optimistically the lack of role clarity for many members of religious orders is the data that suggests the importance of spirituality and a vital relationship with God for many members of religious orders. Structured prayer, however varied the forms, continues to be a value. Individuals feel genuinely called by God to religious life, see an intensified spirituality as desirable, and have found in religious life a context to support that intensification. They are personally and strongly committed to the community, derive satisfaction from belonging, and most intend to remain in religious life.

It is fair to say, however, that the data indicates a stronger ecclesiology than Christology. Individuals emphasize participation in the life of the church and community as foundational to their spirituality. Evidence regarding their relationship to the person of Christ is less clearly drawn, perhaps because of the design of the study itself or maybe because of shifting language schemes used to describe one's spirituality. What is clear from the research is that members' spirituality will define their uniqueness in the church and that their belonging will satisfy their affiliative needs.

The data suggests also that if members of religious orders experience difficulty, it is in the realm of impact and fidelity to vows. The tradition of personal sacrifice that has been the foundation of vowed life has found support for such radical renunciation in the impact that it generates for the mission of the congregation and the church.

Personal understandings of religious life and the commitment required to live the life are very broad. This results in part from a lack of role clarity and from the vast cultural shifts in American society in general which have had a significant influence on religious life. Most religious would see some return to normative behavior as necessary, but they are reluctant to do so if that means returning to the sect-like distinction of religious life of the past.

NOTES

1. Some congregations included with their directories a listing of those members deemed to be too incapacitated to be able to respond to the survey.

2. Exclaustration is a formal state of separation from the congregation. While formal ties between the member and the congregation continue to exist, exclaustration differs significantly from leave of absence in its juridical implications.

3. The authors wish to acknowledge the significant contribution of Martin R. Frankel in the sample design and selection. Dr. Frankel is a senior statistician for the National Opinion Research Center in New York, NY.

4. Dr. Frankel noted that, "with this minimum size, the 95% confidence intervals for sample percentage estimates will always be less than 5%. Furthermore, although the design departs from proportionate allocation, estimates based on the full weighted sample will have an effective sample size in excess of 5,000. This takes into account the loss in statistical precision that occurs when disproportionate weights are applied to the sample in order to compensate for different probabilities of selection across the various strata." (Personal communication.)

5. In this and the following demographic sections, items from the National Survey that related to the issue being discussed are printed in italics.

6. Based on the Retirement Needs Survey (IV) of U.S. Religious reported in April 1992 by Arthur Anderson & Co. to the Tri-Conference Retirement Office (3211 Fourth Street, N.E., Washington, D.C. 20017).

Chapter 5

ROLE CLARITY AMONG
MEMBERS OF RELIGIOUS ORDERS

Vatican II began a process of transformation in the Roman Catholic Church that continues today, resulting in diverse, sometimes contradictory, understandings of religious life. This transformational process results in part from a shift in the interpretative scheme from the church as a culture that is separate from the world to one that is in unity with the world and serves its contemporary needs. Uncertainty is the most common reaction to sweeping organizational change, according to Ashford (1988). During the process of transformation, organizational members will move from a position of clarity to one of ambiguity before they establish a new clarity (Myerson & Martin, 1987). The role transitions accompanying organizational change result in stress for the individual. The amount of stress experienced will depend on factors such as the degree of role ambiguity, the centrality of role to social identity and the amount of self-involvement (Allen & van de Vliert, 1984).

Chapter 4 delineated the principal factors from the National Survey of religious that will have the most significant impact on the future of religious orders themselves. The most pervasive concern to arise from analysis at the level of the social institution of religious life is a lack of role clarity among a significant number of members. This chapter will examine in greater detail the dynamics of role clarity from a theoretical point of view with an expanded review of the results. Then, consideration of the implications for members of religious orders as they attempt to adapt to the ongoing process of transformation in the Roman Catholic Church will follow.

OVERVIEW

Role theory has, for more than five decades, concerned itself with both the structural and interactional facets of individual behavior in organizations (Heiss,

1968). Biddle and Thomas ([1966] 1979) examined the impact of persons who fill certain roles in organizations and, conversely, the influence of organizations or systems on individuals. Roles serve to sustain the action of an organization toward a specific end. Biddle (1979) defined role as patterned human behavior that operates within a social structure to achieve a specified end. Katz and Kahn ([1966] 1978) defined any human organization as a system of roles, which is more defined by the unique properties of patterned behaviors than by the persons who perform them.

Roles are perceived to be controlled by several factors. First, roles are defined by a social identity given with a position or office in an organization. This social position is recognized by various functions performed to specify the role. Second, every role is controlled by at least two additional factors: the expectations of those who are affected by the role and the context within which the role is lived.

Biddle (1979) framed the common propositions that govern role theory. They are restated here to highlight the potential applicability of role to the unique population of members of religious orders.

1. Role theorists assert that some behaviors are patterned and are characteristic of persons within contexts.
2. Roles often are associated with sets of persons who share a common identity.
3. Persons are often aware of roles and are governed by expectations associated with them.
4. Roles persist, in part, because of their consequences to a larger social system.
5. Persons must be socialized into roles.

Roles imply social boundaries among various functions or identities within a broader social structure. Individuals can fill multiple roles depending on the complexity of the context. Stryker and Statham (1985), however, have suggested that when individuals have multiple roles, they organize them according to a salience hierarchy. Identity salience is the location of an identity from among the many roles in the schema or hierarchy of roles. Individuals order their roles in relation to their perceived importance to their self-identity.

A critical facet in role integration is role socialization. Brim ([1966] 1978) defined socialization as the way in which individuals learn position-appropriate behavior in a group from people who hold normative beliefs about what a role should be and how it is rewarded or punished. O'Reilly and Chatman (1986) linked socialization to the process of organizational commitment that involves stages from compliance to identification and, finally, internalization. Organizational commitment intensifies in the first stage as compliance when behavioral standards for a role are clear.

Of particular importance to this study is the question of how Roman Catholicism in the United States today influences the role of members of religious orders.   Graen (1976) argued that the contextual conditions that underpin or surround a role are oftentimes more informative than the role behavior itself. The increasing role of the laity, the dignity of women and a less than clear mandate from Vatican II regarding the distinctive role of religious life, describes in part the context of religious orders today. Within the variety of constructs of role that have been measured, several are relevant to this study, including role overload, role conflict and role ambiguity.

The construct of role ambiguity can be measured both objectively (such as through documentation and policy or procedural statements) and subjectively, based on the subjects' perceptions in regard to their own roles.   The vast majority of studies have involved subjective ratings of role clarity or ambiguity. The role clarity/ambiguity construct was used in this study to examine the ongoing process of organizational change in the Catholic Church, and its current effect on members of religious orders, in order to plan future goals better and to implement them more effectively.

RESULTS

In the National Survey, religious role clarity was defined as the individual's perceived level of understanding regarding his or her purpose and function within the current structure of the church. As indicated in Chapter 4, the role clarity scale consists of two items: "The role of the religious in the church is sufficiently clear to me," and "I know what it means to be a religious in the church today." The alpha reliability coefficient for this scale was .79. Respondents were divided into three groups, indicating high, moderate and low role clarity, as based on their scores for this measure. Subjects responded to a 5-point scale, ranging from 1 (strongly disagree) to 5 (strongly agree), with 3 designated as "neither agree nor disagree." A score of 4.0 was set as the threshold level for inclusion in the high-clarity group. Subjects scoring below 4.0 but above 3.0 were assigned to the moderate-clarity group while those scoring 3.0 or below were assigned to the low-clarity group. Based on these criteria, 59% of the population was high in role clarity, 13% was in the moderate group and 28% was low.

An analysis by vocation (Table 5.1) revealed a different pattern of role clarity for sisters (with 54.6% experiencing high role clarity) from those of brothers and religious priests (65.1% and 68.4%, respectively, in the high clarity group). Based on this finding, brothers and religious priests were combined and cross-gender comparisons of more equal sample sizes were conducted. When brothers and religious priests were combined (N=2,974), 66.8% were high in role clarity compared to 54.6% of sisters (N=3,270), indicating that more male members of religious orders experienced high role clarity than female members of religious orders in the Catholic Church.

Table 5.1
Percentages of High, Moderate and Low Role Clarity by Vocation

Role Clarity	Sisters N=3,270	Brothers N=1,393	Religious Priests N=1,581
Low	33.1	24.3	22.2
Moderate	12.3	10.6	9.4
High	54.6	65.1	68.4

Differences were also seen among the traditions (Table 5.2). A full 70% of subjects in the contemplative tradition experienced high role clarity. The percentage of members in the monastic tradition experiencing high role clarity was 13 points lower (64.4%), followed more closely by members of the apostolic (59.0%) and mendicant (58.4%) traditions.

Table 5.2
Percentages of High, Moderate and Low Role Clarity by Tradition

Role Clarity	Apostolic N=4,273	Contemplative N=230	Mendicant N=774	Monastic N=967
Low	29.5	14.3	30.7	24.8
Moderate	11.5	8.7	10.9	10.8
High	59.0	77.0	58.4	64.4

Table 5.3
Percentages of High, Moderate and Low Role Clarity by Cohort

Role Clarity	19-45 N=1,279	46-60 N=1,946	61-73 N=1,770	74-96 N=1,103
Low	37.5	33.2	24.3	17.0
Moderate	10.6	10.2	11.7	12.1
High	51.9	56.6	64.0	70.9

An examination of role clarity by age (Table 5.3) showed increasing clarity among older members of religious orders. When actual number of years in religious life was examined (Table 5.4), the same pattern of increasing percentages reporting high clarity over time was seen.

Table 5.4
Percentages of High, Moderate and Low Role Clarity by Years in Religious Life

Role Clarity	1-24 yrs. N=1,194	25-38 yrs. N=1,917	39-52 yrs. N=1,875	53-89 yrs. N=1,180
Low	37.3	32.0	25.9	17.9
Moderate	10.4	10.8	11.4	12.1
High	52.3	57.2	62.7	70.0

Level of education was also examined. This analysis showed an inverse relationship between educational level and role clarity (grade school-high school, 75% high role clarity; some college or bachelor's degree, 60%; some graduate work or a doctoral degree, 58%; and other, 65%). The significance of this finding, however, might be questioned because of the size variation between these subpopulations, ranging from 356 subjects in the grade school-high school subgroup to 3,653 in the graduate work/masters degree/doctoral degree group.

Those receiving postsecondary degrees were asked to indicate their most recent field of study. Again, there were large variations in the size of these subpopulations. Members of religious orders with degrees in education (26.6%) and theology (22.9%) constituted the two largest subgroups. In the education group, 56.3% reported high role clarity compared to 62.2% in the theology group.

Levels of role clarity for five other field groups, representing between 10.1% and 3.0% of those with degrees, are presented above in Table 5.5. Of these groups, those in the humanities scored the highest level of role clarity about religious life followed, respectively, by the counselling, social science, business and health professions. Compared to the entire subject population (59% with high religious role clarity), those studying theology and the humanities were slightly higher on this measure, while those in the fields of counselling and social sciences reflected the general population. However, those in business, education and the health professions reported a perceived role clarity that was lower than that of members of religious orders in general. Those whose training was in the health professions showed a dramatically lower level of perceived role clarity than the general population of religious orders.

Table 5.5

Percentages of High, Moderate and Low Role Clarity by Field of Study

Role Clarity	Humanities N=489	Soc'l. Sci. N=289	Health Prof. N=202	Counselling N=186	Business N=150
Low	28.3	29.8	38.1	29.6	29.3
Moderate	10.4	10.7	12.4	10.7	13.4
High	61.3	59.5	49.5	59.7	57.3

The primary ministry in which the subjects were currently involved also was examined in conjunction with perceived role clarity. Disparity in subpopulation size remained. The largest segment of the sample (20.4%) was involved in education, and 58.4% of this subgroup was high in religious role clarity. The second largest segment (12.3%) was involved in parish ministry, with 62.4% reporting high role clarity.

Other ministries are grouped, by similar size, in Tables 5.6, 5.7 and 5.8, with percentages of high, moderate and low role clarity reported. Table 5.6 presents data for subpopulations ranging in size from 6.1% to 5.6% of the sample. Table 5.7 includes fields in the 3% of sample size range, the next largest segment groups. Table 5.8, which reports some of the fields ranging from 1.7% to 1.0% of the sample, was compiled in order to put the social work field, which had the most disparate results (with only 34.7% of the group reporting high role clarity), in a context of appropriate size. Table 5.9 summarizes the percentages of high role clarity by current ministry. This section of the questionnaire also included a response for retirement. Retired individuals comprised 7.3% of the sample population, with 64.3% experiencing high religious role clarity.

Table 5.6

Percentages of High, Moderate and Low Role Clarity by Current Ministry

Role Clarity	Higher Education N=351	Health Care N=343	Educational Admin. N=321
Low	26.2	36.2	30.2
Moderate	12.0	10.2	11.5
High	61.8	53.6	58.3

Note: Includes subpopulations ranging in size from 6.1% to 5.6% of the total.

Table 5.7
Percentages of High, Moderate and Low Role Clarity by Current Ministry

Role Clarity	Formation/ Vocation N=195	Pastoral Visiting N=192	Apostolate of Prayer N=177
Low	27.7	26.0	11.3
Moderate	12.8	14.1	9.0
High	59.5	59.9	79.7

Note: Includes subpopulations around 3% of total sample size.

Table 5.8
Percentages of High, Moderate and Low Role Clarity by Current Ministry

Role Clarity	Counselling N=98	Social Service N=94	Social Work N=72	Communication N=57	Pastoral Counselling N=56
Low	38.8	36.2	51.4	29.8	32.1
Moderate	7.1	9.5	13.9	12.3	12.5
High	54.1	54.3	34.7	57.9	55.4

Note: Includes subpopulations ranging from 1.7% to 1.0% of total sample size.

Respondents were also asked questions about their spiritual activities. These included attendance at liturgies and frequency of prayer. Analysis of this data (Table 5.10) revealed that those most frequently attending Eucharistic liturgy and Liturgy of the Hours had the largest percentage of individuals in the high-clarity category. A consistent pattern also emerged with respect to reports of meditating privately and meeting with a prayer group (Table 5.11). High role clarity is directly correlated with greater involvement in spiritual activities.

Table 5.9
Percentages of High Role Clarity by Current Ministry

Current Ministry	% High Role Clarity	N / % of Population
Apostolate of Prayer	79.7%	141 / 2.5
Parish Ministry	62.4%	440 / 7.7
Higher Education	61.8%	217 / 3.8
Pastoral Visiting	59.9%	115 / 2.0
Formation and Vocation	59.5%	116 / 2.0
Education	58.4%	685 / 1.9
Educational Administration	58.3%	187 / 3.3
Communication	57.9%	33 / 0.6
Pastoral Counseling	55.4%	31 / 0.5
Social Services	54.3%	51 / 0.9
Counseling	54.1%	53 / 0.9
Health Care	53.6%	184 / 3.2
Peace and Justice	43.8%	14 / 0.2
Social Work	34.7%	25 / 0.4

Table 5.10
Percentages of High, Moderate and Low Role Clarity by Attendance at Liturgies

Role Clarity	Every Day	5-6 a Week	2-4 a Week	Once a Week	Less/1 a Week	Almost Never
	Eucharistic Liturgy					
	N=3,933	N=1,027	N=795	N=371	N=44	N=26
Low	21.4	36.9	39.1	49.6	50.0	65.4
Moderate	11.0	13.2	11.3	8.9	13.6	7.7
High	67.6	49.9	49.6	41.5	36.4	26.9
	Liturgy of the Hours					
	N=3,947	N=868	N=462	N=82	N=148	N=667
Low	22.8	36.3	37.4	39.0	40.5	40.9
Moderate	11.6	10.6	9.4	11.0	10.2	12.0
High	65.6	53.1	53.2	50.0	49.3	47.1

Table 5.11
Percentages of High, Moderate and Low Role Clarity by Frequency of Prayer

Role Clarity	Daily	Sev'l. a Week	Once a Week	Spec'l. Occs'n.	Seldom/ Never	Other
		Private Meditation				
	N=4,513	N=1,076	N=168	N=96	N=89	N=35
Low	24.9	37.5	47.1	47.9	47.2	22.9
Moderate	11.5	11.3	6.5	9.4	10.1	11.4
High	63.6	51.2	46.4	42.7	42.7	65.7
		Praying with a Group				
	N=3,013	N=1,412	N=395	N=629	N=378	N=128
Low	22.0	35.0	33.2	35.0	40.2	27.4
Moderate	11.1	11.2	11.1	12.5	11.9	10.2
High	66.9	53.8	55.7	52.5	47.9	62.5

Ten additional scales were constructed, based on the conceptual framework for antecedents and consequences of role clarity. While items were chosen to measure specific antecedents and consequences, scale names were changed in order to represent more accurately items included in them. Table 5.12 lists the alpha reliabilities, group means and levels of significance for these scales. Five of these were antecedent factors: leader individual consideration, active management-by-exception (leader-initiating structure), leader-contingent reward (reward power), structural clarity within the order (formalization) and positive valence of religious life (higher-order need strength).

The remaining five scales were consequences: ministerial (work) satisfaction, congregational commitment, significance of congregation (involvement), propensity to stay and charisma of (confidence in) leader. The high-clarity group had a higher mean score on each of these scales than did the moderate-clarity and low-clarity groups. Levels of significance were better than .0001 on all but one, contingent reward (p < .001).

An examination of mean differences between the high- and low-clarity subjects found the largest difference (.49) on the structural clarity (formalization) scale. This was followed in order of decreasing mean difference by positive valence of religious life (.46), leader charisma (.42), significance of congregation (.41), propensity to stay (.38), leader individual consideration (.32), ministerial satisfaction (.30), commitment (.24), active management by exception (.15) and leader-contingent reward (.10). Some significant differences appear between the high- and low-clarity groups based on these factors.

Table 5.12

Scale Means for High, Moderate and Low Role Clarity (RC) Respondents

Construct	Alpha	Low RC (28%)	Mod RC (13%)	High RC (59%)	Pop. Mean	p
Congregational Commitment	.65	4.43	4.55	4.67	4.58	< .0001
Propensity to Stay	.80	4.16	4.37	4.54	4.41	< .0001
Ministerial Work Satisfaction	.69	3.94	4.05	4.24	4.13	< .0001
Pos. Valence for Religious Life	.64	3.70	3.89	4.16	4.00	< .0001
Ldr. Individual Consideration	.78	3.79	3.96	4.11	4.00	< .0001
Congregational Sign/Involvem't	.86	3.67	3.85	4.08	3.94	< .0001
Structural Clarity	.83	3.32	3.55	3.81	3.64	< .0001
Confidence in Ldr./Charisma	.93	3.23	3.51	3.65	3.51	< .0001
Active Mgmnt. by Exception	.66	2.11	2.20	2.26	2.21	< .0001
Contingent Reward	.82	1.52	1.60	1.62	1.59	< .001

One of the consequence factors, propensity to stay, was also measured separately by a comparison of the responses to questions concerning "primary ministry in which currently involved" and "ministry intending to pursue in the future." Identical responses on these two questions indicates an intention to stay in the current ministry. Among high-clarity respondents, 52.3% indicated that they would remain in their current ministry, while in the low clarity group, 46% intended to stay with their current ministry.

Table 5.13
Correlations for Role Clarity by Antecedent and Consequent Factors

Antecedents		Consequences	
Factor	Correl. Coeffic.	Factor	Correl. Coeffic.
Positive Valence Religious Life	.39	Significance of Congregation	.38
Structural Clarity	.29	Ministerial Satisfaction	.34
Leader Individual Consideration	.18	Propensity to Stay	.31
Active Management by Exception	.11	Congregational Commitment	.25
Leader Contingent Reward	.07	Leader Charisma	.19

Table 5.14
Comparison of Religious Life Futures Project (RLFP) Correlations with Mean Correlations from Fisher and Gitelson (1983)

Correlate	RLFP Correlation	Fisher and Gitelson Mean Correlation
Congregational Signific. Involvement	.38	.26
Ministerial / Work Satisfaction	.34	.35
Propensity to Stay	.31	.32
Commitment	.25	.34
Structural Clarity	.29	.40

Correlation coefficients were also determined for role clarity, and each of these factors is shown in Table 5.13. Correlations for antecedent and consequent factors showed the strongest relationships between role clarity and positive valence for religious life (.39). Other factors—congregational significance and involvement, ministerial satisfaction, propensity to stay, structural clarity and commitment—seem to replicate some of the mean correlations calculated by Fisher and Gitelson (1983) in their meta-analysis of the correlates of role conflict and ambiguity (see Table 5.14).

Four of the scales were determined by factor analysis to correspond to the Bass leadership scales included in the questionnaire. In addition, the spiritual intensity scale (designed specifically to assess member perceptions of leader spirituality) was compared to the high- and low-clarity measures. The results of this analysis are presented in Table 5.15.

Table 5.15
Scale Means for High, Moderate and Low Role Clarity by Leader Behavior

	Role Clarity		
Scales	Low	Mod	High
Spiritual Intensity	3.45	3.70	3.78
Bass Transformational Factors:			
Charisma/ Individual Consideration	3.30	3.50	3.65
Inspirational/ Intellectual Stimulation	3.35	3.44	3.55
Bass Transactional Factors:			
Active Management- by-Exception	2.11	2.20	2.26
Passive Management- by-Exception	2.40	2.25	2.20
Contingent Reward	1.52	1.60	1.62

DISCUSSION

Role clarity for members of religious orders is defined as "the individual's perceived level of understanding regarding his or her purpose and function within the current structure of the church." This measure, as were all the others, was derived through a principal components factor analysis. Due to the nature of the items, the scale is most accurately titled "religious role clarity," as it measures the subjects' understanding of their function and purpose as members of religious orders within the church.

While this construct does encompass the respondents' work or ministerial role, religious role clarity goes beyond this one sphere of life. One's role as a member of a religious order cannot be easily separated from other life roles for the person choosing a religious vocation. Rather, the religious role is considered to be a comprehensive self-identity, one to which an individual generally commits entirely in all facets of the role. This would include various spheres of life and involvement in an intimate spiritual self-understanding that allows one to participate in the life of God in unique ways.

Responses to the questionnaire (N=6,359) indicate that 59% of the members of religious orders perceived their role as clear (high role clarity), 13% indicated their role was moderately clear (moderate role clarity), and the remaining 28% felt that it was less than sufficiently clear (low role clarity). On this measure, 55% of the sisters reported high role clarity, along with 65% of the brothers and 68% of the priests. More than 30% of the women's scores were in the low-role-clarity category, indicating a lack of understanding (or clarity) regarding their role in the church today.

Considering the data by tradition, 77% of the contemplative religious and 64% of the monastics reported high role clarity, while approximately 59% of the apostolic and mendicant members indicated that they had a clear understanding of their role. Thus, clarity regarding role may be more easily established in the future in the first two groups.

High clarity is correlated with age. Fifty-two percent of the youngest members of religious orders reported high role clarity, compared to 71% of the oldest group. This finding parallels research in many professions that points to greater role clarity among those who have a greater tenure in their profession (O'Reilly & Chatman, 1986).

Interestingly, the more highly educated individuals among the population experienced lower role clarity as members of religious orders. Considered by field of study, members of religious orders in the more applied disciplines, such as the business, education and health professions, indicated that they were less clear about their role as members of religious orders in the church when compared to those whose training was in the more theoretical disciplines, such as theology, the humanities and the social sciences. The role demands of health care providers and educators may present pressures that replace or compete with, rather than complement, the current role of members of religious orders in the church. It may well be that other roles take precedence over the religious identity, and this may happen for a variety of reasons.

Survey data were first examined to determine differences in personal and professional characteristics, if any, between high- and low-role-clarity respondents. Relationships between role clarity and antecedent-consequent factors, as proposed by the conceptual framework, were then analyzed. Finally, reported leader behaviors (in response to the Bass scales and the spiritual intensity scale) by high- and low-role-clarity groups were compared.

Personal and Professional Characteristics

High role clarity increased with age and with years in religious life. There was, however, a negative relationship with level of education; that is, role clarity decreased as the amount of formal education increased. These findings confirm previous studies of role clarity that have suggested a weak but positive relationship with age and job tenure, as well as a weak, negative relationship with educational level. While the latter finding may seem counter-intuitive, some have suggested that it results from the increasing job level and complexity that often accompanies higher educational levels (Jackson & Schuler, 1985).

High role clarity also was found to be more likely among men than women. As with any data that divides along male/female lines, a primary question is whether a sex (biological) difference or a gender (cultural/socialized) difference is being witnessed. The literature on role clarity says little about differences between male and female subjects, suggesting that few, if any, differences have been found. The lower level of religious role clarity among women in this sample could result from gender differences in general, or it could be the result of the sisters' role and/or socialization within the church itself (namely, lower autonomy, differences in task identity and power, and lack of access to ordination).

In a study of religious professionals (Richmond, Rayburn, & Rogers, 1985), female clergy reported significantly more role clarity than male clergy. These seemingly contradictory findings could be the result of the different role clarity measures used (Richmond et al. used the Occupational Stress Question-naire). It might also reflect differences in role specificity between the Roman Catholic sisters and clergywomen of other denominations. Future investigation in this area, with the administration of a commonly used measure of role clarity to a subgroup of the sisters' sample, would allow the comparison of role clarity scores with women in broader religious and other professions. It appears that training in the more applied disciplines of business, education or the health professions, as compared with the more theoretical disciplines of theology, the humanities and the social sciences, is associated with lower levels of role clarity (see Table 5.5). The exception to this pattern was training in counselling. Subjects in this field of study mirrored the responses of members of religious orders in general, with 60% reporting high role clarity. It may be noted that the percentage of those actually employed in the field of counselling who reported high role clarity (54%) is below the average of all those who completed the survey. Additionally, the data seem to indicate that the more applied the work

(Tables 5.6-5.8) and the greater the involvement in the world not restricted to Church-related ministry, the lower the role clarity (Table 5.9).

When religious role clarity was examined by tradition, the proportion of those who had high role clarity among members of cloistered groups was significantly greater (77%) than for the religious population as a whole, as well as for samples of each tradition viewed separately. The monastic tradition was slightly higher (64% high role clarity) than the population, while apostolic (59%) and mendicant (59%) religious were closer to the population average of 59% high role clarity. These results seem to continue the pattern of inverse relationship between role clarity and active involvement in the less bounded or restricted context in which most members of apostolic orders work.

Involvement in spiritual activities such as attendance at Eucharistic liturgy, Liturgy of the Hours and frequency of private meditation and group prayer has a positive relationship to religious role clarity. As with most studies of role clarity, due to the survey method of research, the direction and degree of causality cannot be determined here. However, it is interesting to note the degree of association between high role clarity and high involvement in activities that propose to nurture a spiritual life.

Finally, in regard to personal and professional characteristics, it should be noted that, in their meta-analysis, Jackson and Schuler (1985) found that individual characteristics were related less strongly to role clarity than were organizational context variables. This suggests that if the church seeks increased role clarity among members of religious orders in their current ministries, interventions focused on organizational structure and leadership would be likely to have the most impact. The findings of this study also indicate how difficult it seems to be to live a countercultural life-style amid a very active cultural, social and religious engagement with the world at large. Not surprisingly, more restrictive or bounded environments tend to correspond with higher degrees of member role clarity. The dilemmas are clear. Will the Church acknowledge the critical mission of highly-educated women and men religious in institutions and services beyond the limits of the parish? Validating such identity may, in part, increase role clarity and commitment.

Antecedent and Consequent Factors

An examination of the total population response on the antecedent and consequent factor scales (Table 5.12) indicated a high level of congregational commitment (4.58 on a 5-point Likert scale); a strong propensity to stay (4.41); ministerial (work) satisfaction (4.13); a positive valence for religious life (4.00); and above-average (3.94) congregational significance and involvement. They generally agreed (3.64) that structural clarity within their religious order was sufficient. They responded that their leaders often displayed individual consideration (4.00), and they expressed an above-average (3.51) level of confidence in the leadership (leader charisma). Finally, they reported that leaders infrequently used an active management-by-exception (2.21) style of leadership and rarely depended on contingent reward (1.59) as a motivator.

This positive picture of organizational dynamics within the church must be framed within the context of previous studies that found a social desirability factor inhibiting members of religious orders in particular from reporting role strain, and a social desirability bias in role clarity responses in general. It should be noted that a separate measure of propensity to stay in the current ministry, as opposed to the order or religious life, revealed that 50% of the population planned on changing its ministry in the future. This finding seems to contradict the relatively high (4.13) mean score for ministerial satisfaction reported above and may be indicative of the social desirability bias operating in this data. Further, it seems to indicate that religious life is in a state of flux, with many individuals pondering their future ministerial role.

When divided into high-, moderate- and low- clarity groups, high-role-clarity subjects consistently had a higher mean score on each of the scales. This is not particularly surprising because all the scales measure factors that are expected to be positively related to role clarity.

As was noted previously, antecedent and consequent factor correlations replicated some of the mean correlations calculated by Fisher and Gitelson (1983). The largest discrepancy between the Religious Life Futures Project findings and Fisher and Gitelson correlations is seen in the involvement (congregational significance) correlate (see Table 5.14). This discrepancy might be explained in terms of the earlier discussion of the all-encompassing nature of the religious vocation. For members of religious orders, there is no clear separation of life spheres. One obvious consequence of celibacy is that members of religious orders do not enact the parent role, therefore, there is no competing commitment to family life. The result may be a stronger association between this work-related involvement and role clarity for members of religious orders.

Leader Behaviors

The final analysis involved an examination of leader behavior according to the survey results which used the Bass leadership scales. Table 5.15 showed the relationship between the high-, moderate- and low-clarity groups and leadership. The leaders of high-clarity members were rated higher on all the Bass leadership scales except passive management-by-exception. Since passive management-by-exception is the least effective of the leadership behaviors, it is not surprising that individuals who are clear about their role do not see their leaders as less effective. Conversely, the fact that low-role-clarity subjects rated their leaders higher on this scale only serves to strengthen the notion that effective leadership can facilitate greater role clarity.

Leaders for both groups received their highest rating on the spiritual intensity scale, followed by Bass transformational factors of charisma/individual consideration and inspirational/intellectual stimulation. Both sets of leaders were rated lower on the transactional factors, with contingent reward as the lowest of each. High-clarity subjects rated their leaders slightly higher on active management-by-exception than on passive management-by-exception. The order was reversed for the low clarity group.

Jackson and Schuler (1985) made some generalizations, based on their meta-analysis, that may help to shed light on this clear division of the transformational and transactional factors. They suggested that leader consideration, a factor that fits the transformational category, not only clarifies roles but also reduces role conflict. Further, they suggested that it serves an instrumental role, in addition to its socio-emotional one, by contingently rewarding subordinates for desired behavior. Leader-initiating structure, a more transactional behavior, also clarifies role but operates only on an instrumental level and does not have the added benefit of reducing role conflict.

The highest- and lowest-frequency leader behaviors seem clearly to be a function of the population being studied. Spiritual intensity is expected to be a salient feature of religious leadership, whereas, given the professed selflessness of the religious ministry, it is not surprising that leaders rarely attempt to motivate subordinates through contingent reward.

CONCLUSIONS

While the results of this study indicate that the majority of members of religious orders (59%) professed high role clarity, the percentage experiencing low role clarity is significant enough to warrant attention by the church leadership. This is especially true in light of the religious segments where role clarity is at its lowest.

A profile of the religious population would suggest that the prototypical member of religious orders with high role clarity would be an older male of the contemplative tradition, who had entered religious life at an early age. A middle-aged parish priest who is a member of a religious order would probably be moderate in role clarity, based on the data presented here. However, the greater his involvement in addressing the concerns not directly related to pastoral issues, the lower would be his predicted role clarity.

A young sister with a master's degree currently working in a helping profession is most likely to be low in role clarity, compared with other religious professionals. An educated young male choosing the same sort of active ministry also is likely to experience low role clarity, especially if he is involved in the peace and justice movement.

A curious dynamic is operative among younger members of religious orders, particularly women, who identify the importance of active ministry (for instance, among the poor). These individuals, who by these measures reveal lower role clarity, also reveal the slowest rate of increase in membership. Because religious life has, since Vatican II, become so singly identified with a preference for work among the poor, this discrepancy is notable. Those who do the work that the church proclaims as central do not feel at home with their role in the church. This could suggest an alienation from the church among those who are most closely aligned with the church's expressed intention, particularly as outlined in the major social encyclicals and in the documents of the Second Vatican Council.

Other research has demonstrated that ambiguity regarding role can lead to anxiety, reduced ability to meet role requirements, decreased ministerial satisfaction, lower trust and self-confidence, an increased sense of futility and a greater propensity to leave a religious order. The lack of role clarity that a high percentage of members of religious orders experience may contribute to a further diminishment in their number. It could also be that religious orders describe themselves apart from any particular church identity. In addition, there may be some connection between statistics reflecting the equal numbers of women and men entering religious life—in contrast to the approximately three-to-one ratio of prior years—and the greater numbers of women who experience low role clarity. Taken together, this data signals the essential need for improved role clarity if religious orders in the United States are to be revitalized. Without this clarification, the relationship between the church and religious orders could be jeopardized.

Reactions to the stress of role transitions, such as those experienced since Vatican II by members of religious orders who have become more involved in active ministries, include a tendency to fall back on old roles, compartmentalism of conflicting life spheres, and passive or active withdrawal. According to Allen and van de Vliert (1984), the chosen response depends on the perceived legitimacy of the new role, anticipated sanctions, personal capacity to implement the role and the existence of conditions necessary to fill the role properly.

Part of the fear among religious about clarifying their role in the church is that the various operative paradigms will have to be addressed. Most religious have become relatively convinced that their manner of life and ministry is as it should be. Others suffer random drift, attending to any fad that captures their sense of identity. However, religious today, and the church itself, cannot live indefinitely with the experienced role ambiguity. In the face of it, more people will leave religious life, and attracting others to the life will be very difficult. Religious should themselves, along with the leadership conferences in the United States, undertake an aggressive and inclusive study of their role in the church. Postponing the discussion further will further exacerbate the concerns.

Myerson and Martin (1987) have maintained that in the management of change, it is crucial to create a sense of psychological safety in order to allow role ambiguity to be confronted and worked through. Ambiguity can be channeled, or it can be acknowledged as a paradox and legitimized. The least effective strategy in the face of ambiguity is to deny the lack of clarity. In addition, as a clear role definition emerges (however similar or different it may be to what is operative), managing that change and creating a sense of safety as individual members assimilate the new interpretation will be required.

If, indeed, roles are controlled by the social identity derived from a position or office in an organization, it is clear that the social identity for religious orders in the church is lacking. Moreover, if the social position is recognized by various functions that are performed to specify the role, further complications occur. The functions that religious orders historically have served have altered substantially.

Religious orders are no longer willing to be considered—if they ever were thought to be—the work force of the church. However, in saying this, the function becomes less specific. Research has suggested that roles are controlled by at least two additional factors: the expectations of those affected by the role and the context within which the role is lived. In order to clarify the role, it may be necessary to involve the broader church in the dialogue as well as calling on those served by members of religious orders. It could be, for instance, that the poor should have a critical voice in determining the future role of religious orders.

Similarly, the context in which the role is lived will control the social identity. The current context of ministry for members of religious orders, without the larger frame of institutions to support the identity, leaves the social role less evident. Similarly, the political and ecclesial context is shifting dramatically, and the place that religious orders will choose to occupy, or be allowed to occupy, could condition their role in the church and the society.

Finally, if religious orders are to identify more closely with the poor and their condition of life or to increase ministries that seek to ameliorate the ills of society in general, it will be necessary to attract and retain young, highly educated professionals. However, the competing roles of the professions with the vocation to religious life must be integrated more clearly. In other words, the vocation to religious life, and particularly to the apostolic ministry, presumes a context that sees both professional life and vocation as important to ministry. Several strategies can be considered to achieve this goal. As Stryker and Statham (1985) indicated, oftentimes in situations of low role clarity, the context in which the role is lived has greater salience than the behaviors themselves.

In this instance, the context of religious orders in the church must be clarified. Otherwise, competing professions will eclipse the religious identity.

Furthermore, members of religious orders must themselves establish a strong support network of other members of religious orders so that a sense of colleagueship develops. In addition, clarifying the goals and values that underlie the more active ministries will strengthen apostolic commitment.

Finally, dynamic leadership that allows the lack of clarity to be examined and addressed creatively could likely effect a paradoxical resolution. Those most engaged simultaneously in the espoused ideal state of religious life and in their work with the poor could experience the greatest degree of integration and clarity in the church.

Chapter 6

THE MOTIVATION OF PEOPLE WHO CARE

Save for their commitment to prayer and the spiritual life, members of religious orders most often express their commitment to God by providing care and service to those in need. From artistic renderings through listings among providers of health, education and social services to features in various media, members of religious orders are consistently portrayed in care-giving, healing or support roles. Throughout history, the role of members of religious orders has been consistently seen as that of reaching out to the needy, the wounded, and the most abandoned. Those who looked to their services typically sought not only spiritual comfort but also relief from their ills or suffering.

Recognizing this history, and himself possessing a deep interest in investigating the motive structure of those persons who are seen as uniquely caring or as involved in the works of healing, David C. McClelland, Ph.D., a noted personality psychologist, proposed that the study of those members of religious orders who are seen as uniquely caring among their peers be included as part of the Religious Life Futures Project.

Psychological theory supports the notion that persons with a particular personality constellation are attracted to professions that call forth the characteristics of such a personality. The content of vocational tests is based on this assumption, and the corresponding literature is replete with instances that verify this belief. In the theory underlying the Myers-Briggs Type Indicator (MBTI), Isabel Briggs-Myers (1980) reported extensively on the consistency of relationship between the MBTI profiles and professional pursuits. Ukeritis (1984) further attested to the consistency of fit between this theory and the profiles of members of religious orders. In relation to values and decision making, members of religious orders typically indicate a clear preference for harmony over objectivity and opt for caring rather than logical processes.

The authors acknowledge the contributions of David C. McClelland, Ph.D., and Carol Franz, Ph.D., our former colleagues at Boston University, who were instrumental in the design, implementation and writing of this research unit.

BACKGROUND

In more general terms, helping or prosocial behavior has been a subject of intensive study by psychologists for decades (Krebs, 1970; Staub, 1978; Batson, 1987; Dovidio, Allen & Schroeder, 1990; Schaller & Cialdini, 1990). The issue of altruistic versus egotistic helping—whether the motivation for helping is truly to relieve another's distress or to relieve one's own distress that arises from empathy with a person in need—has been the crux of the question in more recent times. The usual paradigm for studying the problem has been to present in various ways (for example, with different scenarios) the situation of a needy person, and then to ask whether the subject feels sympathetic, distressed or sad in response to the situation. Then, one may obtain measures of the willingness of the subject to go to the assistance of the needy person or, perhaps, some other needy person in various ways and under different conditions.

The fact that this paradigm allows for many alternative ways of structuring the situation has led to different conclusions as to why people help. For example, Batson (1987) found that people who were not very distressed by the situation volunteered to help less often if they were provided with an easy escape (being told that others were likely to help the needy person). However, among the subjects highly distressed by the need of another person, providing an easy escape did not lead to much reduction in willingness to help. Batson concluded that people were motivated primarily to relieve the distress of another because, if they had been motivated to relieve their own distress, an easy escape would have served this purpose just as well as volunteering to help. Others have disagreed with this conclusion (Cialdini et al., 1987).

As the number of subtle variations in this type of experiment and their interpretations have increased (Betancourt, 1990), one cannot help wondering if some of the complexities in understanding the basis of helping may have arisen out of the way the studies have been designed. An important limitation, for example, is that many of these studies were designed to explain a *cognitive decision* to help when such a decision is explicitly required. Yet an important aspect of helping is the extent to which the behavior occurs *spontaneously* and, often, over time. Information on this point is not obtained by artificially presenting people with situations in which they must decide to help or not.

The traditional research paradigm presents an additional dilemma in the study of helping behavior insofar as it provides no opportunity to interact with the person to be helped. In fact, there usually is no such person; rather, he or she is a product of the experimenter's imagination. However, an important determinant of everyday helping is the interaction with the person helped. It may, in fact, be that the opportunity for that kind of interaction is what leads many people to help.

Finally, implicit in much of the research on helping behavior has been the notion that helping is automatically a good thing and that its intention and effect are to improve the well-being of another (Wispé, 1972). Social psychologists have been quick to point out, however, that helping behavior is not helpful when it is manipulative, designed to require a response in return, or undermining of independence, power, or self-esteem of the person helped (Fisher, Nadler & Witcher-Alagna, 1982; Nadler, 1986; Daubman, 1991). The traditional research design described above ignores this problem insofar as there is no real recipient in the study whose reaction can be assessed.

A New Research Paradigm

These limitations suggest that knowledge in the area might be advanced by shifting the research paradigm to study what motivates a person who exhibits a consistent pattern of helpful behavior.   One such method involves selecting persons known to be unusually helpful and studying them, using a variety of measures to see how they differ from people who are not perceived to be particularly helpful. In this way, the limitations of the traditional experimental approach would be transcended.   Starting with the perceptions of the people helped, rather than with decisions to help, ensures that the behavior has been helpful and that the nature of the interactions with recipients involved is included as a possible motivating force.   Furthermore people who are seen as helpful have doubtless over time carried out a number of spontaneous acts of helping which frees the investigation from the limits of having information concerning only the determinants of a choice under particular contrived circumstances.

Sources of Hypotheses

To guide the search for ways in which unusually helpful people differed from typical people, previous research provided some possible hypotheses. For example, one might expect that helpful people would be more likely than others to say that they want to relieve other people's suffering or that they are more motivated by egoistic motives like the need for Power (Winter, 1973). However, in view of the limitations of previous research, it seemed desirable to develop hypotheses from another, more direct source: an intensive study of the characteristics of a few caring people widely acknowledged to be extraordinarily helpful. The individuals chosen for study were healers, since healers are known to be often very helpful and are almost universally highly regarded, often with reverence.

One such person is Mother Teresa of Calcutta who has cared for the poorest of the poor, the sick and the dying. Much has been written by Mother Teresa and about her (e.g., Mother Teresa, 1983; Chawla, 1992) so that her chief characteristics are well-known. She draws inspiration from the example of Jesus Christ, another famous healer, whose characteristics are well-documented. By way of contrast, the characteristics and approach of Karmu, an African-American healer (now deceased) who lived in eastern Massachusetts, was intensively studied by David McClelland over a period of 15 years. The advantage of his case is that he did not belong to any particular religious tradition, but had evolved his own special approach to healing drawn from African, Jewish, Christian, Tibetan and "New Age" teachings. He healed the poorest of the poor—outcasts from the American medical system: the street people—as evidenced by the enthusiastic written testimonials of hundreds of them. The details on how he healed and on whether his "medical miracles" were "real" are not relevant here. For purposes of this research project, it is sufficient to know that he was esteemed to be extraordinarily caring, as were Jesus and Mother Teresa.

The most striking aspect of Karmu's approach to healing was that he did not believe that he, personally, was doing the helping or healing. Rather, he described what he did as putting the suffering people in tune, or in touch, with a beneficent power within themselves that performed the actual healing. He believed that he shared in that power and could work with it, or under its direction, in helping others. As Karmu frequently said to patients, "You have the power within you to heal yourself; God gave me the power to put you in touch with it or free you so that it can do its work." Mother Teresa (1983) says something very similar: "I am doing this because I believe I am doing it for Jesus. I am very sure that this is his work. I am very sure that it is he and not me." Similar themes are attributed to Jesus: "The Son can do nothing of himself" (John 5:19); "I and my Father are one" (John 10:30); "It is the Father who dwells in me doing his own work" (John 14:10). This strong belief held by outstanding healers that they are not doing the work, but some other power is doing the work through them, stands in sharp contrast to the psychological notion of the helper as agent or as motivated by self-serving reasons.

The second characteristic of these outstanding healers is that they all focused intensely on the relationship with the person being helped. Each believed that the relationship involved an exchange that was meaningful to both parties and sought primarily to establish that relationship. The relief of suffering was not the primary goal of the contact, but, rather, served as an occasion for establishing a meaningful and rewarding relationship. For Karmu, this was typically reflected in the time he spent in first establishing a relationship with patients. In Mother Teresa's words (1983): "We have a great people among us, only we do not know it. . . . We do not realize the greatness of the poor and how much they give us. It is a wonder. . . . It is not how much we do but how much love we put in the doing—a lifelong sharing of love with others."

Jesus of Nazareth likewise made it clear that his healing encounters were not an end in themselves, but a means of establishing a relationship with him and with God. When a woman touched him to be healed, he went out of his way to find her and convey to her the message, "Your faith has made you whole" (Luke 8:48). A key motive for all the healing activities characteristic of these caring people was the establishment of a deeper, meaningful relationship with the person being helped. None of them entered into the relationship for money. The traditional research paradigm for the study of helping behaviors precludes these types of observation because it does not allow for such relationships.

Finally, all these healers were extraordinarily energized and joyful rather than feeling stressed or burned out from their activities. Once again, this stands in contrast to the experience of many helping professionals who are subject to stress and burnout (Maslach & Jackson, 1982). Karmu was subjected to extraordinary demands for services; he was available 24 hours a day to anyone who walked into his small room. Yet, neither he nor Mother Teresa was ever heard to complain or say things like, "I feel emotionally drained by my work" or "working with people all day is really a strain for me" (items from the Maslach Burnout Inventory). Each clearly found joy in what they were doing. Mother Teresa (1983), in the midst of work which would discourage and sadden most people, says: "Where Jesus is . . . there is joy, there is peace, there is love. And that is why he made himself the Bread of Life to be our life of love and joy. . . . The sisters are always smiling and happy." Or as Jesus himself put it, "That my joy may be in you and your joy may be complete" (John 15:11).

Hypotheses

Based on these three dominant characteristics of people considered to be extraordinarily caring, the following hypotheses were developed:

1. A caring religious, as compared to typical religious, will feel in closer contact with, and greater trust in, a benevolent authority (God) who helps or heals.
2. The caring religious will show signs of greater interpersonal involvement in describing caring experiences than the typical religious.
3. Caring religious will experience more joy in caring, whereas typical members will view caring more often as a response to someone else's need or suffering.

METHOD

Sample

Packets containing information regarding the Religious Life Futures Project and the Caring People component were sent to the major superiors of 56 randomly selected Roman Catholic religious orders of women and men. Included in the packets were an explanatory letter and ten packets of nomination forms, one for the superior's own use and nine for distribution among members who would be "in a good position to know a number of other members of the order or community." Each person receiving forms was asked to nominate as many as three members of their community who were "unusually helpful, thoughtful, understanding or caring persons." They were also asked to give reasons for their nominations, including a particular episode if it came to mind. They were instructed to "keep in mind that we are looking for enduring characteristics and not isolated instances of behaviors." The major superior also was asked to provide names and addresses of "typical" members of the congregation in four different age groups. This was to establish control groups. Of the 56 congregations contacted, 31 (55%) responded.

To identify caring subjects, recommendation by two or more nominators was set as a criterion and comments about the nominations were occasionally used in the final selection. This generated a pool of 57 unusually caring religious: 34 men, drawn from 13 orders, and 23 women, drawn from 12 orders. Fifty-seven of the typical nominees, matched with the caring group on age, sex, geographic location and type of congregation (contemplative, apostolic, monastic or mendicant), were selected for comparison.

Measures

Packets were mailed to each of the 114 subjects. They included a cover letter, the National Survey, and a variety of open-ended and self-report measures, most of which are described below in connection with the hypotheses. The packet also included the five-item Zest Scale (Veroff, Douvan and Kulka, 1981), in which the person rates on a 4-point scale the extent to which they are hopeful, feel useful and have a full life, as well as the NEO-FFI (Costa and McCrae, 1989a), a measure of personality characteristics such as emotional lability, agreeableness, conscientiousness, openness, and extraversion.

To test the first hypothesis, that caring religious, in contrast to typical religious, should feel in closer contact with, and greater trust in, a benevolent authority (God) who helps or heals, the subjects completed a version of the Thematic Apperception Test or Picture-Story Exercise (PSE). It was scored for the three traditional motives: need ($\underline{n}$) for Achievement, need for Affiliation, and need for Power. (For scoring systems, see Smith, 1992.) It was also coded for socialized power motivation (s Power), as described by McClelland and Franz (1992), because it represents the need to act influentially and responsibly on behalf of others (McClelland et al., 1972).

Finally, the PSE was coded for two other dispositional variables directly related to this hypothesis. The first is Affiliative Trust-mistrust, for which a reliable and valid scoring system has been developed by McKay (1992). Those who score high on this variable tend to view relationships as trustworthy, positive and enjoyable, whereas those who score low on it describe relationships in a negative and cynical way. Furthermore, Affiliative Trust is related to better health (McClelland, 1989), and those who score high on this variable show a greater reduction in psychosomatic symptoms than other individuals after participating in a behavioral medicine treatment program (McKay, 1991). It was therefore expected that caring religious would show greater affiliative trust according to this measure, which might contribute to the trust and confidence of those being helped and, consequently, to their well-being.

Oneness motivation (Weinberger and McLeod, 1989) was also scored from the written responses. This reliable scoring system measures the degree to which a person seeks to become one with something outside the self, either through a close personal relationship, being part of a greater whole or through a "merger" or "flow" experience. If the first hypothesis is correct, it seems reasonable to expect that caring religious would tell more stories involving thoughts of being at one with a greater power. To determine if the greater power was God, all subjects were asked the following:

> Sometimes we are aware that we have been part of a "healing experience." The experience may have occurred to you or another person; you may have had an active or passive role in the healing. The healing itself could have taken many forms—spiritual, physical, emotional, psychological. Please describe, in as much detail as possible, a healing experience in which you have been involved recently.

Many of the descriptions dealt with personal healing described in psychological terms. When divine assistance was spontaneously mentioned in describing the healing, it was coded. The expectation was that divine assistance would be mentioned more often by the caring than by the typical religious.

To test the second hypothesis, that the caring religious will show signs of greater interpersonal involvement in describing caring experiences than typical religious, the subjects were asked the following two questions:

1. Please think of a time in your life when you experienced being cared for. How did you feel? Think of the event itself, go over

it in your mind. It could have involved your relationship to God
or Christ, to others in the congregation, to family or friends. It
may have involved medical, psychological or spiritual help you
received, or caring in a loving relationship. Go over the episode
in your mind for about five minutes, and then write out what
happened, especially how you felt. Choose the experience that is
most vivid for you.

2. Being loved and cared for often involves feelings of love in
return. Now, please think of a time when you felt strong love for
someone. This person may have been God or Christ, a friend, a
child, a teacher or a stranger. Go over the episode in your mind
for about five minutes, and then describe it below, especially how
you felt. Choose the experience that is most vivid for you.

Two coding systems, designed to measure degree of interpersonal involvement,
were derived specifically for this study. One centered on whether the caring
relationships were described as growing over time and mutual, while the other
focused on whether the relationships were described as having a meaning or a
wider significance extending beyond the description of what happened. It was
expected that caring religious would score higher on both these signs of greater
personal involvement than would typical religious.

To test the third hypothesis, that caring religious will experience more joy
in caring whereas typical religious will view caring as need-driven, two
measures were used. The first part of this hypothesis was measured simply by
the number of "joy" words used in describing the two caring episodes, which
was expected to be greater among the caring religious. The second part of the
hypothesis was tested by the extent to which subjects mentioned a reason for
caring for another, the reason being either a need in the care giver, such as guilt
or duty, or a special need of the person in some kind of trouble (illness, trauma,
rejection, etc.). In such instances, caring was presented in terms of relieving
tension or distress which, if too high, could lead to the sense of burn out that
is characteristic of some caring professionals (Maslach & Jackson, 1982).

In all instances, free response items and stories were blind coded as to type
of religious by raters who had demonstrated their ability to code to at least an
84% level of agreement with expert coding for the variable in question.

RESULTS

Fairly complete protocols were received from 24 of the typical religious
(11 men, 13 women), and 31 of the caring religious (13 men, 18 women), for
a useable return rate of 47%. The numbers vary slightly in the presentation of
results due to incomplete protocols.

The groups were comparable in age, with the average being 58.6 years for the typical religious and 54.2 years for the caring group. They did not differ significantly from each other in the proportions of different fields of service represented. Overall, 20% came from the field of education, 24% from administration, 27% from the ministry and the remaining 29% from a variety of other areas. The caring religious were less well educated on the average than the typical religious (p < .05), with the difference lying between some graduate work beyond college for caring religious as compared with attaining a master's degree for the typical religious.

Table 6.1

Comparison of Caring and Typical Religious on Various Motivational Characteristics

Story Characteristics	Typical Religious (T) (N=18)		Caring Religious (C) (N=30)		Diff. (C-T)	p
	Mean	SD	Mean	SD		
Number of Words in 6 Stories	919.80	420.50	897.20	423.90	-22.60	ns
n̲ Achievement	7.33	5.53	6.37	4.69	-.96	ns
n̲ Affiliation	9.72	5.53	9.93	3.97	.21	ns
n̲ Power	5.11	3.93	6.30	3.52	1.19	ns
s Power Index	1.56	1.46	1.47	1.41	-.10	ns
Affiliative Trust [a]	4.24	2.04	5.07	2.39	.83	ns
Affiliative Mistrust [a]	1.06	1.06	.41	.56	-.65	< .05
Trust-Mistrust [a]	3.18	1.88	4.66	2.41	1.48	< .05

[a] Outliers were dropped by the Tukey (1977) interquartile range test. For typical religious, N=17; for caring religious, N=29.

Table 6.1 shows the average scores of the typical and caring religious on various motive variables, as scored in the PSE. Because there was no significant difference in protocol length for the two types of religious, raw motive scores were not corrected for number of words in the six stories for comparison of averages. The traditional personal motives involving needs for Achievement, Affiliation and Power did not differentiate between the two groups. The caring religious did not score higher than the typical religious even on the most theoretically relevant variable, socialized power motivation (s Power), which has generally been considered to measure the extent to which a person wants to be influential on behalf of others (McClelland et al., 1972). The s Power index is described in McClelland and Franz (1992).

On the other hand, the first hypothesis receives some support from the fact that, as predicted, the caring people score higher in net Affiliative Trust (positive minus negative Affiliative Trust imagery) and lower in Mistrust. Caring people tend to think more often of other people entering into trustworthy, positive, cooperative rather than exploitative relationships.

Table 6.2 presents the findings for Oneness motivation in terms of the frequency with which various primary types of imagery appeared for the typical and caring religious. The most striking fact is that the caring religious wrote significantly more often about a close interpersonal relationship involving benevolent authority than did the typical religious. This finding directly supports the hypothesis that caring religious will think more often in terms of a benevolent authority.

Table 6.2

Percentages of Typical and Caring Religious Showing Different Aspects of Oneness Motivation in Written Stories

Primary Types of Oneness Imagery	Typical Religious (T) (N=18)	Caring Religious (C) (N=30)	Diff. (C-T)	χ^2
1. Close interpersonal relationship		Percent present		
(a) Benevolent authority	17%	53%	36%	6.24*
(b) Other types	56%	57%	1%	ns
2. Being part of a greater whole	33%	33%	0%	ns
3. Merging or flow experience	50%	37%	-13%	ns

*p < .02

The caring religious also wrote about flow or merger experiences less often than the typical religious. If flow imagery is computed as a percentage of other primary types of oneness imagery, excluding benevolent authority to avoid biasing the result, in only 17% of the caring religious protocols was the flow percentage 25% or more of the total as compared to 50% for the typical religious ($\chi^2 = 3.98$, p < .05). This difference was unexpected but it is consistent with the teaching of the early Christian apostles who warned followers strongly against the dangers of psychic "flow" experiences as substitutes for real oneness with the divine in healing. See Acts 8:9-11; 18-24 for the story of Simon, the sorcerer or magician.

Divine assistance in connection with a healing experience was mentioned by 20% (4 out of 20) of the typical and 60% (15 out of 25) of the caring religious, a statistically significant difference ($\chi^2 = 9.49$, p < .01). This confirms the inference that the greater orientation of the caring religious toward benevolent authority in all likelihood derives from their personal feeling of being closer to, and more directly influenced by, God.

Activity Inhibition (AI) scores were obtained from the stories written for the PSE by counting the number of times the word *not* appeared in the six stories. Among the typical religious, 60% (12 of 20) included 4 or more instances of *not* in their protocols, compared with 33% of the caring religious $\chi^2 = 3.46$, p < .10). Thus, one might infer that the caring religious are less self-controlled or self-controlling than typical religious since the AI score has been associated with a more controlled life style (McClelland et al., 1972). That might mean that caring religious are less concerned about controlling their time and resources. Such a conclusion is consistent with the inference from previous findings that the caring religious are closer to, and more dependent on, God and, therefore, less self-dependent for direction.

Table 6.3 presents results in support of the second hypothesis. Caring religious were hypothesized to show signs of greater interpersonal involvement in describing caring experiences than typical religious. As predicted, the caring religious, as compared to the typical religious, more often gave meaning to the relationship and described relationships as rich, special, developing or mutual.

Caring people also used more "joy" words in describing the relationships. To make certain that the last finding applied to the respondents' own feelings in helping another, a separate analysis was made for self-referent "joy" words in the caring-for-another episode. In this more limited comparison, the caring religious also used significantly more "joy" words than the typical religious. Finally, as expected, significantly more of the typical than the caring religious explained their caring response for another to be due to a need in themselves or the person helped. In short, they described their helping experiences as driven primarily by distress in another or themselves.

Tables 6.4, 6.5 and 6.6 present responses of typical and caring religious to various items on the survey as they relate to the three main hypotheses that guided the study. In general, self-reported feelings and concerns yielded results consistent with the hypotheses but only occasionally were these at accepted levels of significance. Thus, on two of the three items the caring religious reported feeling closer to God (see Table 6.4), but at nonsignificant levels.

Table 6.3
Mean Frequencies of Characteristics Mentioned in Describing
Caring Experiences among Typical and Caring Religious

Characteristics of Descriptions of Two Caring Experiences	Typical Religious (T) (N=21)	Caring Religious (C) (N=27)	Diff. (C-T)
Meaning given to the relationship			
M	.90	1.44	.54*
SD	.81	.50	
Depth of relationship			
M	.38	1.26	.88**
SD	.65	.80	
Joy words			
M	.43	1.19	.76*
SD	.66	1.39	
Self-referent joy words in caring-for episode			
M	.19	.81	.62*
SD	.50	1.16	
Need-driven caring for another [a,b]			
Percent present	64%	26%	

[a] N=22 for typical religious.   [b] χ^2=7.12, p<.05.
*p<.05
**p<.01

On the third item, the trend was in favor of the typical religious. However, a much higher percentage of the caring than typical religious reported that resting in contemplative prayer is very important to them, a finding that is consistent with evidence from their open-ended responses, indicating that they felt themselves to be in closer touch with God.

On five items dealing with greater interpersonal involvement (Table 6.5), and on the sum of their responses to them, the caring religious reported greater involvement than the typical religious, but none of the differences reached accepted levels of significance. Caring religious report higher Zest scores (Veroff et al., 1981), as expected, than did the typical religious. (See Table 6.6.)

Table 6.4
Data Related to Hypothesis 1: Caring Religious in Contrast to Typical
Religious Will Feel in Closer Contact with and Greater Trust in a
Benevolent Authority (God) Which Helps/Heals

	Typical Religious (N=24)	Caring Religious (N=32)
I frequently have:		
A sense of being in the presence of God	58%	74%
A feeling of being embraced by God	38%	48%
An overwhelming feeling of being at one with God or Christ	38%	29%
What is very valuable:		
Resting in contemplative prayer	46%**	84%**

Note: Percentages without a superscript are not significantly different.
**p < .01

On the measure of self-attributed personality characteristics, caring religious were significantly higher in "agreeableness" (Costa and McCrae, 1989a) than were typical religious (mean = 64.45 versus 58.17 respectively). In general, agreeable people tend to be compassionate, good-natured, eager to cooperate and enjoy helping people. Caring men were found to be high in emotional lability (mean = 53.08) and caring women lower in lability (mean 45.89) as compared with typical men and women (F (1,3) = 2.29, p < .10; two-way interaction F (1,3) = 5.83, p < .02). This result suggests that caring men attribute to themselves greater sensitivity and emotion than do typical men; the caring women appear less sensitive or more calm and relaxed even under stressful conditions than the typical women (Costa and McCrae, 1989b). Caring men and women, it seems, respond to experiences in ways that are not sex-stereotyped. Finally, there is no evidence that the typical religious were consciously attracted more to helping those in need, despite the fact that, as Table 6.3 shows, they tend to see helping in terms of responding to needs.

Table 6.5

Data Related to Hypothesis 2: Caring Religious Will Show Greater
Interpersonal Involvement than Typical Religious

	Typical Religious (N=24)	Caring Religious (N=29)
Scale of 1-7 (very typical of me)		
Have sympathetic concern for others		
M	6.04	6.21
SD	.96	.82
Like to care for others		
M	5.67	5.86
SD	1.01	1.03
Warm in my interpersonal relations		
M	5.75	5.97
SD	.94	.77
Making new friends		
M	5.04	5.20
SD	1.27	1.10
Not afraid to let others get close to me		
M	4.75	5.23
SD	1.48	1.14
Sum of interpersonal involvement items		
M	27.25	28.47
SD	3.78	4.25

SUMMARY

The findings provide significant support for the hypotheses derived from studying outstanding healers.

First, members of religious orders who are perceived as unusually helpful, understanding and caring, in contrast to typical religious, feel in closer contact with and experience greater trust in a benevolent authority (God) as evidenced by the following facts:

1. They scored higher in Affiliative Trust and in the benevolent authority aspect of Oneness motivation;
2. They showed a sign of being less self-controlling than other members of religious orders, as shown by their lower Activity Inhibition scores;
3. They more often stated that they find resting in contemplative prayer very valuable; and
4. More often than typical religious, they mentioned divine assistance in connection with a healing experience.

Table 6.6

Data Related to Hypothesis 3: Caring Religious Will Experience More Joy
in Caring While Typical Religious Will See Caring as a Response to
Need

	Typical Religious (N=24)	Caring Religious (N=32)
Scale of 1-4 (nearly always)		
Zest (sum of 5 items)		
M	16.17*	17.73*
SD	2.81	1.74
What is very valuable:		
Visiting the sick	42%	58%
Helping people who are poor	46%	68%
Supporting causes of minorities	38%	52%
Action on behalf of mentally ill or		
retarded persons	29%	23%

Note. Percentages without a superscript are not significantly different.
*p < .02
**p < .01

Second, caring religious showed greater interpersonal involvement in the experience of caring than typical religious, as evidenced by the facts that they more often described caring relationships as special, developing or mutual and that they more often attribute meaning or a wider significance to the relationship described.

Third, caring religious reported more joy in describing caring experiences, as evidenced by the number of "joy" words they used to describe the experiences and by the zest in living that they reported. In contrast, typical religious more often described caring as a response to a need in themselves (as in caring out of duty or a desire to repay someone), or as a response to needs in others (arising, for example, from illness, rejection or trauma).

DISCUSSION

In general, the hypotheses are more strongly supported by spontaneous responses to open-ended questions than by self-reports of relevant attitudes and feelings. This was expected, because self-reports may be more influenced by self-presentation biases than free response answers in which the subject has no clear idea of what kind of answer is most appropriate. For example, typical religious did not report significantly less often than caring religious that they frequently had "A sense of being in the presence of God" (Table 6.4), a reply that might be expected of a devout person.

On the other hand, when there was no suggestion that the answer should relate to religious teachings or norms, as in the item that asked for description of a healing experience, four times as many of the caring as the typical religious spontaneously mentioned God's role in the experience. Caring religious strongly sense that God plays a more active role in their lives than do the typical religious, a difference which was not picked up in a self-report item suggesting a conventional or desirable response.

How do these results fit with conclusions drawn from prior research on helping? They do not fit very well, for a variety of reasons. Traditionally, psychologists have concluded that helping behavior derives either from a desire to relieve the need of another or one's own need to obtain relief from empathy-induced distress. To a certain extent this theorizing has been guided by the implicit assumption about motivation that people must want to do whatever they do. If they achieve, they must want to achieve; if they help, they must want to help. Moreover, subjects are guided by the same implicit assumption so that if they are asked in various, more or less subtle ways why they help, they are apt to answer, "because I want to help." Thus, if subjects say that they feel compassionate about someone in need—which implies that they want to help—they, in fact, say they want to help in order to project a desired, consistent self-image.

To move beyond such obvious connections, one must employ measures that are less influenced than self-reports are by semantic relationships and the need for self-consistency. When this was done in the present study, two interesting findings emerged. The typical religious tended to think of helping in terms of responses to needs, just as psychologists do, and more than the caring religious did. There was no evidence that any of the traditional motives, measured in associative thought or self-report, differentiated the two types of members of religious orders. The caring religious did not score higher than the typical religious on self-reported desires to relieve suffering or on such "self-fulfilling" drives as need for Achievement, need for Affiliation or need for Power, even when the latter was turned into socialized power motivation which reflects a concern for influencing what happens on behalf of others (McClelland, 1975). Hence, there is little evidence here to support traditional self-focussed explanations of the motivation for helping (Batson, 1987; Schaller & Cialdini, 1990).

However, in this study we attempted to explain the motivation for an outcome variable (perceived caring) that was quite different from the one typically employed in research in this area. Our interest here was not to explain a cognitive choice to help but to explain why some people are perceived as helpful over time, when helping has been a response in which they spontaneously engaged. At the very least, these results suggest that these two types of helping have very different determinants and that it would be a serious mistake to assume that what determines a cognitive choice to help tells us anything about what determines spontaneous helpful behavior.

This unique research paradigm also emphasizes relationships as a key aspect of helping and one that traditional research paradigms cannot include. The findings in this study show that establishing a meaningful, developing and mutual relationship with a person in need provides what appears to be a key attraction for helpful people. The findings also show that, for caring people, joy is a key element in helping, yet the traditional paradigm has no way of studying joy in the helping relationship (because no actual relationship is permitted). On the other hand, a large body of evidence from this tradition suggests that happiness or a positive mood is associated with helping (Schaller & Cialdini, 1990). This might mean that people who are generally energetic and cheerful are more likely to help, or that those who find joy in helping relationships specifically are more likely to help. The second possibility seems more likely than the first since there was no evidence that the caring people were happier in general outside the area of caring relationships or higher on self-fulfilling motives associated with a happy mood (Schaller & Cialdini, 1990).

Why, then, do helpful people help? The findings suggest that to answer this question, the simple notion of trying to explain why A acts on B in a helpful way, must be dropped. The reason is that, for truly helpful people, there is a third force in the transaction, that which might be most generally called a "benevolent authority." For members of religious orders in this study, this third force is more simply named "God." The caring person stays in close touch with the third force and wants to share its benevolent influence with others. Thus when encountering a person in need, the immediate impulse for the caring religious is not primarily to relieve his or her suffering but to invite the other person into a three-way relationship in which the divine is deeply involved. The joy and the motivation for the helping that were evidenced in this study come out of establishing a meaningful relationship with the sufferer and sharing the good news that God is present and can help. Helpers of this type do not see themselves as agents in the helping; at most, they are partners with, or assistants to, the real source of helping. Nor do these helpers feel ultimately responsible. For this reason, and also because the helping transaction in itself is joyous, they do not burn out as readily as other helpers.

This description also helps explain why people who are motivated in this way are perceived to be helpful rather than manipulative. Because they so obviously feel that they are not doing the helping and that they want to establish a mutually rewarding relationship, it would be difficult for the people helped to perceive the other as egoistically threatening their self-esteem, interpersonal power or independence (Fisher, Nadler & Witcher-Alagna, 1982).

There are many implications in this research for members of religious orders. Most striking perhaps is the consistency of these findings with both classic and contemporary writers in the area of spirituality who speak of self-emptying (Philippians 2:1-4; Neal, 1977), the vulnerability of the healer (Isaiah 42:1-3; 53:1-5; Nouwen, 1972), and the significance of a spirituality based on the awareness of blessing rather than guilt (Fox, 1983).

Particularly for members of apostolic and mendicant groups, understanding one's own dynamics in relationships with persons in ministerial situations is critical. This is true both for the person in need of ministry and the minister. Education along motivational lines can be pursued and might be included as a part of members' ongoing formation.

As regards candidates and those involved in the initial phases of integration into an order, some assessment of the motive structure and plans to reconcile the gaps between the individual and the profile of a caring person could be pursued.

If religious orders are to continue to undertake seriously their mission of ministry to those who are most in need, understanding the motive structure of the caring person will be a critical factor in ensuring that the work that is done is truly the work of God and not of oneself, and that the energies of the religious orders are channeled in the most effective manner. It long has been an axiom among religious persons that "grace builds on nature." This study provides an excellent resource for building on this truth. The results of this study should also influence religious orders as they clarify their unique contribution to the church and society.

Chapter 7

BRIDGING THE GAP

PARADIGM SHIFTS IDENTIFIED

The first two decades following Vatican II contained enormous energy and dynamic change within and around religious orders in the United States. The boundaries between members of religious orders and the laity, for instance, were relaxed. The sect-like separatism that had differentiated various traditions among the orders was largely eliminated. More permeability and change characterized emerging social, spiritual, ministerial and communal lives of members of religious orders. The attributes of the more static institution that had for so long typified religious orders shifted.

The last ten years, however, have been ones in which the recognition of certain truths became inevitable. For instance, despite the satisfaction of members in ministry, the population of members of religious orders continues to decline in number and increase in age. The increasing awareness of the unique contribution of women and the influence of feminism in the life of the church complements a greater adaptation to changing conditions.

The classic institutional forms of monasticism, apostolic life, cloistered life and mendicantism have, in some instances, been altered substantially, becoming strong social networks with highly fluid concepts of membership and work. Almost suddenly, it seems, members of religious orders in the United States are asking if they are where they intended to be when Vatican II invited the changes to begin.

This research project began with the purpose of identifying those changes that must yet occur if religious life is to remain a vital social institution in American society and the church. Religious life at the levels of the social institution, congregations and individual behavior and beliefs was examined. What is most evident is that the degree of change that has occurred, and continues to occur, is drastic by any standard. Findings reveal that the paradigms that pervaded religious orders prior to Vatican II (namely, those of consistency, objectivity, standardization, compliance and institutional form) have altered irreversibly. Changes that began with Vatican II continue. They parallel American cultural and organizational shifts that consider change as a normative condition for organizations. Nonetheless, the question arises: Is it possible to sustain a social institution as diversified in purpose as religious life without some sense of identity that is agreed on by those who commit their lives to it?

In Chapter 1, four paradigms that appear to operate within organizations were identified. The particular assumptions underlying the functionalist, interpretive, radical-humanist and radical-structuralist paradigms were each specified. To recall, the functionalist paradigm assumes that organizations are oriented to produce an ordered and regulated state of affairs. The interpretive paradigm assumes that organizations are constructed by a variety of subjective interpretive schemes that support particular worldviews. The radical-humanist paradigm assumes that organizations can fail to elaborate subjective experience and are, therefore, largely alienating. Finally, the radical-structuralist paradigm assumes that in organizations or society, some groups dominate others. Change, in this last condition, occurs when those being held in check by the individuals in power begin to transcend domination through constructive action.

Religious orders in the United States today reflect all four paradigms. They include the poles of subjectivity or individualism, on the one hand, and objectivity and a drive toward standardization, on the other. They also tend to be driven by interpretations or preferences for radical change and social regulation. As transformation has occurred over a 30-year period, it has been fostered, experienced and described in ways that depended on some variation of these four organizational paradigms. The interpretive schemes used to describe their lives are rooted more in contemporary idioms than in traditional language and constructs. Where religious orders are most alive, they are extremely vital social and religious organizations.

However, what appears to be happening in the transformation process overall is a movement from the more interpretive paradigm toward the functionalist or structuralist paradigms. This is seen in two distinct ways. For instance, the functionalist assumptions operate in the efforts to determine a single identity or role-state for this population that is regulated, identified by its work or dress and less permeable in membership. For others, however, the radical-structuralist paradigm is more meaningful. The structuralist approach characterizes, for instance, the radical feminist approaches that see the way forward as necessarily eliminating many existing models of power in the church. Both the functionalist and the structuralist paradigms are championed currently as a means of stabilizing religious orders that continue to dwindle.

In the course of the study we observed that while some vibrant groups are organized by principles of social conformity, others that are equally vital were structured to effect radical change. However, this research suggests that while the transformation of religious life continues, the efforts to resolve paradigmatic diversity alone are likely not to resolve the fundamental question of the identity of members of religious orders in the church and society. In fact, the emergent forms will reflect the very diversity that the various paradigms suggest exists.

The challenges that are most pressing relate to consistency of purpose and the credibility of mission. Tushman and Romanelli (1985) suggested that organizational paradigms evolve in either of two ways. The first involves processes of *convergence* that operate through incremental change mechanisms to align and make consistent the complex of dynamics that support an organization's particular orientation to purpose and mission (strategy). The second involves *reorientation*, in which patterns of consistency are reordered dramatically toward a new sense of purpose and alignment with the external environment. They suggest that transformation occurs only when executive leadership has the capacity to engage key interventions in either periods of convergence or reorientation.

This study began with the belief that total reorientation would lead to transformation and that forms of incrementalism were ineffectual, given the scope of change occurring since Vatican II. We have seen, however, that processes of convergence that operate through incremental change mechanisms can indeed be effective, depending on the desired state that is imagined or pursued. For instance, orders that historically have been effective in the functionalist paradigm in some circumstances still operate effectively despite the dominant paradigm shifts occurring in religious life. In these instances, there has not been a radical paradigm shift. Congregations such as the Little Sisters of the Poor, the Benedictine Monks and the Daughters of Charity appear to operate from functionalist assumptions regarding their mission; from that perspective, their paradigms have not shifted dramatically. Therefore, their change processes reflect the dynamics of convergence rather than reorientation.

These orders, from a business perspective, operate primarily from a product orientation. They have a particular delivery system that allows for standardization and a relatively clear sense of purpose. They pray, they teach, they work as social servants, they minister in hospitals. At the level of the social institution, the services of these congregations are often in competition with providers outside the church context. They remain clearly Catholic in order to maintain their independent value orientation and distinctiveness in the marketplace of service. At the congregational level, the focused mission typically requires a degree of conformity among most of the members. At the level of the individual member, the orientation of the congregation exacts a high commitment to the work of the group and a willingness to render authority to a more centralized form of governance.

On the other hand, many, if not most, religious orders interpreted the call for updating as requiring dramatic reorientation after Vatican II. The form of religious life was unfrozen from its assumptions, practices and purposes. The paradigms shifted rapidly from strictest forms of standardization and conformity to expressive forms of individual action that were no longer bound by either top-down control or social conformity. In these orders, the patterns of consistency were reordered dramatically to assume a new sense of mission and alignment with the external environment. Many orders are well on their way to accomplishing this reorientation. The Sisters of Loretto, for instance, shifted their paradigm to incorporate explicitly members of the laity into an intimate collaboration in their life and work. The Sisters of St. Joseph, one of the many congregations known for their outstanding achievements in American education, have reoriented their life and work toward unity and reconciliation, their founding charism. The Alexian Brothers have aligned their dominant works in health care to reflect attention to the external environment. Their efforts on behalf of persons with AIDS are now widely recognized as reorienting many of the assumptions of Catholic health care.

From a business perspective, these orders have changed from a predominantly product orientation to a market orientation. They recognize that their specific charism requires a unique sensitivity to the pressing social needs of the time and they are willing to risk all, even their very existence, to be responsive to a particular need or end. Both the product and market orientations assume a high degree of relevance between the congregation and the society. What is likely to vary most between the two distinct approaches in ministry is the form or structure required to enable the advancement of the mission.

When determining the shifts in paradigms that are occurring, it is clear that the functionalists are in a period of convergence while the structuralists continue to advance reorientation. Both approaches have very strong merit and both have the potential to yield fruitful outcomes.

If the dominant orientation to ministry is to assist society and individuals by delivering some specified form of ministerial care in response to a need, a clear product line may be required. Homeless persons need shelter; persons with AIDS need medical care and comforting support; hungry people need food.

The functionalist paradigm would respond to these needs by delivering some calculated and controlled response to these issues. An order operating with functionalist assumptions would identify those concerns it believes are consistent with their purpose and organize a system of delivery that would then require competent staffing to maintain. Historically, at least, this has been the dominant paradigm. As individual members respond to God's call in vocation, there is some clarity in identifying the type of work one might do in living out that call.

The Jesuits provide an interesting illustration which is, however, limited in its application because of complexity regarding the shifts that are occurring. Ask any individual on the street, Catholic or non-Catholic, what the Jesuits represent in American society and the response will generally be "excellence in education." Although many Jesuits perform numerous other highly necessary and valued ministries for the church, including spiritual direction, direct service of the poor and pastoral ministry, they continue to be recognized for the excellent product they deliver, particularly in higher education. However, in attempts to come closer to their charism, the Jesuits have identified a faith that does justice as a critical concern. For the Jesuits, the product of educational excellence does not translate, or has not easily translated, into a convergence between their espoused mission of a faith that works for justice and the product of education. In fact, many Jesuits challenge the validity of institutions to accomplish this end.

The research would suggest that most members of religious orders operate from the belief that reorientation is occurring, that is, that the functionalist paradigm and the product orientation are insufficient. They believe that the former structures of religious orders will not work in the contemporary world. The national leadership conferences of women and men religious appear to operate from the perspective of reorientation as well. However, the success of reorientation can only happen if a new sense of purpose and alignment occurs in relation to the external environment. This is the point at which many of the efforts at reorientation have not succeeded. For example, some religious orders have adopted as a primary focus the preferential option for the poor. This is stated throughout the research, in the Visioning Groups, the National Survey and various studies of leadership. Unfortunately, for a host of reasons, reorientation to this fundamental purpose has been stalled. Dialogue with the external environment has been eclipsed by concerns internal to the orders such as diminished personnel, retirement needs, financial limits and institutional relinquishment. Moving from a product orientation (for example, providing education) to a market orientation (such as serving those needs that are consistent with a congregation's purpose and valued by the society) requires a different structure, different resources and a different way of perceiving work. Some orders have managed to integrate the product and the market orientations into one cohesive system. Ironically, these instances tend to occur in those congregations with a tradition of serving the poor through a complex, integrated network of services. These orders often operate from the functionalist paradigm, enacting convergence processes involving incremental change, and often are oriented by social regulation. They have been effective in attracting membership and conducting ministry that is perceived as important to the society and the church.

This implies that both convergence and reorientation perspectives have validity. Incremental change, as well as radical, discontinuous change, must be motivated by a clear sense of what a group wishes to become. Vast literatures and intense debates regarding the type of change required to be faithful to the Gospel call to follow Jesus have emerged during the 30 years since Vatican II. Determining exactly how a congregation will serve heightens awareness of what the congregation will do to express itself in the society and the church, a predominantly product orientation. Exploring who a congregation will serve focuses attention on the needs that are evident and pressing, and usually involves proceeding from a market orientation. For a religious congregation, a mission that addresses a real need is likely to yield greater resources to accomplish these ends.

Present Gaps Experienced by Members of Religious Orders

As congregations undertake change processes, either of convergence or reorientation, a gap will always remain between what they aspire to become and where they stand at present. This gap is to be expected, given the orientation of religious orders to Gospel ideals. We have identified several ideal states, as imagined by the visionary members and some leaders of the orders, and the actual lived reality: the gaps, so to speak, between the espoused and the operative values. Gaps exist between perceptions of leaders and members, as well as among various age cohorts and different segments or populations in the church. For example, those who believe reorientation is the only hope for religious orders and those who believe in convergence processes that occur through modest incremental change efforts are distant.

What follows is an elaboration of some of the gaps that were identified in the research. It is not intended to reinstate "perfectionistic" or conformist inclinations, but rather to evidence the frame within which the action of God occurs. They are put forward from the data gathered from the various units of the research project, reflecting on the lived experience of members of religious orders, their ideals and their vision. The exploratory and empirical perspectives of the more than 10,000 individual sisters, brothers and religious priests who were invited to participate in some part of the research provides a lens into the current experience and the desired future of religious life. The model of change proposed will hopefully advance the process of transformation into what can be a window of opportunity for focus. This option has a limited life, and failure to respond will significantly restrict religious life.

Gaps exist between the ideal of religious life as it has been espoused since Vatican II and the lived reality of members of religious orders. The question arises about how to resolve these gaps between the vision and the reality. Some would argue that institutionalizing the forms of religious orders is the way forward. For instance, they would propose to sharpen the distinctions between the lay and the religious vocations, both theologically and practically. Others would argue that the transformation is still on its way to some yet unidentified new and vibrant state, and that the process of moving forward supersedes the outcome. However, either approach to transformation must first address the desired state it hopes to achieve in whatever process it adopts.

The history of religious life is replete with examples of orders that expand and contract along with the political and social dynamics of the church and society. For instance, following the massive upheaval of the French Revolution in Europe, Benedictine foundations declined from nearly 2,000 to approximately 20 by 1815. In contrast, the Daughters of Charity in Europe during the nineteenth century attracted nearly 700 novices a year through the period of industrialization (Langlois, 1984). Their responsiveness to the alienated and subjected worker, the enormous poverty of the time and the enhancement of the dignity of women through this apostolic endeavor yielded a strength that was seemingly unparalleled in the history of religious orders. Observing the historical facts is necessary but not sufficient to describe how and whether a transformation of the vibrant social institution of religious life may have been initiated in the past and if it can be anticipated or directed in our time.

The quality of national, congregational and individual leadership is essential to the successful implementation of the change and reorientation process. However, in this study the perspectives of leaders did not necessarily correspond with those of the members of religious orders on several key dimensions. In some instances, the imagination of leaders outpaced that of members. In other contexts, leaders appeared to have been selected to retain the status quo. One of the fundamental tasks of leadership is to name the dynamics and keep the group focused on bridging the gap between the ideals and the actual life of the congregation.

Naming the gaps that exist in the lives of members of religious orders can help give direction to the future. Narrowing the gap between the ideals set forth for individuals, congregations and religious life and their current practice is part of the process of transformation. What follows is a formulation of those gaps and some of the major issues to be considered as the future of religious life in the United States is shaped.

Resolving Discrepancies

A significant gap between their own self-identity and the actual strength they can exert in the world exists for members of religious orders. The inconsistencies between their espoused values and their operative ones leads members to feel a discrepancy that is increasingly challenged by those who remain. This section explores what happens psychologically as individuals and groups become aware of the fact that they are not who they say they are.

Using the espoused value of the "preferential option" for the poor as an example, the structures, life-styles and ministries of the apostolic orders do not yet reflect that singularly strong espoused commitment to minister for and among the poor. This is a discrepancy: members of congregations do not express behaviorally or in intention the degree of commitment to participate in an activity that has become increasingly an espoused value for many congregations and quite explicitly by the church.

While it is true that sisters, members of apostolic groups and members of religious orders in the 19-45 age group yielded the highest means, in their respective groupings, regarding their intention to engage in work with poor people, the degree of disagreement concerning the belief that this is a unique identifying attribute of religious life is significant. If service to the poor is espoused but not lived, individuals will resolve the dissonance more likely by altering the priority given to this value rather than by altering their behavior to support this espoused belief. In other words, members of religious orders might likely deemphasize the preferential option for the poor and adjust their self-definition to correspond to what it is that they are actually doing. The following section explores how to resolve this dissonance and what is likely to happen if it is not resolved.

An Example: Attitude-Behavior Congruence in Service of the Poor

Since the time of Vatican II, religious orders have been called to attend more closely to those in society who are poor. Although Catholic social teaching during the last century, and several apostolic religious orders for many more years, have emphasized the special love that should be shown to the poor, apostolic religious life is identified increasingly with this unique vocation or mission. To the extent that religious orders espouse the "preferential option" for the poor and live by that promise, they will achieve some measure of social credibility. The research indicates, however, that many members of religious orders are not necessarily committed to service to those in most need as a uniquely defining characteristic of religious life. Among the members, many do not intend to commit to this effort even though, theologically and ideologically, they seem to believe it is somehow important to being members of religious orders.

The relationship between attitudes and behavior has been examined by social psychologists from the first decades of the century up to the present (Halberstadt & Ellyson, 1990). The relationship between attitudes and behavior is, therefore, critical to resolving discrepancies. Allport (1935) proposed that attitudes are developed through four processes. The first of these is the integration of repeated responses to specific situations. The second, differentiation, develops as the infantile attitudes of approach and avoidance and matures into specific patterns of action and avoidance. A third mechanism is through traumatic experience and the fourth, the imitation of role models by analogy. If we consider how attitudes toward serving the poor emerge through these four processes, we might develop some sense of the complexity of attitude formation. If we couple that with the requirement of behavioral consistency once the attitudes are formed, we will see how difficult it is to act in a manner consistent with belief.

Festinger (1964) theorized that cognitive dissonance is created by inconsistencies between attitudes and behaviors. Dissonance is an unpleasant state of arousal in which cognitions and behaviors vary. If behavior does not correspond to attitudes, a sense of dissonance, in which the individual becomes psychically uncomfortable with the distance between the two phenomena, is said to develop. In order to reduce discomfort, the individual must change either behavior or cognition.

Situations create dissonance through a number of mechanisms. Raising inconsistent cognition and behaviors to consciousness focuses attention on it. Likewise, self-focused attention (that is, calling attention to discrepancies) tends to heighten dissonance (Wicklund & Brehm, 1976). When considering the attitudes of members of religious orders toward working with the poor, cognitive dissonance is pronounced in the relationship between the leaders' raising of the issue and followers' attitudes and behaviors. A near match between the percentage of leaders who describe themselves as committed to and prepared for working with the poor initially seems to indicate that leaders who are committed and prepared pass this on to followers.

This study's data indicates a highly significant correlation between the ability of the leader to mobilize a collective sense of action and the followers' attitude toward working with the poor. Likewise, leaders who convey a sense of mission to followers also are more likely to have followers who are both committed to and prepared for working with the poor. According to the theory of cognitive dissonance, this is a predictable result of leaders' ability to heighten cognitive awareness of the value of serving the poor. Essentially, cognitive dissonance is raised when leaders heighten awareness of the inconsistency between an attitude and a behavior. In order to reduce this experience, followers develop behaviors that are consistent with their attitudes about the importance of working with the poor.

The pitfall that leaders need to avoid when dealing with an attitude they want to instill in followers is that a suitable behavioral outlet must be available. In essence, if the leader is able to demonstrate the importance of serving the poor but followers find no behavioral outlet through which to express their convictions, it is likely that they will change attitudes in order to reduce cognitive dissonance or will likely leave religious life.

A paradox related to cognitive dissonance and behavior is that the greatest attitude change occurs when the choice is apparently the highest. In other words, in order to instill the attitude of service to the poor, the skillful leader must demonstrate that such a form of service is a choice. Members of apostolic orders become entirely frustrated when the congregation espouses service among the poor but retains traditional ministries that, in fact, have little to do with the poor. Consciously or unconsciously, individual members react strongly to discrepancies between the espoused value and how the order actually allocates finances and personnel to the work of the congregation. Similarly, monastics and contemplatives, who do not view service of the poor generally as part of their charism or tradition, are likely to experience dissonance in more subtle ways. Given the importance of work and prayer in their lives, the greatest dissonance will arise when these values are not lived to the fullest. Moreover, the data does suggest that monastics, for instance, do not participate in liturgical prayer as often as they believe they should.

Since recent Catholic social encyclicals, Vatican II and congregational constitutions have emphasized the special relationship between religious orders and the poor, dissonance will intensify for many members of apostolic religious orders until the behavior, both individually and collectively, is linked to that value. These religious orders have a difficult time, however, moving rapidly in response to new forms of poverty for many reasons already delineated in the study. Existing commitments, the awareness of the shifting paradigms, the density of information provided from sources outside the orders themselves, escalating social needs, the high affiliation needs of members (which may inhibit mission) or, simply, lack of competent members limit the capacity of orders to see or respond to the most pressing human needs. Leadership can, however, emphasize clearly this preference through policies, placement practices and the activation of resources through value-based budget allocation processes. Demonstration projects also can be established within orders' works to portray clearly the desired direction the order seeks to pursue. Without either models or outlets through which members can express this commitment, emphasizing the poor will only frustrate conscientious members. Similarly, for monastics and contemplatives, modeling the tradition consistently in prayer and work will reduce the dissonance that members may feel in response to strongly espousing these values but not actualizing them in practice.

Mysticism and Prophetism

Contemplation and action are often juxtaposed in spiritual writings. On one hand, the mystery of God acting within individuals listening to the words of Christ and transformed by their power is part of the dynamic of contemplation. On the other, the constitutive mission of the Roman Catholic Church that is identified in the works of justice and mercy is part of the dynamic role of the prophet in society and the church. The prevailing espoused orientation of religious orders since Vatican II has been toward the prophetic, emphasizing systemic and personal service to the poor as a fundamental distinguishing attribute of the vocation to religious life. In the Visioning Groups research unit, the contemplative dimension was listed as the most important element in the transformation of religious life. The prophetic dimension was ranked second. Since Vatican II, the prophetic dimensions of religious life have been emphasized increasingly among the apostolic orders. The contemplative dimension, more characteristic of the monastic and cloistered traditions, has been relatively deemphasized compared to the prophetic. Interestingly, the majority of participants in the Visioning Groups were involved in very strong prophetic apostolates, and they are the individuals who most strongly emphasize the contemplative dimension to ground what they do.

The research concludes that the apostolic traditions of religious life will survive to the extent that they are attentive to the larger social and ecclesial environment in which they minister. Those that are most responsive to pressing human need and motivated by the love of Christ will be vitalized as long as their efforts are consistent with their tradition. This is the dramatic change that is still required regardless of the operative paradigm. Their purpose must be clear and their efforts to achieve, unencumbered.

The data indicates that the apostolic orders are likely to emphasize increasingly the prophetic tradition. This will result, for a period of time, in considerable retraining of membership. For many, this may require relinquishing a functional specialization or professional career. For others, it will mean tailoring a professional identity to serve the needs of those who are poor. For congregations, assuming the prophetic stance will require a significant reallocation of resources and personnel to accomplish that fundamental vision. Their institutions will be measured as effective to the extent that they assist the poor directly or advocate on their behalf. Concretely, the commitment will mean abandoning some institutions or works that do not respond to this direction. Conversely, it may mean establishing entirely new foundations or institutions clearly responsive to need. In addition, it may mean that lucrative salaries associated with the professions may have to be relinquished in order to serve a more transcendent purpose. Until the external perception of apostolic religious orders is congruent with their self-definitions (that is, until they do what they profess), their membership is likely to remain limited in numbers and their social credibility will be threatened.

Several other dynamics mitigate against increasing membership to either the prophetic or mystical lines of religious life. First, many congregations have vague boundaries. Some orders have established lay association programs that accord equal rights to members and affiliates. In these instances, aside from the belief about a vocation as a unique call, there is little to be gained by the enormous sacrifice to the vowed life as compared to the affiliate requirements for membership. Organizations and orders that appear strong have a dual formula of both a high cost for membership and high commitment rituals and practices to differentiate this group from any other. Until religious orders again understand the dynamics of commitment to prophetic and mystical witness, they are not likely to see dramatic increases in membership.

Second, as they become smaller, religious orders will be forced to be extremely conscientious in their use of resources. The paradoxical resolution of decline can happen if concerns with survival yield to a passion for the mission and doing the work that, consistent with a particular charism, the society and the church both value. Without external validation, resources will be difficult to secure.

Third, mendicantism, in the strict sense of begging, likely will be sustained or revived either by new groups that have very limited resources or by those that choose the condition of the poor. The evidence that orders relinquish resources for the sake of becoming poor is very weak. Finally, an essential element that will distinguish apostolic ministry from either social activism or contemplative life will be a supporting spirituality that realistically reflects in prayer and action the life of the apostle in the world.

The monastic tradition likely will rebound more notably by virtue of having reclaimed its foundational purpose and form. The monastics' greatest challenge will be to interpret for this time in history how the traditions of prayer ground their lives and make their form of religious life sustainable. The research indicates that conceptions of Eucharist and pious practice, which have so long been a constitutive part of the monastic tradition, are under revision. The traditional practices of Liturgy of the Hours and Eucharist are seemingly not central to the lives of a fair percentage of monastics. It is equally apparent from the research that monastic life that deviates clearly from purpose or engages too ambitiously in apostolic life leads to fragmentation and role confusion among the members. The role of apostolic ministry among monastics appears increasingly common but may diffuse their identity. For instance, for monastics to assume primary responsibility for diocesan parish life appears to be in conflict with their core identity. However, for both personal and financial reasons, this practice is increasingly common.

Perhaps less energetically, some cloistered groups will evolve into stricter observance and varieties of neomysticism that include all forms of spiritual wisdom—from "New Age" to Islam—to advance the solitary discipline of the awareness of God in the world. In many respects, the dynamics affecting monastics appear to have a similar impact on cloistered religious. For either group, adapting to the times while being faithful to centuries of tradition may be the greatest challenge.

Sponsorship, Corporate Witness and Individual Placement

The research indicates a gap between how members regard institutions sponsored by their orders and the work they currently do. The data suggests that more than 90% of members are willing to work in sponsored institutions. While willingness does not necessarily reflect competence to undertake a position, it is interesting to observe how strong is the willingness to support sponsored institutions in this manner at a time when policies and practices of placement reflect other priorities. It is also interesting to consider that, in fact, such policies and practices of personnel distribution or assignment, as well as the general decline of institutions, may be undermining both collective action and institutional viability. The espoused value of institutions and the willingness of individuals to work in them is at variance with the dominant models of ministerial placement. In addition, placement is oftentimes out of step with preparation or competence. Religious women often report difficulty in finding ministerial placement or the competence required to get particular jobs. The gap between willingness and readiness deserves attention.

The concept of career paths and training an individual into a professional field, while once quite prevalent among members of religious orders, has become less common. However, if orders continue to provide professional services or products, commensurate training will be required. It is probably true that the priority in the past may have been to emphasize the professional identity of religious more strongly than the vocational call to ministry. Increasingly, however, individual religious are not prepared to function to capacity in ministerial situations that are in competition now with laity or individuals. For instance, hospital executives are today so highly specialized that to function in the role, priority must be given to distinctive competencies. Between decreasing executive mentorship opportunities for members of religious orders in the health field and the general decline in membership, the probability of having executives of hospitals emerging from within a sponsoring religious congregation is low.

The application of dissonance theory applies here as well. For example, many religious orders that continue to sponsor hospitals or health systems have restructured their attitudes regarding the importance of having someone in the order serve in an executive capacity. Many justifications are advanced: Some believe it is now incompatible with the primary role of ministerial service and vocation to seek executive roles, while others acknowledge that training or mentoring individuals into the role is too costly financially or from the standpoint of resource allocation. Still others have shifted attention to the emerging role of mission effectiveness in hospitals, seeing this role as the conduit of sponsoring values, while another faction simply regards these areas as the domain of lay leaders. In fact, the shift from a product orientation to a market orientation to ministry is probably operative. Congregations now regard the poor as the primary focus of ministry and look less and less to the context in which that will take place. However, this very attitude may undermine valid institutional placement.

The strong support of sponsored institutions suggests that individual members of religious orders see institutional ministry as providing a means to express a fundamental vocation or desire. Yet, institutions have, for many orders, become too costly to continue, impossible to staff and often inconsistent with the order's vocational mission as established in recent years. Many members of religious orders have said in various facets of the research that institutions are a viable conduit of mission and ministry. However, the demographics on Roman Catholic institutions in the United States are startling. Overall, a more than 25% decline is seen in all areas of delivery: health, education and social service. Consequently, religious orders are becoming increasingly driven by a mission to the poor but are less able to respond to those needs through institutional means. Ironically, institutions often provide for the possibility of economies of scale and social credibility for service to populations that others are unwilling to serve. They also provide a context to accomplish collectively far more than any person can accomplish individually.

Members of religious orders clearly support sponsored institutions, but years of deinstitutionalization and strong positions that denigrate the importance of religious institutions have decoupled many congregations from their sponsored works. Corporate restructuring of major health and educational institutions has, in some instances, separated totally the sponsoring order from the sponsored work. For example, colleges previously sponsored by religious congregations have established lay boards and independent corporations that leave nothing but moral authority to the sponsor. Similarly, sponsored institutions, which for so long provided a base of operational power and independence for members of religious orders, have suffered significant losses in religious personnel despite the apparent willingness among members to work in them.

How can the discrepancy be understood, and what can be done to alter the current trends toward consolidation or relinquishment? New foundations that demonstrate ambitiously the charisms of religious orders are not very prevalent. However, new foundations that dramatically reflect a corporate commitment and the willingness of members to join the shared project enhance the internal sense of collective action as well as external perception of a contribution to the society.

An example might be helpful: a century-old order on the East Coast whose charism and history serve the needs of women recently began to rededicate one of its nearly abandoned inner-city facilities to educating women who had not received their high school diploma. One older member with a background in inner-city ministry and education was assigned to assess the needs and to develop programs. In relatively short order, this sister discovered that these women often came with children who needed to be cared for while the women attended school. She set up a child-care center to provide for them while the mothers were in class.

The child-care center staff discovered that many of the children were malnourished while a few of them were abused or drug-addicted. The child-care facility networked with a hospital run by the order in a neighboring suburb to obtain limited treatment. Eventually, a health clinic was established on the site, because it was determined that both the mothers and the children were in need of nutritional counseling or other medical services. The health clinic and related volunteers discovered that many of the women who came for schooling were also pregnant. Prenatal classes and parenting classes then evolved to meet that need.

Within one year of its inception, 12 sisters had asked to work in the ministry. Most of these women left their individual ministries, which were very similar to this work, to join this program. What was different, however, was that the order could actualize its values and the sisters could achieve together a scale of operation and networking that they could not have achieved in individual ministries. The facility now has an operating budget of more than $1.2 million, most of which is donated by neighboring corporations and small businesses that are willing to invest in the emerging work force. The irony is that, in the course of restructuring the corporation, the congregation established a lay board to govern the new organization. In so doing, it also separated the assets of the congregation, alienated the congregation's oldest property and essentially made the sisters employees of the corporation.

On the other hand, the movement of some orders to accomplish direct service among individuals who are poor through systemic means or institutional resources tends to characterize the more proactive and, in some instances, the financially stronger orders. Examples of the conversion of assets from previously strong institutional bases to alternative institutions that provide housing, neighborhood health care or educational resources demonstrate the attempts to transform institutions in such a way that they relate directly to the fundamental charism of the order and, in certain instances, to the poor.

Even among orders that are quite small, examples of the application of institutional resources to address a focal problem can serve as demonstration projects that will gradually narrow the gap between espoused and operative values in religious orders. As the gap in identity narrows, orders will become stronger or clearly move toward dissolution because they are no longer perceived as relevant to the church or society. However, if they demonstrate credible witness with little discrepancy between what they espouse and how they act, the vitality of religious life as a social institution will be observable.

Involvement and Influence

Results of the National Survey in particular revealed a discrepancy between the reported level of involvement by members in their religious orders and their perceived sense of influence. Ratings of involvement, including both the current level of activity and desired future state, were consistently higher than reported levels of perceived influence in the present and desired influence for the future. The hypothesis of dissatisfaction and discontent that such data would suggest was, in fact, verified in some of the qualitative interviews and written responses. It is further substantiated in the phenomenon of internal migration, whereby highly functional and influential members of religious orders have moved into realms of ministry that enable them to have a sense of influence.

An examination of the dynamics in religious orders over the past three decades raises several additional questions with regard to influence and involvement. To begin, has the rhetoric of participation and collegiality raised the expectations of members of religious orders regarding the potential for influence beyond the point of being realistic? The years immediately following the Second Vatican Council were marked by intense work among members of religious congregations, frequently involving myriad committees, on updating constitutions and rewriting government, formation and placement documents. These processes entailed broad consultation, lengthy meetings and, frequently, tedious debate. The emphasis was placed, however, on hearing each person's voice, and many changes came about during these years.

As the updating of these documents and structures is brought to conclusion, orders are left with members who have become accustomed to broad consultation and intense involvement in determining the policies and plans of their orders. Does the opportunity for involvement and influence at such a broad level continue for members of religious orders? Which items are most appropriately left to administration so that the greater number of members may devote themselves to ministry? It appears that unreal expectations relative to areas in which members of religious orders might appropriately expect to exercise their influence in congregational matters have been created.

As congregations moved to update their structures, many evolved from medieval hierarchies that were modeled on the dominant form of government at the time of their founding to democratic processes (one person, one vote) that reflect the current system of civil government. Assumptions regarding the applicability of democratic forms of governance to religious life were made with little or no conversation regarding the appropriateness of this move. Centuries-old notions of obedience were dismissed and replaced with concepts such as "listening to the Spirit" which, while challenging, lack a history of experience to provide a context that produces consistency in form or process.

Finally, there is a gap between the members' reported desire for influence and their willingness to assume positions of leadership or administration that will provide entrée into those realms. For example, the number of those who project ministry in congregational leadership or administration is half the number of those currently involved in these areas. Minimal interest is expressed by members of religious orders in preparing for positions of potential influence. It seems that members report a desire for influence but are reluctant to pay the price.

Identified Boundaries and Permeability

A significant gap continues between those who view religious orders as distinct social entities with very exact boundaries and those who see them as far more permeable. Few would dispute the observation that religious orders historically represent some of the most strongly bounded institutions in society. It was characteristic of most orders prior to Vatican II that once having entered a religious order, a person's entire identity would be engaged by the collective forces or social control mechanisms and policies of the group. Membership had very specific rewards and consequences. Most orders functioned as, and resembled, sects. Members often assumed new names, wore distinctive garb and renounced family ties. Most of these practices began to change prior to Vatican II, and that change continues today. In some orders, boundaries have become entirely fluid. Membership, although still a fairly significant construct among older members of religious orders, carries less salience among younger members of religious orders. Younger members would not necessarily consider the religious order their primary or their only reference group, whereas most older members of religious orders still would.

Boundaries within and between religious orders provide a frame of reference for individuals who are members. Some sense of boundaries helps in articulating or interpreting reality. They serve to link individuals to one another and also to separate them. As noted in Chapter 1, boundaries are essentially features that either differentiate one tradition from another (Cherns, 1976); pose actual or symbolic barriers to the access to or transfer of information, goods, services or people (Katz & Kahn, [1966] 1978) or serve as points of external exchange with other organizations, clients, peers, competitors or other entities (Friedlander, 1987).

In the period since Vatican II, religious orders have been engaged significantly in boundary negotiation. The operative paradigms each have their own assumptions about the nature of boundaries. For instance, functionalists require clear boundaries to relate well. They regulate behavior in order to produce an efficient outcome in ministry. Their boundaries are defined largely by what they do. The structuralists, on the other hand, would maintain that religious life as a state of life in the church must have its own autonomy and not be subjected to the hierarchical authority of the church because hierarchy is a form of power that ultimately subordinates all other forms. They could, however, suggest that whoever participates in the ministry of an order and shares its charism is, therefore, "part of" the group. Specifying the boundaries of religious identity is one of the significant tasks facing leaders and members of the orders.

Many religious orders have, to a large extent, lost their distinctiveness. The absence of boundaries, even between orders, has led to the homogenization of a group that was previously viewed more complexly. Monks want to know, for instance, who they are in relation to the apostolic tradition. Conversely, members of apostolic religious orders want to know how their spirituality is distinct from that of the monastic tradition. Similarly, vowed members want to know how the rights of affiliates are determined. These boundaries are difficult to describe concisely. They can be psychological, physical, symbolic, financial, spiritual or philosophical in character. All serve, however, to define, at least partly, how a group needs to operate within its context to be effective. When boundaries become too open or indistinct, the order risks becoming overwhelmed and losing its identity, whereas, if its boundaries are too exclusive, the order may lose touch with its primary constituents.

Mother Teresa of Calcutta, the Nobel prize winner, established the Missionaries of Charity to accomplish an international mission among the poorest of the poor. She is thought by many American members of religious orders to reflect an irretrievable or, for some, an undesirable form of religious life. However, she nonetheless maintains clear boundaries in the organization with a clearly focused mission. Curiously, the order is the fastest growing order in the world today. The dynamics of commitment deserve serious attention without implying that mimicking this form is either possible or desirable. The underlying psychological and anthropological frames may be useful to American religious orders.

In contrast, the fusion of groups within organizations occurs when boundaries are less clear. Boundaries alter as shifts in self-identity occur. Moving from a fixed identity to an alternative unfreezes assumptions and actions at the individual and group levels and introduces competing interpretations of a group's direction and the members' sense of self. As boundaries are negotiated and as alternative paradigms emerge to explain the life and direction of a group, there is likely to be considerable conflict among the original and developing interpretive schemes and the subgroups espousing them. Groups that hold one particular new perspective, for example, are likely to find themselves in conflict with individuals or groups who espouse the original perspective or a different new one. The conflict may take various forms. One perspective may clearly dominate those holding different perspectives and may be separated from other views, or leaders of the organization may acknowledge the potential value of, and thus encourage, interaction between several different perspectives.

Boundaries must be maintained if religious orders are to remain as distinct entities in the church. The documents of Vatican II and the prevailing drift among religious orders over these past 30 years may suggest that religious orders are no longer distinct in either their contribution to the church and society or their relevance as separate agencies. Establishing boundaries between members and lay associates or affiliates will only make sense if the value of religious orders is observed. Otherwise, religious orders will become voluntary agencies with highly permeable boundaries, characterized by lower-order requirements for membership and exerting a lesser impact than was previously the case.

Women and Men Religious in the Church

One of the unique attributes of the study was that it incorporated the perspectives of sisters, brothers and religious priests. In the study, these social variables influenced the sampling plan, analysis plan and interpretation of the results. Significant differences between the beliefs and practices of men and women were expected, and in some instances, the differences were confirmed. In many other instances, however, the similarity of opinions was notable. Contrary to assertions in much of the popular treatment of women religious in the church, their counterparts among the male population of members of religious orders did not differ dramatically on key dimensions. This section will elaborate areas of divergence and congruence.

Among the differences identified between women and men, we conclude that women in the study, in general, scored higher in positive affect and lower in negative affect than men, rated themselves as more satisfied with ministry and community living, and were more satisfied with their leaders. They were also very strongly committed to their congregation and its mission. They were less strategic in their orientation than the males, planned fewer long-range projects, exhibited less sanctioning behavior toward members and, generally, were lower in achievement orientation. Women showed less aspiration for further education than male members of religious orders. Women were more inclined to complete master's level studies than to pursue doctoral degrees.

Male members of religious orders tended to plan projects that reflect attention to the future, to employ fewer consensual processes, to be more likely to have a doctoral degree, and to have a higher degree of role clarity than women. They were less satisfied with community life, perceived their leaders as less transformational and, generally, showed fewer signs of positive affect than women religious.

Women enter religious life today at approximately the same rate as men, as compared to the three-to-one ratio of previous decades in this century. This ratio most likely reflects two dynamics: the increasing opportunities for women in other professions, including church ministry, and the experience of alienation of women in the church. The decrease in membership of women in religious orders should be less a concern than the alienation that women and men religious feel from the church itself. What has been identified as a perceived lack of role clarity among members of religious orders, lowered respect for the magisterium of the church and general support of sponsored institutions that are rapidly dwindling in number are but a few of the systemic issues facing women and men in religious orders in the church.

CONCLUSIONS: SHAPING THE FUTURE OF RELIGIOUS LIFE

If religious life is to continue as a vital force in the church and the world, changes must occur in most religious congregations in the United States. Fidelity to the spirit of the founder and responsiveness to critical and unmet human needs are basic to the ongoing mission of religious communities.

While individual examples abound, members of religious orders have acted collectively in only limited ways on behalf of absolute human needs, new forms of poverty and demands that seemingly outstrip the capacity of any group to respond. Vatican II called members of religious orders to a return to the "spirit of the founder." Most congregations have engaged in much study and devoted great efforts to move in this direction, but the absence of corporate commitment to embody the groups' responses to current unmet needs in light of Gospel imperatives stands in contrast to the collective vision and action, rooted in God, that marked the birth of most apostolic, monastic and cloistered congregations.

Religious life as a social institution in American society is at a crossroads. To achieve a viable future, members of religious orders as a group, as well as individual members, must confront the forces that currently restrain them and reinforce those dynamics that will allow them, in fact, to be responsive to absolute human need in the context of their particular charism. A future marked by significant revitalization will emerge for those congregations that are rooted in their relationship with God and that, in a spirit of fidelity to their founding purpose and responsiveness to absolute human need, confront the current gap between the Gospel and the culture.

The research concludes with an equation of sorts (depicted in Figure 7.1) that can be applied to all congregational traditions in varying degrees. The interaction of eight critical factors in the context of personal and collective conversion will move congregations from their current states to their desired futures. The research also concludes that for other groups, the restraints on advancement are severe and may lead to decline. What follows is a brief summary of the conclusions drawn from the various facets of the study.

Individualism and Vocation

Since Vatican II, shifting paradigms of vocation and concomitant cultural trends have deemphasized the distinctiveness of the religious life. The research suggests that the personal call to holiness of all Christians, reiterated in Vatican II, affected religious life and our understanding of it. Members of religious orders reported ambivalence about their current state while they concurrently celebrated the advances of the laity in the church since Vatican II. The age of experimentation in the church paralleled vast cultural shifts in American society toward individualism, cultural assimilation and the democratization of authority.

Figure 7.1
Shaping the Future of Religious Life

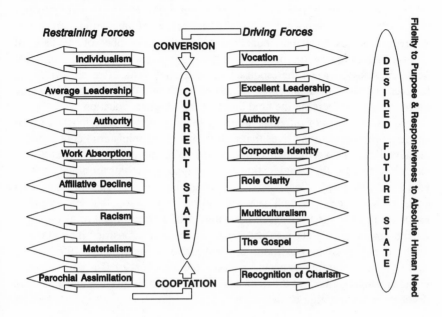

For their part, members of religious orders have spent at least 20 years focused largely on the internal reorganization of congregational life. This structural perspective, combined with a heightened psychological awareness, left many individuals weary of the bureaucratization of vocation at a time when individualism was escalating in society, and in religious life as well. For many, the dynamics of change itself presented an additional burden. The impulse to generosity among some members of religious orders is being eclipsed by self-preoccupation, psychological decompensation, stark individualism and a lessening of the willingness to sacrifice.

For others, the reaction is the opposite. In these congregations we observe individuals who, regardless of age, know the distinctiveness of their vocation to religious life. Their profile includes a radical dependence on God, whom they see as a benevolent authority, and a capacity to enter the life of another for the sake of that other and not in order to meet their own personal—even though seemingly altruistic—needs. They also possess a deep desire for oneness with God and with others. They are deeply committed to their congregation where, by objective standards, the costs of their work and membership are very high.

Recent literature on the theology of religious life has espoused as normative for members of religious orders a commitment to the preferential option for the poor (Vatican Synod Secretariat, 1992). Such attentiveness to the poor has been seen by some as constitutive of the religious vocation. However, a discrepancy exists between this espoused value and the action of many individuals and congregations. A small but, nonetheless, significant number of members of religious orders feel no personal commitment to this espoused value. Resolving the discrepancy between the espoused and operative values that are evident in the lives and work of members of religious orders will decrease the dissonance felt by many and increase the credibility of the religious vocation.

Many members of religious orders have migrated to the periphery of their congregation, often living lives that reflect significant ministerial contributions but have little to do with their congregation or religious life. For many such persons, a call by the congregation to participate in its vocation and mission would be welcome. For others, the dynamics of individualism and inner authority have come to dominate any notion of vocation that entails either obedience or even discernment of the will of God in the context of a congregational commitment. Recent research has shown how intensified individualism can be transformed into extraordinary collective action (Chang, 1993). The future lies in the ability to decide between the high cost of Gospel living in a religious congregation and the demands of an exclusively private understanding of vocation to the religious life.

Leadership

The research presents a profile of outstanding leaders of religious orders. They are men and women grounded deeply in faith, who are able to acknowledge the centrality of God in their lives. They have a high need to achieve personally and have a clear sense of the impact that the congregation could have. Moreover, they are characterized by objectivity and compassion. With all these attributes, the outstanding leaders do not have a strong need to belong to the very groups they are attempting to lead, and yet they find meaning precisely in that context of faith, membership and impact. The outstanding leader has a clear vision of the future and successfully employs the means to both gain the support of the congregation for the direction and implement the decisions of the group.

Several factors inhibit the exercise of effective leadership in religious orders. The nature of authority is widely contested, consensual decision-making processes have little form, membership is generally unwilling to relinquish authority to those given responsibility and the concept of personal "call" often eclipses any willingness to work on behalf of the congregational ends. Furthermore, those elected to leadership are, in some instances, the individuals least likely to succeed because they are elected to fill the need of a group that lacks ambition or the will to move forward.

Effective leaders, on the other hand, are rooted in an awareness that they act with, and on behalf of, God. They treat members as though they were equally responsible for the life of the congregation yet do not compromise the clarity of their role as leader. Effective leaders understand how to position the congregation strategically to be responsive to human needs, and they generally are granted authority by their members. Whether in apostolic, mendicant, monastic or cloistered congregations, leaders understand the importance of focus and a clear identity in order to retain optimism and productivity among the members. The impulses to extremes of reformism or restorationism can be contained by a focus on building competencies over ideologies.

Authority

Authority in religious life, as in the church itself, is perhaps the most pressing question for members of religious orders. T. Monroe (personal communications, April 8, 1991) described the nature of authority to be that of providing protection, direction and order for the sake of the group. Authority in many American institutions, including religious life, has undergone deconstruction. Variable understandings of consensus, subsidiarity, discernment and leadership have diffused the conception of authority. This, coupled with dynamics of individualism, limited understandings of obedience and the separation of one's spiritual life from the life of the Christian community, has made the exercise of authority extremely difficult.

Demorath and Williams (1992) suggest that the emphasis on democratic processes in the church in general has led to the "protestantization" of Catholicism. They suggest that this may yield greater legitimacy but attenuated power, both internally and externally. Religious authority among the orders and within the orders spans a democratic spectrum that varies substantially from the past.

The abuses of authority in the past have made individuals reluctant to endorse authority in any way. Members of religious orders, in particular, are clear in their lowered respect for the magisterial authority of the church and the U.S. hierarchy in general. Moreover, within their own congregations, the interpretations of authority vary widely. The favorable resolution of the issues of authority will contribute to moving religious life toward its fundamental purposes. However, a failure to address issues of authority will further restrain revitalization efforts.

Work and Corporate Identity

The period of the 1960s and 1970s has been referred to as an age of "deconstructionism," in which structures of American life, industry, family and religion have been disassembled. The convergence of American deconstructionism and the post-Vatican II world produced a massive unraveling of the forms and structures of religious life. During this time, the institutions being sponsored or staffed by members of religious orders experienced a dramatic decline. Without making a judgment as to the validity of the institutions themselves and the known negative impact they seemed to have on particular members of religious orders, they did, in many instances, provide a locus of corporate identity. At present, many congregations lack a sense of corporate identity. Members often remain because of a high need to belong to the group, but a lack of clarity regarding the group's mission focus offers little to attract the commitment or capture the passion of potential new members.

The orders that appear to be most successfully rebounding or stabilizing in the United States are several monasteries, both male and female, that have carefully reinstated monastic practices and a sense of clarity regarding their life and work. It is also significant to note that monastic communities, particularly men's groups, that have retained the classic traditions of monasticism have not had to rely as much on compensation from parochial work.

A related dynamic for members of religious orders involves becoming identified solely with one's work. For developmental reasons, this results from a lack of corporate identity and from the absence of community and spiritual support. Under the guise of the motto, "We are more than what we do," many individual members of religious orders and groups have relinquished the power of corporate witness for a variety of individual commitments in effective but unconnected ministerial positions. The emphasis on individual ministry, or, at times, on simply procuring a position has eclipsed the symbolism of and statement of commitment and permanence previously made by corporate commitments.

Affiliative Decline and Role Clarity

The most compelling result of the study indicates that a significant percentage of members of religious orders no longer understand their role and function in the church. This lack of role clarity can result in lowered self-confidence, a sense of futility, greater propensity to leave religious life and significant anxiety. The younger members of religious orders experienced the least clarity, and among them, women experienced less clarity than their male counterparts. Whatever clarity existed among men seemed to emerge from the definitiveness of ordination for priests and from the incumbent role requirements, as well as the clarity, of the lay vocation for brothers. Women members are divided on the concept of consecrated life as it is distinct from or equal to that of their female lay counterparts. For sisters, brothers and religious priests, Vatican II reinforced substantially the role of laity in the church but did not help to clarify for members of religious orders the unique contribution of their vocation as members of religious orders in the church.

A related dynamic is regarded as affiliative decline. The data indicates that individuals who are currently members of religious orders obtain a high degree of satisfaction from membership in their congregation. In many instances, what holds them to their commitment to religious life is their personal need for a sense of affiliation, rather than their sense of communal purpose or mission. Communal bonding continues in spite of 30 years of membership decline. Congregations will continue to decline if affiliative motives are stronger than a concern for the mission of the church and the extension of the charism. As the median age for members of religious orders continues to increase, yielding control of the congregation to those younger members who understand, and are able to present, a compelling vision of the group's mission may be critical.

Racism and Multiculturalism

The project delineates a profile of American members of religious orders that is 96% white. Despite the radical increases of African-Americans, Hispanics, Asians and other ethnic groups in the U.S. population, religious orders do not reflect proportional increases. The research indicates that a complex dynamic of unconscious racism makes it very difficult for minority populations to penetrate rather homogeneous orders. Most younger members of religious orders acknowledge that members of ethnically distinct populations find incorporation into their religious order to be quite difficult. Older members, while believing they are open to minority participation, cannot easily adapt to the cultural demands that heterogeneity in a religious order requires.

Ethnically distinct groups feel their culture to be, not unwelcome, but generally unrecognized. To the extent that this remains the dynamic of religious orders, minority populations will likely develop religious orders in the tradition of the classical disciplines of monasticism and apostolic life, but they may well do so independently of the existing congregations. In other words, they will establish ethnically distinct contexts in which their culture can be lived more fully. Among minority groups themselves, the research suggests that the prevalent discontent observed in mainstream orders relative to pious practices, authority and discipline are not their concerns. Their structure of faith, ecclesiology, female and male relationships, understandings of the vows and relationship to the church each present a very different dynamic, as a function of their unique cultures.

Materialism and the Gospel

The research suggests that religious orders of the future will derive their mission and their life in common from a firm relationship with the person of Jesus, grounded in communion with the Word. Members of religious orders must focus on the gap that exists between the evident culture and the Gospel community. Because of the strength of the forces of materialism in the United States, conscious efforts will be made to define themselves within the culture while retaining very distinctive values. They will be recognized by their simplicity of life, by their visible presence among the most abandoned and by their joy in serving God.

The research also indicates that at the present time, members of religious orders are often unaware of the degree of their assimilation into the mainstream culture and how invisible they have become to those who most would call out to them. The costs of belonging to a religious congregation have diminished as the former rigor of the vowed life has diminished. Most members of religious orders, however, would agree that to remain distinctive in the world, this trend toward assimilation must be reversed. In a related dynamic, clearly defining the boundaries and expectations of membership will be part of that revitalization.

Charisms and Parochial Assimilation

Religious orders have arisen classically in the midst of the church to serve emerging or unmet human needs. They have been historically quite independent of, yet complementary to, the hieratic order of the church. The "consecrated life," as it has been known in the past, today is being assimilated into either the lay state for brothers and sisters or the clerical state for religious priests. The complementary structures of the hierarchy and the charisms of the church are being blended into a predominantly parochial view. This is due, in part, to the absence of a vibrant declaration by Vatican II about the clear role of members of religious orders in the church. The decline of sponsored institutions among religious orders has also altered the independence of their members. Moreover, the decreased numbers of diocesan clergy, at a time when the parish is defined as the primary locus of ecclesiology, has led to an increasing dependence and pressure on religious orders to staff diocesan operations.

The increasingly widespread insertion of members of religious orders into diocesan and parochial positions, to the point where such commitments take precedence over involvements in the lives of their congregations, is a growing phenomenon in the United States. This trend, which is known as parochial assimilation, has had a dramatic effect on most religious orders, probably most significantly among women. It easily can lead to a compromise of the prophetic role of members of religious life.

Many congregations that appear to be vital have chosen not to be assimilated into the exclusively parochial context. They tend to exact a higher cost among their members as regards belonging, and are characterized by a focused mission that clearly serves the church.

Summary

These eight dynamics operate to varying degrees in religious orders that have undertaken substantial renewal. The dynamics affect the social institution of religious life in American society and in the church, the congregations and the individuals. The resolution of the change process, however, is deeply affected by the individual and communal choices made along the way. The critical component in the change effort is to imagine a desirable future for a congregation and reinforce that movement by consistency in choices based on values and the traditions of the order.

For the transformation of religious life to shift from a pattern of consistent numerical decline, surely the will of God must also be considered. No formula, regardless of its scientific underpinnings, can create will where little exists in congregations nor diminishment where commitment abounds. Consideration of these dynamics may give focus to the complex task of vitalizing religious life. Our own conviction is that there are many reasons to be hopeful about the future of religious life. Some individual members of religious orders live their charisms with such vigor and ease that one can only conclude that God sustains them. In addition, the data, in its various formats, attests to the will of many religious to move forward. Personal conversion to those forces that will support a future consistent with the dual dynamic of fidelity to purpose and responsiveness to absolute human need will nonetheless continue to be threatened by significant cultural, personal and collective resistance. Transformation occurs in both subtle and emphatic ways—in nuances of language and in radical restructuring to advance the mission. The commitment of individual religious to the action of God in the world can transform the world and those who dwell in it. Understanding more thoroughly where we are today, we hope, will enable members of religious orders to chart a course that responds creatively to the Gospel challenges before us as members of the faith community who have a unique gift to offer the church.

Appendix A

POPULATION STATISTICS, 1962-1992

Table A.1
United States Population Statistics

Population	1962	1972	1982	1992	% Change 1962-1992
U.S. Total	180,940,947	205,074,905	225,993,945	254,476,684	40.6
U.S. Catholics	42,876,665	48,390,990	51,207,579	58,267,424	35.9

Source: Official Catholic Directory 1962, 1972, 1982, and 1992.

Table A.2
Religious Sisters, Brothers and Priests

Group	1962	1972	1982	1992	% Change 1962-1992
Sisters	173,351	146,914	121,370	99,337	-42.7
Brothers	11,502	9,740	7,880	6,603	-42.6
Priests	21,807	20,694	22,572	17,989	-17.5
TOTALS	206,660	177,348	151,822	123,929	-40.0

Source: Official Catholic Directory 1962, 1972, 1982, and 1992.

Table A.3
Roman Catholic Institutional Statistics

Institutions	1962	1972	1982	1992	% Change 1962-1992
Parochial Elementary Schools	10,177	8,877	7,761	7,176	-29.5
Private Elementary Schools	453	329	318	266	-41.3
Diocesan High Schools	1,566	1,086	882	875	-44.1
Private High Schools	869	729	588	525	-39.6
Colleges and Universities	278	260	237	235	-15.5
Diocesan Seminaries	98	106	86	79	-19.4
Religious Seminaries	447	326	217	156	-65.1
General Hospitals	816	718	635	628	-23.0
Patients Treated	14,140,884	22,895,125	36,723,368	47,635,520	236.9

Source: Official Catholic Directory 1962, 1972, 1982, and *1992.*

Appendix B

COMPONENTS AND ELEMENTS
USED IN VISIONING GROUPS

Table B.1
**Components of a Future Vision of Religious Life in the Catholic Church in
    the United States**

Component	Definition
Contemplative Attitude	Religious in 2010 will have a contemplative attitude toward all creation. They will be attentive to and motivated by the presence of the sacred in their own inner journeys, in the lives of others, and throughout creation. Recognizing contemplation as a way of life for the whole church, they will see themselves and their communities as centers of spirituality and the experience of God. This awareness will distinguish religious more than any social categories that define them.
Prophetic Witness	Being converted by the example of Jesus and the values of the Gospel, religious in the year 2010 will serve a prophetic role in church and society. Living this prophetic witness will include criticizing societal and ecclesial values and structures, calling for systemic change and being converted by the marginalized with whom we serve.
Intentional Communities	In 2010 religious communities will be characterized by inclusivity and intentionality. These communities may include persons of different ages, genders, cultures, races, and sexual orientation. They may include persons who are lay or cleric and married or single, as well as vowed and/or unvowed members. They will have a core group and persons with temporary and permanent commitments.

Table B.1 (continued)

Component	Definition
Intentional Communities, cont.	These communities will be ecumenical and possibly interfaith; faith sharing will be constitutive of the quality of life in this context of expanded membership. Such inclusivity will necessitate a new understanding of membership and a language to accompany it. Permanent commitment will be more a function of intentionality than of specified norms of membership. Religious life will still include congregations of permanently vowed members.
Conversion*	Religious continue to penetrate the social order and the church in 2010 by their intense focus on personal conversion to God expressed through a vowed commitment and witnessed in their mission. Personal conversion then leads to transformation of interpersonal relationships, community, and the social and global order.
Charism	By the year 2010, religious groups will have reexamined, reclaimed and set free the charisms of their founders. Corporate ownership of a focused vision gives meaning and expression to mission and ministry. Some groups who share similar visions/charisms have already joined together.
Preferential Option for the Poor	Religious in 2010 will be investing their resources in direct service with and advocacy for structural change on behalf of the poor and marginalized. They will minister where others will not go. Their own experience in listening to and learning from the poor and marginalized will shape all aspects of their lives.
Distributed Power	Religious in 2010 have replaced models of domination and control with principles of mutuality drawn from feminist and ecological insights, so that collaborative modes of decision making and power sharing are normative. Priorities for service will be generated and shaped in the local arena, while impetus for such action will be influenced by global awareness.
Global Spirituality	Animated by their deep conviction of the oneness of creation, religious in 2010 will live and work in a manner that fosters participation and harmony among all people, healthy personal and interpersonal relationships, reverence for the earth, and integration of spirituality and technology on behalf of the gospel.

Table B.1 (continued)

Component	Definition
Cultural Interdependence	Radical demographic changes will, by the year 2010, alter the face of our local church and our congregations. Our interactions with persons of various cultures and races have uncovered our enduring racism, prejudices and intolerance and called us to deeper inculturation, interdependence and openness to being evangelized by others. Global interdependence among nations will require a flexible orientation to mission among religious.
Living with Less	Religious in the year 2010 will be transformed by the poor, living a simpler life-style that includes reverence for the earth. They will develop a spirituality that will free them to be more authentic witnesses by letting go of nonessentials, by being content with what is enough, and by sharing their resources with the poor. An alternative motivation for the above might be economic circumstances beyond our control.
Community Life*	Religious in the year 2010 will be known by their example of the possibility of authentic community life within the community of the church. Communal living of the vowed life will be one of their distinguishing features. Community life will be life-giving for the individual religious and it will further nurture growth in holiness.
"We Are Church"	An essential element of religious life in 2010 will be our ability to accept the concept that "we are church." As people of God, we will assume our priestly role of shared leadership in the life and worship of the local church. We will support all members of the church as equals in diverse ministries.
Commitment Focus*	In the year 2010, religious, by their love for all people, their simplicity of life, and their availability and attentiveness to the voice of God expressed through the vows of chastity, poverty and obedience, and by their willingness to live interdependently with others in community, will offer a viable alternative to what is and speak of what is to be.

* Items that did not appear in the original listing of "Transformative Elements" but were added by the researchers as a result of the process described in the text.

Table B.2
Essential Elements in Church Teaching on Religious Life
in the Roman Catholic Church

Element	Definition
Consecration by Public Vows	The vows are a triple expression of a single yes to the one relationship of total consecration. They are the act by which the religious "makes himself or herself over to God in a new and special way." (*Lumen Gentium*, 44)
Communion in Community	Communion is rooted in religious consecration itself. For religious, communion in Christ is expressed in a stable and visible way through community life. Every religious must normally live under the authority of a local superior in a community of the institute to which he or she belongs. Community living entails a daily sharing of life according to specific structures and provisions established in constitutions. Sharing of prayer, work, meals, and leisure are among the valuable factors.
Evangelical Mission	The consecrated person is one who is sent to do the work of God in the power of God. This saving work of Christ is shared by means of concrete services mandated by the church in the approval of constitutions. The mission itself is undertaken as a community responsibility. The works of all the members are directly related to the common apostolate, which the church has recognized as expressing concretely the purpose of the institute.
Prayer	Religious life cannot be sustained without a deep life of prayer, including individual, communal and liturgical. The habit of prayer is necessary if the religious is to have that contemplative vision of things by which God is revealed in faith in the ordinary events of life.
Asceticism	Religious life itself is an ongoing, public, visible expression of Christian conversion. It calls for the leaving of all things and the taking up of one's cross to follow Christ throughout the whole of life. This involves the asceticism necessary to live in poverty of spirit and of fact; to love as Christ loves; and to give up one's own will for God's sake to the will of another who represents him, however imperfectly.
Public Witness	The totality of religious consecration requires that the witness to the Gospel be given publicly by the whole of life. The visibility of this witness involves the forgoing of standards of comfort and convenience that would otherwise be legitimate. It requires a restraint on forms of relaxation and entertainment. To ensure this public witness, religious willingly accept a pattern of life that is not permissive but largely laid down for them. They wear a religious garb that distinguishes them as consecrated persons, and they have a place of residence that is properly established by their institute.

Table B.2 (continued)

Element	Definition
Relation to the Church	Religious life has its own place in relation to the divine and hierarchical structure of the church. It is not a kind of intermediate way between the clerical and lay conditions of life, but comes from both as a special gift of the entire church.
Formation	Religious formation fosters growth in the life of consecration to the Lord. The discernment of the capacity to live a life that will foster this growth according to the spiritual patrimony and provisions of a given institute and the accompanying of the life itself in its personal evolution in each member in community are the two main facets of formation.
Government	The government of apostolic religious, like all other aspects of their life, is based on faith and on the reality of their consecrated response to God in community and mission. These women and men are members of religious institutes whose structures reflect the Christian hierarchy, of which the head is Christ himself. They have chosen to live vowed obedience as a value in life. They therefore require a form of government that expresses these values and a particular form of religious authority.

Source: *Essential Elements in Church Teaching on Religious Life*, 1983.

Appendix C

COMPETENCIES OF LEADERS
OF RELIGIOUS ORDERS

Table C.1
**Frequency of Occurrence of Competency Levels for Typical (T) and
Outstanding (O) Religious Leaders**

COMPETENCY LEVEL		Frequency	t value	p
I. GOAL AND ACTION COMPETENCIES				
1. Achievement				
1. Wants to do the job well or right.	T O	.667 1.956	-2.78	.009
2. Sets and acts to achieve measurable goals.	T O	.167 .565	-1.64	.112
3. Innovates, finds new unique ways to improve performance.	T O	.167 .435	-1.28	.208
2. Efficiency				
1. Uses own specific methods of measuring outcomes against a standard of excellence.	T O	1.917 .478	1.46	.169
2. Makes specific changes to improve efficiency.	T O	.667 .609	.17	.864
3. Initiative				
1. Works extra hours, makes extra visits to houses, when not required to do so.	T O	.333 .522	-.80	.429

Table C.1 (continued)

COMPETENCY LEVEL		Frequency	t value	p
3. Initiative (continued)				
2. Creates opportunities or minimizes potential problems by unique extra effort in the immediate future (next 1-2 months).	T O	1.083 1.870	-1.72	.097
3. Starts new projects or activities to deal with opportunities or problems over the next year.	T O	1.333 2.087	-1.29	.208
4. Anticipates, plans, acts to create opportunities or avoid problems in the farther future (over a year ahead.)	T O	1.167 2.043	-1.72	.095
II. INTELLECTUAL/COGNITIVE COMPETENCIES				
4. Information Seeking				
1. Is objective/views issues from many perspectives.	T O	.417 1.087	-1.77	.086
2. Asks direct questions, consults available resources.	T O	3.083 2.261	1.04	.309
3. Research: digs deeper, conducts surveys, or does formal research.	T O	1.750 1.391	.73	.471
5. Conceptual Thinking				
1. Uses simple concepts, "rules of thumb" to identify and solve problems.	T O	2.750 1.565	1.24	.232
2. Makes sense of unpredictable and uncertain situations.	T O	3.667 4.174	-.37	.718
3. Concept creation: sees things in new ways; generates and tests hypotheses or formulates a metaphor.	T O	2.250 2.652	-.46	.648
4. Finding meaning: sees the significance in terms of over-arching philosophical, religious or societal trends.	T O	1.667 2.956	-1.54	.136
6. Analytical Thinking				
1. Simple lists of items, tasks, priorities, resources and elements.	T O	.833 .783	.10	.920

Table C.1 (continued)

	COMPETENCY LEVEL		Frequency	t value	p

6. Analytical Thinking (continued)

2.	Works out component, causal-chain, sequential, "if-then" relationships.	T O	.917 1.652	-1.05	.301
3.	Translates, organizes or condenses specialized or diverse sources of information into practical, understandable reports.	T O	.750 .652	.21	.835

III. PEOPLE COMPETENCIES

7a. Responsiveness to Members' Needs

1.	Maintains clear communication with members. Monitors their satisfaction/dissatisfaction.	T O	2.083 1.174	1.16	.264
2.	Works to add value for the members, to make things better for them in some way.	T O	1.750 1.348	.59	.562
3.	Works with a long-term perspective on members' problems.	T O	.917 .956	-.09	.931

7b. Responsiveness to Needs of Client Groups

1.	Maintains clear understanding of clients' needs, satisfactions/dissatisfactions.	T O	.583 .391	.59	.561
2.	Works to make things better in some way for client groups.	T O	.167 .435	-1.35	.187
3.	Focuses on long-term benefits for client groups.	T O	.250 .609	-1.47	.151

8. Developmental

1.	Supervising: gives instructions, guidance to members or staff.	T O	.750 .261	1.66	.119
2.	Counseling/coaching: gives feedback for developmental purposes, counsels after setbacks.	T O	2.250 1.130	1.87	.078
3.	Training: arranges for formal training responsive to needs that goes beyond what has been routinely provided.	T O	1.333 .261	2.70	.018

Table C.1 (continued)

COMPETENCY LEVEL		Frequency	t value	p
8. Developmental (continued)				
4. Mentoring: delegates to prepare others to assume leadership positions by providing them with opportunities to develop their abilities.	T O	.250 .565	-.99	.332
9. Interpersonal Understanding				
1. Understands and is influenced by the feelings of others: empathy.	T O	1.833 3.522	-2.13	.041
2. Establishes good relationships with others.	T O	1.250 1.087	.34	.738
3. Understands complex causes of others' long-term, underlying problems.	T O	1.333 1.087	.47	.645
IV. ORGANIZATIONAL COMPETENCIES				
10. Mission Orientation				
1. Mentions importance of mission; models good, loyal behavior; states commitment to organization mission and goals.	T O	4.083 4.087	.00	.997
2. Mentions specific planning activities sponsored to reflect on mission.	T O	1.750 2.087	-.62	.538
3. Develops a new or renewed sense of mission.	T O	1.167 1.087	.15	.879
11. Community Leadership				
1. Manages meetings well, in a way that goes beyond routine job requirements.	T O	.917 1.217	-.57	.578
2. Uses formal authority to set and maintain group norms.	T O	3.583 2.522	1.22	.234
3. Team consensus.	T O	1.500 2.870	-2.46	.019
4. Participatively solicits inputs, team-builds, develops consensus.	T O	1.167 1.565	-.52	.608
5. Positions self as leader so that others buy into the mission, goals, climate, policy. Has genuine charisma.	T O	.167 .522	-1.70	.099

Table C.1 (continued)

COMPETENCY LEVEL		Frequency	t value	p
12. Directiveness, Personal Assertiveness				
1. Directs: tells others what to do; gives directions.	T O	3.000 2.391	.76	.453
2. Assertively asks and says "No."	T O	1.583 .870	.90	.384
3. Confronts others openly and directly.	T O	1.667 1.956	-.52	.608
4. Uses reward and punishment to control behavior; threatens, terminates.	T O	1.333 .522	1.51	.155
13. Impact and Influence				
1. Shows intention or desire to have a specific effect or impact.	T O	2.333 4.826	-2.45	.020
2. Direct persuasion: takes action to persuade others.	T O	1.083 2.565	-2.41	.022
3. Develops a complex influence strategy, involving two or more steps.	T O	1.500 1.913	-.68	.505
V. PERSONAL COMPETENCIES				
14. Self-Confidence	T O	3.000 3.739	-1.02	.317
15. Positive Expectations	T O	3.500 4.913	-1.02	.314
16. Negative Reactions	T O	4.500 5.696	-.56	.579
17. Concern for Moderation, Control of Excess	T O	1.083 2.521	-.56	.582
18. Stress Resistance, Energy Level	T O	1.833 1.783	.08	.939

Table C.2
Correlations among Competencies: All Leaders

Competency	1	2	3	4	5	6	7	8	9
1. Achievement	-								
2. Initiative: Short-term	.07	-							
3. Initiative: Long-term	.52**	.40*	-						
4. Objectivity	.17	.03	.07	-					
5. Information Seeking	.27	.25	.16	-.08	-				
6. Conceptual Thinking	.17	.18	.18	.49**	-.02	-			
7. Finding Meaning	.12	.35*	.21	.48**	-.10	.25	-		
8. Analytical Thinking	.31	.25	.45**	.16	.18	.37*	.06	-	
9. Resp. to Members	-.03	.11	.25	.24	.12	.26	.36*	.25	-
10. Resp. to Clients1	.12	.30	.24	.05	.11	.33	.08	.75	.16
11. Resp. to Clients2	-.03	.01	.13	.20	-.15	.15	.24	.18	-.03
12. Developmental	-.36*	.15	-.17	-.22	.23	.07	-.25	.20	.22
13. Mentor	.26	-.12	.22	-.11	.00	-.09	.22	.14	.28
14. Empathy	.11	.02	.21	.55**	-.04	.35*	.52**	.12	.27
15. Interpersonal Understanding	.08	.02	-.03	.22	.26	.19	.18	.10	.40*
16. Mission Orientation	.08	.27	.24	-.27	.07	.15	.25	.18	.35*
17. Community Leadership	.03	-.19	-.05	.27	-.01	.17	-.07	.04	.19
18. Command Authority	.12	.41*	.30	.17	.13	.31	.26	.56***	.50**
19. Consensual Authority	.16	.33	.22	.24	-.09	.13	.38*	-.12	-.05
20. Directiveness	-.11	.01	-.23	-.05	-.06	-.14	-.14	-.07	.03
21. Socialized Power	.58**	.14	.41*	.45**	.22	.40*	.45**	.40*	.22
22. Self-Confidence	.40*	.10	.35*	.04	.03	.23	.12	.39*	.27
23. Positive Expectations	.12	.38*	.30	.57**	-.04	.42*	.57**	.31	.12
24. Negative Expectations	.09	.03	-.07	.34*	-.12	.12	.07	.02	-.21
25. Moderation	.31	.34*	.12	.27	.13	.37*	.56**	.16	.26
26. Stress	.28	-.02	.17	.15	.01	.26	-.14	.03	.04
27. Support	.21	.29	.34*	.05	.11	.22	.16	-.00	.10
28. Dynamism	-.02	.00	-.15	.29	.10	.27	.26	-.09	.00

Table C.2 (continued)

Competency	10	11	12	13	14	15	16	17	18
1. Achievement									
2. Initiative: Short-term									
3. Initiative: Long-term									
4. Objectivity									
5. Information Seeking									
6. Conceptual Thinking									
7. Finding Meaning									
8. Analytical Thinking									
9. Resp. to Members									
10. Resp. to Clients1	-								
11. Resp. to Clients2	.06	-							
12. Developmental	.23	-.02	-						
13. Mentor	-.05	-.07	-.04	-					
14. Empathy	.16	.46**	-.17	.01	-				
15. Interpersonal Understanding	.38*	-.17	.17	.10	.25	-			
16. Mission Orientation	.06	.27	.07	.29	.08	-.06	-		
17. Community Leadership	-.02	-.17	-.02	-.02	.23	.05	-.08	-	
18. Command Authority	.52**	-.17	.20	.14	.17	.15	.29	.21	-
19. Consensual Authority	-.16	.03	-.43**	-.01	.29	-.14	.16	.13	-.07
20. Directiveness	.08	-.02	.07	-.14	-.03	-.02	.10	.23	.35*
21. Socialized Power	.27	.28	-.33	.04	.36*	.22	.24	-.08	.16
22. Self-Confidence	.17	.20	-.10	.17	.06	-.02	.36*	.01	.30
23. Positive Expectations	.18	.36*	-.14	-.21	.65**	-.04	.09	.03	.38*
24. Negative Expectations	.19	.14	-.32	-.09	.35*	.12	-.05	.33	.22
25. Moderation	.08	.13	-.22	.01	.33	.10	.46**	.07	.38*
26. Stress	-.04	-.22	.08	.37*	.11	.34*	-.12	.23	.10
27. Support	-.03	.06	.02	.02	.42*	.17	.11	-.06	.11
28. Dynamism	-.06	.08	-.24	-.07	.22	.08	.16	.08	-.16

Table C.2 (continued)

Competency	19	20	21	22	23	24	25	26	27	28
1. Achievement										
2. Initiative: Short-term										
3. Initiative: Long-term										
4. Objectivity										
5. Information Seeking										
6. Conceptual Thinking										
7. Finding Meaning										
8. Analytical Thinking										
9. Resp. to Members										
10. Resp. to Clients1										
11. Resp. to Clients2										
12. Developmental										
13. Mentor										
14. Empathy										
15. Interpersonal Understanding										
16. Mission										
17. Community Leadership										
18. Command Authority										
19. Consensual Authority	-									
20. Directiveness	-.34*	-								
21. Socialized Power	.20	-.14	-							
22. Self-Confidence	.17	.12	.34*	-						
23. Positive Expectations	.32	-.10	.37*	.17	-					
24. Negative Expectations	.05	.58***	.11	.10	.23	-				
25. Moderation	.40*	.06	.37*	.47**	.50**	.21	-			
26. Stress	-.14	.08	-.15	.06	-.03	.31	.09	-		
27. Support	.46**	-.27	-.03	.32	.42**	.02	.46**	.37*	-	
28. Dynamism	.37*	-.35*	.35*	.02	.28	.13	.36*	-.14	.06	-

* p < .05
** p < .01
***p < .001

THE NATIONAL SURVEY

The National Survey which was distributed to 9,999 religious priests, brothers and sisters in October 1990 appears on the following pages.

INSTRUCTIONS

Please review the following instructions before you begin work on this questionnaire.

+ Read each question carefully and mark your answer *in this question booklet according to the instructions* that precede each section. There are **no right or wrong answers** to these questions. Please try to answer every question. If you must skip a question, do not mark anything in the space provided.

+ Answer each question as honestly and openly as possible. Your responses to this questionnaire are entirely confidential. Your name will never be attached to your responses, nor will your responses ever be considered individually.

+ Having someone record your answers, translate the questions, or help in any other way necessary is acceptable if visual, lingual or other factors affect your ability to respond to this questionnaire. Please be sure that the answers you select reflect **your** thoughts and feelings, and not those of the person assisting you.

+ If you have any additional comments you believe might help us to understand better the future of religious life in the United States please write them in the space provided at the end of the questionnaire.

+ When you have filled out the questionnaire as completely and candidly as possible, please review your responses. Be sure that no pages have been skipped, and that when a question requires only one response, only one response has been chosen.

+ Send the completed questionnaire to us in the prepaid return envelope as soon as possible, preferably by **November 15, 1990.** Remember, if for some reason you have received the questionnaire near, or after, the return date, we would appreciate your returning it to us as soon as possible.

+ Your participation in this effort is very important. Your input will contribute to the validity of the results and further our understanding of the future of religious life.

Thank you for your cooperation.

Please circle the number that corresponds to your response, or fill in the blank where appropriate.

1. Your present age: _____

2. Race/Ethnicity:

   Caucasian 1

   Black/African-American 2

   Mexican-American 3

   Other Hispanic 4

   Asian-American 5

   Native American 6

   Asian or Pacific Islander 7

   Other *(specify)* 8

   _____

3. State or foreign country where you were born:

   _____

4. Are you a citizen of the United States?

   a. Yes _____   b. No _____

5. Number of siblings _____

6. Your position in family _____
   (oldest, 3rd of 6, etc.)

7. MBTI type (if known): _____

8. Vocation:

   Sister 1

   Brother 2

   Priest 3

9. Are you in formation?

   a. Yes _____   b. No _____

10. Are you permanently professed?

    a. Yes _____   b. No _____

11. Are you ordained?

    a. Yes _____   b. No _____

    c. IF YES, in what year? _____

12. Number of years in religious life: _____

13. Year first entered religious life: _____

14. Age at entrance: _____

15. Have you ever been a member of another congregation?

    a Yes _____   b. No _____

    c. IF YES, for how long? _____

    d. IF YES, how long have you been a member
       of your present congregation? _____

16. Have you ever held a position of provincial, abbatial
    leader or other major superior in your congregation?

    a. Yes _____   b. No _____

    c. IF YES, please circle office(s) you have held:

       Superior/Superioress General 1

       President of Monastic Federation 2

       Abbot/Abbess 3

       Provincial/Vicar Provincial 4

       President of Congregation 5

       Prior/Prioress 6

       Leadership Team
       (with equal authority) 7

    d. Total years as a leader: _____

17. Tradition:

    Apostolic 1

    Monastic 2

    Contemplative 3

    Mendicant 4

    Evangelical 5

18. What is the highest level of education or degree you
    have completed?

    Grade school 1

    High school 2

    Some college/technical degree 3

    Associate degree 4

    Bachelor's degree 5

    Some graduate school 6

    Master's degree 7

    Doctoral degree 8

    Other *(specify)* 9

    _____

19. Was your most recent degree granted by a Catholic
    institution?

    a. Yes _____   b. No _____

Choose your response to Questions 20 and 21 from the following listing of fields of study. Write the appropriate code in the blank provided.

Medicine	01	Agriculture and related subjects	11
Law	02	Business and administration	12
Biological sciences	03	Theology and related subjects	
Physical sciences	04	(church history, catechetics, etc.)	13
Social sciences	05	Art	14
(including history)		Counselling	15
Humanities		Pastoral Counselling	16
(including philosophy)	06	Health professions	17
Mathematics	07	Other *(specify)*	18
Engineering	08		
Education	09		
Social work	10	Does not apply	00

20. If you have received a higher degree, what is the field of study that represents your highest qualification? *If your highest degree is in more than one field, please select ONLY the code that corresponds to your most RECENT degree.* _____

21. If you are currently enrolled in a degree program, or you plan to begin full-time or part-time study at any college or university in the near future, indicate the field of study. _____

Choose your response to Questions 22 and 23 from the following listing of ministries. Write the appropriate code in the blank provided.

		Eucharistic ministry	14
Parish ministry	01	Business and finance	15
Hospital administration	02	Art	16
Congregational/provincial leadership	03	Retreat ministry	17
Congregational/provincial administration	04	Prison ministry	18
Social service	05	Social work	19
Educational administration	06	Apostolate of prayer	20
Higher education	07	Counselling	21
Engineering	08	Pastoral counselling	22
Education	09	Retirement	23
Health care	10	Formation/vocation	24
Communication	11	Peace and justice	25
Pastoral visiting of the elderly, hospice patients, or others	12	Other *(specify)*	26
Agriculture	13		

22. The primary ministry in which you are currently involved. *(Select only ONE)* ____

23. The ministry you intend to pursue in the future. *(Select only ONE)* ____

24. I work approximately _____ hours per week in my primary job.

Circle the number that corresponds to your response for the following questions. Please choose only one response.

25. Over a typical week, how often is Eucharistic liturgy a part of your routine?

    Every day 1

    5-6 times 2

    2-4 times 3

    Once a week 4

    Less than once a week 5

    Almost never 6

26. Over a typical week, how often is the Liturgy of the Hours a part of your routine?

    Every day 1

    5-6 times 2

    2-4 times 3

    Once a week 4

    Less than once a week 5

    Almost never 6

27. In what context do you usually find yourself at Eucharistic liturgy?

    Your local parish 1

    Another parish 2

    A religious congregation 3

    Institution (e.g., school, hospital) 4

    Covenant community 5

    Other *(specify)* 6

28. How often do you pray or meditate privately?

    Seldom or never 1

    Only on very special occasions 2

    About once a week 3

    Several times a week 4

    Daily (regardless of number of times) .. 5

    Other *(specify)* 6

29. Other than celebration of the Eucharist, how often do you pray with a group?

    Seldom or never 1

    Only on very special occasions 2

    About once a week 3

    Several times a week 4

    Daily (regardless of number of times) .. 5

    Other *(specify)* 6

30. Which of the following statements best describes your feelings? *Choose ONE code.*

    I find attending Mass has become so difficult for various reasons that I no longer attend 1

    I find attending Mass is not difficult at all. It is usually a very important form of prayer and worship for me. 2

    I find attending Mass difficult, but it remains a very important form of prayer and worship for me. 3

    I find attending Mass is not difficult, but it is not a very important form of prayer and worship for me. 4

Choose your response to Questions 31 and 32 from the following listing of living situations. Write the appropriate code in the blank provided.

Alone	01	In a mixed community of men and women religious	05
In a community with more than one other person of my congregation	02	In a community which includes men and women, married and celibate	06
With one other member of my congregation	03	With an elderly or ill parent/relative	07
With member(s) of other congregations (same sex)	04	, Other *(specify)*	08

_____

31. At present I live   _____   32. In the future, I expect to live   _____

Listed below are some statements about your present living situation. To what extent do you agree or disagree with each statement? Please choose only ONE response per statement.

	Strongly Disagree	Disagree	Neither Agree nor Disagree	Agree	Strongly Agree
33. I am satisfied with my present living situation.	1	2	3	4	5
34. My congregation allows me sufficient freedom in determining my living situation.	1	2	3	4	5
35. My present living situation detracts from my prayer life.	1	2	3	4	5
36. My present living situation enhances my sense of belonging to my congregation.	1	2	3	4	5
37. Ministry is the primary factor in determining my living situation.	1	2	3	4	5

This scale consists of a number of words that describe different feelings and emotions. Read each item and mark the appropriate answer in the space next to that word. Indicate to what extent you generally feel this way, that is, how you feel on the average.

1 very slightly or not at all	2 a little	3 moderately	4 quite a bit	5 extremely

38.	_____ interested	45.	_____ hostile	52.	_____ nervous
39.	_____ distressed	46.	_____ enthusiastic	53.	_____ determined
40.	_____ excited	47.	_____ proud	54.	_____ attentive
41.	_____ upset	48.	_____ irritable	55.	_____ jittery
42.	_____ strong	49.	_____ alert	56.	_____ active
43.	_____ guilty	50.	_____ ashamed	57.	_____ afraid
44.	_____ scared	51.	_____ inspired		

Please indicate your agreement with the following statements by circling the appropriate number. Remember that there are no right or wrong answers. Select only ONE response per statement.

	Strongly Disagree	Disagree	Neither Agree nor Disagree	Agree	Strongly Agree
58. The role of religious in the Church is sufficiently clear to me.	1	2	3	4	5
59. Religious life is not as important as it once was to the Church.	1	2	3	4	5
60. The laity have assumed most of the responsibilities previously held by religious.	1	2	3	4	5
61. I know what it means to be a religious in the Church today.	1	2	3	4	5
62. Women religious are essentially lay women who choose to live the common life and to profess vows.	1	2	3	4	5
63. Religious priests regard their priesthood as more important than they regard membership in their congregation.	1	2	3	4	5
64. My life as a religious is more meaningful to me today than it was in the past.	1	2	3	4	5
65. I am satisfied with the job that I currently hold.	1	2	3	4	5
66. I think being a religious is important to the job I hold.	1	2	3	4	5
67. If I had to do it all over again, I would still choose to become a religious.	1	2	3	4	5
68. I would encourage others to pursue a vocation in my congregation today.	1	2	3	4	5
69. Religious brothers are essentially lay men who choose to live the common life and to profess vows.	1	2	3	4	5
70. My congregation inspires the very best in me.	1	2	3	4	5
71. Leadership in my congregation inspires my loyalty.	1	2	3	4	5
72. I am careful to use opportunities to nurture my spiritual life.	1	2	3	4	5
73. The vows have been a great source of freedom for me.	1	2	3	4	5
74. I believe that in the future other vows will substitute for the traditional vows of poverty, chastity and obedience.	1	2	3	4	5
75. I feel adequately prepared to work with the poor.	1	2	3	4	5
76. I meet regularly with a spiritual guide or spiritual director.	1	2	3	4	5
77. Some agreed upon structure is important to effectively living the common life.	1	2	3	4	5
78. My personal preference would be (is) to live alone.	1	2	3	4	5
79. A diversity of ministries makes living a community life difficult.	1	2	3	4	5

		Strongly Disagree	Disagree	Neither Agree nor Disagree	Agree	Strongly Agree
80.	That which most unites community members is their commitment to a single ministry.	1	2	3	4	5
81.	I derive great satisfaction from living with other religious.	1	2	3	4	5
82.	The future will see more communities of men and women living together.	1	2	3	4	5
83.	Personality differences make living in common difficult.	1	2	3	4	5
84.	Common life requires that someone in the group take a position of leadership (e.g., a local superior).	1	2	3	4	5

85. *Consider the three traditional vows of poverty, chastity, and obedience. In COLUMN A below please rank the vows in order of the meaning they hold for you, with 1 signifying the most meaningful for you and 3 signifying the least meaningful for you.*

86. *Consider the three traditional vows of poverty, chastity, and obedience. In COLUMN B below please rank the vows in order of the difficulty you experience living them, with 1 signifying the most difficult for you to live and 3 signifying the least difficult for you to live.*

COLUMN A - (Meaningfulness)   COLUMN B - (Difficulty)

Poverty   _____   Poverty   _____

Chastity   _____   Chastity   _____

Obedience   _____   Obedience   _____

To what extent do you agree or disagree with each of the following statements? For each, circle the code under the heading which best fits your PRESENT thinking. Please choose only ONE response per statement.

		Strongly Disagree	Disagree	Neither Agree nor Disagree	Agree	Strongly Agree
87.	I feel I am an important part of my congregation.	1	2	3	4	5
88.	My opinions are considered in decisions made about my congregation.	1	2	3	4	5
89.	I would like to have more influence in establishing the future of my congregation.	1	2	3	4	5
90.	I feel isolated from the important things happening in my congregation.	1	2	3	4	5
91.	I am willing to participate in implementing decisions of my congregation.	1	2	3	4	5
92.	My congregation has clear policies (e.g. personnel procedures) that assist me as I make choices about my work and ministry.	1	2	3	4	5
93.	Lines of accountability within my congregation are clear.	1	2	3	4	5
94.	When I am uncertain about something within my congregation, I know exactly with whom to speak to have it clarified.	1	2	3	4	5

	Strongly Disagree	Disagree	Neither Agree nor Disagree	Agree	Strongly Agree
95. I look forward to being with members of my congregation.	1	2	3	4	5
96. I am personally involved in my congregation.	1	2	3	4	5
97. The important things that happen to me directly involve my congregation.	1	2	3	4	5
98. Members of my congregation agree on what our congregation's goals are.	1	2	3	4	5
99. Declaring a homosexual orientation would not exclude an individual from being admitted to my congregation.	1	2	3	4	5
100. Although there is increasing talk about religious working with the poor, I feel little commitment to that.	1	2	3	4	5
101. I am willing to contribute more than is normally expected in order to help my congregation fulfill its mission.	1	2	3	4	5
102. I feel little loyalty to my congregation.	1	2	3	4	5
103. I find that my values and my congregation's values are similar.	1	2	3	4	5
104. Members of minority groups may feel uneasy in my congregation.	1	2	3	4	5
105. I intend to remain a member of my congregation for the rest of my life.	1	2	3	4	5
106. I am proud to tell others that I am part of my congregation.	1	2	3	4	5
107. It would take little change in my present circumstances to cause me to leave my congregation.	1	2	3	4	5
108. There is little to be gained by remaining with my congregation indefinitely.	1	2	3	4	5
109. Often, I find it difficult to agree with my congregation's policies on important matters relating to its members.	1	2	3	4	5
110. Inclusion of lay associates as members of my congregation may undermine what it means to be a member of my congregation.	1	2	3	4	5
111. I care about the future of my congregation.	1	2	3	4	5
112. For me this is the best of all possible congregations to which I could belong.	1	2	3	4	5
113. Deciding to enter this congregation was a mistake on my part.	1	2	3	4	5
114. My closest friends are members of my religious congregation.	1	2	3	4	5
115. The mission of my congregation is clear.	1	2	3	4	5
116. I would prefer to work outside the corporate commitment of my congregation.	1	2	3	4	5

Listed below are some statements regarding aspects of life as a religious. To what extent do you agree or disagree with each statement as a description of religious life as you experience it? Please select only ONE response per statement.

	Strongly Disagree	Disagree	Neither Agree nor Disagree	Agree	Strongly Agree
117. I know what is expected of me as a religious.	1	2	3	4	5
118. In general, it is easy to work with the hierarchy in the Church.	1	2	3	4	5
119. Being a religious presents challenges that I enjoy.	1	2	3	4	5
120. Being a religious gives meaning to my life in a way no other vocation can.	1	2	3	4	5
121. Religious in this country are at the service of the institutional Church.	1	2	3	4	5
122. In general, there is conflict between religious and the laity.	1	2	3	4	5
123. The bishops of the Church should be influential in determining the future of religious life.	1	2	3	4	5
124. Congregations should consider merging when they are too small to carry out their mission.	1	2	3	4	5
125. It is necessary for religious to work together with the hierarchy of the Church so that the mission of the Church can be accomplished.	1	2	3	4	5
126. In general, members of the Church hierarchy have a clear picture of what religious do.	1	2	3	4	5
127. It is necessary for religious to work together with the laity so that the mission of the Church can be accomplished.	1	2	3	4	5
128. The institutional Church must clarify the role of religious for religious life to remain viable.	1	2	3	4	5
129. In general, members of the laity have a clear picture of what religious do.	1	2	3	4	5
130. What happens in the institutional Church is very important to me.	1	2	3	4	5
131. In general, members of the laity are easy to work with.	1	2	3	4	5
132. The role of religious in the Church was clearer before laity became involved in the Church.	1	2	3	4	5
133. In general, there is conflict between religious and the hierarchical Church.	1	2	3	4	5

Questions 134-149 list various aspects of your life as a religious. Indicate your level of satisfaction with each by choosing ONE response per item.

	Very Dissatisfied	Dissatisfied	Neither Dissatisfied nor Satisfied	Satisfied	Very Satisfied
134. My current work in ministry	1	2	3	4	5
135. My personal health	1	2	3	4	5
136. My spiritual life	1	2	3	4	5
137. My psychological stability	1	2	3	4	5
138. My sexual integration	1	2	3	4	5
139. My relationships with peers	1	2	3	4	5
140. My current living situation	1	2	3	4	5
141. My opportunities for continuing education	1	2	3	4	5
142. My opportunities for continuing formation	1	2	3	4	5
143. My relationships with members of my local community	1	2	3	4	5
144. My relationship with my local superior	1	2	3	4	5
145. My relationship with my major superior	1	2	3	4	5
146. My competence in the work that I perform for the Church	1	2	3	4	5
147. My role as a religious in the Church today	1	2	3	4	5
148. My relationship with the laity with whom I work	1	2	3	4	5
149. My relationship with my congregation	1	2	3	4	5

150. By the year 1995, I will still be a member of my religious congregation. *(Circle ONE code).*

    Definitely not 1

    Undecided 2

    Probably 3

    Definitely 4

151. I intend to remain a member of my religious congregation

    For the rest of my life 1

    Until I discern God calling me elsewhere . 2

    For at least 5 years 3

    For only a short time 4

    Undecided 5

A list of possible reasons for leaving your congregation follows. Please read the list and consider the following question. In your response, you may choose up to three reasons. Place a 1 next to the most likely reason. Should you have additional reasons, write 2 and 3 next to the second and third most likely reasons. Regardless of your responses to Questions 150 and 151, please give serious consideration to this item.

152. If I should ever decide to leave my congregation, it probably would be for the following reason(s):

My congregation is moving in a direction that conflicts with my calling/values/vision.   _____

I feel called to a lifestyle that is more life giving.   _____

My congregation no longer meets my needs. Therefore, I choose to leave.   _____

I see little hope for the future of religious life.   _____

My congregation has become so middle class that the vow of poverty is no longer meaningful.   _____

I no longer feel called to the simplicity of life that the vow of poverty requires.   _____

I seek a more intimate relationship which is incompatible with my current commitment to celibacy/chastity. _____

I need greater independence from authority and more personal freedom than the vow of obedience entails.   _____

I cannot continue my affiliation with the institutional Church.   _____

Our diminished size jeopardizes the effectiveness of our congregational structures.   _____

The role of religious in the Church is no longer unique or distinct.   _____

I experience my congregation as a dysfunctional system. Therefore, I choose to leave.   _____

I cannot envision any reason for ever leaving my congregation.   _____

Other *(specify)*:   _____

_____

Below are some statements about the nature and relevance of religious life. For each, circle the code under the heading which best fits your PRESENT thinking. Please select only ONE code per statement.

	Strongly Disagree	Disagree	Neither Agree nor Disagree	Agree	Strongly Agree
153. Religious life is a purely human phenomenon subject to radical reconsideration even to the point of allowing its disappearance.	1	2	3	4	5
154. Church institutions provide a conduit for the effective exercise of ministry by religious.	1	2	3	4	5
155. Poverty means dependence on the congregation for all of one's material needs.	1	2	3	4	5
156. For religious life to be relevant today, there should be a re-emphasis of its contemplative dimension.	1	2	3	4	5
157. Various congregations with the same apostolates or similar ways of life should be merged or united.	1	2	3	4	5
158. I would be pleased if the changes that continue in religious life would slow down or cease.	1	2	3	4	5

	Strongly Disagree	Disagree	Neither Agree nor Disagree	Agree	Strongly Agree
159. Religious life has been a major factor in my ministerial happiness and success.	1	2	3	4	5
160. The vow of chastity is so essential to religious life that religious life would not survive without it.	1	2	3	4	5
161. In my experience as a religious, I see that there is seldom, if ever, any real conflict for men religious between being a member of a congregation and being an effective priest.	1	2	3	4	5
162. In the future, temporary commitment will be the norm for religious life.	1	2	3	4	5
163. A religious congregation should require that its members live together.	1	2	3	4	5
164. Poverty requires members of a congregation to contribute their income to the congregation or local house.	1	2	3	4	5
165. Each member of the congregation should be allowed to involve herself/himself in various movements and demonstrations without hindrance from her/his community.	1	2	3	4	5
166. In its efforts toward renewal, my congregation has not recaptured the original spirit of our Founder/ress.	1	2	3	4	5
167. I have been faithful to my vow of obedience.	1	2	3	4	5
168. Updating has created disorder and confusion which is harmful to my congregation.	1	2	3	4	5
169. I have been faithful to my vow of chastity.	1	2	3	4	5
170. Religious life is so tied to institutions that its prophetic role is almost snuffed out.	1	2	3	4	5
171. Renewal in my congregation has been marginal.	1	2	3	4	5
172. Each local community should have the right to choose its own members.	1	2	3	4	5
173. A religious congregation should require uniformity in dress for its members.	1	2	3	4	5
174. At the time of my perpetual vows, I was well aware of the implications of my vow of chastity.	1	2	3	4	5
175. Optional celibacy for religious would hamper vocations to religious life.	1	2	3	4	5
176. Poverty shields religious from the realistic cares of everyday human living.	1	2	3	4	5
177. The leadership conferences of women and men religious (LCWR & CMSM) should consider forming one conference of major superiors.	1	2	3	4	5
178. The spirit of poverty is meaningless without poverty in fact.	1	2	3	4	5

	Strongly Disagree	Disagree	Neither Agree nor Disagree	Agree	Strongly Agree
179. For religious life to be relevant today, there should be a return to stricter discipline.	1	2	3	4	5
180. I have been faithful to my vow of poverty.	1	2	3	4	5
181. All major superiors should be elected directly by the entire religious membership.	1	2	3	4	5
182. Religious life is a permanent element in the Church.	1	2	3	4	5
183. There is no need for a local superior in a community of mature religious.	1	2	3	4	5
184. Looking over the last twenty years, renewal has left me disenchanted with religious life.	1	2	3	4	5
185. In the future, lifelong commitment for religious life will be the norm for religious life.	1	2	3	4	5

During the past two or three years how often have you experienced each of the following? Select ONE response on each line.

	Frequently, if not always	Fairly often	Sometimes	Once in a while	Not at all
186. A sense of being in the presence of God	1	2	3	4	5
187. A feeling of being afraid of God	1	2	3	4	5
188. A feeling of great hope about the future of religious life	1	2	3	4	5
189. A deep feeling of being personally loved by Christ here and now	1	2	3	4	5
190. A feeling that I am seriously depressed	1	2	3	4	5
191. A feeling of being tempted by the devil	1	2	3	4	5
192. A feeling of being embraced by God	1	2	3	4	5
193. A feeling of being unable to identify the God who originally called me to a vocation	1	2	3	4	5
194. A feeling of wanting to leave religious life	1	2	3	4	5
195. A feeling of being at one with God or Christ	1	2	3	4	5
196. A desire to join another group more committed than my congregation to values in which I believe	1	2	3	4	5
197. A clear sense that membership in my congregation is the appropriate choice for me	1	2	3	4	5

How do you evaluate the following activities as contributing to your spiritual and personal fulfillment? If you do not engage in a particular activity, choose the "I do not do this" code. Please select only ONE code on each line.

	I do not do this	No Value	Doubtful Value	Somewhat Valuable	Very Valuable
198. Visiting the sick	1	2	3	4	5
199. Helping people who are poor	1	2	3	4	5

	I do not do this	No Value	Doubtful Value	Somewhat Valuable	Very Valuable
200. Participating in some significant social justice activities	1	2	3	4	5
201. Private devotion to Mary, e.g., rosary	1	2	3	4	5
202. Small group discussions of spiritual issues	1	2	3	4	5
203. Supporting the causes of minority peoples	1	2	3	4	5
204. Action on behalf of mentally ill or retarded persons	1	2	3	4	5
205. Regular confession (monthly)	1	2	3	4	5
206. Working for better political leadership	1	2	3	4	5
207. Spiritual reading	1	2	3	4	5
208. Providing recreational opportunities for the young or deprived	1	2	3	4	5
209. Having a good time at a social gathering	1	2	3	4	5
210. Personal donations of money to worthy causes	1	2	3	4	5
211. Literature, drama, film, art	1	2	3	4	5
212. Celebrating prayer led by a woman	1	2	3	4	5
213. Experiencing nature	1	2	3	4	5
214. Praying in common with members of my community	1	2	3	4	5
215. Reading about global issues	1	2	3	4	5
216. Participating in ecumenical activity	1	2	3	4	5
217. Praying with charismatic groups	1	2	3	4	5
218. Making an annual retreat	1	2	3	4	5
219. Engaging in aerobic exercise	1	2	3	4	5
220. Playing competitive sports	1	2	3	4	5
221. Participating in non-traditional religious rituals	1	2	3	4	5
222. Resting in contemplative prayer	1	2	3	4	5

*Listed below are descriptive statements about **leadership**. Choose the person or group in your congregation to whom you consider yourself accountable and keep them in mind as you complete this section. For each statement, we would like you to judge how frequently it fits the person or group you have in mind. Choose ONE response for each statement.*

	Frequently, if not always	Fairly often	Sometimes	Once in a while	Not at all
223. Is content to let me continue to do my job in the same way.	1	2	3	4	5
224. Talks optimistically about the future.	1	2	3	4	5
225. Treats me as an individual rather than just a member of the group.	1	2	3	4	5

	Frequently, if not always	Fairly often	Sometimes	Once in a while	Not at all
226. Things have to go wrong for him/her to take action.	1	2	3	4	5
227. Persuades me to go beyond my own self-interest.	1	2	3	4	5
228. Works out agreements with me on what I will receive if I do what needs to be done.	1	2	3	4	5
229. Is alert for failure to meet standards.	1	2	3	4	5
230. Shows the value of questioning assumptions.	1	2	3	4	5
231. Articulates a vision of future opportunities.	1	2	3	4	5
232. Listens to my concerns.	1	2	3	4	5
233. Provides reasons to change my way of thinking about problems.	1	2	3	4	5
234. Talks about special rewards for good work.	1	2	3	4	5
235. Shows s/he is a firm believer in "If it ain't broken, don't fix it."	1	2	3	4	5
236. Focuses attention on irregularities, mistakes, exceptions and deviations from what is expected of me.	1	2	3	4	5
237. If I don't bother him/her, s/he doesn't bother me.	1	2	3	4	5
238. Provides advice when it is needed.	1	2	3	4	5
239. Serves as a role model for me.	1	2	3	4	5
240. Makes me back up my opinions with good reasoning.	1	2	3	4	5
241. Introduces new projects and new challenges.	1	2	3	4	5
242. Monitors performance for errors needing correction.	1	2	3	4	5
243. As long as work meets minimal standards, s/he avoids trying to make improvements.	1	2	3	4	5
244. Avoids getting involved when important issues arise.	1	2	3	4	5
245. Shows how to look at problems from new angles.	1	2	3	4	5
246. Sets high standards for herself/himself and others.	1	2	3	4	5
247. Tells me what to do to be rewarded for my efforts.	1	2	3	4	5
248. Avoids making decisions.	1	2	3	4	5
249. Problems have to be chronic before s/he will take action.	1	2	3	4	5
250. Mobilizes a collective sense of mission.	1	2	3	4	5
251. Points out what I will receive if I do what is required.	1	2	3	4	5
252. Keeps careful track of mistakes.	1	2	3	4	5
253. Serves as teacher or coach as necessary.	1	2	3	4	5
254. Instills pride in being associated with him/her.	1	2	3	4	5

	Frequently, if not always	Fairly often	Sometimes	Once in a while	Not at all
255. Engages in words and deeds which enhance her/his image of competence.	1	2	3	4	5
256. Makes me aware of strongly held values, ideals, and aspirations which are shared in common.	1	2	3	4	5
257. Demonstrates a strong conviction in her/his beliefs and values.	1	2	3	4	5
258. Projects a powerful, dynamic, and magnetic presence.	1	2	3	4	5
259. I am ready to trust him/her to overcome any obstacle.	1	2	3	4	5
260. I have complete confidence in him/her.	1	2	3	4	5
261. In my mind, s/he is a symbol of success and accomplishment.	1	2	3	4	5
262. Displays extraordinary talent and competence in whatever s/he decides to undertake.	1	2	3	4	5
263. Inspires loyalty to the congregation.	1	2	3	4	5
264. Summons me to faith in Jesus and the Gospel.	1	2	3	4	5
265. Speaks about global concerns.	1	2	3	4	5
266. Has a sense of mission which s/he transmits to me.	1	2	3	4	5
267. Challenges me to spiritual growth.	1	2	3	4	5
268. Focuses attention of members on the poor.	1	2	3	4	5
269. Gives personal attention to members who seem neglected.	1	2	3	4	5

	Very Dissatisfied	Dissatisfied	Neither Dissatisfied nor Satisfied	Satisfied	Very Satisfied
270. In all, how satisfied are you with the person or group you are rating as a leader?	1	2	3	4	5

271. Please indicate the person or group whom you had in mind as you responded to the leadership questions (Questions 223-270). *Choose ONE code.*

Resident superior (not major superior) of my local community 1

Non-resident regional, district, or sectional superior (not of province or congregation) 2

Abbot, Prioress, etc. of my monastery, cloister 3

Major Superior of my province (not congregation) 4

General Superior of my congregation 5

Leadership team of my province 6

Leadership team of my congregation 7

Other *(specify)* 8

272. I am willing to work in an institution sponsored by my congregation.   a. Yes _____   b. No _____

273. I am willing to live in an institution sponsored by my congregation.   a. Yes _____   b. No _____

274. *Listed below are various lifestyles of religious. Choose the ONE that would most appeal to you if you were on the verge of making a religious commitment today:*

Same sex celibate community 1

Mixed sex celibate community 2

Mixed sex community including celibate, married, and single persons 3

Living alone with affiliation with other members of my congregation 4

Living in absolute solitude 5

Other *(describe)* 6

_____

275. *Below is a list of several attitudes or behaviors that may be important to the future of religious life. Please rank order, that is, arrange the list according to the priority that you would give to each item in terms of their actual importance to your own future as a religious. The most important item would receive a 1, while the least important item would receive a 7.*

    a. Engaging in some contemplative activity   _____

    b. Working on behalf of the poor and marginalized   _____

    c. Living in harmony with the earth and all of creation   _____

    d. Engaging in the ministry of the Church universal   _____

    e. Modelling my life on the values of my founder/ress   _____

    f. Participating in work that heightens global awareness   _____

    g. Acting on behalf of the reign of God   _____

Some possible threats to religious life are listed below. Indicate the degree to which you feel each issue is a threat to religious life by circling ONE code.

	Not at all	A little	Moderately	Quite a bit	Extremely
276. Individualism	1	2	3	4	5
277. Financial independence from community	1	2	3	4	5
278. Lack of clarity about the role of religious	1	2	3	4	5
279. Apathy	1	2	3	4	5
280. Sexual needs	1	2	3	4	5
281. Becoming too settled	1	2	3	4	5
282. Unwillingness to grant authority to others	1	2	3	4	5
283. Pessimism about the future	1	2	3	4	5
284. Loss of faith	1	2	3	4	5
285. Involvement of the hierarchy in religious life issues	1	2	3	4	5
286. Loss of conviction about the vows	1	2	3	4	5

	Not at all	A little	Moderately	Quite a bit	Extremely
287. The belief that more relevant work can be done outside religious life	1	2	3	4	5
288. The increased role of the laity in the Church	1	2	3	4	5
289. Lack of corporate identity of the congregation	1	2	3	4	5
290. American culture	1	2	3	4	5
291. Affluent lifestyle	1	2	3	4	5
292. Technology	1	2	3	4	5
293. The laity	1	2	3	4	5
294. Capitalism	1	2	3	4	5
295. Charismatic communities	1	2	3	4	5
296. Lack of personal prayer	1	2	3	4	5
297. Unconscious racism	1	2	3	4	5
298. Homosexuality	1	2	3	4	5
299. Liberation theology	1	2	3	4	5
300. Increased understanding of co-dependence	1	2	3	4	5
301. Disillusionment with religious leadership	1	2	3	4	5
302. Loss of meaningful rituals	1	2	3	4	5
303. Controversy concerning forms of worship	1	2	3	4	5
304. Communidades de base (base Christian communities)	1	2	3	4	5
305. Recognition that religious life supports an oppressive system	1	2	3	4	5
306. Lack of minority vocations	1	2	3	4	5
307. Emphasis on professionalism	1	2	3	4	5
308. Feminism	1	2	3	4	5

Some possible influences on religious life are listed below. Indicate the degree to which you feel each of these issues or events would favorably influence the future of religious life by circling ONE code.

	Not at all	A little	Moderately	Quite a bit	Extremely
309. A clearer definition of what it means to be a religious	1	2	3	4	5
310. A more rigorous structure of religious life	1	2	3	4	5
311. More community prayer	1	2	3	4	5
312. A conservative repositioning of the Church	1	2	3	4	5
313. The reintroduction of religious garb	1	2	3	4	5

	Not at all	A little	Moderately	Quite a bit	Extremely
314. Technology	1	2	3	4	5
315. Feminist theology	1	2	3	4	5
316. Mixed communities of men and women	1	2	3	4	5
317. More individuals joining my congregation	1	2	3	4	5
318. The ordination of women	1	2	3	4	5
319. A married clergy	1	2	3	4	5
320. Communities that include married couples and families	1	2	3	4	5

321. By the year 2010, I expect that my congregation: *(Choose ONE code)*

will have a significantly greater number of members 1

will have approximately the same number of members 2

will have a significantly smaller number of members 3

will no longer be in existence 4

will have merged or united with another congregation (monastery, etc). 5

Complete each of the following statements by indicating the phrase that best describes the degree of change in your perception. Please choose only ONE response per statement.

	More than it was when I took my vows	Less than it was when I took my vows	About the same as it was when I took my vows
322. My level of satisfaction as a religious today is	1	2	3
323. My commitment to prayer is	1	2	3
324. My belief in Jesus Christ is	1	2	3
325. My commitment to the celibate way of life is	1	2	3
326. My happiness with the role of religious life in the Church today is	1	2	3
327. My awareness of the significance of religious life is	1	2	3
328. My belief that religious life is a gift to give to the Church is	1	2	3
329. My choice to live simply is	1	2	3
330. My respect for the Magisterium of the Church is	1	2	3
331. My love of religious life is	1	2	3

Please complete the following analogies in the form "A" is to "B" as "C" is to "D." For example, rose is to flower as cat is to animal.

332. Religious life is to the Church as

_____ is to _____

333. The vows of poverty, chastity, and obedience are to religious life as

_____ is to _____

334. The common life is to religious life as

_____ is to _____

335. Please feel free to add any additional concerns you may have regarding religious life or this study.

THANK YOU FOR THE EFFORT YOU HAVE MADE IN COMPLETING THIS QUESTIONNAIRE!

Appendix E

RESPONSES TO THE NATIONAL SURVEY

As outlined in Chapter 4, each of the 9,999 surveys was coded with an identification number. Upon receipt of the survey or of information concerning the potential respondent, a disposition code was assigned to each of the identification numbers.

Descriptions of the disposition codes and the number of responses in each of the disposition categories, listed by vocation and tradition, appear in the following tables.

Table E.1
Disposition Codes and Descriptions

DISPOSITION	DESCRIPTION
ELIGIBLE, DID RESPOND	
COMP	Completed survey has been received
ELIGIBLE, DID NOT RESPOND	
LANG	Survey returned incomplete because of language problem
REFN	Negative refusal to participate as indicated by a note or letter
REFP	Positive refusal to participate as indicated by a note or letter
UNUS	Survey returned empty or with more than 100 questions unanswered or with missing ID number
CHNG	Change of address received; survey not yet returned
SENN	Second survey sent after subject requested another survey during follow-up phone call
SENT	Sent a new copy of survey as a result of address change or some indication that it was not received in the first mailing
RETR	Will return questionnaire or has returned questionnaire
NOT ELIGIBLE	
INFI	Subject unable to complete survey due to illness
DEAD	Subject deceased
LEFT	Subject left religious life
UNKNOWN	
ANSF	No answer after two attempts to reach by phone; detailed message left with another or on answering machine
UNKN	Survey returned; new address unknown; unable to obtain new address or phone
DISC	Telephone disconnected
NOCT	No contact after two tries
PHOS	Phone out of service, unable to make any further contact
(BLANK)	No disposition

Table E.2
Number of Respondents in Each Disposition Category

Disposition Code	Apostolic			Mendicant		
	Sisters	Brothers	Priests	Sisters	Brothers	Priests
COMP	2,560	1,004	787	294	180	313
LANG	11	3	1	2	0	0
REFN	3	4	6	0	0	3
REFP	79	46	61	6	11	15
UNUS	60	28	13	3	5	12
CHNG	19	4	15	1	0	4
SENN	56	84	101	15	30	31
SENT	4	13	15	2	3	3
RETR	24	16	13	3	2	7
INFI	304	55	52	32	16	14
DEAD	46	27	26	6	2	8
LEFT	6	38	8	1	12	6
ANSF	15	13	21	1	2	7
UNKN	19	35	28	3	11	10
DISC	5	3	1	0	0	1
NOCT	124	134	147	18	17	49
PHOS	0	4	0	0	0	0
(NONE)	255	163	170	11	30	55
TOTALS	3,590	1,674	1,465	398	321	538

Table E.2 (continued)

Disposition Code	Contemplative			Monastic			Total
	Sisters	Brothers	Priests	Sisters	Brothers	Priests	
COMP	123	72	38	375	285	328	6,359
LANG	2	0	0	0	2	0	21
REFN	1	1	1	0	5	1	25
REFP	15	4	2	6	17	12	274
UNUS	12	4	0	8	14	7	166
CHNG	0	0	1	3	10	23	80
SENN	3	7	7	5	25	42	406
SENT	1	0	0	0	8	16	65
RETR	1	0	0	2	3	2	73
INFI	25	6	3	45	22	34	608
DEAD	3	4	2	8	7	14	153
LEFT	2	11	0	3	30	13	130
ANSF	2	0	0	0	1	4	66
UNKN	2	0	1	4	11	14	138
DISC	0	0	0	0	0	0	10
NOCT	1	28	15	10	42	49	634
PHOS	0	0	0	0	0	0	4
(NONE)	1	24	22	8	22	26	787
TOTALS	194	161	92	477	504	585	9,999

THE NATIONAL SURVEY:
FACTORS AND ITEMS

FACTORS DERIVED FROM THE RELIGIOUS FUTURES PROJECT, ALPHA COEFFICIENTS FOR EACH FACTOR, ITEM NUMBERS IN THE SURVEY AND ITEMS COMPRISING EACH FACTOR[1]

Role Clarity: Alpha = .79

> 58. The role of religious in the Church is sufficiently clear to me.
> 61. I know what it means to be a religious in the Church today.

Permanent Commitment: Alpha = .73

> 162. In the future, temporary commitment will be the norm for religious life.
> 185. In the future, lifelong commitment for religious life will be the norm for religious life.

External Authority (Influence): Alpha = .82

> 310. A more rigorous structure of religious life.
> 313. The reintroduction of religious garb.
> 312. A conservative repositioning of the Church.
> 158. I would be pleased if the changes that continue in religious life would slow down or cease.
> 311. More community prayer.

Systemic Change: Alpha = .75

203. Supporting the causes of minority peoples.
206. Working for better political leadership.
200. Participating in some significant social justice activities.
204. Action on behalf of mentally ill or retarded persons.
216. Participating in ecumenical activity.

Hierarchical Alliance: Alpha = .83

118. In general, it is easy to work with the hierarchy in the Church.
126. In general, members of the Church hierarchy have a clear picture of what religious do.
123. The bishops of the Church should be influential in determining the future of religious life.
125. It is necessary for the religious to work together with the hierarchy of the Church so that the mission of the Church can be accomplished.
130. What happens in the institutional Church is very important to me.
285. Involvement of the hierarchy in religious life issues.
154. Church institutions provide a conduit for the effective exercise of ministry by religious.
133. In general, there is conflict between religious and the hierarchical Church.
128. The institutional Church must clarify the role of religious for religious life to remain viable
84. Common life requires that someone in the group take a position of leadership.

Diversity: Individual Items

99. Declaring a homosexual orientation would not exclude an individual from being admitted to my congregation.
104. Members of minority groups may feel uneasy in my congregation.
110. Inclusion of lay associates as members of my congregation may undermine what it means to be a member of my congregation.

Expanding Lay Roles (Threat): Alpha = .79

293. The laity.

288. The increased role of laity in the Church.
304. *Communidades de base* (base Christian communities).
295. Charismatic communities.
300. Increased understanding of co-dependence.
299. Liberation theology.

Greater Inclusion: Alpha = .85

320. Communities that include married couples and families.
319. A married clergy.
318. The ordination of women.
316. Mixed communities of men and women.
315. Feminist theology.

Cultural Threats: Alpha = .71

290. American culture.
291. Affluent lifestyle.
294. Capitalism.
292. Technology.

Commitment to the Poor: Individual Item

100. Although there is increasing talk about religious working with the poor, I feel little commitment to that.

Anomie: Alpha = .85

284. Loss of Faith.
286. Loss of conviction about the vows.
279. Apathy.
283. Pessimism about the future.
278. Lack of clarity about the role of religious.
282. Unwillingness to grant authority to others.
296. Lack of personal prayer.
289. Lack of corporate identity of the congregation.
301. Disillusionment with religious leadership.
287. The belief that more relevant work can be done outside religious life.

Spiritual Intensity: Alpha = .93

263. Inspires loyalty to the congregation.
264. Summons me to faith in Jesus and the Gospel.
265. Speaks about global concerns.
266. Has a sense of mission which s/he transmits to me.
267. Challenges me to spiritual growth.
268. Focuses attention of members on the poor.
269. Gives personal attention to members who seem neglected.

Charisma/Individual Consideration: Alpha = .95

261. In my mind s/he is a symbol of success and accomplishment.
259. I am ready to trust him/her to overcome any obstacle.
260. I have complete confidence in him/her.
262. Displays extra ordinary talent and competence in whatever s/he decides to undertake.
239. Serves as a role model for me.
258. Projects a powerful, dynamic and magnetic presence.
256. Makes me aware of strongly held values, ideals, and aspirations which are shared in common.
254. Instills pride in being associated with him/her.
257. Demonstrates a strong conviction in her/his beliefs and values.
246. Sets high standards for herself/himself and others.
245. Shows how to look at problems from new angles.
238. Provides advice when it is needed.
253. Serves as teacher or coach as necessary.
232. Listens to my concerns.
250. Mobilizes a collective sense of mission.

Intellectual Stimulation/Inspirational: Alpha = .86

227. Persuades me to go beyond my own self-interest.
233. Provides reasons to change my way of thinking about problems.
240. Makes me back up my opinions with good reasoning.
230. Shows the value of questioning assumptions.
231. Articulates a vision of future opportunities.
241. Introduces new projects and new challenges.
224. Talks optimistically about the future.
225. Treats me as an individual rather than just a member of the group.

Laissez-Faire: Alpha = .82

249. Problems have to be chronic before s/he will take action.
243. As long as work meets minimal standards, s/he avoids trying to make improvements.
226. Things have to go wrong for him/her to take action.
248. Avoids making decisions.
244. Avoids getting involved when important issues arise.
235. Shows s/he is a firm believer in "if it ain't broken, don't fix it."
237. If I don't bother him/her, s/he doesn't bother me.

Active Management by Exception: Alpha = .65

252. Keeps careful track of mistakes.
242. Monitors performance for errors needing correction.
236. Focuses attention on irregularities, mistakes, exceptions and deviations from what is expected of me.
229. Is alert for failure to meet standards.

Contingent Reward: Alpha = .82

251. Points out what I will receive if I do what is required.
247. Tells me what to do to be rewarded for my efforts.
234. Talks about special reward for good work.
228. Works out agreements with me on what I will receive if I do what needs to be done.

Community Living: Alpha = .85

140. My current living situation.
33. I am satisfied with my present living situation.
35. My present living situation detracts from my prayer life.
143. My relationship with members of my local community.
36. My present living situation enhances my sense of belonging to my congregation.

Involvement: Alpha = .63

91. I am willing to participate in implementing decisions of my congregation.
96. I am personally involved in my congregation.
101. I am willing to contribute more than is normally expected in order to help my congregation fulfill its mission.

Influence: Individual Item

88. My opinions are considered in the decisions made about my congregation.

Ongoing Development (Influence): Alpha = .82

141. My opportunities for continuing education.
142. My opportunities for continuing formation.

Procedural Clarity: Alpha = .86

92. My congregation has clear policies (e.g., personnel procedures) that assist me as I make choices about my work and ministry.
93. Lines of accountability within my congregation are clear.
94. When I am uncertain about something within my congregation, I know exactly with whom to speak to have it clarified.
103. I find that my values and my congregation's values are similar.
109. Often, I find it difficult to agree with my congregation's policies on important matters relating to its members.
115. The mission of my congregation is clear.
98. Members of my congregation agree on what our congregation's goals are.

Effects of Renewal: Alpha = .61

166. In its efforts toward renewal, my congregation has not recaptured the original spirit of our Founder/ress.
170. Religious life is so tied to institutions that its prophetic role is almost snuffed out.
171. Renewal in my congregation has been marginal.

Support of Sponsored Institutions: Individual Items

272. I am willing to work in an institution sponsored by my congregation.
273. I am willing to live in an institution sponsored by my congregation.

Oneness with God: Alpha = .84

195. A feeling of being at one with God or Christ.
189. A deep feeling of being personally loved by Christ here and now.
192. A feeling of being embraced by God.
186. A sense of being in the presence of God.

Intensified Spirituality: Alpha = .66

328. My belief that religious life is a gift to give to the Church is . . .
327. My awareness of the significance of religious life is . . .
324. My belief in Jesus Christ is . . .
323. My commitment to prayer is . . .

Structured Prayer: Alpha = .65

205. Regular confession (monthly).
201. Private devotion to Mary, e.g., rosary.
207. Spiritual reading.
218. Making an annual retreat.
214. Praying in common with members of my community.

Congregational Commitment: Alpha = .86

105. I intend to remain a member of my congregation for the rest of my life.
106. I am proud to tell others that I am part of my congregation.
107. It would take little change in my present circumstances to cause me to leave my congregation.
108. There is little to be gained by remaining with my congregation indefinitely.
111. I care about the future of my congregation.

112. For me this is the best of all possible congregations to which I could belong.

Affiliation: Alpha = .85

87. I feel I am an important part of my congregation.
95. I look forward to being with members of my congregation.
97. The important things that happen to me directly involve my congregation.
81. I derive great satisfaction from living with other religious
149. My relationship with my congregation.
68. I would encourage others to pursue a vocation in my congregation today.

Faithfulness to Vows: Alpha = .69

167. I have been faithful to my vow of obedience.
169. I have been faithful to my vow of chastity.
180. I have been faithful to my vow of poverty.

Works of Mercy: Alpha = .64

198. Visiting the sick.
199. Helping people who are poor.

NOTE

1. For statistical analysis of factors and individual items, questions written in the negative to avoid response bias were recoded. All scores reported in the text relating to the National Survey have been adjusted accordingly.

REFERENCES

Albert, S., & Whetten, D.A. (1985). Organizational identity. Research in organizational behavior, 7, 263-295.

Allen, V.L. & van de Vliert, E. (1984). A role theoretical perspective on transitional processes. In V.L. Allen and E. van de Vliert (Eds.), Role transitions: Explorations and explanations. New York: Plenum Press.

Allport, G.W. (1935). Attitudes. In C. Murchison (Ed.), Handbook of social psychology. Worcester, MA: Clark University Press.

Argyris, C. (1982). Reasoning, learning and action. San Francisco: Jossey-Bass.

Ashford, S.J. (1988). Individual strategies for coping with stress during organizational transitions. Journal of Applied Behavioral Science, 24(1), 19-36.

Ashforth, B.E., & Mael, F. (1989). Social identity theory and the organization. Academy of Management Review, 14(1), 20-39.

Ault, J. (Producer & Director). (1991). Irwin Miller: Portrait of a trustee [Film]. New York, NY: National Conference of Christians and Jews.

Baltzell, E.D. (1979). Puritan Boston and Quaker Philadelphia: two Protestant ethics and the spirit of class authority and leadership. New York: Free Press.

Bartunek, J.M. (1984). Changing interpretive schemes and organizational restructuring: The example of a religious order. Administrative Science Quarterly, 29(3), 355-372.

Bartunek. J.M., & Ringuest, J.L. (1987). Spanning new boundaries during organizational transformation. Paper presented at the Academy of Management meeting, New Orleans.

Bass, B.M. (1985). Leadership and performance beyond expectations. New York: Free Press.

Bass, B.M., & Avolio, B.J. (1990). The implications of transactional and transformational leadership for individual, team, and organizational development. Research in Organizational Change and Development, 4, 31-272.

Batson, C.D. (1987). Prosocial motivation: Is it ever truly altruistic? In L. Berkowitz (Ed.). Advances in experimental social psychology (Vol. 20, pp.65-122). New York: Academic Press.

Beckhard, R. (1988) The executive management of transformational change. In R.H. Kilmann, & T.J. Covin (Eds.), Corporate Transformation: Revitalizing organizations for a competitive world (pp. 89-101). San Francisco: Jossey Bass.

Beckhard, R., & Harris, R.T. (1977). Organizational transitions: Managing complex change. The Addison-Wesley series on organization development. Reading, MA: Addison-Wesley.

Bellah, R.N., Madsen, R., Sullivan, W.M., Swidler, A., & Tipton, S.M. (1985). Habits of the heart Berkeley: University of California Press.

Bellah, R.N., Madsen, R., Sullivan, W.M., Swidler, A., & Tipton, S.M. (1991). The good society. New York: Alfred A. Knopf, Inc.

Beres, M.E. & Musser, S.J. (1987). Avenues and impediments to transformation: Lessons from a case of bottom-up change. In R.H. Kilmann & T.J. Covin (Eds.), Corporate transformation: Revitalizing organizations for a competitive world (pp. 152-182). San Francisco: Jossey Bass.

Betancourt, H. (1990). An attribution-empathy model of helping behavior: Behavioral intentions and judgments of help-giving. Personality and Social Psychology Bulletin, 16(3), 573-591.

Biddle, B.J. (1979). Role theory: Expectations, identities, and behaviors. New York: Academic Press.

Biddle, B.J., & Thomas, E.J. (Eds.). (1966, 1979). Role theory: Concepts and research. Huntington, NY: Robert E. Krieger.

Boyatzis, R.E. (1982). The competent manager: A model for effective performance. New York: John Wiley & Sons.

Brim, O.G., Jr. (1966). In Katz, D., & Kahn, R. (1966, 1978). The social psychology of organizations. New York: Wiley Inc.

Cada, L. et al. (1979). Shaping the coming age of religious life. New York: Seabury Press.

Chang, P. (1993). An institutional analysis of the evolution of the denominational system in American Protestantism, 1790-1980. Unpublished doctoral dissertation. Stanford University, CA.

Chawla, N. (1992). Mother Teresa. New Delhi, India: Gulmohur Press.

Cherns, A. (1976). The principles of sociotechnical design. Human Relations, 29(8), 783-792.

Cialdini, R.B., Schaller, M., Houlihan, D., Arps, K., Fultz, J. & Beaman, A.L. (1987). Empathy-based helping: Is it selflessly or selfishly motivated? Journal of Personality and Social Psychology, 52(4), 749-758.

Congregation for Religious and Secular Institutes. (1983). Essential elements in the church's teaching on religious life as applied to institutes dedicated to works of the apostolate, May 31, 1983: Vatican City.

Daly, R.J., Buckley, M.J., Donovan, M.A., Fitzgerald, C.E., & Padberg, J.W. (Eds.). (1984). Religious life in the U.S. church: The new dialogue. New York: Paulist Press.

Daubman, K.A. (1991). The self-threat of receiving help: A comparison of the threat-to-self-esteem model and the threat-to-interpersonal-power model. Unpublished manuscript, Gettysburg College.

Deal, T.E., & Kennedy, A.A. (1982). Corporate cultures: The rites and rituals of corporate life. Reading, MA: Addison-Wesley.

Demerath, N.J. III., & Williams, R.H. (1992). A bridging of faiths. Princeton: Princeton U. Press.

Diener, E., Larsen, R.J., Levine, S., & Emmons, R.A. (1985). Intensity and frequency: Dimensions underlying positive and negative affect. Journal of Personality and Social Psychology, 48(5), 1253-1265.

Dovidio, J.F., Allen, J.L., & Schroeder, D.A. (1990). Specificity of empathy-induced helping: Evidence for altruistic motivation. Journal of Personality and Social Psychology, 59(2), 249-260.

Ebaugh, H.R.F. (1993). Women in the Vanishing Cloister. New Brunswick, NJ: Rutgers University Press

Ebaugh, H.R.F. (1984). Leaving the convent: The experience of role exit and self-transformation. In J.A. Kotarba & A. Fontana (Eds.), The existential self in society. Chicago: University of Chicago Press.

Festinger, L. (1964). Conflict, decision, and dissonance. Stanford: Stanford University Press.

Fisher, C.D., & Gitelson, R. (1983). A meta-analysis of the correlates of role conflict and ambiguity. Journal of Applied Psychology, 68 (2), 320-333.

Fisher, J.D., Nadler, A., & Witcher-Alagna, S. (1982). Recipient reactions to aid. Psychological Bulletin, 91(1), 27-54.

Foley, N. (Ed.). (1988). Claiming our truth: Reflections on identity by United States women religious. Silver Spring, MD: Leadership Conference of Women Religious.

Fox, M. (1983). Original blessing. Santa Fe, New Mexico: Bear & Company.

Friedlander, F. (1987). The ecology of work groups. In J. Lorsch (Ed.), Handbook of organizational behavior (pp. 301-314). Englewood Cliffs, NJ: Prentice-Hall.

Graen, G. (1976). Role-making processes within complex organizations. In M. Dunnette (Ed.), Handbook of industrial and organizational psychology. Chicago: Rand-McNally.

Halberstadt, A.G., & Ellyson, S.L. (1990). Social psychology readings. New York: McGraw-Hill Publishing Company.

Hannan, M.T., & Freeman, J. (1986). Where do organizational forms come from? Sociological Forum, 1(1), 50-72.

Heiss, J. (Ed.). (1968). Family roles and interaction. Chicago: Rand-McNally.

Jackson, S.E., & Schuler, R.S. (1985). A meta-analysis and conceptual critique of research on role ambiguity and role conflict in work settings. Organizational Behavior and Human Decision Processes, 36(1), 16-78.

Jacobs, R. (1991). Moving up the corporate ladder: a longitudinal study of motivation, personality and managerial success in women and men. Unpublished doctoral dissertation, Department of Psychology, Boston University.

Katz, D., & Kahn, R.L. (1978). The social psychology of organizations (2nd ed.). New York: John Wiley & Sons.

King, E. (Ed.) (1991). CARA Formation directory for men and women religious 1992. Washington, D.C.: CARA/Georgetown University.

Krebs, D.L. (1970). Altruism - an examination of the concept and a review of the literature. Psychological Bulletin, 73, 258-302.

Kuhnert, K.W., & Lewis, P. (1987). Transactional and transformational leadership: A constructive development analysis. Academy of Management Review, 12(4), 648-657.

Langlois, C. (1984). Le catholicisme au feminin. Paris: Les Editions du Cerf.

LCWR (1985). Reflections upon the religious life of U.S. women religious. In N. Foley (Ed.), Claiming our truth (pp.173-181). Silver Spring, MD: Leadership Conference of Women Religious.

Lozano, J. (1986). Life as parable: Reinterpreting the religious life. New York: Paulist Press.

Lumen Gentium. (1964). Dogmatic constitution of the church. In W.M. Abbott (Ed.), The documents of Vatican II (pp. 14-101) (J. Gallagher, Trans.). New York: Guild Press.

Maslach, C., & Jackson, S.E. (1982). Maslach burnout inventory. In G.S. Sanders & J. Suls (Eds.) Social psychology of health and illness (pp.227-251). Hillsdale, NJ: Erlbaum

McClelland, D.C. (1961). The achieving society. New York: Van Nostrand.

McClelland, D.C. (1975). Power: The inner experience. New York: Irvington.

McClelland, D.C. (1980). Motive dispositions: The merits of operant and respondent measures. In L.Wheeler (Ed.), Review of personality and social psychology (Vol.1, pp.10-41). Beverly Hills, CA: Sage.

McClelland, D.C. (1985) Human motivation. New York: Cambridge University Press.

McClelland, D.C. (1989). Motivational factors in health and disease. American Psychologist, 44(4), 675-683.

McClelland, D.C., & Boyatzis, R.E. (1982). The leadership motive pattern and long term success in management. Journal of Applied Psychology, 67, 737-743.

McClelland, D.C., Davis, W.B., Kalin, R., & Wanner, E. (1972). The drinking man: Alcohol and human motivation. New York: Free Press.

McClelland, D.C., & Franz, C.E. (1992). Motivational and other sources of work accomplishments in mid-life: A longitudinal study. Journal of Personality, 60, 679-707.

McClelland, D.C., Sturr, J., Knapp, R.H., & Wendt, H.W. (1958). Obligation to self and society in the United States and Germany. Journal of Abnormal and Social Psychology, 56, 245-255.

McDonough, E. (1991). Beyond the liberal model: Quo vadis? Review for Religious, 50 (2), 171-188.

McKay, J.R. (1992). Affiliative trust-mistrust. Chapters 17-18 in C.P. Smith (Ed.), Motivation and personality: Handbook of thematic content analysis. New York: Cambridge University Press.

Molinari, S.J., & Gumpel, S.J. (1987). Chapter VI of the dogmatic constitution "Lumen Gentium" on religious life. Rome.

Monroe, T. (1992). Reclaiming Competence. Review for Religious, 51(3), 432-452.

Morgan, G. (1980). Paradigms, metaphors, and puzzle solving in organization theory. Administrative Science Quarterly, 25(4), 605-622.

Mother Teresa (1983). Words to love by. Notre Dame, Indiana: Ave Maria Press.

Myers, I.B., & Myers, P.B. (1980). Gifts differing. Palo Alto, CA: Consulting Psychologists Press.

Myerson, D. (In preparation). Living with ambiguity: How hospital social workers construct meaning and identity from ambiguity. Doctoral dissertation, Stanford University, Palo Alto.

Myerson, D., & Martin, J. (1987). Organizational cultures and the denial, channeling, and acknowledgement of ambiguity. In R. Boland, M. McCaskey, L. Pondy, & H. Thomas, (Eds.), Managing ambiguity and change. N.Y.: Wiley.

Nadler, A. (1986). Self-esteem and the seeking and receiving of help: Theoretical and empirical perspectives. In B.A. Maher & W.B. Maher (Eds.) Progress in experimental personality research (Vol.14, pp.115-163). New York: Academic Press.

Neal, M.A. (1977). A socio-theology of letting go. New York: Paulist Press.

Nouwen, H.J.M. (1972). The wounded healer. New York: Doubleday & Company, Inc.

Nygren, D. (1988). Contextual correlates of religious leadership: Structure, climate and leader attitudes. Dissertation Abstracts International, 8722587.

Nygren, D., & Piedmont, R. (1988). Issues of status, power and role differentiation in male religious identity: Results of a national survey. In P. Armstrong (Ed.), Who are my Brothers? (187-224). Staten Island, NY: Alba House.

Nygren, D., & Ukeritis, M. (1992). Research executive summary: Future of religious orders in the United States. Origins, 22(15), 257-272.

Nygren, D., & Ukeritis, M. (1993). Future of Religious Orders in the United States. Review for Religious, 52(1), 6-55.

Official Catholic Directory. (1962, 1972, 1982, 1992). New Providence, NJ: P.J. Kenedy & Sons.

O'Reilly, C., III, & Chatman, J. (1986). Organizational commitment and psychological attachment: The effects of compliance, identification, and internalization on prosocial behavior. Journal of Applied Psychology, 71(3), 492-499.

Padberg, J.W. (1984). Memory, vision and structure: Historical perspectives on the experience of religious life in the church. In R.J. Daly, M.J. Buckley, M.A. Donovan, C.E. Fitzgerald, & J.W. Padberg, (Eds.), Religious life in the U.S. Church: The new dialogue (pp. 64-78). New York: Paulist Press.

Pope John Paul II (July 7, 1983). Letter to U.S. Bishops on Religious Orders. Origins, 13(8), 129-133.

Richmond, L.J., Rayburn, C., & Rogers, L. (1985, September). Clergymen, clergywomen, and their spouses: Stress in professional religious families [Special issue: Family-career linkages]. Journal of Career Development, 12(1), 81-86.

Rosener, J.B. (1990). Ways women lead. Harvard Business Review, November-December, 119-125.

Schaller, M., & Cialdini, R.B. (1990). Happiness, sadness and helping. In E.T. Higgins, & R.M. Sorrentino. (Eds.) Handbook of motivation and cognition (Vol.2, pp.265-296). New York: Guilford Press.

Schneiders, S.M. (1986). Women and the world. New York: Paulist Press.

Schneiders, S.M. (1991). Beyond patching. New York: Paulist Press.

Senge, P.M. (1990a). The fifth discipline: The art and practice of the learning organization. New York: Doubleday Currency.

Senge, P.M. (1990b). The leader's new work: Building learning organizations. Sloan Management Review, 32(1), 7-23.

308

REFERENCES

Smith, C.P. (Ed.). (1992). Motivation and personality: Handbook of thematic content analysis. New York: Cambridge University Press.

Staub, E.(1978). Positive forms of social behavior. New York: Academic Press.

Strauss, A.L. (1987). Quantitative analysis for social scientists. Cambridge: Cambridge University Press. (pp. 28-32).

Stryker, S., & Statham, A. (1985). Symbolic interaction and role theory. In G. Lindzey & E. Aronson (Eds.), The handbook of social psychology (3rd ed.), I, 311-378.

Sundstrom, E., De Meuse, K.P., & Futrell, D. (1990). Work teams: Applications and effectiveness. American Psychologist, 45 (2), 120-133.

Tipton, S.M. (1982). Getting saved from the sixties: Moral meaning in conversion and cultural change. Berkeley, CA: University of California Press.

Tukey, J.W. (1977). Exploratory data analysis. Reading, MA: Addison-Wesley.

Tushman, M.L., & Romanelli, E. (1985). Organizational evolution: A metamorphosis model of convergence and reorientation. Research in organizational behavior, 7, 171-222.

Ukeritis, M. (1984). [MBTI profiles of members of religious orders and ministerial preference]. Unpublished raw data.

Vatican Synod Secretariat. (1992). Consecrated life in the church and the world. Lineamenta, Nov. 20, 1992: Vatican City.

Veroff, J., Douvan, E., & Kulka, R.A. (1981). The inner American: A self-portrait from 1957 to 1976. New York: Basic Books.

Watson, D., Clark, L.A., & Tellegen, A. (1988). Development and validation of brief measures of positive and negative affect: The PANAS scales. Journal of Personality and Social Psychology, 54(6), 1063-1070.

Weigel R.H. & Newman L.S. (1976). Increasing attitude-behavior correspondence by broadening the scope of the behavioral measure. In A. Halberstadt & S. Ellyson (Eds.) Social psychology readings. New York: McGraw-Hill Publishing Company.

Weinberger, J., & McLeod, C. (1989). A scoring system for Oneness motivation in the McClelland-Atkinson tradition. Unpublished paper, Derner Institute, Adelphi University, Garden City, NY.

Wicklund, R.A. & Brehm, J.W. (1976). Perspectives on cognitive dissonance. New York: John Wiley & Sons.

Wispé, L. (1972). Positive forms of social behavior: An overview. Journal of Social Issues, 28, 1-19.

Wittberg, P. (1991). Creating a future for religious life. New York: Paulist Press.

Woodward, E. (1987). Poets, prophets, and pragmatists: A new challenge to religious life. Notre Dame, IN: Ave Maria Press.

INDEX

About the Authors

DAVID J. NYGREN is a psychologist at DePaul University in Chicago.

MIRIAM D. UKERITIS is a psychologist at DePaul University in Chicago. Both she and David Nygren are members of religious orders.